MCSE Training Guide: TCP/IP

Internetworking with Microsoft TCP/IP on Windows NT 4.0 Exam Objectives		Located Here	
Exam Section	Exam Objective	Chapter/Section/Page	Questions/Exercises
Planning	Given a scenario, identify valid network configurations	Chapter 4 - Subnetting, p. 118	Chapter 4 - Review Questions 3, 7, 8
Installation and Configuration	Given a scenario, select the appropriate services to install when using Microsoft TCP/IP on a Microsoft Windows NT Server computer	Chapter 1 - Services, p. 24	
	On a Windows NT Server computer, configure Microsoft TCP/IP to support multiple network adapters	Chapter 1 - Installing TCP/IP, p. 14	
	Configure scopes by using DHCP Manager	Chapter 6 - Creating Scopes, p. 208	Chapter 6 - Exercises 6.2 , 6.3, 6.4; Review Question 2
	Install and configure a WINS server	Chapter 9 - Installing a WINS Server, p. 297	Chapter 9 - Test Yourself Questions 5, 8, 10; Review Questions 1, 3, 4, 5, 7, 12, 13, 16, 17, 19, 24; Exercises 9.1, 9.6
	Install and configure a WINS server - Import LMHOSTS files to WINS	Chapter 9 - Adding Entries to WINS from an LMHOSTS File, p. 300	Chapter 9 - Exercise 9.5; Review Questions 8, 18
	Install and configure a WINS server - Run WINS on a multihomed computer	Chapter 9 - Installing a WINS Server, p. 208	Chapter 9 - Exercise 9.11
	Install and configure a WINS server - Configure WINS replication	Chapter 9 - Replication, p. 303	Chapter 9 - Test Yourself Questions 3, 4, 5, 9; Exercises 9.6, 9.7; Review Questions 7, 13, 21, 22, 25
	Install and configure a WINS server - Configure static mappings in the WINS database	Chapter 9 - Registering Non-WINS Clients with Static Entries, p. 299	Chapter 9 - Review Questions 8, 19
	Configure subnet masks	Chapter 4 - Subnetting p. 118	Chapter 4 - Exercise 4.1
	Configure a Windows NT Server computer to function as an IP router	Chapter 5 - Building a Multihomed Router, p. 180	Chapter 5 - Test Yourself Question 2; Review Question 10
	Configure a Windows NT Server computer to function as an IP router - Install and configure the DHCP Relay Agent	Chapter 6 - Installing the DHCP Relay Agent, p. 200	Chapter 6 - Test Yourself Question 3; Review Question 2
	Install and configure the Microsoft DNS Server service on a Windows NT Server computer	Chapter 13 - Installing the DNS Service, p. 429	Chapter 13 - Exercises 13.1, 13.2; Review Questions 4, 9
	Install and configure the Microsoft DNS Server service on a Windows NT Server computer - Integrate DNS with other name servers	Chapter 13 - Integration with WINS, p. 440; Configuring as an IP Forwarder, p.435	Chapter 13 - Test Yourself Question 4; Review Questions 3, 5, 9, 13
	Install and configure the Microsoft DNS Server service on a Windows NT Server computer - Connect a DNS server to a DNS root server	Chapter 12 - Using the Cache File to Connect to Root-Level Servers, p.415	Chapter 12 - Review Questions 9, 13
	Install and configure the Microsoft DNS Server service on a Windows NT Server computer - Configure DNS server roles	Chapter 12 - Types of DNS Servers, p. 401; Chapter 13 - Roles for a Microsoft DNS Server, p. 434	Chapter 13 - Test Yourself Question 5; Review Question 3

Internetworking with Microsoft TCP/IP on Windows NT 4.0 Exam Objectives		Located Here	
Exam Section	Exam Objective	Chapter/Section/Page	Questions/Exercises
	Configure HOSTS and LMHOSTS files	Chapter 7 - The LMHOSTS File, p. 244; The HOSTS File, p. 251; Chapter 10 - LMHOSTS File, p. 353; Chapter 11 - Configure HOSTS File, p. 374; Configure LMHOSTS Files p. 376	Chapter 7 - Exercise 7.1; Review Questions 5, 10, 14, 15; Chapter 10 - Review Question 16; Chapter 11 - Test Yourself Question 1
	Configure a Windows NT Server computer to support TCP/IP printing	Chapter 14 - Printing Utilities, p. 480	Chapter 14 - Review Question 8
	Configure SNMP	Chapter 15 - Installing and Configuring SNMP, p. 512	Chapter 15 - Review Questions 8, 9, 11, 12, 13, 16
Connectivity	Given a scenario, identify which utility to use to connect to a TCP/IP-based Unix host	Chapter 14 - Microsoft TCP/IP Utilities, p. 471	
	Configure a RAS server and dial-up networking for use on a TCP/IP network	Chapter 17 - Dial-Up Networking, p. 597; The RAS Server, p. 603	
	Configure and support browsing in a multiple-domain routed network	Chapter 10 - Browsing in an IP Internetwork, p. 352	Chapter 10 - Test Yourself Questions 1, 2, 3
Monitoring and Optimization	Given a scenario, identify which tool to use to monitor TCP/IP traffic	Chapter 14 - Troubleshooting Utilities, p. 483	
Troubleshooting	Diagnose and resolve IP addressing problems	Chapter 3 - IP Addresses Defined, p. 91; Chapter 16 - TCP/IP Configuration Parameters, p. 536	Chapter 16 - Test Yourself Questions 3, 4, 5; Exercise 16.2; Review Questions 1, 3, 7, 9, 13
	Use Microsoft TCP/IP utilities to diagnose IP configuration problems	Chapter 14 - Troubleshooting Utilities, p. 483; Chapter 16 - Tools Used to Troubleshoot TCP/IP Configuration Problems, p. 545	Chapter 16 - Review Question 7; Test Yourself Questions 1, 6; Exercises 16.1, 16.2
	Identify which Microsoft TCP/IP utility to use to diagnose IP configuration problems	Chapter 14 - Troubleshooting Utilities, p. 483; Chapter 16 - Tools Used to Troubleshoot TCP/IP Configuration Problems, p. 545	Chapter 16 - Review Questions 1, 2, 12, 14
	Diagnose and resolve name resolution problems	Chapter 7 - nbtstat, p. 258; Chapter 16 - Name Resolution Problems, p. 559; Chapter 11 - Configure LMHOSTS Files, p. 376; Chapter 13 - NSLOOKUP, p. 449	Chapter 7 - Review Question 4; Exercise 7.1; Chapter 13 - Exercise 13.4; Review Questions 3, 4, 12

EMMETT DULANEY   JOHN WHITE
SHERWOOD LAWRENCE   RAYMOND WILLIAMS
ROBERT SCRIMGER   KEVIN WOLFORD
ANTHONY TILKE

MCSE
TRAINING GUIDE

TCP/IP

New Riders

MCSE Training Guide: TCP/IP

By Emmett Dulaney, Sherwood Lawrence, Robert Scrimger, Anthony Tilke, John White, Raymond Williams, and Kevin Wolford

Published by:
New Riders Publishing
201 West 103rd Street
Indianapolis, IN 46290 USA

Printed in the United States of America 1 2 3 4 5 6 7 8 9 0

Library of Congress Cataloging-in-Publication Data

CIP data available upon request

ISBN: 1-56205-747-2

Warning and Disclaimer

This book is designed to provide information about TCP/IP. Every effort has been made to make this book as complete and as accurate as possible, but no warranty or fitness is implied.

The information is provided on an "as is" basis. The authors and New Riders Publishing shall have neither liability nor responsibility to any person or entity with respect to any loss or damages arising from the information contained in this book or from the use of the discs or programs that may accompany it.

New Riders is an independent entity from Microsoft Corporation, and not affiliated with Microsoft Corporation in any manner. This publication may be used in assisting students to prepare for a Microsoft Certified Professional Exam. Neither Microsoft Corporation, its designated review ICV, nor New Riders warrants that use of this publication will ensure passing the relevant Exam. Microsoft is either a registered trademark or trademark of Microsoft Corporation in the United Stated and/or other countries.

Publisher	*David Dwyer*
Executive Editor	*Mary Foote*
Managing Editor	*Sarah Kearns*

Acquisitions Editors
Julie Fairweather,
Nancy Maragioglio,
Steve Weiss

Development Editor
Rob Tidrow

Project Editor
John Sleeva

Copy Editors
Margo Catts,
Cliff Shubs,
Sharon Wilkey

Technical Editor
Lance Skok

Software Product Developer
Steve Flatt

Software Acquisitions and Development
Dustin Sullivan

Team Coordinator
Stacey Beheler

Manufacturing Coordinator
Brook Farling

Book Designer
Glenn Larsen

Cover Designer
Jay Corpus

Cover Production
Casey Price

Director of Production
Larry Klein

Production Supervisor
Victor Peterson

Graphics Image Specialists
Sadie Crawford,
Wil Cruz

Production Analysts
Dan Harris
Erich J. Richter

Production Team
Lori Cliburn,
Pamela Woolf

Indexer
Tim Wright

About the Authors

Emmett Dulaney is a consultant for D. S. Technical Solutions in central Indiana. An MCSE, CNE, OS/2 Engineer, and LAN Server Engineer, he has taught continuing education courses for Indiana University-Purdue University of Fort Wayne for more than seven years, and has authored or coauthored over a dozen books. He can be reached at edulaney@iquest.net.

Shey Lawrence When Sherwood Lawrence is not tracing TCP/IP packets and troubleshooting connectivity issues, he spends his time tracing down his free time and troubleshooting why he has so little of it left. He contends that the undeniable proof that black holes exist in the universe sucking up space and time sits squarely in the middle of his desk, bathing him in for medical therapy can be sent to the author by contacting him through his company's Web site at www.atlasconsulting.com.

For almost 20 years, **Robert Scrimger** has done everything with computers except design the boards (yet) and sell them. In the last eight years his primary endeavor has been training, starting with many different applications and moving in the last few years to work exclusively with network operating systems and client/server applications. Rob is a Microsoft Certified Systems Engineer on both 3.51 and 4.0 and a Microsoft Certified Trainer.

Anthony Tilke is a network consultant and engineer. He is both Microsoft- and Novell-certified with MCSE and MCNE designations to his credit. After administering his first network in 1987, Anthony started to change his career from an economic analyst to a network engineer. With a transitional period as a statistical programmer and graduate student, Anthony dedicated himself to a career in networking by 1992. His career has included the design, implementation, and management of large networks and messaging systems for public sector clients. More recently, Anthony has been a senior network engineer for a Micrsoft Solution Provider, and Novell Platinum reseller in the Pacific Northwest. A 1985 magna cum laude graduate from Pace University in New York, Anthony has written software reviews for *PC* magazine. He can be reached at anthony@compuserve.com.

John White currently works as a senior systems administrator. He is heavily involved in the implementation and support of Windows NT systems worldwide. John was a UNIX and NetWare systems administrator before joining the world of Windows NT. Prior to becoming a systems administrator, he was a biochemistry major at Trent University. He now lives in Ottawa, Canada with his wife Viviana.

Raymond Williams is a Microsoft Certified Trainer (MCT) and consultant. He currently works for GSE Erudite as a network instructor. Raymond is a Microsoft Certified Systems Engineer as well as a Certified NetWare Instructor and Certified NetWare Engineer. He has worked as a systems analyst and design engineer for many companies during his five years experience. He thouroughly enjoys the computer industry and what it has to offer, and finds pleasure in sharing the information with others.

Kevin B. Wolford is an MCSE, MCT, Master CNE, and CNI. He has had several careers, including technical writer, pension actuary, and trainer. He is the lead Windows NT trainer for GSE Erudite Software in Salt Lake City, Utah. You alos can see Kevin in training videos produced by Keystone Learning Systems of Provo, Utah. Kevin enjoys explaining complex, technical things in a simple manner.

Trademark Acknowledgments

Contents at a Glance

Table of Contents

13   Implementing Microsoft DNS Servers   427

14   Connectivity in Heterogeneous Environments   467

15   Implementing the Microsoft SNMP Service   499

Introduction

MCSE Training Guide: TCP/IP is designed for advanced end-users, service technicians, and network administrators who are considering certification as a Microsoft Certified Systems Engineer (MCSE), Microsoft Certified Product (MCP) Specialist or as a Microsoft Certified Solution Developer (MCSD). The TCP/IP exam (Exam 70-59: "Internetworking with Microsoft TCP/IP on Microsoft Windows NT 4.0") tests your ability to implement, administer, and troubleshoot information systems that incorporate TCP/IP as well as your ability to provide technical support to users of Microsoft Windows NT employing TCP/IP protocols.

Who Should Read This Book

This book is designed to help advanced users, service technicians, and network administrators who are working for MCSE certification prepare for the MCSE "Internetworking with Microsoft TCP/IP on Microsoft Windows NT 4.0" exam (#70-59).

This book is your one-stop-shop. Everything you need to know to pass the exam is in here, and Microsoft has certified it as study material. You do not *need* to take a class in addition to buying this book to pass the exam. However, depending on your personal study habits or learning style, you may benefit from taking a class in addition to the book or buying this book in addition to a class.

This book also can help advanced users and administrators who are not studying for the MCSE exam but are looking for a single-volume reference on TCP/IP implementation.

How This Book Helps You

This book takes you on a self-guided tour of all the areas covered by the MCSE TCP/IP exam and teaches you the specific skills you need to achieve your MCSE certification. You'll also find helpful hints, tips, real-world examples, exercises, and references to additional study materials. Specifically, this book is set up to help you in the following ways:

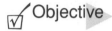 Objective

▶ **Organization.** This book is organized by major exam topics. Every objective you need to know for the "Internetworking with Microsoft TCP/IP on Microsoft Windows NT 4.0" exam is covered in this book; we've include a margin icon, like the one in the margin here, to help you quickly locate these objectives. There are pointers at different elements to direct you to the appropriate place in the book if you find you need to review certain sections.

▶ **Deciding how to spend your time wisely.** Pre-chapter quizzes are at the beginning of each chapter to test your knowledge of the objectives contained within that chapter. If you already know the answers to those questions, you can make a time-management decision accordingly.

▶ **Extensive practice test options.** Plenty of questions are at the end of each chapter to test your comprehension of material covered within that chapter. An answer list follows the questions so you can check yourself. These practice test options will help you decide what you already understand and what requires extra review on your part. The CD-ROM also contains a sample test engine that will give you an accurate idea of what the test is really like.

You'll also get a chance to practice for the certification exams using the test engine on the accompanying CD-ROM. The questions on the CD-ROM provide a more thorough and comprehensive look at what your certification exams really are like.

Note

For a complete description of New Riders' newly-developed test engine, please see Appendix D, "All About TestPrep."

For a complete description of what you can find on the CD-ROM, see Appendix C, "What's on the CD-ROM."

For more information about the exam or the certification process, contact Microsoft at:

Microsoft Education: Call (800) 636-7544

Internet: `ftp://ftp.microsoft.com/Services/MSEdCert`

World Wide Web: `http://www.microsoft.com/train_cert/default.htm`

CompuServe Forum: `GO MSEDCERT`

Understanding What the "Internetworking with Microsoft TCP/IP on Microsoft Windows NT 4.0" Exam (#70-59) Covers

The "Internetworking with Microsoft TCP/IP on Microsoft Windows NT® 4.0" exam (#70-59) covers five main topic areas, arranged in accordance with test objectives. On the CD-ROM that comes with this book, you'll find document lpr70-59.doc, which is the exam preparation guide prepared by Microsoft. lpr70-59.doc describes what you will be tested on and suggests ways to prepare for the exam. The exam objectives, listed by topic area, are covered in the following sections.

Hardware and Software Needed

As a self-paced study guide, much of the book expects you to use Windows NT Server and follow along through the exercises while you learn. Microsoft designed their implementation of TCP/IP to operate in a wide range of actual situations, and the exercises in this book encompass that range. However, the exercises require only a single stand-alone Windows NT computer running TCP/IP Server. The computer should meet the following criteria:

- ▶ Computer on the Microsoft Hardware Compatibility List
- ▶ 486DX2 66-Mhz (or better) processor for Windows NT Server
- ▶ 16 MB of RAM (minimum) for Windows NT Server
- ▶ 340-MB (or larger) hard disk for Windows NT Server
- ▶ 3.5-inch 1.44-MB floppy drive
- ▶ VGA (or Super VGA) video adapter
- ▶ VGA (or Super VGA) monitor
- ▶ Mouse or equivalent pointing device
- ▶ Two-speed (or faster) CD-ROM drive (optional)
- ▶ Network Interface Card (NIC)
- ▶ Presence on an existing network, or use of a 2-port (or more) mini-port hub to create a test network
- ▶ MS-DOS 5.0 or 6.*x* and Microsoft Windows for Workgroups 3.*x* preinstalled
- ▶ Microsoft Windows 95 (floppy version)
- ▶ Microsoft Windows NT Server (CD-ROM version)

It is somewhat easier to get access to the necessary computer hardware and software in a corporate business environment. It is harder to allocate enough time within the busy workday to complete a self-study program. Most of your study time may occur after normal working hours, away from the everyday interruptions and pressures of your regular job.

Tips for the Exam

Remember the following tips as you prepare for the MCSE/MCSD certification exams:

▶ **Read all the material.** Microsoft has been known to include material not specified in the objectives. This course has included additional information not required by the objectives in an effort to give you the best possible preparation for the examination, and for the real-world network experiences to come.

▶ **Complete the exercises in each chapter.** They will help you gain experience using the Microsoft product. All Microsoft exams are experienced-based and require you to have used the Microsoft product in a real networking environment. Exercises for each objective are placed at the end of each chapter.

▶ **Take each pre-chapter quiz to evaluate how well you know the topic of the chapter.** Each chapter opens with one essay question per exam objective covered in the chapter. Following the quiz are the answers and pointers to where in the chapter that objective is covered.

▶ **Complete all the questions in the "Review Questions" sections.** Complete the questions at the end of each chapter—they will help you remember key points. The questions are fairly simple, but be warned, some questions may have more than one answer.

▶ **Review the exam objectives in the Microsoft Preparation Guide.** Develop your own questions for each topic listed. If you can make and answer several questions for each topic, you should pass.

Note

Although this book is designed to prepare you to take and pass the "Internetworking with Microsoft TCP/IP on Microsoft Windows NT 4.0" certification exam, there are no guarantees. Read this book, work through the exercises, and take the practice assessment exams.

When taking the real certification exam, make sure you answer all the questions before your time limit expires. Do not spend too much time on any one question. If you are unsure about an answer, answer the question as best you can and mark it for later review when you have finished all the questions. It has been said, whether correctly or not, that any questions left un-answered will automatically cause you to fail.

Remember, the object is not to pass the exam, it is to understand the material. Once you understand the material, passing is simple. Knowledge is a pyramid; to build upward, you need a solid foundation. The Microsoft Certified System Engineer and Solution Developer programs are designed to ensure that you have that solid foundation.

Good luck!

New Riders Publishing

The staff of New Riders Publishing is committed to bringing you the very best in computer reference material. Each New Riders' book is the result of months of work by authors and staff who research and refine the information contained within its covers.

As part of this commitment to you, the NRP reader, New Riders invites your input. Please let us know if you enjoy this book, if you have trouble with the information and examples presented, or if you have a suggestion for the next edition.

Please note, though: New Riders staff cannot serve as a technical resource during your preparation for the Microsoft MCSE/MCSD certification exams or for questions about software- or hardware-related problems. Please refer to the documentation that accompanies Windows NT Server or to the applications' Help systems.

If you have a question or comment about any New Riders' book, there are several ways to contact New Riders Publishing. We will respond to as many readers as we can. Your name, address, or phone number will never become part of a mailing list or be used for any purpose other than to help us continue to bring you the best books possible. You can write us at the following address:

New Riders Publishing
Attn: Publisher
201 W. 103rd Street
Indianapolis, IN 46290

If you prefer, you can fax New Riders Publishing at (317) 817-7448.

You also can send e-mail to New Riders at the following Internet address:

slayton@.mcp.com

NRP is an imprint of Macmillan Computer Publishing. To obtain a catalog or information, or to purchase any Macmillan Computer Publishing book, call (800) 428-5331.

Thank you for selecting *MCSE Training Guide: TCP/IP*!

Chapter 1

Introduction to TCP/IP

This chapter helps you prepare for the exam by covering the following objectives:

 Objectives

> ▶ Install and configure TCP/IP
>
> ▶ On a Windows NT Server computer, configure Microsoft TCP/IP to support multiple network adapters
>
> ▶ Given a scenario, select the appropriate services to install when using Microsoft TCP/IP on a Microsoft Windows NT computers

The Exam

The "Internetworking with Microsoft TCP/IP on Microsoft Windows NT 4.0" exam (Exam 70-059) is one of the most crucial exams in the MCSE track. Although Microsoft does not require the exam, almost all MCSE candidates are choosing it as one of their electives. In fact, it is the most popular elective Microsoft offers. Furthermore, you can use the exam to obtain more than one certification. In addition to being an MCSE elective, the TCP/IP exam is one of three exams required to be a Microsoft Certified Product Specialist (MCPS) with an Internet Systems specialty.

In preparing for this exam, you learn some of the most useful networking skills you can have. TCP/IP is widely used on a variety of networks. Although TCP/IP has its roots in the Unix operating system and in the Internet, it often is used to connect different network operating systems into one heterogeneous network. Of course, a knowledge of TCP/IP is vital for establishing and maintaining Internet connections because TCP/IP is the Internet's protocol. However, a growing number of businesses are choosing to distribute vital internal information through intranets. Although intranets use mainly Web and FTP publishing (contained in Microsoft's Internet Information Server or IIS), once again, all these services depend on the TCP/IP protocol. (An intranet is a network intended strictly for internal use. For example, many companies use a Web server on a corporate intranet to distribute employee handbooks, phone lists, internal job listings, and shared work.)

Three Exam Preps in One Book

People prepare for exams in many ways. Some rely on their experience for the basic knowledge of a product and then fill in the details with a book such as this. Others take a Microsoft authorized course to learn the basics and the detailed information covered on the test. However, many Microsoft students end up buying additional materials to supplement the course information or to learn the material from a different point of view. Some people also purchase sample tests designed to duplicate the testing environment. Exam candidates who use a variety of sources to prepare for exams pass with higher scores and with fewer attempts, usually on the first try.

This book contains three different types of information that, when used together, can greatly improve your chances of passing the TCP/IP exam.

This book contains the same information that you would receive in Course 688, Internetworking Microsoft TCP/IP on Microsoft Windows NT 4.0, the Microsoft authorized course for this topic. Microsoft Certified Trainers, who present the authorized course each week, wrote this book. The authors explain TCP/IP in ways that are easy to understand. They also add information to provide a more thorough explanation of TCP/IP and the ways it is used in networking. These additional insights and explanations are typical of the type of information you receive from a top-notch Microsoft Certified Trainer. Therefore, you can read this book, answer the review questions, and do the exercises as a substitute for taking the Microsoft course. Microsoft has approved this book, certifying that the book contains all the information you need to know to pass the Microsoft TCP/IP test.

For those who have some experience with TCP/IP or who have taken the Microsoft course, this book is an excellent supplementary source. This book contains information not available in Microsoft courses, including a more detailed treatment of each topic. It has many more review questions that more thoroughly test your knowledge of each chapter. The exercises focus on the key concepts of TCP/IP, helping you review the most important principles with hands-on practice.

A set of sample exams is also included with this book. The test engine looks and feels like a Microsoft exam, complete with time limits and a score at the completion of the test. Authors well acquainted with the TCP/IP exam wrote the test questions, which are similar in scope and level of difficulty to those on the Microsoft TCP/IP exam. Each question in the sample test has a written explanation of the answers, which can be read only at the conclusion of the test. The answers can help you see the thinking required to correctly answer questions and to eliminate answers that don't apply.

Microsoft has made their tests extremely difficult. Test candidates must know material from the authorized Microsoft curriculum as well as information from other sources. Microsoft wants to pass only those candidates who truly know how to implement TCP/IP in a variety of environments. The *MCSE Training Guide: TCP/IP* was designed with one purpose in mind—to give all the resources you need to master TCP/IP and demonstrate your competence by passing the TCP/IP test.

What Is on the Test?

The Microsoft TCP/IP exam has questions from nine areas. Each chapter of this book is devoted to one of these areas. A test question can cover information from more than one area. In fact, test questions often cover several different areas to test your breadth of knowledge and your understanding of how the different components of TCP/IP work together.

Each chapter in this book includes appropriate references to other related components and how they work together, so you learn how all the pieces of TCP/IP work together. The review questions at the end of each chapter focus mainly on the material in that chapter; the sample test questions on the CD-ROM incorporate several sections into one question, more like actual test questions.

The following sections describe each part of the TCP/IP test and the type of information you are expected to know. The chapters that correspond to the test sections contain a thorough explanation of these concepts. You can use this summary as a useful final review to determine whether you are comfortable with all the topics listed here.

TCP/IP Architecture

This section covers the protocols and utilities that make up TCP/IP. These topics are covered in Chapter 2 of this book. The following list shows what you are expected to know from this area:

▶ What does each protocol in the TCP/IP suite do?

▶ How are these protocols combined to make a network connection?

▶ What are the TCP/IP utilities and how are they used? (Some tools are used for troubleshooting, which is covered in another section, but many utilities can be used to test your initial installation and to make various TCP/IP connections.)

▶ How was TCP/IP developed (its history) and how are changes made to the TCP/IP standards?

This section also covers the addressing scheme of TCP/IP and how it can be used to subnet a network. This is covered in Chapters 3 and 4. This list shows major topics you need to understand about addressing and subnetting:

▶ How are TCP/IP addresses structured?

▶ What do the four numbers (octets) that make up an address represent?

▶ How does the subnet mask divide the address into a network address and a host address?

▶ What type of subnet mask is needed to support a given number of subnets and hosts?

▶ What is supernetting and how does it work?

TCP/IP Routing and Name Resolution

This section covers how TCP/IP packets are sent from the host to the target and how this traffic can be directed with HOSTS and LMHOSTS files. This is covered in Chapters 5, 8, 9, and 10 of the book. (Chapters 11 and 12 more thoroughly describe WINS and DNS.) The following list shows what you need to know about TCP/IP routing:

▶ How does TCP/IP decide whether the target is a local or remote computer?

▶ How does TCP/IP decide if a computer is on a local or remote subnet?

▶ What role does the default gateway address play in routing?

▶ How do you configure LMHOSTS and HOSTS files to re-solve TCP/IP addresses?

▶ How can you link information from a Unix HOSTS file into my Microsoft TCP/IP environment?

▶ If you don't use a static HOSTS or LMHOSTS file to resolve addresses, what other means are available to do this?

Installing TCP/IP on Windows NT Computers

This section covers installing TCP/IP on a Windows NT computer and how TCP/IP is configured through the Windows NT inter-face. Chapter 5 of this book describes this area. The following list shows what you need to know for this test section:

▶ Where in the NT interface is the new protocol installed?

▶ How do you configure TCP/IP with a manual IP address?

▶ How do you configure TCP/IP to automatically receive an IP address from a DHCP server?

▶ How do you configure other components of the TCP/IP address, such as using a DNS server or a WINS server?

▶ How do you assign multiple IP addresses to one network card?

The Dynamic Host Configuration Protocol (DHCP)

This section covers how clients can receive a TCP/IP address and other configuration information from a DHCP server. This is de-scribed in Chapter 6 of this book. The following list shows what you are expected to know from this area:

▶ How do you set up a DHCP server?

▶ What types of NT platforms can you install DHCP on?

▶ What clients can receive an address from DHCP?

▶ What additional configuration information can the client receive from DHCP?

▶ Where does a DHCP server have to be located on the network so clients can communicate with the server and receive an address?

▶ How do you set up a scope of TCP/IP addresses?

▶ How do you reserve an IP address for a specific client?

▶ What properties can you specify in addition to the address?

▶ How do you assign a Default Gateway, a WINS address, or a DNS server address along with the TCP/IP address?

▶ How do you set up scopes with multiple DHCP servers?

▶ How do you resolve the TCP/IP address for DHCP clients? (Chapters 8 and 9 more thoroughly describe WINS.)

▶ How often is a DHCP lease renewed?

▶ What happens on the client if a lease expires?

▶ How should you configure the lease life for various scenarios? (Using DHCP for a one-time assignment of addresses suggests a different lease life than using DHCP to manage a limited pool of addresses for brief Internet sessions.)

The Windows Internet Name Service (WINS)

This section covers how WINS automatically collects TCP/IP address and NetBIOS name mappings. This is described in Chapters 8 and 9 of the book. The following list shows what you need to know for the test:

▶ How do you install a WINS server?

▶ What NT platforms can WINS be installed on?

▶ How is a WINS database built?

▶ How can you view the WINS database?

▶ How can you add static entries to the WINS database?

▶ How can you import entries from a HOSTS file into the WINS database?

▶ How can you configure WINS to use a DNS server to resolve addresses that are not in its database?

▶ What clients can register their names and addresses with WINS?

▶ What clients can resolve addresses using WINS?

▶ How do clients need to be configured so they can use WINS?

▶ How can you configure WINS servers to replicate their databases?

▶ What are the two types of replication and when would I use each type?

▶ Where do you locate WINS servers on the network and how many WINS servers do you need?

▶ How does a client use a secondary WINS server?

The Domain Name System

This section covers how you can use DNS to resolve domain names or aliases to individual TCP/IP addresses. This is described in Chapters 11 and 12 of the book. You need to know the following:

▶ What does a DNS server do and what type of information is in a DNS database?

▶ How do you install a DNS server?

▶ What type of Windows NT platforms does DNS run on?

▶ Given a network configuration, where do you locate the DNS server so it is accessible to all DNS clients?

▶ Do you need more than one DNS server?

▶ How do you add entries to DNS?

▶ How do you add a zone and how do you add a record?

▶ How can you link DNS to WINS?

▶ How can you link your DNS server to other DNS servers?

▶ How does DNS resolve a name when other servers are linked to it?

▶ How does DNS server resolve Internet names?

▶ Can a non-Microsoft network (such as Unix) resolve names using a Microsoft DNS server?

Browsing in a TCP/IP Internetwork

This section covers the definition of browsing and how a browse list is built. This is described in Chapter 10 of the book. You should know the following for the test:

▶ How are different computers involved in the browsing process?

▶ How is browsing through TCP/IP different than browsing with other protocols?

▶ What is the difference between a Domain Master Browser and a Master Browser?

▶ What happens to browsing when a Master Browser goes down?

▶ What happens to browsing when a Domain Master Browser goes down?

▶ How do you configure the Domain Master Browser so you can browse other domains?

▶ How is the WINS server used to browse multiple domains?

▶ When do you have to create an LMHOSTS file to browse multiple domains?

▶ Does DNS play a role in browsing?

▶ What do you have to do when a Primary Domain Controller (PDC) goes down to preserve the browsing in my domain?

Implementing the Microsoft SNMP Service

This section covers what role SNMP (Simple Network Management Protocol) has in the TCP/IP suite of protocols and how you can use SNMP for troubleshooting. This is described in Chapter 15 of the book. For the test, you should know the following:

▶ What is SNMP used for?

▶ How do you install SNMP?

▶ What does SNMP expose in TCP/IP that can be used by troubleshooting and monitoring utilities?

▶ What Microsoft utilities use SNMP?

▶ What computers have to be running SNMP so they can be involved in troubleshooting?

▶ How can you customize a tool to extract SNMP information?

▶ How do I configure SNMP so troubleshooting information is available to other applications?

Performance Tuning and Optimization

This section covers what traffic TCP/IP generates as it is used for network communications. Once you understand that process, you can tune it to reduce network traffic and increase response time for clients. For the test, you should know the following:

▶ What are the steps involved in setting up a TCP/IP connection, such as the handshaking that connects a host to its target?

▶ When does TCP/IP use directed packets and when does it use broadcasts?

▶ Do broadcasts generate more traffic?

▶ How can I streamline communications?

▶ Where on different network segments can you locate DHCP, WINS, and DNS servers to improve response time and reduce network traffic?

▶ What tools are available to monitor TCP/IP communications and what information can each tool give me?

▶ What type of packets can I see using Network Monitor?

Troubleshooting TCP/IP

This chapter covers resolving TCP/IP communication problems, which can draw on any of the other chapters. The overall process is described in the Chapter 16. For the test, you should know the following:

▶ How can you use PING to verify a TCP/IP installation?

▶ What address do you PING to test basic functions of the TCP/IP stack on the computer?

▶ What address do you PING to test the capability to communicate with remote hosts?

▶ What information can you get using the IPCONFIG utility?

▶ How can you see if a client got a DHCP address and any additional configuration information it received?

▶ How can you fix name resolution with WINS or DNS servers?

▶ Why is the client getting a DHCP address from the wrong server?

How the Internetworking TCP/IP Test Differs from Other Microsoft Exams

In general, the Internetworking TCP/IP test is like other Microsoft tests; it has the same multiple-choice format. However, you need to know a few little quirks about this test to enhance your chances of passing. You can accustom yourself to these quirks as you take the sample tests so you will not falter under the time pressure of the real exam.

First, you need to know how to use the Windows Calculator. Each exam question provides access to the Calculator. This is the same Calculator located in the Accessories group in Windows 95 or Windows NT. Figure 1.1 shows a question from Microsoft's TCP/IP assessment test, available in the Microsoft Roadmap. Note the Calculator button at the top right of the question.

Figure 1.1

The Windows Calculator is accessed by selecting the Calculator button.

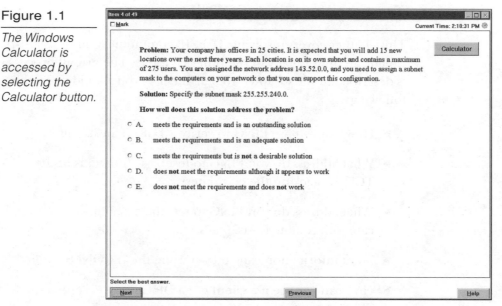

The Calculator is provided to help convert numbers easily from binary to decimal as you work with subnet masks and TCP/IP addresses. However, you can use only the Calculator's scientific mode to convert from decimal to binary. When you first open the Calculator, it is in standard mode. However, after you switch to scientific mode, the Calculator remains in that mode for the rest of the test. Figure 1.2 shows switching the Calculator from standard to scientific mode from the View menu.

Figure 1.2

Switch from standard to scientific mode from the View menu.

You should become comfortable with converting numbers from binary to decimal and from decimal to binary. To convert a decimal number to binary, select the Dec button, then enter the number. Now select the Bin button. The binary number displays. When you use this number for TCP/IP addresses or subnet masks, be sure to add enough leading zeros to the number so you have eight binary digits. You need to make sure you use eight digits because you are dealing with octets. Figure 1.3 shows the final step of converting decimal 240 to binary 11110000. In this figure, the user has just selected Bin after entering 240 in decimal. A complete description of binary arithmetic, the TCP/IP addressing scheme, and subnet masking is contained in Chapter 3.

Figure 1.3

The result of converting decimal 240 to binary.

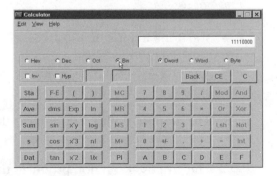

 Tip

Memorize the binary-to-decimal conversion tables in Chapter 3. Then you will know that a subnet mask of 255 indicates all eight digits of that octet are the network ID whereas a subnet of 240 uses only four digits for the network ID. I use the calculator on the test, but only as a tool to check my math. If you know the conversion tables, you should be able to recognize any mistakes you make with the calculator. You should be so used to converting these numbers that you will know when something just doesn't look right.

Microsoft has introduced a new type of question on many of the NT 4.0 exams. In these questions, you are presented with a scenario, a required result, and two optional results. The question also presents a proposed solution. You are asked to evaluate the solution as to whether it meets the required and optional results. The following is a sample question:

Scenario: It is a hot day and you are very thirsty. You want a drink.

Required results:

> ▶ Quench thirst.

> ▶ Replace fluids lost to heat.

Optional desired results:

> ▶ The drink should be cold.

> ▶ The drink should stimulate you.

Proposed solution:

> ▶ You drink a hot cup of coffee.

A. The proposed solution produces both the required result and the desired optional results.

B. The proposed solution produces the required result but only one of the desired optional results.

C. The proposed solution produces the required result but does not produce any of the desired optional results.

D. The proposed solution does not meet the required result.

In this question, the coffee would replace bodily fluids and quench the thirst (assuming you are a coffee drinker). The drink is hot, so it does not meet one of the optional results, but the caffeine in the coffee would stimulate the drinker, meeting the other optional result. The correct answer would be B.

This question has nothing to do with TCP/IP, but it does show the format of these types of questions. Often the same scenario is used for three or four consecutive questions. You should study the scenario carefully, because it is typically used again. However, each question usually presents a different proposed solution, so study the solution for each question carefully.

Once you understand the scenario and proposed solution, the trick is now to answer the test question correctly. Note that the required results can have more than one requirement. If any of the required results are not met by the solution, you can immediately choose answer D (the proposed solution does not produce the required results). There is no need to examine the optional desired results because the required result must work so you can move on to the optional ones.

If you have determined that the required result is produced, you can examine the optional desired results. Note that there are always two optional results. You merely need to decide how many of these are produced by the proposed solution. Answer A indicates both optional results are produced; answer B indicates only one is produced; and answer C indicates none of the optional results are produced. Remember that each of these answers depends on all the required results being produced. If the required results are completely fulfilled, then you should choose answer D.

Installing TCP/IP

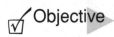 The rest of this book is dedicated to working with TCP/IP. It therefore seems that a logical place to start is installing the protocol.

To install TCP/IP protocol support, complete the following steps:

1. Open the Network Settings dialog box (double-click the Network icon in the Control Panel).

2. Click Add in the Protocols tab to open the Select Network Protocol dialog box.

3. Select TCP/IP Protocol in the Network Protocol list and choose OK.

4. The next prompt asks, "Do you wish to use DHCP?" If this computer will obtain its IP address from DHCP, choose Yes. If this computer will be configured with a static IP address, choose No.

5. When prompted, supply the path where Setup can locate the driver files.

6. Choose Close to exit the Network settings dialog box. After recalculating the bindings, Setup shows you a Microsoft TCP/IP Properties dialog box that will, at first, be blank.

7. If more than one adapter has been installed, select the adapter to be configured in the Adapter list. (You should configure each adapter with a valid IP address for the subnet they are on.)

8. If this computer will obtain its address configuration from DHCP for any of the network adapters, click the Obtain an IP address from a DHCP server radio button.

9. If this computer will be configured with static addresses, click the Specify an IP address radio button and complete the following fields:

   IP Address (Required)

   Subnet Mask (Required. Setup will suggest the default subnet mask appropriate for the IP address you enter.)

   Default Gateway

10. Choose OK and restart the computer to activate the settings.

Services

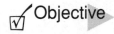 Objective ▶ After you have installed the TCP/IP protocol, you will be able to install several different services that work on the TCP/IP protocol. The following is a list of the services that you may need to install.

▶ **Internet Information Server (IIS).** IIS provides you the capability to share information to any type of computer that can use the TCP/IP protocol. IIS includes FTP, Gopher, and WWW servers.

▶ **Line Printer Daemon.** This server enables you to share printers with many different types of hosts, including main frames
and Unix-based hosts.

▶ **Dynamic Host Configuration Protocol (DHCP).** DHCP provides automatic configuration of remote hosts, making management of a TCP/IP environment easy.

▶ **DHCP Relay Agent.** This extends the capabilities of the
DHCP service by allowing it to work across various different
subnets.

▶ **Windows Internet Name Service (WINS).** Without the ability
to find another computer on the network, you would never
be able to communicate. The WINS server provides a centralized method of name management that is both flexible
and dynamic.

▶ **Simple Network Management Protocol Agent (SNMP).** In
areas where you will use SNMP managers, or even if you want
to track the performance of your TCP/IP protocols, you will
want to install the SNMP agent.

▶ **Domain Name Server (DNS).** Whereas the WINS server provides the capability to find NetBIOS names, the DNS server
works with host names to allow you to integrate your systems
into the Internet or to resolve hosts on the Internet.

These services are covered in detail through the course of this
book.

Chapter

Architectural Overview
of the TCP/IP Suite

2

This chapter will help you prepare for the exam by covering the basics of WINS. This information is the basis for all the information that will follow in this book.

Test Yourself! Before reading this chapter, test yourself to determine how much study time you will need to devote to this section.

1. You are trying to explain the architecture of TCP/IP to a fellow co-worker who has never used it. Your co-worker is familiar with other protocols and is also familiar with the OSI model. How many layers do you tell your co-worker TCP/IP has and to how many of them does it map in the OSI model?

2. The president of your company calls you into a meeting and asks you about the transition you're planning for the corporate-wide network to the TCP/IP protocol. The president expresses some concern about getting locked into a proprietary protocol that will put the company at the mercy of a software company. How do you respond?

3. Your network administrator has told you to integrate your IBM mainframes, NetWare servers, Macintosh clients, and Windows 95, and NT machines with a common protocol. Is TCP/IP able to connect all these different systems together?

4. During a test, you are asked which protocol in the TCP/IP suite is responsible for the routing and delivery of datagrams on the network. Which protocol do you say provides this functionality?

5. Your company has set up a streaming audio/video server that is accessible over your intranet. For some reason, you are unable to see any streaming content through your Web browser. You want to use Network Monitor to help determine whether the datagrams are actually being sent out onto the network. Which transport protocol is best suited for this type of data?

6. One of your users has been reading up on the Unix environment because the company is planning to migrate to the TCP/IP protocol. This user is worried that the Windows network is using the NetBIOS API, and that NetBIOS doesn't work over TCP/IP. Is this a valid concern?

Answers are located at the end of the chapter.

Introduction

Operating systems, networks, and protocols are all designed with a particular framework, or architecture, in mind. Although they may vary from vendor to vendor, it is this fundamental architecture that defines how all the components of a machine, operating system, and protocol fit together.

All computers in a network environment rely on network protocols to enable them to communicate with one another. Network protocols are designed and written to fit into the overall computing framework, or architecture, of the operating system running on a machine. Historically, and even today, defining how these protocols are developed is important. After operating systems such as Microsoft Windows NT began to support multiple protocols running on a machine at the same time, it became even more critical to have a clear idea of how various protocols function in relation to the operating system, and with each other.

This chapter begins with an introduction to physical network architectures. An understanding of the different types of networks is fundamental to understanding the benefits of TCP/IP, as well as many of the services provided by Microsoft, such as the Dynamic Host Configuration Protocol (DHCP) and the Windows Internet Name Service (WINS).

Without an understanding of networks in general, an appreciation of how TCP/IP works is much more difficult to reach. Therefore, this chapter briefly examines various physical network architectures before discussing the architecture of the TCP/IP protocol suite. Those readers not already familiar with physical network architectures may find this a welcome introduction, and those readers who are already familiar may find a review quickly puts points in perspective.

After a review of physical networks, the discussion turns to the Open Systems Interconnect (OSI) model, probably the most common industry architecture for defining how protocols interact with themselves and with each other. This chapter discusses the seven layers of the OSI model and the functionality of each of these layers.

After this, TCP/IP is introduced in terms of how it is managed and how it evolves through the use of Request For Comments (RFCs). It will introduce how TCP/IP maps to a four-layer model rather than a seven-layer model, while demonstrating how the functionality of each layer of the model is still maintained. Within these four layers, the reader discovers that TCP/IP is made up of more than just the TCP and IP protocols and consists of five primary protocols. This chapter serves as an introduction to these protocols as well as the Application Programming Interfaces (APIs) supported with Microsoft's implementation of TCP/IP.

Introductory Concepts—Network Basics

The subjects covered in this section represent the basic knowledge required to understand the architecture of TCP/IP. This section on network basics is intended to review basic network concepts and provide the larger picture within which to see how the TCP/IP architecture comes together.

The Components of a Network

Put simply, a *network* is a collection of machines that have been linked together both physically and through software components to facilitate communication and sharing of information among them. By this definition, a network might be as simple as the computers shown in figure 2.1. In fact, figure 2.1 shows the simplest kind of network that can be created: two machines connected by a piece of coaxial cable. This example is deceptively simple and hides a fairly complex arrangement of pieces that must work together to enable these two machines to communicate.

Figure 2.1

A network in the simplest terms.

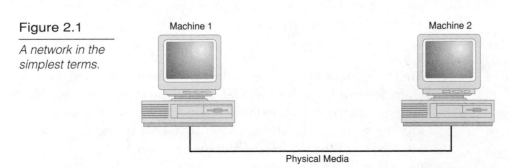

Look at figure 2.2, which shows each of the components, both hardware and software, required to enable communication between these two machines.

Figure 2.2

Network components.

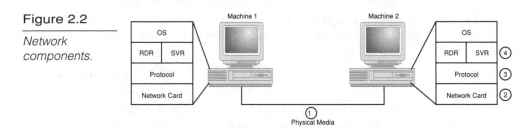

Observe that the first requirement for a network is a physical connection. A number of communication methods can be used to establish a physical connection: 10Base-T Ethernet, 10Base-2 Ethernet, Token Ring, FDDI, and others. Each connection type has pros and cons in terms of ease of installation, maintenance, and expense (see table 2.1). The following table reflects some generalizations about each type of media as a means to connect computers together. Unless you plan to run a wireless network, you need some kind of physical connection between machines for transferring data back and forth.

Table 2.1

Network Connection Types

Connection Type	Installation	Maintenance	Expense	Notes
10Base-2 Coaxial	Easy	Easy	Cheap	Traffic seen by all machines on a coax segment
10Base-T Unshielded Twisted Pair	Moderately easy	Easy	Moderately inexpensive	Traffic can be easily isolated
Token Ring	Moderately difficult	Difficult	Expensive	Traffic isolated, large data throughput
FDDI (Fiber)	Difficult	Difficult	Very expensive	Immune to electrical disturbances, very large data throughput

The second requirement for a network is appropriate hardware, such as a network card in the machine that acts as the interface to the network. The hardware provides the appropriate connection the machine needs to communicate with other machines across the wire. Physical networks can have different connection methods, depending on what has been installed. For example, if the physical network consists of coaxial cable, a BNC connector attaches the machines to the network; whereas if the physical network uses unshielded twisted-pair cabling, RJ-45 connectors connect the machines to the network. It is very difficult to connect an unshielded twisted pair network card to a network that uses coaxial cable and vice versa. Conversion devices and intermediary pieces can be purchased to allow for this kind of mixing, but you're generally better off buying a network card that supports your physical media inherently. This prevents an additional source of error when troubleshooting network connection problems.

Some network cards support multiple connection types for easy implementation. Naturally, a network card in the machine requires machine resources, including interrupts and memory addresses. These features need to be available for the network card to function.

Your third requirement in setting up a network is to install a network protocol. A network protocol is software installed on a machine that determines the agreed-upon set of rules for two or more machines to communicate with each other. One common metaphor used to describe different protocols is to compare them to human languages.

Think of a group of people in the same room who know nothing about each other. In order for them to communicate, this group has to determine what language to speak, how to handle identifying each other, whether to make general announcements or have private conversations, and so on. If machines are using different protocols, it is equivalent to one person speaking French and another person speaking Spanish. Machines that have different protocols installed are not able to communicate with each other. Common protocols in the Microsoft family include: NetBEUI (NetBIOS Extended User Interface), NWlink

(NDIS compliant version of Novell's IPX/SPX), DLC (Data Link Control), AFP (Appletalk File Protocol), and TCP/IP (Transmission Control Protocol/Internet Protocol).

The fourth and final key to the networking equation is having an operating system that is network-aware. Examples of operating systems that are network-aware include Windows NT, Windows 95, Windows for Workgroups, DOS, Unix, and Novell. Most operating systems are network-aware, but until now almost all applications were written to ask for local resources (hard drives) on the machine. Applications have only recently become fully network-aware and still generally use local drives to access resources.

Because applications still use local drives, it falls upon the operating system to be able to redirect (thus the name of the redirector) local resource requests to other machines out on the network. Figure 2.3 illustrates why you map or connect network drives to virtual local drives. The operating system knows the resources are on another machine, but the applications do not. In figure 2.3, the application thinks that drive x: is actually on the local machine. The operating system is responsible for acting on behalf of the application when a resource on the network is requested. Here the I/O manager redirects the save request from the application and sends it to the network redirector. To have a network, your operating system must have the appropriate networking components installed, otherwise the operating system cannot utilize resources that reside over a network connection.

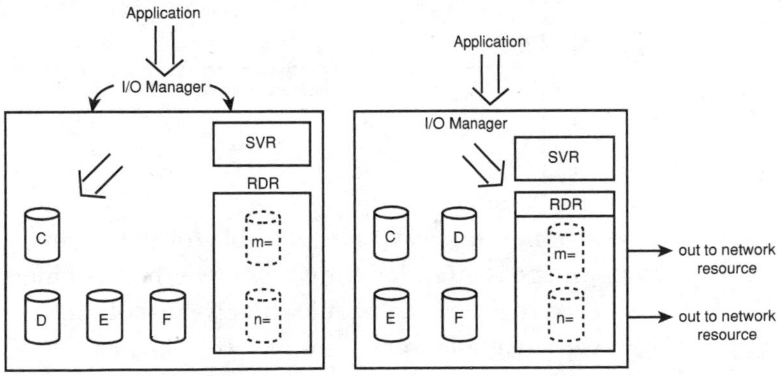

Figure 2.3

A network redirection for an application.

The Physical Address

As long as the four criteria discussed in the preceding section are met, creating a network is relatively simple. All that is necessary now is some way to distinguish machine A from machine B in a way the network cards can understand. This is done by using a physical address, the unique identifier assigned to a network card. This unique identifier is often referred to as the Mac address, the hardware address, or the ethernet address, but these all represent the same thing. For simplicity, this chapter refers to this identifier as the physical address.

A physical address is a 48-bit address represented by six sections of two hexadecimal values, for example 00-C0-DF-48-6F-13. It is assigned by the manufacturer of the network card before it is shipped to be sold. This identifier is designed to be unique and is often used to help identify a single machine on a network. At this level of the networking model, the Physical layer, data being passed over the network appears to be nothing more than the transmission and error-checking of voltage (1s and 0s) on the wire. These 1s and 0s are transmitted in a certain sequence based on the type of network used. This sequence is referred to as a frame. Within the frame, various pieces of information can be deciphered. The first active component to receive and process the voltage being transmitted onto the network is the network card. Figure 2.4 shows an example of what a standard ethernet frame looks like and the components to which an ethernet card is designed to pay attention.

Figure 2.4

A standard IEEE 802.3 (ethernet) frame.

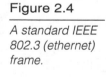 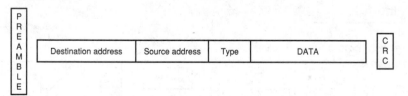

The network card is responsible for determining whether the voltage is intended for it or some other machine. Each network card is given a set of rules that it must obey. First it listens to the preamble to synchronize itself so it can determine where the data within the frame begins. After it determines where the data begins, it discards both the Preamble and the Frame Check

Sequence before continuing to the next process. In the second process, the network card deciphers the data to determine for what physical address the frame is destined. If the destination address matches the physical address of the network card, it continues to process the information and pass the remaining data on for further action. If the destination address specifies some other machine's physical address, it silently discards the data within the frame and starts listening for other messages.

On a machine running Windows NT 4.0, it is relatively easy to determine its IP address. Complete the following steps:

1. From the Start menu, select Programs, Command Prompt.

2. After the command prompt window appears, type **IPCONFIG /all.**

3. Read the information provided by the IPCONFIG utility until you see a section called "Ethernet address." The value represented is the physical address of the machine.

If a network card discards the preamble and determines that the destination physical address is a broadcast, for example FF-FF-FF-FF-FF-FF, this means the message is intended for all machines connected on that network segment. Whenever a network card receives a broadcast, it assumes the data is relevant and passes the data to the rest of the system for further processing. Network protocols such as NetBEUI use broadcasts to begin communication with a single machine on the network, requiring all machines on the network segment to listen, process the frame, and allow higher layers in the networking model to discard the information. Network protocols such as TCP/IP, although capable of broadcasting, typically determine the specific physical address of the destination machine, eliminating a great deal of broadcast traffic.

Figures 2.5 and 2.6 illustrate the difference between the two types of methods in terms of the processing a machine initiates when receiving a broadcast or directed frame.

Figure 2.5

A broadcast frame using NetBEUI.

Figure 2.6

A directed frame using TCP/IP.

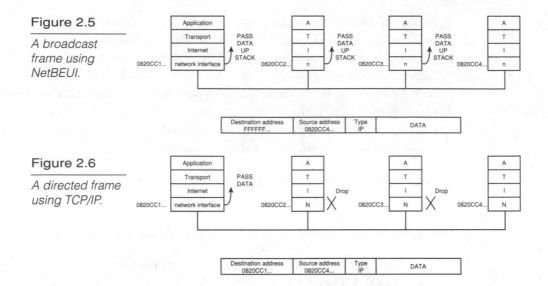

In figure 2.5, each machine on the network opens up the frame and discovers a broadcast address, indicating it must pass the data up to higher layers for processing. In figure 2.6, only one machine passes the data up to the higher networking layers, while the other machines silently discard the frame as uninteresting data.

It would be unfair to say that TCP/IP does not utilize any broadcasts to communicate, but in general, machines on a network using NetBEUI spend more time deciphering broadcast traffic than machines on a TCP/IP network. This is primarily because NetBEUI is optimized for use on a local area network (LAN), where bandwidth and resources are plenty. NetBEUI is also enormously easy to install and configure and requires almost no ongoing intervention on behalf of the user. It's only significant weakness is that it is not a routeable protocol, meaning that it has no addressing characteristics that allow packets to be moved from one logical network to another.

TCP/IP, on the other hand, is designed for wide area network (WAN) environments where routers are the common connection method between two locations. Because of its routability and almost surgical (precise and efficient) use of bandwidth resources, it is clearly the favorite for this type of environment. However, it does require significantly more knowledge and experience on the user's part to install and configure it correctly before it can be utilized. This is probably why Microsoft deems it necessary to test user's and administrator's knowledge of this protocol (that is, they don't have a test dedicated to NetBEUI or NWLink).

Network Topologies

In the seemingly never-ending competition to maximize the amount of data that can be pushed through a piece of wire, numerous network topologies have been tried and tested. Initially, companies offered wholesale solutions for customers wanting to utilize various software packages. The problem was that these solutions typically required certain network protocols and certain hardware be in place before anything would work. This was often referred to as "monolithic" networking because these solutions were rarely interoperable with other applications or hardware.

After a company committed to a particular type of network, they were stuck with that network, and it was just too bad if a really useful application was released for a different network architecture. Accommodating a brand new application or suite of applications sometimes required removing the old network and installing another one. Administrators therefore wanted to make sure they were planning for the longest term possible. In an effort to sell administrators on the benefits of a particular networking package, companies developed network configurations for maximizing network performance. Performance was typically rated by how well a network architecture maximized available bandwidth. The strategies and implementation details for achieving these goals could be broken down into three general configurations. These evolved into the Bus, Ring, and Star configurations. It is helpful to understand how each of these developed.

The Bus Configuration

The bus configuration has its roots with coaxial cable in simple networks where desktop machines are simply connected together so that they can share information with each other. Traffic, here defined as voltage applied to the wire by any machine that needs to communicate, is applied to the bus, or the wire connecting the machines (see fig. 2.7).

Figure 2.7

The bus configuration.

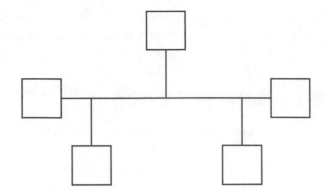

Any time a machine needs to access information from another machine, it simply sends out a sequenced variation of voltage in a frame that the destination machine can understand, process, and respond to. Notice in this configuration (fig. 2.7) that other machines on the network are also listening for frames and will open the frame up long enough to determine whether it is destined for them as well.

In this configuration, clients and servers can be randomly placed on the network, because they are all capable to listening to frames sent by a machine. The main selling point behind this type of network is that it is somewhat simple to set up, and can scale fairly well with the addition of relatively inexpensive hardware, such as repeaters or bridges. The keyword here is relatively. Remember, adding more machines to a bus type network simply adds more machines that will be competing for the wire to transmit.

One problem with this type of network architecture occurs when two machines try to communicate and send their frames on the wire at the same time. This is the electrical equivalent of a train wreck for 1s and 0s, or what is commonly referred to as a collision on the network. Any machine listening on the network for frames has no idea what to make of the chaotic confusion that results from a collision. Imagine trying to listen to fifteen or twenty people trying to talk at the same time to different people, and even possibly in different languages. Thankfully, network cards are designed with algorithms to alleviate some of the chaos surrounding collisions and ground rules for avoiding them in the future. One common design called Carrier-Sense Multiple Access with

Collision Detection (CSMA/CD) implements a standard set of rules for the transmission of frames on a network.

This simple concept (CSMA/CD) defines the relative politeness of machines on the network. When a network card wants to use the wire to transmit data, it listens first to determine whether another machine is already in the process of transmitting. If the network is idle (silent), the machine may transmit its own frames. If, in the course of transmitting, another network card also begins to transmit, a collision occurs. Each network card is instructed to stop transmitting, wait a random amount of time, and then listen again before trying to retransmit the data.

At the blazing speeds that data is transferred, it might seem that collisions are not a problem, and on small networks this is true; however, as networks grow in size and as the data being transferred between machines increases, the number of collisions also increases. It is possible to put so many machines on a network segment that the capability of machines to communicate is slowed down, if not stopped altogether. If too many machines try to communicate at the same time, it is nearly impossible for network cards to transmit data without collisions. This scenario is often referred to as saturating your bandwidth (the amount of sustainable data transfer rate) and should be avoided if at all possible.

To conceptualize this, just imagine the traffic on any rural road and how the traffic increases as the surrounding area becomes more developed. More and more people move into the area and use the roads until it becomes somewhat congested. A quick trip to the store may have taken five minutes initially, but now it takes fifteen minutes to run to the store, despite the fact that the distance hasn't changed. Further development and growth of the area into, say, a metropolitan city, leads to more people and more traffic, until eventually the trip to the store takes two hours because of the constant traffic jams. The usual effect of this is frustration and a commitment not to go to the store during rush hours.

The scenario described above can happen with computer networks as well. The inability to access resources in a timely manner because of saturated bandwidth can lead to productivity losses and frustrated users. One method that has been used to help reduce collisions is specifying a smaller frame size for sending data. By specifying small frame sizes, network cards must stop more often to allow other network cards the opportunity to transmit. This means computers can only send a small amount of data at any one time.

The Ring Configuration

The ring configuration (see fig. 2.8) provides an alternative method for the transmission of data from one computer to another over a network segment. This configuration relies on a token-passing method. In this type of network, one of the machines is designated to be the creator of a token. The token is the vehicle that carries all network communication, and it is sent from one machine to another in a circular loop, until it travels all the way around. A token has two basic states: In Use and Free. If a network card receives the token and the token is Free, it has permission to place data in the token, address the token for a destination address, and flag the token as In Use. This token is passed from network card to network card, each silently ignoring it, until it reaches its destination. After the destination address receives the frame, it formulates a reply, readdresses the token, and sends it back to the originator of the message. Again, the token is passed from one network card to another until the token reaches its origin. Assuming communication between the two machines is done, the originator of the communication releases the token by setting its flag to "Free" and passes it on to the next network card.

Figure 2.8

The ring configuration.

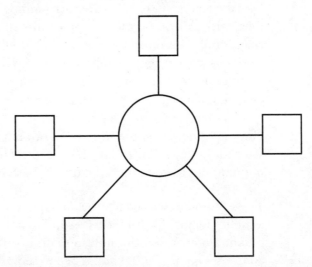

To conceptualize this method, think of a classroom of five students. At any one time a shoebox (the token) is in the hands of one of the students. It starts off empty (no lid, no tag) and is passed around from student to student. After a student decides to send a message, he or she assembles the message, places it inside the shoebox, and puts a lid on the shoebox with a tag indicating who is to receive the message.

Each time a student receives the shoebox, he or she checks to see whether the box has a lid and a tag. If it does have a lid, the student looks at the tag to determine for whom the message is intended. If the lid is on, but the tag isn't addressed to her, the student simply passes it to the next student. A student is only allowed to send a message to any of the others when he receives the shoebox and it is empty. Only if the shoebox is empty can a student put a message into the shoebox.

The only student that can remove the lid permanently is the original sender. After the communication is complete, the sender then removes the lid and passes the empty shoebox to the next student. Notice the absence of any type of collision detection. In a ring - based network, the only communication occurring on the network is by the machine that currently has control of the token. The risk of collisions has been completely eliminated. Not only that, but the lack of collisions means network cards don't have to be quite so polite and can send much larger frames. Larger frame sizes equate to much larger amounts of data being transmitted at any one time.

So where is the drawback? Look at our example again. Student four passes the shoebox with a message to student five. The shoebox is sitting on student five's desk, but student five actually skipped school that day. The ring has essentially been broken (machine crash) and the communications network is down. Without the capability to pass the token to student one, the other students are out of luck. Also, imagine the students are wearing blindfolds and can only identify the students to their immediate left and their immediate right through touch. Therefore, if a student (or machine) on a ring-based network is moved, the student has to learn who its neighbors are again before communications can be reestablished.

As with bus-based networks, software and hardware implementations have been developed to eliminate some of these problems, but ring networks are typically more expensive and more difficult to maintain and service. The main selling point behind this type of configuration is the amount of data that can be transferred at one time through the significantly larger frame sizes.

The Star Configuration

The star configuration (see fig. 2.9) is designed primarily to reduce the traffic with which any one machine has to compete to communicate on the network. It operates in almost the same way as the Bus configuration, with one exceptional difference. Through the implementation of smart hardware, in this case a fast switch in the center of the diagram, machines never have to worry about collisions with each other. The switch isolates the network segments so that collisions do not occur between network cards. All data is designed to flow through the switch. A virtual circuit is created between two machines to allow them to communicate with each other, and this virtual circuit lasts only as long as is necessary to transfer data. After the machines finish communicating, the virtual circuit is destroyed and the segments are isolated from each other once again.

Figure 2.9

The star configuration.

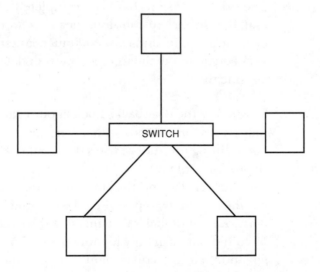

To visualize this, you might think of the switch in the middle acting as telephone operators did back in the days when connections were made between a caller and receiver by plugging the cables into their respective sockets. Switches are performing essentially the same task, just significantly quicker than a person can do it. Again, the connection lasts only as long as the two machines are communicating.

After the machines stop, the connection is broken, and the path between the two machines no longer exists. In a very small environment, each machine is assigned a port on the switch; in most situations, however, this is not terribly practical. Switches of this kind are typically very expensive and would not be used for a small number of machines. Most switches are used in hybrid configurations, where additional hubs are used to provide more available bandwidth to up to hundreds of machines.

The key characteristic of this type of configuration is that each machine with its own port receives the maximum sustainable bandwidth that the medium can carry, because each machine only sees the traffic for the connections it has established. This is one of the more expensive solutions to minimizing bandwidth bottlenecks, but it works very well when implemented.

Hybrid Configurations

These three basic network configurations have been modified and hybridized in the last couple of years so that each has several variations. But in the past, businesses had to chose which configuration they were going to use based not only on the merits of each implementation, but on which software they intended to use. This didn't make too many in the industry happy, understandably. A company producing network interface cards had to know exactly what kinds of programs would be run so that they could support those applications. At the same time, a programmer or software company couldn't complete the authoring of software until they knew what kind of physical network the software would be running on.

Hardware companies were unhappy; software companies were unhappy; and businesses faced with millions of dollars of upgrade investment every time there was a software or operating system conversion were decidedly unhappy.

All this unhappiness led the industry to develop several models for developing networks. These models typically include agreed-upon layers that distribute tasks among various manufacturers and programmers in the industry. This means that software companies can spend their time worrying about improving their software, not about network card standards. And for network card manufacturers, they can spend their time worrying about getting more throughput from their cards, rather than worrying about whether it can support the most popular application of the day. One of the most well-known of these models is the Open Systems Interconnect, or OSI model

The OSI Model

The OSI model takes networking tasks and divides them into seven fundamentally different layers to make it easier for the industry to move forward and evolve. With the tasks segregated into functional units, a person writing the code for a network card doesn't have to worry about what applications are going to be run over it; conversely, a programmer writing an application doesn't have to worry about who manufactured the network card. However, to make this work, everything must be written to comply with the boundary specifications between each of the seven layers of the model. Although the TCP/IP protocol suite only maps to a four-layer model, these four layers provide the same functionality as each of the seven layers of the OSI model.

This chapter examines the functionality of each of the seven layers first and then describes the function of the boundary layers between them. A good understanding of these layers will provide the proper background for looking at the four layers of the TCP/IP protocol suite.

The Physical Layer

The first layer is the Physical layer. This is the only layer that is truly connected to the network in the sense that it is the only layer concerned with how to interpret the voltage on the wire—the 1s and 0s. This layer is responsible for understanding the electrical rules associated with devices and for determining what kind of medium is actually being used (cables, connectors, and other mechanical distinctions). TCP/IP does not function at this level, leaving these tasks instead for the network cards to handle.

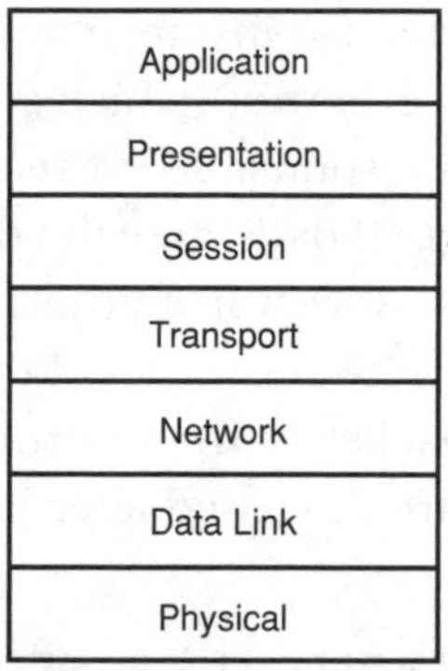

Figure 2.10

The seven layers of the OSI model.

Application
Presentation
Session
Transport
Network
Data Link
Physical

The Data Link Layer

The second layer is the Data Link layer. This layer is responsible for the creation and interpretation of different frame types based on the actual physical network being used. For instance, ethernet and token-ring networks support different and numerous frame types, and the Data Link layer must understand the difference between them. This layer is also responsible for interpreting what it receives from the Physical layer, using low-level error detection and correction algorithms to determine when information needs to be re-sent. Network protocols, including the TCP/IP protocol suite, do not define physical standards at the physical or Data Link layer, but instead are written to make use of any standards that may currently be in use. The boundary layer in between the Data Link layer and Network layer defines a group of agreed-upon standards for how protocols communicate and gain access to these lower layers. As long as a network protocol is appropriately written to this boundary layer, the protocols should be able to access the network, regardless of what media type is being used.

The Network Layer

The third layer of the OSI model is the Network layer. This layer is mostly associated with the movement of data by means of addressing and routing. It directs the flow of data from a source to a destination, despite the fact that the machines may not be connected to the same physical wire or segment, by finding a path or route from one machine to another. If necessary, this layer can break data into smaller chunks for transmission. This is sometimes necessary when transferring data from one type of physical network to another, for instance, token-ring (which supports larger frame sizes) to ethernet (which supports smaller frame sizes). Of course, it is also responsible for reassembling those smaller chunks into the original data after the data has reached its destination. A number of protocols from the TCP/IP protocol suite exist in this layer, but the network protocol that is responsible for routing and delivery of packets is the IP protocol. More on this protocol and the others are discussed later in the chapter.

The Transport Layer

The fourth layer is the Transport layer. This layer is primarily responsible for guaranteeing delivery of packets transmitted by the Network layer, although it does not always have to do so. Depending on the protocol being used, delivery of packets may or may not be guaranteed. When it is responsible for guaranteeing the delivery of packets, it does so through various means of error control, including verification of sequence numbers for packets and other protocol-dependent mechanisms. TCP/IP has two protocols at this layer of the model, Transmission Control Protocol (TCP) and User Datagram Protocol (UDP). UDP may be used for non-guaranteed delivery of packets and TCP may be used to guarantee the delivery of packets.

The Session Layer

The fifth layer is the Session layer. This layer is responsible for managing connections between two machines during the course of communication between them. This layer is the one which determines whether it has received all pertinent information for the session and whether it can stop receiving or transmitting data. This layer also has built-in error correction and recovery methods. TCP/IP utilizes two Application Programming Interfaces (APIs)—Windows Sockets and NetBIOS—for determining whether all information has been sent and received between two connected machines.

The Presentation Layer

The sixth layer is the Presentation layer. This layer is primarily concerned with the conversion of data formats from one machine to another. One common example is the sending of data from a machine that uses the ASCII format for characters to a machine that uses the EBCDIC format for characters, typically IBM mainframes. The Presentation layer is responsible for picking up differences such as these and translating them to compatible formats. Both EBCDIC and ASCII are standards for translating characters to hexadecimal code. Letters, numbers, and symbols in one format must be translated when communicating with machines using a different format. This is the responsibility of the Presentation layer.

The Application Layer

The seventh layer is the Application layer. This is the last layer of the model and acts as the arbiter or translator between users' applications and the network. Applications that want to utilize the network to transfer data must be written to conform to networking APIs supported by the machine's networking components, such as Windows Sockets and NetBIOS. After the application makes an API call, the Application layer determines with which machine it wants to communicate, whether a session should be set up between the communicating machines, and whether the delivery of packets needs to be guaranteed.

The Layer Relationship

Between each layer is a common boundary layer. For instance, between the Network layer and the Transport layer is a boundary that both must be able to support. It is through these boundary layers that one layer of the networking model communicates and shares valuable and necessary information with the layer above or below it. In fact, each time a layer passes data to the layer below, it adds information to it, and each time a layer receives data it strips off its own information and passes the rest up the protocol stack. Figure 2.11 illustrates how each layer of the networking model adds and then strips away information.

Figure 2.11

Passing data up and down the model.

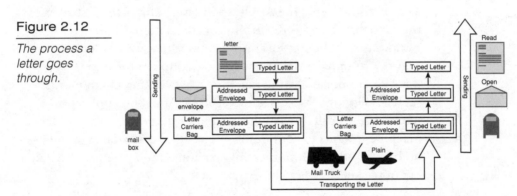

PH=Presentation Layer Header
SH=Session Layer Header
TH=Transport Layer Header
NH=Network Layer Header
DLH=Data Link Header

One of the most common and useful analogies used to describe the networking model is to imagine the process a letter goes through to get to its destination. Figure 2.12 shows a sample of the process.

Figure 2.12

The process a letter goes through.

After looking at figure 2.12, what would happen if any of these steps broke down? The letter would not be received. The same thing happens on computer networks such as the one in figure 2.11. If any of the steps in the process break down, messages are not received. Error checking is applied to the model to keep the communications process from breaking down, just as the postal service runs in any kind of weather. But sometimes packets still get lost in the shuffle.

Messages sent from one computer to another move in the same manner. Messages from one layer are packaged and placed into the next layer. Each step of the process has little to do with the preceding or following step. The kind of envelope used has nothing to do with whether you wrote the message in English, French, or German, and it certainly doesn't matter what the message was. In the same way, where you actually address the envelope, California, Florida, or Hawaii, has absolutely nothing to do with what kind of envelope you use. The only common link between the address and the message is the envelope itself.

Lastly, it doesn't matter which vehicle: boat, plane or train, the postal service uses to deliver the envelope to its destination address, as long as it gets there. Each layer depends upon the other layers, but is only mildly related in terms of functionality to the others. With this introduction to networks and networking, the architecture of TCP/IP can be both more easily understood and appreciated.

Introduction to TCP/IP

The Transmission Control Protocol/Internet Protocol (TCP/IP) is an industry-standard suite of protocols designed to be routeable, robust, and functionally efficient. TCP/IP was originally designed as a set of wide area network (WAN) protocols for the express purpose of maintaining communication links and data transfer between sites in the event of an atomic/nuclear war. Since those early days, development of the protocols has passed from the hands of the government and has been the responsibility of the Internet community for some time.

The evolution of these protocols from a small four-site project into the foundation of the worldwide Internet has been extraordinary. But, despite more than 25 years of work and numerous modifications to the protocol suite, the inherent spirit of the original specifications is still intact.

Installing Microsoft's TCP/IP as a protocol on your machine or network provides the following advantages:

▶ **An industry-standard protocol.** Because TCP/IP is not maintained or written by one company, it is not proprietary or subject to as many compatibility issues. The Internet community as a whole decides whether a particular change or implementation is worthwhile. Naturally, this slows down the implementation of new features and characteristics compared to how quickly one directed company might make changes, but it does guarantee that changes are well thought out, that they provide functionality with most, if not all other implementations of TCP/IP, and that a set of specifications is publicly available that can be referenced at any time over the Internet, detailing how the protocol suite should be used and implemented.

▶ **A set of utilities for connecting dissimilar operating systems.** Many connectivity utilities have been written for the TCP/IP suite, including the File Transfer Protocol (FTP) and Terminal Emulation Protocol (Telnet). Because these utilities use the Windows Sockets API, connectivity from one machine to another is not dependent on the network operating system used on either machine. For example, a Unix FTP server could be accessed by a Microsoft FTP client to transfer files without either party having to worry about compatibility issues. This functionality also allows a Windows NT machine running a Telnet client to access and run commands on an IBM mainframe running a Telnet server, for example.

▶ **A scalable, cross-platform client-server architecture.** Consider what happened during the initial development of applications for the TCP/IP protocol suite. Vendors wanted to be able to write their own client/server applications, for instance, SQL server and SNMP. The specification for how to write applications was also up for public perusal. Which operating systems would be included? Users everywhere wanted to be able to take advantage of the connectivity options promised through utilizing TCP/IP, regardless of the operating system they were currently running. Therefore the Windows Sockets API was established, so that applications utilizing the TCP/IP protocol could write to a standard, agreed-upon interface. Because the contributors included everyone, and therefore every kind of operating system, the specifications for Windows Sockets on TCP/IP were written to make the operating system transparent to the application. Microsoft TCP/IP includes support for Windows Sockets and for connectivity to other Windows Sockets-compliant TCP/IP stacks.

▶ **Access to the Internet.** TCP/IP is the de facto protocol of the Internet and allows access to a wealth of information that can be found at thousands of locations around the world. To connect to the Internet, though, a valid IP address is required. Because IP addresses have become more and more scarce, and as security issues surrounding access to the Internet have been raised, many creative alternatives have been established to allow connections to the Internet. However, all these implementations utilize gateways or firewalls that act on behalf of the requesting machines.

Now that you understand the benefits of installing TCP/IP, you are ready to learn about how the TCP/IP protocol suite maps to a four-layer model.

The Four Layers of TCP/IP

TCP/IP maps to a four-layer architectural model. This model is called the Internet Protocol Suite and is broken into the Network Interface, Internet, Transport, and Application layers. Each of these layers corresponds to one or more layers of the OSI model. The Network Interface layer corresponds to the Physical and Data Link layers. The Internet layer corresponds to the Network layer. The Transport layer corresponds to the Transport layer, and the Application layer corresponds to the Session, Presentation, and Application layers of the OSI model. Figure 2.13 illustrates these relationships.

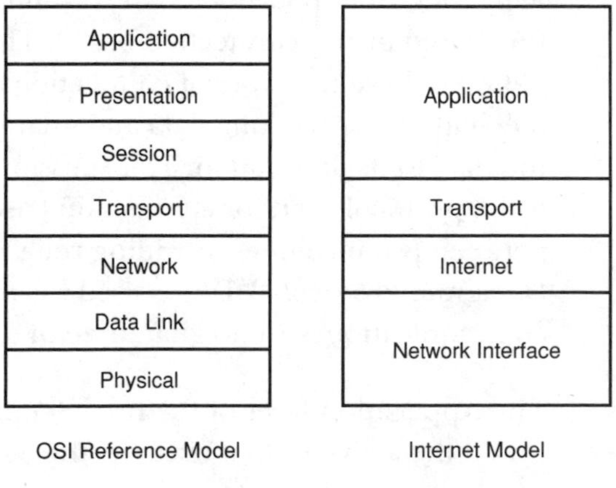

Figure 2.13

Layers in the TCP/IP protocol suite.

OSI Reference Model	Internet Model
Application	
Presentation	Application
Session	
Transport	Transport
Network	Internet
Data Link	Network Interface
Physical	

Each of the four layers of the model is responsible for all the activities of the layers to which it maps.

The Network Interface layer is responsible for communicating directly with the network. It must understand the network architecture being used, such as token-ring or ethernet, and provide an interface allowing the Internet layer to communicate with it. The Internet layer is responsible for communicating directly with the Network Interface layer.

The Internet layer is primarily concerned with the routing and delivery of packets through the Internet Protocol (IP). All the protocols in the Transport layer must use IP to send data. The Internet Protocol includes rules for how to address and direct packets, fragment and reassemble packets, provide security information, and identify the type of service being used. However, because IP is not a connection-based protocol, it does not guarantee that packets transmitted onto the wire will not be lost, damaged, duplicated, or out of order. This is the responsibility of higher layers of the networking model, such as the Transport layer or the Application layer. Other protocols that exist in the Internet Layer are the Internet Control Messaging Protocol (ICMP), Internet Group Management Protocol (IGMP), and the Address Resolution Protocol (ARP). Each of these is described in more detail later in this chapter.

The Transport layer maps to the Transport layer of the OSI model and is responsible for providing communication between machines for applications. This communication can be connection-based or nonconnection-based. The primary difference between these two types of connections is whether there is a mechanism for tracking data and guaranteeing the delivery of the data to its destination. Transmission Control Protocol (TCP) is the protocol used for connection-based communication between two machines providing reliable data transfer. User Datagram Protocol (UDP) is used for nonconnection-based communication with no guarantee of delivery.

The Application layer of the Internet protocol suite is responsible for all the activities that occur in the Session, Presentation, and Application layers of the OSI model. Numerous protocols have been written for use in this layer, including Simple Network Management Protocol (SNMP), File Transfer Protocol (FTP), Simple Mail Transfer Protocol (SMTP), as well as many others.

The interface between each of these layers is written to have the capability to pass information from one layer to the other. Figure 2.14 illustrates how each layer adds its own information to the data and hands it down to the lower layers. It also illustrates how that data is then stripped off by the corresponding layer of the receiving machine, until what is left is only the information needed by that layer.

Figure 2.14

Layers in the TCP/IP protocol suite.

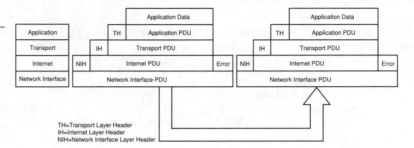

The interface between the Network Interface layer and the Internet layer does not pass a great deal of information, although it must follow certain rules. Namely, it must listen to all broadcasts and send the rest of the data in the frame up to the Internet layer for processing, and if it receives any frames that do not have an IP frame type, they must be silently discarded.

The interface between the Internet layer and the Transport layer must be able to provide each layer full access to such information as the source and destination addresses, whether TCP or UDP should be utilized in the transport of data, and all other available mechanisms for IP. Rules and specifications for the Transport layer include giving the Transport layer the capability to change these parameters or to pass parameters it receives from the Application layer down to the Internet layer. The most important thing to remember about all of these boundary layers is that they must use the agreed upon rules for passing information from one layer to the other.

The interface between the Transport layer and the Application layer is written to provide an interface to applications, whether or not they are using the TCP or UDP protocol for transferring data. The interface utilizes the Windows Sockets and NetBIOS APIs to transfer parameters and data between the two layers. The Application layer must have full access to the Transport layer to change and alter parameters as necessary.

The layers provide only guidelines, though; the real work is done by the protocols that are contained within the layers. This chapter describes the TCP/IP protocol as being a suite of protocols, not just two (TCP and IP). In fact, six primary protocols are associated with TCP/IP:

▶ Transmission Control Protocol (TCP)

▶ User Datagram Protocol (UDP)

▶ Internet Protocol (IP)

▶ Internet Control Message Protocol (ICMP)

▶ Address Resolution Protocol (ARP)

▶ Internet Group Management Protocol (IGMP)

Figure 2.15 shows where each of these protocols resides in the architectural model. Each protocol has a graphic to help you visualize the type of communication that is being achieved through these protocols. The telephone is meant to represent TCP; the letter is meant to represent UDP; the security guard is meant to represent ICMP; the cable TV is meant to represent IGMP; the detective is meant to represent ARP; and the mail truck/phone operator is meant to represent IP. Each of these protocols and the details of their implementation is discussed in the following sections.

Transmission Control Protocol

The first protocol that lives in the Transport layer is the Transmission Control Protocol (TCP). This protocol is a connection-based protocol and requires the establishment of a session before data is transmitted between two machines. TCP packets are delivered to sockets or ports. Because TCP sets up a connection between two machines, it is designed to verify that all packets sent by a machine are received on the other end. If, for some reason, packets are lost, the sending machine resends the data. Because a session is established and delivery of packets is guaranteed, there is additional overhead involved with using TCP to transmit packets.

Figure 2.15

Protocols within the layers of the TCP/IP protocol suite.

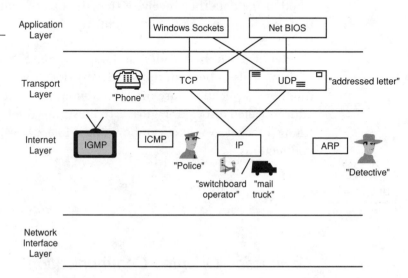

To understand TCP further, you must understand ports and sockets, connection-oriented communications, sliding windows, and acknowledgments. The following sections cover each of these areas.

Ports and Sockets

The communication process between the Transport layer and the Application layer involves identifying the application that has requested either a reliable or unreliable transport mechanism. Port assignments are the means used to identify application processes to the Transport layer. Ports identify to which process on the machine data should be sent for further processing. Specific port numbers have been assigned by the Internet Assigned Numbers Authority (IANA), specifically those from 1 to 1023. These port assignments are called the well-known ports and represent the ports to which standard applications listen. Defining these standard port numbers helps eliminate having to guess to which port an application is listening so that applications can direct their queries or messages directly. Port numbers above the well-known port range are available for running applications, and work in exactly the same way. In this case, however, the client or user has to be able to identify to which port the application is connecting. Ports can be used by both TCP and UDP for delivering data between two machines. Ports themselves do not care whether the data they receive is in order or not, but the applications running on those ports might.

To identify both the location and application to which a stream of data needs to be sent, the IP address (location) and the port number (application) are often combined into one functional address called a socket. Figure 2.16 illustrates the format for defining a socket. A socket can be defined for either TCP or UDP connections.

Figure 2.16

Definition of a socket.

IP address	+	Port	=	Select
131.107.2.200		137		131.107.2.200(137)

Connection-Oriented Communication

The Transmission Control Protocol (TCP) is a connection-based protocol that establishes a connection, or session, between two machines before any data is transferred. TCP exists within the Transport layer, between the Application layer and the IP layer, providing a reliable and guaranteed delivery mechanism to a destination machine. Connection-based protocols guarantee the delivery of packets by tracking the transmission and receipt of individual packets during communication. A session is able to track the progress of individual packets by monitoring when a packet is sent, in what order it was sent, and by notifying the sender when it is received so it can send more. Figure 2.17 illustrates how TCP sets up a connection-oriented session between two machines.

The first step in the communication process is to send a message indicating a desire to synchronize the systems. This is equivalent to dialing a phone number and waiting for someone to answer. The second step is for the machine to send an acknowledgment that it is listening and willing to accept data. This step is equivalent to a person answering the phone, and then waiting for the caller to say something. The third step is for the calling machine to send a message indicating that it understands the receiving machine's willingness to listen and that data transmission will now begin.

Figure 2.17

Connection-based communication.

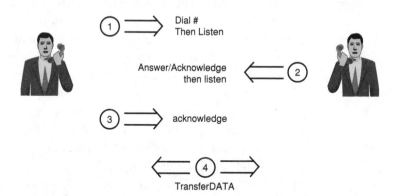

1 ⟹ Dial #
Then Listen

Answer/Acknowledge
then listen ⟸ 2

3 ⟹ acknowledge

⟸ 4 ⟹
TransferDATA

After the TCP session has been created, the machines begin to communicate just as people do during a phone call. In the example of the telephone, if the caller uses a cellular phone and some of the transmission is lost, the user indicates she did not receive the message by saying "What did you say? I didn't hear that." This indicates to the sender that he needs to resend the data.

Figure 2.18 illustrates the format of a TCP header. The header includes all the parameters that are used to guarantee delivery of packets and to provide error-checking and control. Notice that the header specifies a source and destination port for the communication. This tells the machine where it is supposed to send the data, and from where the data came.

Figure 2.18

The TCP datagram parameters.

0										1										2										3	
0	1	2	3	4	5	6	7	8	9	0	1	2	3	4	5	6	7	8	9	0	1	2	3	4	5	6	7	8	9	0	1

Source Port	Destination Port
Sequence Number	
Achknowledgement Number	

Data Offset	Reserved	U R G	A C K	P S H	R S T	S Y N	F I N	Window
Checksum								Urgent Pointer
Options							Padding	
data								

Included in the header are sections defining the sequence numbers and acknowledgment numbers that help verify the delivery of a datagram. A datagram or packet is simply the data that is being transferred to the destination machine. This data often has to be broken up into smaller pieces (datagrams) because the underlying network can only transmit so much data at one time. Other parameters include the SYN and FIN options for starting and ending communication sessions between two machines, the size of the window to be used in transferring data, a checksum for verifying the header information, and other options that can be specific implementations of TCP/IP. The last part of the frame is the actual data being transmitted. A full discussion of each of these parameters is beyond the scope of this book or the TCP/IP test. More academic texts and RFCs on the Internet describe in fuller detail the specifications for each parameter. I recommend looking for sources that speak to you in your language. Some resources are engineering texts; some are much too simple. Look for a happy medium to begin with and work your way into the more complex.

During the initialization of a TCP session, often called the "three-way handshake," both machines agree on the best method to track how much data is to be sent at any one time, acknowledgment numbers to be sent upon receipt of data, and when the connection is no longer necessary because all data has been transmitted and received. It is only after this session is created that data transmission begins. To provide reliable delivery, TCP places packets in sequenced order and requires acknowledgment that these packets reached their destination before it sends new data. TCP is typically used for transferring large amounts of data, or when the application requires acknowledgment that data has been received. Given all the additional overhead information that TCP needs to keep track of, the format of a TCP packet can be somewhat complex.

Try to visualize TCP as being similar to a phone call. Imagine Shey decides to call Kim on the phone. Shey picks up the phone and dials Kim's phone number. This is equivalent to TCP sending out a synchronization request to another machine. Kim happens to have caller ID and can identify Shey before picking up the phone. Kim decides to speak to Shey and picks up the phone with a greeting, something like "Hi," indicating her willingness to communicate.

This is equivalent to a machine sending an acknowledgment that it has received a synchronization request and is willing to respond. Shey now says "Hi," indicating that he has heard Kim and is ready to communicate, in the same way that a sending machine verifies that it has received the other machine's willingness to communicate. Now Shey and Kim can talk about anything they want, secure in the knowledge that their messages are being received.

After the transfer of data is complete, the TCP session is broken down in a similar three-step fashion. In the case of Shey and Kim, Shey may indicate his need to get off the phone because he's run out of things to say. Kim says, "Oh, no problem, goodnight." Shey ends the three step sequence by saying "Goodnight." Machines use the same type of process to break down a TCP session. The sending machine indicates that it has run out of data to send and wants to close the connection. The receiving machine indicates it has received all the data and that closing the connection is fine. The sending machine then simply closes the connection.

Sliding Windows

For an exercise covering this information, see end of chapter.

TCP uses the concept of sliding windows for transferring data between machines. Sliding windows are often referred to in the Unix environment as streams. Each machine has both a send window and a receive window that it utilizes to buffer data and make the communication process more efficient. A window represents the subset of data that is currently being sent to a destination machine, and is also the amount of data that is being received by the destination machine. At first this seems redundant, but it really isn't. Not all data that is sent is guaranteed to be received, so they must be kept track of on both machines. A sliding window allows a sending machine to send the window data in a stream without having to wait for an acknowledgment for every single packet.

A receiving window allows a machine to receive packets out of order and reorganize them while it waits for more packets. This reorganization may be necessary because TCP utilizes IP to transmit data, and IP does not guarantee the orderly delivery of packets. Figure 2.19 shows the send and receive windows that exist on machines that have TCP/IP installed. By default, window sizes in

Windows NT are a little more than 8 KB in size, representing eight standard ethernet frames. Standard ethernet frames are a little more than 1KB apiece.

Figure 2.19

Send and receive windows.

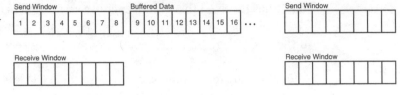

Packets do not always make it to their destination, though. TCP has been designed to recover in the event that packets are lost along the way, perhaps by busy routers. TCP keeps track of the data that has been sent out, and if it doesn't receive an acknowledgment for that data from the destination machine in a certain amount of time, the data is re-sent. In fact, until acknowledgment for a packet of data is received, further data transmission is halted completely.

Acknowledgments

Acknowledgments are a very important component necessary to ensure the reliable delivery of packets. As the receiving window receives packets, it sends acknowledgments to the sending window that the packets arrived intact. When the send window receives acknowledgments for data it has sent, it slides the window to the right so that it can send any additional data stored in memory. But it can only slide over by the number of acknowledgments it has received. By default, a receive window sends an acknowledgment for every two sequenced packets it receives. Therefore, assuming no network problems, if the send window in figure 2.20 sends eight packets to the receive window on the other machine, four acknowledgment packets come back. An acknowledgment for packets 1 and 2, 3 and 4, 5 and 6, and 7 and 8. The sending window slides over to the next eight packets waiting to be sent and sends those out to the receiving window. In this manner, the number of acknowledgments sent over the network is reduced, and the flow of traffic is increased.

Figure 2.20

*Sliding after re-
ceiving acknowl-
edgments.*

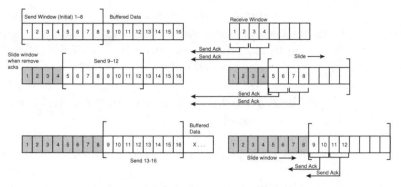

As long as the acknowledgments begin flowing back regularly from
the receiving machine, data flows smoothly and efficiently. However, on busy networks, packets can get lost and acknowledgments
may be delayed. Because TCP guarantees delivery and reliability of
traffic flow, the window cannot slide past any data that has not been
acknowledged. If the window cannot slide beyond a packet of data,
no more data beyond the window is transmitted, TCP eventually
has to shut down the session, and the communication fails.

Each machine is therefore instructed to wait a certain amount of
time before either retransmitting data or sending acknowledgments for packets that arrive out of sequence. Each window is
given a timer: the send window has the Retransmit Timer and the
receive window has the Delayed Acknowledgment Timer. These
timers help define what to do when communication isn't flowing
very smoothly.

In the sending window, a Retransmit Timer is set for each packet,
specifying how long to wait for an acknowledgment before making the assumption that the packet did not get to its destination.
After this timer has expired, the send window is instructed to
resend the packet and wait twice as long as the time set on the
preceding timer. The default starting point for this timer is
approximately 3 seconds but is usually reduced to less than a
second almost immediately. Each time an acknowledgment is
not received, the Retransmit Timer doubles. For instance, if the
Retransmit Timer started at approximately 1 second, the second
Retransmit Timer is set for 2 seconds, the third for 4 seconds, the
fourth, 8 seconds, up to a fifth attempt that waits 16 seconds. The
number of attempts can be altered in the Registry, but if after

these attempts an acknowledgment still cannot be received, the TCP session is closed and errors are reported to the application. Figure 2.21 illustrates the resending of data after the first Retransmit Timer has expired.

The Registry location for changing the number of times to retry a transmission is in the following subkey:

`HKEY_LOCAL_MACHINE\SYSTEM\CurrentControlSet\Services\Tcpip\Parameters`

The Registry parameter and value is:

`TcpMaxDataRetransmissions (REG_DWORD).`

The default value is 5.

Figure 2.21

Retransmission of data after the Retransmit Timer has expired.

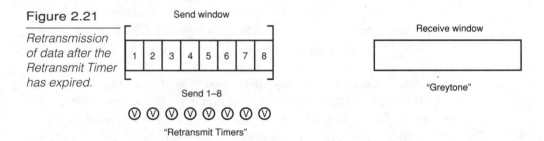

In the receiving window, a Delayed Acknowledgment Timer is set for those packets that arrive out of order. Remember, by default an acknowledgment is sent for every two sequenced packets, starting from the left-hand side of the window. If packets arrive out of order (if, for instance, 1 and 3 arrive but 2 is missing), an acknowledgment for two sequenced packets is not possible. When packets arrive out of order, a Delayed Acknowledgment Timer is set on the first packet in the pair. In the parenthetical example, a Timer is set on packet number 1. The Delayed Acknowledgment Timer is hard-coded for 200 milliseconds, or $\frac{1}{5}$ the Retransmit Timer. If packet 2 does not show up before the Delayed Acknowledgment Timer expires, an acknowledgment for packet 1, and only packet 1, is sent. No other acknowledgments are sent, including those for packets 3 through 8 that might have appeared. Until packet 2 arrives, the other packets are considered interesting, but useless. As data is acknowledged and passed to the Application layer, the receive window slides to the right, enabling more data to be received. Again though, if a packet doesn't show up, the window is not enabled to slide past it. Figure 2.22 illustrates the Delayed Acknowledgment Timer in action.

Figure 2.22

Setting of the Delayed Acknowledgment Timer for out-of-sequence packets.

Send window

"Greytone"

missing DATA

| 1 | | 3 | 4 | 5 | | | | |

Ⓥ

"Delayed Acknowledgement Timer"

User Datagram Protocol

The second protocol that lives in the Transport layer is the User Datagram Protocol, or UDP. This protocol is a nonconnection-based protocol and does not require a session to be established between two machines before data is transmitted. UDP packets are still delivered to sockets or ports, just as they are in TCP. But because UDP does not create a session between machines, it cannot guarantee that packets are delivered or that they are delivered in order or retransmitted if the packets are lost. Given the apparent unreliability of this protocol, some may wonder why a protocol such as UDP was developed. Figure 2.23 illustrates the relative simplicity of the address format of UDP compared to TCP.

Figure 2.23

The UDP datagram format.

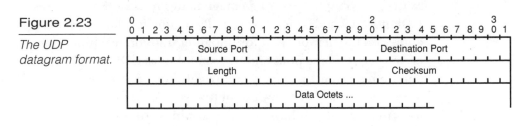

Notice that sending a UDP datagram has very little overhead involved. A UDP datagram has no synchronization parameters or priority options. All that exist are the source port, destination port, the length of the data, a checksum for verifying the header, and then the data.

There are actually a number of good reasons to have a transport protocol that does not require a session to be established. For one, very little overhead is associated with UDP, such as having to keep track of sequence numbers, Retransmit Timers, Delayed Acknowledgment Timers, and retransmission of packets. UDP is quick and extremely streamlined functionally; it's just not guaranteed. This makes UDP perfect for communications that involve broadcasts, general announcements to the network, or real-time data.

For an exercise covering this information, see end of chapter.

Try to visualize UDP as being similar to a postcard. In order for Shey to send a message to Kim, all Shey needs to know is Kim's address. Shey can write his message on the postcard, put Kim's address on it and put it in the mailbox to be sent. Shey does not have to verify that Kim is at home to send the postcard on its way. If Kim is at home when the mailman arrives, the postcard is read and the message is received. Notice that unless Kim responds back to Shey through mail or by phone, Shey can never really know whether the postcard was received. That is the nature of nonconnection-oriented protocols. Delivery is not guaranteed. If the mailman is eaten by the neighbor's dog, or the sorting machine at the post office eats the postcard, or a tornado takes out the mail truck, Shey may never know it, and Kim may never know there was a message intended for her.

In terms of applications, the same methodology is true. For instance, the Simple Network Management Protocol (SNMP) uses UDP ports 67 and 68 for occasionally polling for data from machines on the network and for initiating traps on machines when errors occur. These polls and traps are sent as UDP broadcasts and do not require a session to be established to communicate a message. Think about how useful that is. Does it make any sense for a machine that is having a catastrophic error of some sort to have to go through the business of establishing a TCP session, just to tell you the machine is going down? No, it doesn't. It makes perfect sense however, to let the last gasping breath of a machine be a broadcast message that it's in serious trouble.

Another really good use for UDP is in streaming video and streaming audio. Not only does the unguaranteed delivery of packets enable more data to be transmitted (because a broadcast has little to no overhead), but the retransmission of a packet is pointless, anyway. In the case of a streaming broadcast, users are more concerned with what's coming next than with trying to recover a packet or two that may not have made it. Compare it to listening to a music CD and a piece of dust gets stuck in one of the little grooves. In most cases, the omission of that piece is imperceptible; your ear barely notices and your brain probably filled in the gap for you anyway. Imagine instead that your CD player decides to guarantee the delivery of that one piece of data that it can't quite get, and ends up skipping and skipping indefinitely. It can definitely ruin the listening experience. It is easier to deal with an occasional packet dropping out to have as fulfilling a listening experience as possible. Thankfully, UDP was developed for applications to utilize in this very same fashion.

Internet Protocol

A number of protocols are found in the Internet layer, including the most important protocol in the entire suite, the Internet Protocol (IP). The reason that this is probably the most important protocol is that the Transport layer cannot communicate at all without communicating through IP in the Internet layer. Figure 2.24 illustrates that at one point or another all Transport layer traffic is passed through IP, with no exceptions. IP is responsible for the handling, addressing, and routing of packets on a network. It is a connection-less delivery system, and delivery of packets is not guaranteed. Reliability is provided by the higher layers, either through TCP or by higher-layer applications.

Figure 2.24

IP protocol layer.

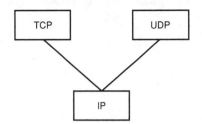

In figure 2.24, the IP protocol is referred to by a mail truck and a telephone operator icon, because IP is responsible for the delivery of packets whether they use connection-based or non-connection-based communications. Delivery and routing are not guaranteed, even though for the most part they work seamlessly.

IP also has a number of parameters that can be set. Figure 2.25 illustrates a sample datagram for IP and the various characteristics that can be configured.

Figure 2.25

An IP packet on the network.

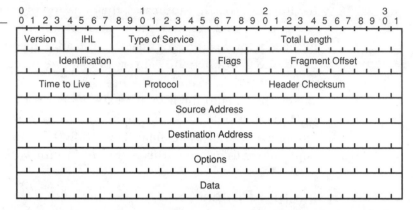

Of the parameters that can be controlled and set in the IP packet in figure 2.25, pay close attention to the Time to Live, the Protocol, Source Address, and the Destination Address. These parameters are what specify where a datagram is supposed to be sent, where it came from, how long a packet has to get to its destination before it is discarded by the network, and to what protocol (such as TCP or UDP) the data should be passed.

Addressing

The most fundamental element of the Internet Protocol is the address space that IP uses. Each machine on a network is given a unique 32-bit address called an Internet address or IP address. Addresses are divided into five categories, called classes. There are currently A, B, C, D, and E classes of addresses. The unique address given to a machine is derived from the Class A, B, or C addresses. Class D addresses are used for combining machines into one functional group, and Class E addresses are considered experimental and are not currently available. For now, the most important concept to understand is that each machine requires a unique address and IP is responsible for maintaining, utilizing, and manipulating it to provide communication between two machines. The whole concept behind uniquely identifying machines is to be able to send data to one machine and one machine only, even in the event that the IP stack has to broadcast at the Physical layer. Figure 2.26 illustrates how IP can distinguish between machines even when the frame is sent as a broadcast at the physical address layer.

Figure 2.26

An IP packet on the network.

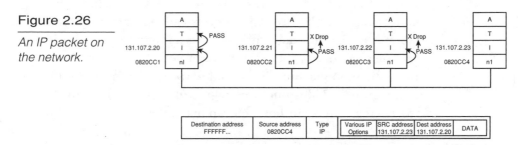

If IP receives data from the network interface layer that is addressed to another machine or is not a broadcast, its directions are to silently discard the packet and not continue processing it.

IP receives information in the form of packets from the Transport layer, from either TCP or UDP, and sends out data in what are commonly referred to as datagrams. The size of a datagram is dependent upon the type of network that is being used, such as token-ring or ethernet. If a packet has too much data to be transmitted in one datagram, it is broken into pieces and transmitted through several datagrams. Each of these datagrams has to then be reassembled by TCP or UDP. More on fragmentation and reassembly is discussed in the "Fragmentation and Reassembly" section later in this chapter.

Broadcasts

Despite the fact that IP was designed to be able to send packets directly to a particular machine, at times it is preferable to send a message to all machines connected to a physical segment. IP supports broadcasts at the Internet layer and if it receives a broadcast datagram from the Network Interface layer, it must process the packet as if it had been addressed to it.

Fragmentation and Reassembly

Fragmentation and reassembly occurs when data is too large to be transmitted on the underlying network. Combining a token-ring and ethernet network is the most common example. Token-ring networks support much larger frame sizes and therefore support larger datagram sizes. It may also be the case that the Transport layer sends the Internet layer more data than one datagram can handle. In either of these cases, IP must break down the data into manageable chunks through a process called fragmentation. After data is fragmented, each datagram gets a fragment ID, identifying it in the sequence so that each fragment can be reassembled at the destination machine. This whole process is transparent to the user. Figure 2.27 illustrates the fragmentation and reassembly process that can occur between two machines.

Figure 2.27

Fragmentation and reassembly.

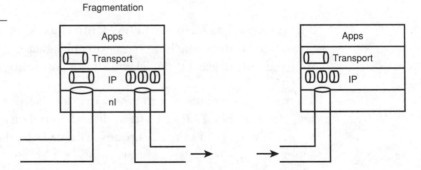

After the fragments have been received and reassembled at the destination machine, the data can be sent up to the higher layers for processing.

Routeability

IP is responsible for routing IP datagrams from one network to another. Machines on a network can be configured to support routing. With routing, when a machine receives a datagram that is neither addressed to it nor is a broadcast, it is given the additional responsibility of trying to find where the datagram should be sent so that it can reach its destination. Not all machines on a TCP/IP network are routers. But all routers have the capability to forward datagrams from one network to another. Connections to the Internet are often through one form of router or another.

Time To Live

The Time to Live (TTL) specification is set in Windows NT to a default of 128. This represents either 128 hops or 128 seconds, or a combination of the two. Each time a router handles a datagram, it decrements the TTL by one. If a datagram is held up at a router for longer than one second before it is transmitted, the router can decrement the TTL by more than one.

One way to visualize how the TTL works is to think of a deadly poison. Each time a datagram is sent out on to the network, it is injected with this deadly poison. The datagram has only the length of time specified in the TTL to get to its destination and receive the antidote for the poison. If the datagram gets routed through congested routers, traffic jams, narrow bandwidth communication avenues, and so on it just might not make it. If the TTL expires before the datagram reaches its destination, it is discarded from the network.

Although this concept may seem strange at first, in reality it prevents datagrams from running around a network indefinitely wreaking havoc with bandwidth and the synchronization of data. Imagine a scenario in which 100 datagrams are sent to a machine. Twenty-five of them have to be resent because the Retransmit Timer on the sending machine expired. After the communication is complete and the session broken down, suddenly 25 packets appear out of nowhere hitting the destination machine. It may be that these 25 packets got rerouted through some extremely slow network path and were never discarded. At least in this case the destination machine can just ignore the datagrams. However, in routed environments it would be pretty easy to set up infinite loops where packets would bounce in between two routers indefinitely.

So here we have TCP, UDP, and IP working together to provide both connection-oriented and non-connection-oriented communication. These three protocols work together to provide communication between two machines.

For an exercise covering this information, see end of chapter.

Consider an example that helps to illustrate exactly how each of these protocols works and the functionality required by them. In this illustration, Bob would like to send a message to Kim. The message is an invitation to a New Year's Eve party.

Think of TCP as being similar to a telephone call. Bob picks up the phone and dials Kim's number. If Kim is home and wants to receive calls, she picks up the phone, indicating that she is home and available to communicate. Kim answers with a greeting of some sort, such as "Hi," indicating to Bob that he should speak. Bob then chooses the appropriate response to Kim's "Hi," such as, "Hey, this is Bob, I'm glad you're home." After this pleasant exchange, the session has been created and Bob can send his message of friendship to Kim. If, however, Bob replies with a response such as "Goodbye," rather than "Hey," the communication breaks down because Kim would think, "How strange," and hang up the phone before any communication can occur. And certainly, if Kim is not at home, no data can be transferred.

Think of UDP now. Here communication can be achieved simply by Bob placing a written invitation in an envelope, addressing it properly, and placing the envelope in his mailbox with the flag up. Bob does not have to verify that Kim is currently at home to send the message. Delivery of the message is not guaranteed, however, because the only way for Bob to know whether the message got there would be for him to receive some indication from Kim, either by mail or by phone. Until Kim responds, Bob has no idea whether the mailman was attacked by a dog, or if perhaps the invitation is currently sitting under a stack of bills on Kim's desk. The point is, Bob has no way to know.

Now how did IP play into the picture? IP serves both kinds of communications methods, but in and of itself does not guarantee delivery of data. Consider how this applies to the example. For the telephone conversation, IP acts similarly to the old-style operator who connects the call. The operator can make the connection and deliver the available resources, but it's still up to Bob to say the correct things, and it's still up to Kim to answer the phone. For the mailed invitation, IP acts as the mailman. The mailman checks to see whether the address is properly formatted and routes it to the appropriate delivery method, until it eventually lands in Kim's mailbox. No guarantees are made here in terms of delivery of the mail.

Internet Control Message Protocol

Internet Control Message Protocol (ICMP) is part of the Internet layer and is responsible for reporting errors and messages regarding the delivery of IP datagrams. It can also send "source quench" and other self tuning signals during the transfer of data between two machines without the intervention of the user. These signals are designed to fine-tune and optimize the transfer of data automatically. ICMP is the protocol that warns you when a destination host is unreachable, or how long it took to get to a destination host. In figure 2.24, ICMP is represented by a policeman. If it helps, think of ICMP as the Internet Control Military Police, the protocol that's always watching over your shoulder.

ICMP messages can be broken down into two basic categories: the reporting of errors and the sending of queries. Error messages include the following:

▶ Destination unreachable

▶ Redirect

▶ Source quench

▶ Time exceeded

The Destination unreachable error message is generated by ICMP when an IP datagram is sent out and the destination machine either cannot be located or does not support the designated protocol. For instance, a sending machine may receive a Destination host unreachable message when trying to communicate through a router that does not know to which network to send a datagram.

The first important thing to realize about Redirect messages is that these are only sent by routers in a TCP/IP environment, not individual machines. A machine may have more than one default gateway defined for redundancy. If a router detects a better route to a particular destination, it forwards the first packet it receives, but sends a redirect message to the machine to update its route tables. In this way, the machine can use the better route to reach the remote network.

Sometimes a machine has to drop incoming datagrams because it has received so many it can't process them all. In this case, a machine can send a Source quench message to the source, indicating it needs to slow up transmission. The Source quench message can also be sent by a router if it is in between the source and destination machines and is encountering trouble routing all the packets in time. Upon receiving a Source quench message, the source machine immediately reduces its transmissions. However, it continues to try to increase the amount of data as time progresses to the original amount of data it was sending before.

The Time exceeded error message is sent by a router whenever it drops a packet due to the expiration of the TTL. This error message is sent to the source address to notify the machine of a possible infinite routing loop or that the TTL is set too low to get to the destination.

ICMP also includes general message queries. The two most commonly used are the following:

▶ Echo request

▶ Echo reply

The most familiar tool for verifying that an IP address on a network actually exists is the Personal Internet Groper (PING) utility. This utility uses the ICMP echo request and reply mechanisms. The echo request is a simple directed datagram that asks for acknowledgment that a particular IP address exists on the network. If a machine with this IP address exists and receives the request, it is designed to send an ICMP echo reply. This reply is sent back to the destination address to notify the source machine of its existence. The PING utility reports the existence of the IP address and how long it took to get there.

ICMP serves a number of functions, but primarily acts as the messenger for what is happening during the communication process. (Remember, you should think of ICMP as standing for the Internet Control Military Police.) For instance, in the mail example, if Bob improperly formats his address, ICMP (the police) come knocking on Bob's door to notify him of his error. Or if Bob sends so many letters to Kim that Kim's mailbox cannot hold them all, causing a considerable overflow at the post office, ICMP (the police) knock on Bob's door and politely ask him to reduce his transmissions. In the phone call scenario, if Bob dials the wrong number, ICMP (the police) are right there to warn Bob about the error of his ways. Or if Bob talks Kim's poor ear off and doesn't let her get a word in edgewise, ICMP (the police) kindly step in on Kim's behalf and remind Bob that conversations are supposed to work both ways.

Internet Group Management Protocol

For an exercise covering this information, see end of chapter.

Internet Group Management Protocol (IGMP) is a protocol and set of specifications that allow machines to be added and removed from IP address groups, utilizing the class D range of addresses mentioned earlier. IP allows the assignment of class D addresses to groups of machines so that they may receive broadcast data as one functional unit. Machines can be added and removed from these units or groups, or be members of multiple groups. The reason for assigning the cable television icon to this protocol in figure 2.24 is based on how both cable TV and IGMP work. Both work in fundamentally the same way.

For instance, when you want to receive the premium channels, you pay more money and the cable company alters your cable box so that you can receive the premium channels. You have therefore joined the group of people who receive the premium cable channels. All you have to do to remove yourself from this group is stop paying your bill. And presto, several months later, you no longer get the premium channels you once had. If you are not a subscriber, you never see the pay channels. But if you want premium channels you can get a wide range of choices, just as you can be a member of a number of Class D addresses, or IGMP groups, to receive broadcasts.

Most implementations of the TCP/IP protocol stack support this on the local machine; however routers designed to broadcast IGMP messages from one network to another are still in the experimental stage. Routers are designed to initiate queries for multicast groups on local network segments to determine whether they should be broadcasting on that segment. If at least one member of an IGMP group exists or responds with a IGMP response, the router processes IGMP datagrams and broadcasts them on the segment.

Address Resolution Protocol

Unless IP is planning to initiate a full broadcast on the network, it has to have the physical address of the machine to which it is going to send datagrams. For this information, it relies on Address Resolution Protocol (ARP). ARP is responsible for mapping IP addresses on the network to physical addresses in memory. This way, whenever IP needs a physical address for a particular IP address, ARP can deliver. But ARP's memory does not last indefinitely, and occasionally IP will ask for an IP address that is not in ARP's memory. When this happens, ARP has to go out and find one. This is why ARP is represented by the detective icon in figure 2.24.

ARP is responsible for finding a map to a local physical address for any local IP address that IP may request. If ARP does not have a map in memory it has to go find one on the network. ARP uses local broadcasts to find physical addresses of machines and maintains a cache in memory of recently mapped IP addresses to physical addresses. Although this cache does not last indefinitely, it enables ARP to not have to broadcast every time IP needs a physical address.

As long as the destination IP address is local, all ARP does is a local broadcast for that machine and returns the physical address to IP. IP, realizing that the destination IP address is local, simply formulates the datagram with the IP address above the physical address of the destination machine. Figure 2.28 shows how that process happens.

Figure 2.28

A datagram destined locally.

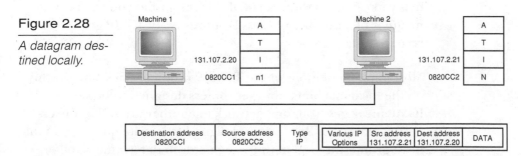

But IP does not always need to send datagrams to local IP address-es. In fact, often the destination address is on a remote network where the path may include several routers along the way. The hardest thing to realize conceptually is that ARP operates so close to the network interface layer that it is really only good for finding local physical addresses. This is true even in environments where routers exist. ARP never reports a physical address that exists on a remote network to IP. Figure 2.29 illustrates what would happen if ARP was capable of responding with a physical address from a remote network. IP datagrams specify exactly which physical ad-dress is supposed to listen to their message. In the example in figure 2.29, then, the datagram is sent out onto the network, and the router, which also has a physical address, simply ignores the packet. Not exactly what was intended.

Figure 2.29

IP asking ARP for a remote physical address.

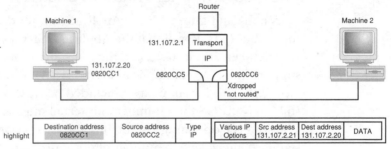

This packet is transmitted on segment A

To get the packet to the other network, the router is supposed to listen to the packet and forward it on. The only way to get it to listen to the packet, though, is to either do a broadcast, or send the packet to the router's physical address. IP is smart enough to realize that the destination IP address is on a remote network and that the datagram must be sent to the router. However, it has no idea what the physical address of the router is, and thus relies on ARP to discover that for it.

To route a packet, IP asks ARP whether it has the physical address of the router, not of the destination machine. This is one of the more subtle and elegant features of the TCP/IP suite, in that it cleverly redirects packets based upon what layer is being commu-nicated with. After IP receives the physical address of the router from ARP, it formulates the datagram, placing the destination IP address directly above the router's physical address. Figure 2.30 illustrates how this interaction actually works and how elegant this system of routing really is.

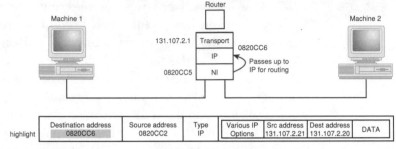

The Network APIs, Windows Sockets, and NetBIOS

Notice that in figure 2.31, the Application layer does not have protocols, but APIs. Recall that the Application layer provides the interface between applications and the transport protocols. Microsoft supports two APIs for applications to use: Windows Sockets and NetBIOS. This functionality is included because Microsoft networks still use NetBIOS for a number of internal mechanisms within the Windows NT operating system. It is also used because it provides a standard interface to a number of other protocols as well. TCP/IP, NetBEUI, and NWLink all have a NetBIOS interface to which applications can be written to use networking protocols. Strict Unix flavors of TCP/IP may not support the NetBIOS interface and may only support Windows Sockets as their API; Microsoft's implementation of TCP/IP therefore includes support for both.

The Windows Sockets interface defines an industry standard specification for how windows applications communicate with the TCP/IP protocol. This specification includes definitions for how to use the transport protocols and how to transfer data between two machines, including the establishment of connection-oriented sessions (TCP three-way handshake) and non-connection-oriented datagrams (broadcasts). The Windows Sockets API also defines how to uniquely address packets destined for a particular application on another machine. The concept of a socket (the combination of the TCP/IP address and the port

number) is a common example of the relative ease of uniquely
identifying a communications path. Because of the ease and
standardization of the Windows Sockets specifications, this API
is enjoying a tremendous amount of exposure and success, particularly in terms of its use in Internet applications.

Figure 2.31

*APIs in the Appli-
cation layer.*

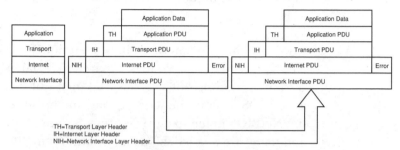

Windows Sockets uniquely identifies machines through their IP
address, so machine names in the TCP/IP environment are entirely
optional. Given that it is tremendously more difficult for users to
remember a hundred IP addresses over some form of an alias for
these machines, a name space was created to help identify machines on a TCP/IP network. A name space is a hierarchical naming scheme that uniquely identifies machine aliases to IP addresses.
This scheme allows two machines to have the same alias as long as
they are not in the same domain. This is very useful for people, but
entirely unnecessary for applications, since applications can use the
IP address. This is why you can use any alias you want to establish a
connection to a particular machine. As long as the name resolution
method (DNS, hosts file) returns a valid IP address, a communication path can be created. The IP address is what's most important.
With the NetBIOS API, the IP address is only part of the information necessary to establish communication between two machines,
and the name of the machine is required.

The NetBIOS API was developed on local area networks and has
evolved into a standard interface for applications to use to access
networking protocols in the Transport layer for both connection-
oriented and non-connection-oriented communications. NetBIOS
interfaces have been written for the NetBEUI, NWLink, and

TCP/IP protocols so that applications need not worry about which of these protocols is providing the transport services. Because each of these protocols supports the NetBIOS API, all the functionality for establishing sessions and initiating broadcasts is provided. Unlike Windows Sockets, NetBIOS requires not only an IP address to uniquely identify a machine, but a NetBIOS name as well.

Every machine on a network must be uniquely identified with a NetBIOS name. This name is required for establishing a NetBIOS session or sending out a broadcast. When utilizing names through a NetBIOS session, the sending machine must be able to resolve the NetBIOS name to an IP address. Because both an IP address and name are needed, all name resolution methods have to supply the correct IP address before successful communication can occur.

The Microsoft TCP/IP stack supports connection-oriented and non-connection-oriented communications established through either of these popular APIs. Microsoft includes NetBT (NetBIOS over TCP/IP) for applications that would like to utilize the Net-BIOS API over a TCP/IP network. This small, seemingly insignificant piece of software is what prevents your machine from having to run two protocols, one for Windows Sockets, and one for Net-BIOS. By providing NetBT with Microsoft's TCP/IP protocol stack, all NetBIOS calls an application may initiate are supported.

RFCs

Anyone interested in learning more about TCP/IP can find out more by reading the series of published standards called Request For Comments (RFCs). These standards can be thought of as the living documents of the Internet and are constantly under various stages of completion, acceptance, or planned obsolescence. Each enhancement or feature to the TCP/IP protocol is described by a particular RFC number. Whenever a significant change to a feature is recommended or suggested, and enough of the Internet community agrees on the change, a new RFC is created to discuss the new implementation and place it under further study.

RFCs are referred to as the living documents of the Internet because RFCs are never updated or deleted, much like the Constitution of the United States. Every addition or change is an amendment to the original. Therefore changes require the creation of a new RFC number, and always reference the original RFC they are intended to replace or enhance.

To keep track of whether RFCs are current, under progress, or no longer used, a classification system was created indicating the status of any individual RFC. These classifications are Required, Recommended, Elective, Limited Use, and Not Recommended. When you read an RFC, you may notice that different terminology is used. For instance, in the case of a particular implementation detail that is Required, the terminology used in the RFC says that this implementation must be used. In the case of a recommended implementation, the RFC uses the word "should." The elective portions are discussed in terms of how a protocol may do a particular feature. And of course, for those implementations that are not recommended, the use of "should not" is often seen. To view Internet RFCs, check out the following URL:

```
http://ds.internic.net/ds/dspg1intdoc.html
```

Exercises

Exercise 2.1: Using Netstat to Generate Statistics (TCP)

1. From the Start menu, choose Programs, Command Prompt.

2. At the command prompt, type > **netstat -s -p tcp**.

What appears is a statistics report for the TCP protocol as well as a display of any TCP sessions that are currently in use.

Exercise 2.2: Using Netstat to Generate Statistics (UDP)

1. From the Start menu, choose Programs, Command Prompt.

2. At the command prompt, type > **netstat -s -p udp**.

What appears is a statistics report for the UDP protocol.

Exercise 2.3: Using Netstat to Generate Statistics (IP)

1. From the Start menu, choose Programs, Command Prompt.

2. At the command prompt, type > **netstat -s -p ip**.

What appears is a statistics report for the IP protocol.

Exercise 2.4: Using Netstat to Generate Statistics (ICMP)

1. From the Start menu, choose Programs, Command Prompt.

2. At the command prompt, type > **netstat -s -p icmp**.

What appears is a statistics report for the ICMP protocol.

Review Questions

The following questions will test your knowledge of the information in this chapter:

1. You're talking with a few of the programmers in your department about an application they are working on. They tell you it is designed to use a connection-oriented protocol to communicate over the network. Which protocol in the TCP/IP protocol suite provides connection-oriented communications?

   A. Transmission Control Protocol

   B. User Datagram Protocol

   C. Internet Control Message Protocol

   D. Address Resolution Protocol

2. Several machines on the network utilize DHCP and WINS in order to get their IP address information and to resolve NetBIOS names to IP addresses, respectively. What protocol allows these machines to resolve an IP address to a hardware address?

   A. Internet Control Protocol

   B. DHCP address resolution manager

   C. WINS address resolution manager

   D. Address Resolution Protocol

3. An NT server in your environment needs to be able to communicate with other machines on the Internet using a DNS server to resolve names to IP addresses. Which command line utility displays whether a machine has been configured with the IP address of a DNS server?

   A. Netstat –N

   B. Nbtstat –N

   C. IPCONFIG

   D. PING

4. Several programmers are discussing the design of a new application to be written for your company and a heated debate ensues over whether the application should use Windows Sockets or NetBIOS. Half the programmers think TCP/IP supports Windows Sockets only and half think TCP/IP supports both Windows Sockets and NetBIOS. Who is correct in this argument?

    A. Programmers who say Windows sockets only

    B. Programmers who say NetBIOS only

    C. Programmers who say neither

    D. Programmers who say both are supported

5. The Dallas office is having trouble communicating with the Orlando office over the company's wide area networks links. There are several routers in between these two offices and you suspect some of them may be slow or not functioning at all. Which utility would be useful in determining the path and time that packets are taking to get from the Dallas office to the Orlando office?

    A. Tracert

    B. Netstat

    C. Nbtstat

    D. Ipconfig

6. You will be implementing DHCP in your environment and want to know how relay agents actually transmit DHCP requests from one network segment to another. What Internet resource is available to you for finding the specifications for a particular protocol or service?

    A. Request for Comments

    B. Netstat

    C. Nbtstat -Trace

    D. Network Monitor

7. One of your users calls and says that she cannot connect to the network. She can't logon to the NT domain and she can't use network neighborhood. As part of your trouble-shooting steps, you find out that the user can ping every IP address on the network successfully. Not only that but she seems to be able to FTP, HTTP, and Telnet wherever she wants to. Which of the following do you think might be the source of the error?

   A. NetBIOS API isn't functioning properly

   B. DNS isn't configured

   C. Telnet is an unpredictable program

   D. Windows sockets isn't functioning properly

8. Kristin is a user in the advertising department who is writing a document in Word. This is a very important document that must be transferred immediately to the remote office. If you had to select which protocol would be best for this type of transfer, which protocol would you choose?

   A. User Datagram Importance Protocol

   B. Internet Control Messaging Protocol

   C. Transmission Control Protocol

   D. Important Packet Protocol

9. Paul is a user who seems to be having some issues with connecting to another network segment on the other side of a router. Despite repeated attempts to route packets to the other side, Paul is unsuccessful. In an attempt to help Paul with his problem, you will need to determine which layer is responsible for the routing of IP packets. Which layer would that be?

   A. Network layer

   B. Transport layer

   C. Internet layer

   D. Application layer

10. Daphne works in the engineering department and is rather savvy with computers. She has informed you that you will be implementing a program that works at the Application layer and uses NetBIOS to communicate with a remote network computer. In order to test whether this application will work, which of the following would be a valid test?

    A. Ping destination computer

    B. Ping hostname of destination computer

    C. Tracert to destination machine

    D. NetView destination machine

11. During the troubleshooting of a problem, you take a trace to discover what is going on. As you are analyzing the packets, you discover a "Redirect" packet that appears to have come from a router. Which protocol is capable of generating such a packet?

    A. Transmission Control Protocol

    B. User Datagram Protocol

    C. Internet Group Management Protocol

    D. Internet Control Message Protocol

12. Some of the programmers in your environment are interested in writing a new program to communicate on the network. They have been studying IP and want to know if there is any way to direct packets to a group of users without having to send a broadcast to everyone. They don't want the program to keep lists. They want to be able to do this at the IP level. Which protocol would you suggest they take a closer look at?

    A. Internet Group Therapy Protocol

    B. Internet Group Protocol

    C. Internet Group Management Protocol

    D. Address Resolution Protocol

13. You've been given the task of troubleshooting a program failure because of your vast IP experience with ports and sockets. As part of this troubleshooting, you've been given access to the program code. This code seems to be having trouble communicating with its server component located on 7.23.70.1. The program uses TCP as its transport but still seems to not be running correctly. What additional piece of information is necessary in order for the client to communicate with the server?

    A. NetBIOS functionality

    B. 32-bit session utility

    C. Server Port definition

    D. Windows sockets Name resolution

Review Answers

1. A

2. D

3. C

4. D

5. A

6. A

7. A

8. C

9. C

10. D

11. D

12. C

13. C

Answers to the Test Yourself Questions at the Beginning of the Chapter

1. The TCP/IP protocol suite maps to a 4-layer networking model. Each of the layers corresponds to one or more of the OSI layers. These four layers map to all seven layers that exist in the OSI model. See "The Four Layers of TCP/IP."

2. Tell the president TCP/IP is an industry-standard suite of protocols that is not owned or developed by one company. The Internet community works on the establishment of these standards and the evolution of the protocols, and no implementation is considered mandatory until the whole community agrees upon a good implementation. See "RFCs."

3. TCP/IP has been developed as a cross-platform, client/server suite of protocols and enables IBM mainframes, NetWare servers, Macintosh clients, Windows 95, and Windows NT machines to be integrated together. See "Introduction to TCP/IP."

4. The IP protocol is responsible for routing and delivery of datagrams. See "Internet Protocol."

5. UDP is the best protocol for delivering streaming data, because it is much quicker and more streamlined, not requiring the overhead of verifying the delivery of datagrams. See "User Datagram Protocol."

6. This is an unnecessary concern, because Microsoft's TCP/IP protocol stack includes NetBT (NetBIOS over TCP/IP), which enables all NetBIOS API calls to utilize TCP/IP as a protocol. See "The Network APIs, Windows Sockets, and NetBIOS."

Chapter

IP Addressing

This chapter helps you prepare for the exam by covering the following objective:

▸ Diagnose and resolve IP addressing problems

Test Yourself! Before reading this chapter, test yourself to determine how much study time you will need to devote to this section.

1. How many layers does the OSI networking model have? The TCP/IP networking model?

2. How many classes of addresses are there?

3. What class of address can have 65,534 hosts per network?

4. How many bits long is a IPv6 address?

5. What two methods can you use to configure a TCP/IP address?

Answers are located at the end of the chapter.

Overview

A network protocol suite such as TCP/IP has to have a methodology by which devices on the network can identify each other at every level of the network model. TCP/IP provides identification at the Internet layer of the TCP/IP networking model in the form of IP addressing. Refer to Chapter 2 for a discussion of the four layers.

 Tip

> Remember that the Internet layer of the TCP/IP networking model is equivalent to the Network layer of the OSI Reference Model.

Networked devices such as a computer or printer in a TCP/IP network rely on an identification scheme similar in concept to a postal system. In order for me to send a letter to you, I will have to submit the letter to my local postal system. For the system to deliver the correspondence, I will have to enclose it in an envelope clearly marked with the country, ZIP/postal code, city, street, and name identifying you and where you live. I will also include my return address, in order for the letter to be returned if you have changed your address or for you to write back.

In order to send information from one component to another through a TCP/IP network the information, like our correspondence, must contain the address of the recipient and the sender.

Instead of a letter this information is packaged, at the Internet Layer of the TCP/IP networking model, in units known as datagrams. The addresses are represented by 32-bit numbers called IP addresses.

TCP/IP Addressing Methods

When a device, such as a server or workstation, is attached to a TCP/IP network, it is commonly referred to as a *host*. Each host connected through a TCP/IP network must have the capability to communicate with every other host on the network as needed—security considerations notwithstanding. This capability to communicate is not just limited to the Internet layer of the TCP/IP architecture. Rather, a host has to be able to communicate at all four layers: the Process/Application layer, Host-to-Host layer, Internet layer, and Network Access layer. Each layer of the model uses its own addressing method to communicate with a remote TCP/IP host.

Addressing at the Process/Application layer is provided using host names. This naming method allows hosts to be configured with easily remembered names. This is a significant advantage, since the Process/Application layer is the level seen directly by users. Host naming will be discussed later in Chapter 11, "Host Name Resolution."

 Note

As a Windows NT administrator, you will undoubtedly be responsible for providing names for your servers. Please be kind to yourself and others. Use a name that makes sense in the context of your network and the location of your server. In a global economy, your network can easily expand beyond your wildest dreams. You might find it difficult to explain to your international colleague the significance of a domestically popular cartoon character. Check out RFC 1178 for recommended guidelines for naming a computer.

Port numbers are the addressing methods used at the Host-to-Host layer. These numbers are used to describe the interface to software processes operating on the host.

The Internet layer uses IP addresses. The current version of IP, IPv4, uses a 32-bit address. This amounts to a seemingly inexhaustible 4,294,967,296 addresses available. I emphasize "seemingly," because as the Internet and world markets continue to expand at incredible rates, the current method of IP addressing will not keep up. This chapter concentrates on IP addressing elements, in addition to future trends these elements will follow.

Table 3.1 summarizes the addressing method used in each of the TCP/IP architecture.

Table 3.1

Addressing Method in the TCP/IP Architecture

TCP/IP Architecture	Addressing Method
Process/Application	Host name
Host-to-Host	Port number
Internet	IP address
Network Access	Hardware address (MAC address)

IP Addresses Defined

Objective

Every device connected to a TCP/IP network requires at least one IP address and must be unique within that network. An IP address is commonly represented in dotted decimal notation. Here are some examples of IP addresses shown in dotted decimal form.

207.21.32.12

10.1.2.34

120.224.21.253

As in these examples, all IP addresses are 32 bits long and are comprised of four 8-bit segments known as *octets*. Representing IP addresses in dotted decimal notation makes them a lot easier to read than in the machine friendly binary format. As you will see in the next section, however, the capability to convert IP addresses to-and-from binary format is required for configuring your TCP/IP network and for the exam. The following is an example of an IP address shown in dotted decimal and its equivalent binary notation.

```
Dotted Decimal          Binary
207.21.32.12            11001111 00010101 00100000 00001100
```

Conversion Between Decimal and Binary Numbers

The term *bit* is commonly used to describe a 1 or 0 and is a contraction of the words *bi*nary digi*t*. Binary means a value of 2, and therefore bit patterns use a base 2 system, whereas decimal numbers us a base 10 system. For the purpose of converting IP addresses between decimal and binary, think of each decimal number as being mapped to an 8 digit binary number. For example, the IP address 207.21.32.12 can be represented as shown in table 3.2.

Table 3.2

Conversion of 207.21.32.12 to Decimal		
Decimal Value	Bits	Binary Value
207	128+64+0+0+8+4+2+1	11001111
21	0+0+0+16+0+4+0+1	00010101
32	0+0+32+0+0+0+0+0	00100000
12	0+0+0+0+8+4+0+0	00001100

Table 3.3 shows possible values of each bit in an octet.

Table 3.3

Possible Values of Each Bit in an Octet							
Bit	8	7	6	5	4	3	2	1
Value	128	64	32	16	8	4	2	1

 Note

This means that the binary number 11010 is the same as 16 + 8 + 2 or 26.

Network ID and Host ID

Although an IP address is a single value, it is divided into two pieces of information: the network ID and the host ID of the networked device.

The network ID identifies the systems that are located on the same physical network. All systems on the same physical network must have the same network ID, and the network ID must be unique to the local segment. In this case, local is defined as being on one side of a router.

The host ID identifies a workstation, server, router, or other TCP/IP device within a network. The host address for each device must be unique to the network ID. A computer connected to a TCP/IP network uses the network ID and host ID to determine which packets it should receive or ignore and to determine which devices are to have the opportunity of receiving its transmissions.

Throughout the world, TCP/IP networks vary greatly in size and scope. In order to accommodate the wide range of network design needs, IP addresses have been divided into classes.

IP Address Classes Defined

The IP address is 32 bits in length and is used to identify both the host address and the address of the network in which the host resides. An address class is defined to allocate the minimum number of bits that are to be used as the network ID. The remaining bits can be used to further subdivide the network using subnet masks and to define the host ID.

Table 3.4 illustrates the currently available IP address classes:

Table 3.4

Classes of IP Addresses Available Under IPv4					
IP Address Class	First Octet		Start in Binary	Number of	
	Minimum	Maximum		Networks	Hosts
Class A	1	126	1	126	16,777,214
Class B	128	191	10	16,384	65,534
Class C	192	223	110	2,097,152	254
Class D	224	239	1110		
Class E	240	247	11110		

Note

Class D addresses are used for Multicasting (for example Real Audio broadcasts across the Internet. Class E are experimental. Neither of these address classes can be used as a host ID.

Let's revisit the one of the sample IP address shown in table 3.2. Based on our newly acquired knowledge of IP address classes, we see that IP address 207.21.32.12 is a Class C address. Note that the first octet is 207, and falls within the range of a Class C network. In addition, the binary equivalent of 207 is 1101111. Since the first three most significant bits are 110, we can again confirm that this is a Class C address.

Reasons for Using Specific Address Classes

If you are new to TCP/IP, you may be asking yourself "Why are there different classes of IP addresses, and how can I use them?" First of all, the Internet community has defined the different types of IP addresses in order to accommodate the needs of networks of different sizes. A network with less than 255 devices (workstations, routers, printers, and so) can be assigned a Class C network address. However, a large organization with up to 65,534 devices will need at least a Class B address.

Second, as long as you are not connecting your internal network directly to the public Internet, you can use any valid Class A, B, or C address you want. However, any device that is connected directly to the Internet, must be assigned a network ID from the Internet community. The organization responsible for administering the assignment of the network ID portions of IP addresses for network devices directly connected to the Internet is the Internet Network Information Center (InterNIC). They can be reached at www.internic.net.

Note   RFC 1918 defines the methodology for IP address allocation for private networks.

For most private networks (intranets) on the border of the public Internet, IP addresses are either assigned dynamically (see Chapter 6, "Dynamic Host Configuration Protocol") or statically by an Internet Service Provider (ISP). The ISP maintains responsibility for administering IP network IDs assigned by InterNIC. Three examples of ISPs, which dynamically assign IP addresses, commonly used by individuals for dial-up access are CompuServe, America Online, and Prodigy. Typically, a private network requiring access to the Internet will use a direct connection to an ISP through a router. In these cases, the ISP will provide a network ID to the private network. This address will be a unique statically assigned address provided to the ISP from InterNIC. These commercial services are usually provided by larger ISPs, including MCI, AT&T, and GTE.

Classes Defined

We have already discussed the reason behind the provision of separate classes of IP addresses. Now we will discuss in more detail, the definition for each class of IP address. Before continuing, the following table and figure will help clarify the differences between host and network IDs. Table 3.5 illustrates the publicly available IP address classes (A to C) and their corresponding network and host ID components.

Table 3.5

Network and Host ID Assignments

IP Address Class	IP Address	Network ID	Host ID
Class A	a.b.c.d	a	b.c.d
Class B	a.b.c.d	a.b	c.d
Class C	a.b.c.d	a.b.c	d

Again, it is important to understand that the IP address consists of two parts: a network ID and a host ID. As shown in table 3.4, the most significant bits (MSBs) are used to determine how many bits are used for the network ID and the host ID. Figure 3.1 diagrams the placement of the MSBs within each of the five classes of IP addresses.

Figure 3.1

The placement of the most significant bits.

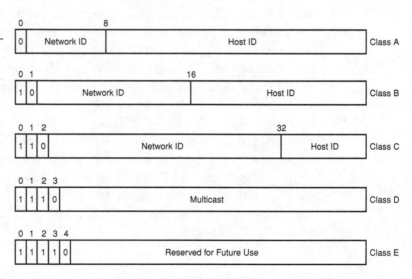

▶ **Class A** addresses are assigned to networks with extremely large numbers of hosts (networked devices). The MSB is set to 0, and is combined with the remaining seven bits of the first octet to complete the network ID. This leaves the last 3 octets, or 24 bits to be assigned to subnet masking and to hosts. As we saw in table 3.3, this allows for 126 (2^7-2) networks with up to 16,777,214 (2^{21}-2) hosts per network. An example of a Class A address is 10.1.2.34 where 10.0.0.0 is the network and 0.1.2.34 is the host.

▶ **Class B** addresses are assigned to networks with no more than 65,534 (2^{16}-2) hosts (networked devices). The MSBs are set to 10, and are combined with the remaining 14 bits of the first two octets to complete the network ID. This leaves the last 2 octets, or 16 bits to be assigned to subnet masking and to hosts and allows for 16,384 (2^{14}) networks. Each of these networks can have as many as 65+ thousand hosts. An example of a Class B address is 120.224.21.253 here the network is 120.224.0.0 and the host is 21.253.

▶ **Class C** addresses are assigned to small networks with a more limited number of hosts. The MSBs are set to 110, and are combined with the remaining 21 bits of the first three octets to complete the network ID. This leaves the last octet available to be assigned to subnet masking and to hosts, allowing for 2,097,152 (2^{21}) networks with up to 254 (2^8-2) hosts per network. An example of a Class B address is 207.21.32.12 which is a network of 207.21.32.0 with a host ID of 0.0.0.12.

▶ **Class D** addresses are reserved for multicast groups. Multicast addresses are assigned to groups of hosts that are cooperating, or are related in some manner. Each host in a multicast group has to be configured to accept multicast packets. The MSBs of a class D address are set to 1110. The remaining bits are uniquely assigned to each group of hosts. Microsoft NT supports class D addresses for applications such as Microsoft Net-Show.

▶ **Class E** addresses are an experimental class of IP addresses reserved for use in the future. The MSBs for class E addresses are 1111.

Note   You may be wondering why there are only 126 Class A networks, rather than 128 (2^8). As will be discussed in the next section: a network ID of all 0s is not allowed, and the Class A network ID of 127 is reserved. Read on to find out why!

IP Addressing Guidelines

As discussed earlier, a network administrator can choose to use any IP address he or she likes for an internal TCP/IP network (intranet). However, the following information should be kept in mind as these are notable exceptions:

▶ The network ID of 127 is reserved as the loopback address. It is also used in diagnostics.

▶ A network ID of all 1s or all 0s is never assigned to an individual network.

▶ A host ID of all 1s or all 0s is never assigned to an individual host.

▶ The value 255.255.255.255 represents the broadcast address.

The IP address 127.b.c.d, with b,c and d each being any number between 0 and 255, represents a software loopback address. Any packet sent to this address will be returned to the application without transmission to the network. That is, the information is returned to host from which it originates, without being sent out to the network. The packet is being copied from the transmit to receive buffer on the same host. Hence the name "loopback address." This address can be used as a check to see that TCP/IP software has been installed correctly. For example, executing a **ping 127.0.0.1** command on a Windows NT server will request a packet to be sent to itself. A return of this packet will imply a successful installation of TCP/IP. However, the return of this packet will not necessarily imply a successful configuration of TCP/IP. See Chapter 16, "Troubleshooting Microsoft TCP/IP," for more information.

Host ID values of all 0s are not assigned to individual hosts, because these addresses represent the network itself. For example, the IP address of 207.21.32.0 represents the Class C network 207.21.32. Similarly, the IP address of 10.0.0.0 represents the class A network 10. The IP address containing all 1s in the Host ID segment of the address, the address is known as a directed broadcast. For example, the IP address of 207.21.32.255 would be the address a packet is sent to if it is to be received by all hosts on the Class C network 207.21.32. Similarly, a packet sent to an address of 10.255.255.255 would be received by all hosts in the Class A network 10.

A network ID of all 0s is not defined. As seen in table 3.3, the valid range of Class A networks is 1 to 126, and not 0 to 126. Similarly, a network ID containing all 1s is not defined.

The address 255.255.255.255 is referred to as the local broadcast. This type of broadcast address can be used in a local area network, or intranet, where a broadcast will never cross a router boundary.

Assigning Network IDs

Whether you are configuring your TCP/IP LAN to connect to the public Internet, or not, you must follow specific guidelines for assigning IP addresses to networks and hosts.

Each and every physical network compliant with the TCP/IP protocol suite must have a unique network address. If the network is connected to the public Internet, the connecting network must have a network ID assigned by the InterNIC. However, all other networks may be assigned any valid network ID. Figure 3.2 provides an illustration of two intranets connected via a WAN link through the public Internet. Let's say that the network administrator of LAN A had already configured his network using a class A network ID. In this case, the network ID was 10.0.0.0. Meanwhile, his colleague in a separate physical location decides to use a Class B network address of 120.224.0.0 for her LAN. Fortunately for the two of them, they didn't have to change network IDs when management decided to connect these separate LANs via the public Internet. Instead, their company was assigned a class C address of 207.21.32.0 from the InterNIC, and they were able to connect LAN A with LAN B using a WAN link provided to them by an ISP.

Figure 3.2

A network addressing example of two TCP/IP LANs or intranets connected via a WAN link.

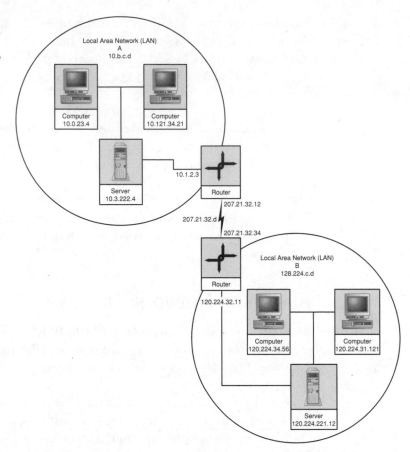

Assigning Host IDs

Just as every connected TCP/IP network must have a unique network ID, every IP addressed host within a network must be unique within that network. Figure 3.2 shows that all hosts have been assigned IP addresses unique within their networks. As can be seen, hosts do not just include computers and servers, but they also include ports on routers. By definition, a router allows for transmission of packets between different networks. As such, an IP router requires at least two network interfaces, or ports.

 Note

An IP host with more than one network interface is called a *multi-homed host*.

Addressing with IP Version 6

As was discussed earlier in this chapter, 4,294,967,296 (2^{32}) may seem like an awful lot of IP addresses. However, we saw that many of these addresses are not available for private networks. And of those, many have been used up in the exponential growth of hosts connected to the public Internet. No fear! The Internet powers that be—Internet Engineering Task Force (IETF)—have risen to the challenge.

The current definition of the IP address is known as version 4, or Ipv4. This version has not been upgraded on the public Internet since 1970. However, the Internet community does not sleep. Indeed, there have been many proposals for extending the addressing scheme on the Internet. The winner is IP Version 6 (Ipv6), formerly referred to as IP next Generation (IpnG). What about Ipv5?—no such animal.

Note | RFC 1883 specifies version 6 of the Internet Protocol (IPv6) as defined by the IETF.

The current version (Ipv4) of IP addressing uses a space of 4 octets. Ipv6 uses 16! These addresses are not commonly represented in dotted decimal form. Nor are they typically represented in binary form. But, to make things more challenging (yet take up less space) they are represented in 8 octet pairs in hexidecimal format! Here's an example:

```
3E0F:ACDE:11FE:2312:34A9:FE34: 1BAF:CABE
```

Not only does Ipv6 offer many times the address space of IPv4 (2^{128} addresses instead of just 2^{32}), but it boasts other benefits to take the Internet well into the future. These benefits include simplified header format, enhanced support for real-time data and built-in expandability through the use of extension headers.

By moving non-essential fields out of the base header and into extension headers allows for a significant increase in efficiency. For example, real-time data transmissions can be guaranteed a fixed band-width through a new field in the header.

Review Questions

1. Which of the following is the loopback address?

    A. 127.0.0.1

    B. 0.0.0.0

    C. 1.1.1.1

    D. 128.0.0.1

2. What class of address is 21.34.55.55?

    A. Class A

    B. Class B

    C. Class C

    D. Illegal

3. What class of address is 223.75.234.239?

    A. Class A

    B. Class B

    C. Class C

    D. Illegal

4. What class of address is 223.322.232.127?

    A. Class A

    B. Class B

    C. Class C

    D. Illegal

5. What class of address is 192.192.232.127?

    A. Class A

    B. Class B

    C. Class C

    D. Illegal

6. What class of address is 1.1.1.1?

   A. Class A

   B. Class B

   C. Class C

   D. Illegal

7. What class of address is 44.12.256.254?

   A. Class A

   B. Class B

   C. Class C

   D. Illegal

8. What class of address is 126.122.243.34?

   A. Class A

   B. Class B

   C. Class C

   D. illegal

9. By default, what is the Network ID for the address
   201.102.21.12?

   A. 201.0.0.0

   B. 201.102.0.0

   C. 201.102.21.0

   D. 0.0.0.12

10. By default, what is the Network ID for the address
    121.212.112.122?

    A. 121.0.0.0

    B. 121.212.0.0

    C. 121.212.112.0

    D. 0.0.0.122

11. By default, what is the Network ID for the address 198.81.91.119?

   A. 198.0.0.0

   B. 198.81.0.0

   C. 198.81.91.0

   D. 0.0.0.119

12. By default, what is the Host ID for the address 179.79.234.234?

   A. 179.0.0.0

   B. 0.0.234.234

   C. 0.79.234.234

   D. 0.0.0.234

13. By default, what is the Host ID for the address 41.1.6.222?

   A. 41.0.0.0

   B. 41.1.6.0

   C. 0.1.6.222

   D. 0.0.0.222

14. By default, what is the Network ID for the address 201.44.45.54?

   A. 0.0.0.54

   B. 0.0.45.54

   C. 201.44.0.0

   D. 201.44.45.0

15. By default, what is the Host ID for the address 201.44.45.54?

   A. 0.0.0.54

   B. 0.0.45.54

   C. 201.44.0.0

   D. 201.44.45.0

Review Answers

1. A

2. A

3. C

4. D

5. C

6. A

7. D

8. A

9. C

10. A

11. C

12. B

13. C

14. D

15. A

Answers to the Test Yourself Questions at the Beginning of the Chapter

1. The OSI model has seven layers whereas the TCP/IP model has four.

2. There are five classes of addresses: classes A–C are used for host addresses, class D addresses are for multicasting and class E is experimental.

3. Class B addresses provide 65.534 hosts per network.

4. Current IP addresses are 32 bits long, the new version of IP (IPv6) will use addresses 128 bits long.

5. Addresses can be configured manually or by using a DHCP server.

Chapter

Subnetting

This chapter helps you prepare for the exam by covering the following objectives:

 Objectives

▶ Configure subnet masks

▶ Given a scenario, identify valid network configurations

Test Yourself! Before reading this chapter, test yourself to determine how much study time you will need to devote to this section.

1. What are the three components of a TCP/IP Address?

2. How does the subnet mask divide a TCP/IP address into its components?

3. What subnet mask is used for a Class A network without subnets?

4. How can the wrong subnet mask prevent you from communicating with remote hosts?

5. How does a subnet mask determine the number of subnets that can be created on a network?

Answers are located at the end of the chapter.

Introduction

A TCP/IP address typically has two components: the *network ID* of the address, which specifies the general location of the host, and the *host ID*, which uniquely identifies an individual host after the network is located. In most cases, you will need to break your network into smaller more manageable pieces—notably you will segment your network for performance. If you are using TCP/IP these segments are referred to as subnets.

A subnet is really a subnetwork of a TCP/IP internetwork. An *internet* or *internetwork* is a group of computers linked together using TCP/IP technology. An internet can be either a portion of the Internet (the worldwide network of publicly interconnected TCP/IP networks) or a private corporate or enterprise internetwork. Such private internetworks are usually called intranets to show that they are internal to an enterprise and not part of the Internet.

The term *network* is used when it is not necessary to distinguish between individual subnets and internetworks. A subnet is simply a subdivision of a network. You create a subnet by carefully choosing the IP addresses and subnet masks for your hosts. This process is known as *subnet addressing* or *subnetting.* The term *subnetworking* or *subnetting* refers to the use of a custom subnet mask to subdivide a single network ID into multiple network IDs.

An IP address consists of four octets, which are numbers between 0 and 255. These are strung together with periods to look like this example 200.20.5.59. This number is a representation of a 32 binary number—made easier for humans to understand. Part of the address identifies the host's network or subnet, and part of the address identifies the host. The subnet mask specifies what portion of the TCP/IP address identifies which part. A subnet mask can also specify how much of the address will instead specify a subnet ID.

The subnet mask is used by the Internet layer (IP layer) to route a TCP/IP packet to its proper destination. When a TCP/IP address is combined with a subnet mask, the TCP/IP protocol determines whether the destination is on the local subnet or not.

If the destination address is on a different subnet than the sender is, then it is determined to be on a remote network and the packet is routed appropriately—normally through the default gateway. If the destination address is on the local subnet, the packet is not routed but sent directly to the destination host.

If a network has a small number of hosts that are all on the same segment that is no connection to any other network, they are all given the same network ID. Subnets are not needed in this case. If the network is larger, however, with remote segments connected by routers (an internetwork), then each individual subnet needs a different network ID. It is possible to assign a different network ID to each network segment, but organizations are usually given only one network ID for the entire organization. A subnet mask must then be used to use part of the host ID as the subnet ID. When assigning IP addresses and subnet masks, you must know how many subnets are required and the maximum number of hosts that are on each subnet. Then you can use a subnet mask that allows enough hosts on each subnet while allowing for enough subnets within the entire network.

Depending on the subnet mask selected, the internetwork can either have a lot of subnets with fewer hosts on each subnet, or a smaller number of subnets with a larger number of hosts on each subnet. The purpose of this chapter is to show how to determine the proper subnet mask to be used to meet the addressing requirements.

This chapter discusses the following topics:

- ▶ Subnet masks, host IDs, and network IDs

- ▶ The limitations of using a default subnet mask

- ▶ Subnetting—how to increase the number of subnets on the network by using a custom subnet mask

- ▶ Three different procedures for subnetting an internetwork

- ▶ Shortcuts to reduce the time it takes on the exam to subnet a network ID

The Purpose of Subnet Masks

A TCP/IP address is like a calendar date. The IP address has two components; a network ID and a host ID. The network ID may include a subnet ID. A date also has several components, such as a month, a day, and a year.

The subnet mask is used by the internet layer to determine which part of the IP address is the network ID and which part is the host ID. The subnet mask also can be used to determine whether a subnet is defined and to find the ID of that subnet. Calendar dates are also represented with a numbering scheme that communicates which part of the date is the month, day, and year.

As table 4.1 shows, dates are listed with the month first, then the day, then the year (in the United States, at least). If the year is in the 1900s, it is common to omit the first two digits in the year. Americans are so used to this type of date scheme that they rarely stop to think about it. The TCP/IP subnet mask specifies that the octets of the IP address marked as 255 are the network ID and octets marked by 0 are the host ID. When subnetting you will begin to see other numbers appear instead of just 0 and 255.

Table 4.1

IP Address:	200.20.16.5
Subnet Mask:	255.255.255.0
Network ID:	200.20.16
Host ID:	5
Date:	4/27/87
Date Scheme:	Month/Day/Year
Month:	4
Day:	27
Year:	1987

It's important to understand the correct date scheme when inter-preting a date. For example, in Europe the orders of months and days are reversed. The date 12/6/69 is 12 June 1969 in Europe, whereas in the United States this date is interpreted as December 6, 1969. Similarly, with subnets, an understanding of the TCP/IP addressing scheme is necessary to decipher the IP address into the components of network ID, subnet ID, and host ID.

With a TCP/IP address, the address always follows the same for-mat of four octets separated by periods. You can define different subnet masks, however, so that the address is interpreted differ-ently. In table 4.2, the same IP address listed in table 4.1 is used, but with a different subnet mask. The address now specifies a subnet.

Table 4.2

IP Address:	11001000 00010100 00010000 00000101
Subnet Mask:	11111111 11111111 11111111 00000000
Network ID:	11001000 00010100 00010000 00000000
Host ID:	00000000 00000000 00000000 00000101

The TCP/IP address and subnet mask are made up of four 8-bit octets that, for ease of use, are viewed in decimal format rather than binary format. However, the address and subnet mask are actually binary so that IP understands them.

Any part of the subnet mask with 1s specifies the network portion of the address; 0s in the subnet mask specify the host portion of the address. The 1s are always at the first of the subnet mask, be-cause an IP address always specifies the network portion of the address first. The host ID is specified by the remaining numbers of the IP address, which correspond to the 0s at the end of the subnet mask. In a subnet mask, note that the 1s are always grouped together and the 0s are always grouped together. The subnet mask basically divides the IP address into two pieces: the network ID and the host ID. The subnet mask simply indicates how many of the higher-order bits are devoted to the network ID and how many of the lower-order bits are devoted to the host ID.

The subnet mask determines how many host IDs are available. In the example in table 4.2, there is a maximum of 254 different hosts on the network 200.20.16 (200.20.16.1 through 200.20.16.254). If you want to have more hosts on one network, you have to use a different addressing scheme. For example, if you use a subnet mask of 255.255.0.0, the address is interpreted as shown in table 4.3.

Table 4.3

IP Address	200.20.16.5
Subnet Mask	255.255.0.0
Network ID	200.20
Host ID	16.5

With this subnet mask, two octets are available for the host ID. Using two octets allows you to have (256*256)-2 (you cannot use all 0s or all 1s) hosts on the network 200.20.

As noted, there are two cases that are not allowed for the host ID, these are where all bits are set to either 1 or 0. In these two cases the addresses are interpreted to mean a broadcast address (all 1s) or "this network only," (all 0s). Neither of these destinations is valid for a host ID. Thus, the number of valid addresses is $(2^n)-2$, where n is the number of bits used for the host ID.

The example in table 4.2 has fewer combinations of network IDs (because only two octets are used for the network) than in the example in table 4.1 (in which three octets are used for the network). Bear in mind that you cannot always chose the subnet mask that allows you the greatest number of host IDs. For example, if the hosts are on the Internet, you must use a certain set of IP addresses assigned by the Internet address assignment authority, InterNIC.

Because the number of IP addresses available today is limited, you usually do not have the luxury to choose an addressing scheme that gives exactly the combination of host and network ID you require. Suppose you are assigned the network ID 139.20 and have a total of 1,000 hosts on three remote networks. A Class B network using the default subnet mask of 255.255.0.0 only has one network (139.20) yet allows 65,534 hosts.

Using the Subnet Mask

This section will look at exactly how a subnet mask is used to determine which part of the IP address is the network ID and which part is the host ID. The IP layer performs binary calculations on the IP address and the subnet mask to determine the network ID portion of the IP address.

The computation TCP/IP performs is a logical bitwise "AND" of the IP address and the subnet mask. The calculation sounds complicated, but all it really means is that the address in its true 32-bit binary format is logically "ANDed" with the subnet mask (also a 32-bit binary number). This extracts the network ID.

Performing a bitwise AND on two bits results in 1 (or TRUE), if the two values are both 1. All other cases return a 0. In the examples (tables 4.1, 4.2 and 4.3) the numbers 255 or 0 are used for the subnet mask. In binary, 255 means all the bits in that octet are 1; 0 means they are 0.

1 AND 1 results in 1

1 AND 0 results in 0

0 AND 1 results in 0

0 AND 0 results in 0

In the example in table 4.1, the IP address 200.20.16.5 is "ANDed" with the subnet mask 255.255.255.0. Because 1 and "n" always returns "n" and because the first three octets are all 1s, this example simply duplicates the first three octets leaving the network ID of 200.20.16.

Table 4.4 illustrates the calculation that is performed.

Table 4.4

Example of a Bitwise AND Operation

	Decimal Notation	Binary Notation
IP address:	200.20.16.5	11001000 0001010000010000 00000101
Subnet mask:	255.255.255.0	11111111 1111111111111111 00000000
IP address AND Subnet mask:	200.20.16.0	11001000 0001010000010000 00000000

Determining the network ID is very easy if the subnet mask is made up of only 255 and 0 values. Simply "mask" or cover up the part of the IP address corresponding to the 0 octet(s) of the subnet mask. For example, if the IP address is 15.6.100.1 and the subnet mask is 255.255.0.0, then the resulting network ID is 15.6.

For more complicated subnet masks, you can use the Windows Calculator in scientific view to convert between decimal and binary numbers, and use the "AND" button to perform a logical "AND." For example, you can enter the number 240, select And, enter 35, and then select =. This gives you the decimal answer to the "AND." You can then convert the result to binary if desired. Or you can enter the numbers in binary, converting the result to decimal when you are finished. However, you must use the same number system for both of the operands in the "AND" process when using the Windows Calculator.

You may have to use a subnet mask with values other than 255 and 0 if you need to subdivide your network ID into individual subnets. If you are not using subnets, you can use the default subnet mask that Microsoft TCP/IP assigns when configuring the IP address.

Understanding Default Subnet Masks

Microsoft TCP/IP assigns a subnet mask to an IP address by default that can then be changed if needed. Table 4.5 shows the subnet mask that appears in the subnet mask field when an IP address is entered in the Microsoft TCP/IP Configuration dialog box.

Table 4.5

Default Subnet Masks

Class	IP Address	Default Subnet Mask
A	001.y.z.w to 126.y.z.w	255.0.0.0
B	128.y.z.w to 191.y.z.w	255.255.0.0
C	192.y.z.w to 223.y.z.w	255.255.255.0

In Chapter 3, the discussion of the TCP/IP addressing scheme focused on the different classes of IP addresses and the number of different networks and hosts per network that are available for each of the IP address classes. These values were based on the default subnet masks. See table 4.6 for a summary.

Table 4.6

Maximum Number of Networks and Hosts per Network in TCP/IP

Class	Using Default Subnet Mask	Number of Networks	Number of Hosts per Network
A	255.0.0.0	126	16,777,214
B	255.255.0.0	16,384	65,534
C	255.255.255.0	2,097,152	254

If the hosts on your internetwork are not directly on the Internet, you are free to choose the network IDs that you use. For the hosts and subnets that are a part of the Internet, however, the network IDs you use must be assigned by InterNIC.

 Note

> InterNIC—the Internet Network Information Center—is responsible for assigning network IDs for use on the Internet, among other things. You can visit InterNIC at www.internic.net.

If you are using network IDs assigned by InterNIC, you do not have the choice of choosing the address class you use. Using the address assigned by InterNIC, the number of subnets you use is normally limited by the number of network IDs assigned by InterNIC, and the number of hosts per subnet is determined by the class of address. Fortunately, if you are not assigned enough network addresses you can subdivide your network into a greater number of subnets by choosing the proper subnet mask. However, if you subnet your network, you have fewer possible hosts on each subnet.

Many companies today are avoiding the addressing constraints and security risks of having their hosts directly on the Internet by setting up private networks with gateway access to the Internet. Having a private network means that only the Internet gateway host needs to have an Internet address. For security, a firewall can be set up to prevent Internet hosts from directly accessing the company's network.

Subdividing a Network

Internetworks are networks comprised of individual segments connected by routers. The reasons for having distinct segments are as follows:

▶ They permit physically remote local networks to be connected.

▶ A mix of network technologies can be connected, such as ethernet on one segment and token ring on another.

▶ They allow an unlimited number of hosts to communicate by combining subnets, even though the number of hosts on each segment is limited by the type of network used.

▶ Network congestion is reduced as broadcasts and local network traffic are limited to the local segment.

Each segment is a subnet of the internetwork, and requires a unique network ID or specifically a subnet ID.

Subnetting

 The following are the steps involved in subnetting a network:

1. Determine the number of network IDs required for current use and also for planning future growth needs.

2. Determine the maximum number of host addresses that are on each subnet, again allowing for future growth.

3. Define one subnet mask for the entire internetwork that gives the desired number of subnets and allows enough hosts per subnet.

4. Determine the resulting subnet network IDs that are used.

5. Determine the valid host IDs and assign IP addresses to the hosts.

The following sections describe each of these steps in detail.

Step 1: Determine the Number of Network IDs Required

The first step in subnetting a network is to determine the number of subnets required while planning for future growth. A unique network ID is required for each subnet and each WAN connection.

Step 2: Determine the Number of Host IDs per Subnet Required

Determine the maximum number of hosts IDs that are required on each subnet. A host ID is required for:

▶ Each TCP/IP computer network interface card.

▶ Each TCP/IP printer network interface card.

▶ Each router interface on each subnet. For example, if a router is connected to two subnets, it requires two host IDs and therefore two IP addresses.

When determining the number of subnets and hosts per subnet that are needed in your internetwork, it is very important to plan for growth! The entire internetwork should use the same subnet mask; therefore the maximum number of subnets and hosts per subnet is predetermined when the subnet mask is chosen.

To illustrate the need for growth planning, consider an internetwork with two subnets. Each subnet has 50 hosts and the subnets are connected by a router. The network administrator is authorized by InterNIC to use the network ID 200.20.16 to put all the hosts on the Internet. As the following sections explain, a subnet mask of 255.255.255.192 creates two logical subnets on the internetwork, each allowing a maximum of 62 valid host IDs. In the future, if another segment is added or more than 62 hosts are needed on one segment, the network administrator needs to do the following: choose a new subnet mask, shut down every computer on the network to reconfigure the subnet mask, reconfigure a lot of the network software, and probably look for another job.

 Note

When deciding on a subnet mask to use, make sure you allow for the number of subnets on the network and the number of hosts per subnet to increase substantially beyond current needs.

Step 3: Define the Subnet Mask

The next step is to define for the entire internetwork one subnet mask that gives the desired number of subnets and allows enough hosts per subnet.

As shown previously, the network ID of an IP address is determined by the "1s" of the subnet mask, shown in binary notation. To increase the number of network IDs, you need to add more bits to the subnet mask.

For example, you are assigned a Class B network ID of 168.20.0.0 by InterNIC. Using the default Class B subnet mask 255.255.0.0, you have one network ID (168.20.0.0) and about 65,000 valid host IDs (168.20.1.1 through 168.20.255.254). Suppose you want to subdivide the network into 4 subnets.

First, consider the host 168.20.16.1, using the subnet mask 255.255.0.0. In binary notation, it is represented as shown in table 4.7.

Table 4.7

IP address:	10101000.00010100.00010000.00000001
Subnet Mask:	11111111.11111111.00000000.00000000
Network ID:	10101000.00010100.00000000.00000000

Remember, the subnet mask 1 bits correspond to the network ID bit in the IP address.

By adding additional bits to the subnet mask, you increase the bits available for the network ID and thus create a few more combinations of network IDs.

Suppose that in the example in table 4.7 you add three bits to the subnet mask. The result increases the number of bits defining the network ID and decreases the number of bits that define the host ID. Thus, you have more network IDs, but fewer hosts on each subnet. The new subnet mask is:

```
Subnet Mask:      11111111      11111111      11100000      00000000
```

As you have three extra bits in the network ID, you now have six different network IDs. All 0s or all 1s are not allowed, because these are reserved for the broadcast-type addresses. All 0s mean "this network only," and all 1s mean broadcast. Table 4.8 shows all the possible subnet IDs using the network ID of 168.20.0.0 with a subnet mask of 255.255.224.0.

Table 4.8

Network IDs	Decimal Equivalent
10101000.00010100.001	168.20.32.0
10101000.00010100.010	168.20.64.0
10101000.00010100.011	168.20.96.0
10101000.00010100.100	168.20.128.0
10101000.00010100.101	168.20.160.0
10101000.00010100.110	168.20.192.0

Note that if you use only two additional bits in the subnet mask, you are only able to have two subnets. The network IDs that result in table 4.8 are as follows:

     10101000.00010100.01   168.20.64.0

     10101000.00010100.10   168.20.128.0

Therefore, you must use enough additional bits in the new subnet mask to create the desired number of subnets while still allowing for enough hosts on each subnet.

After you determine the number of subnets you need to create, calculate the required subnet mask as follows:

1. Add 1 to the number of subnets needed and convert the result to binary format. (Like the host ID, the subnet ID cannot be all 0s or all 1s—adding 1 avoids these possibilities.) You may want to use the Windows Calculator in Scientific view.

2. The number of bits you used to write the required subnets in binary is the number of additional bits that you add to the default subnet mask. You also need to include any 0 bits in the count. For example, if you need eight subnets that is the binary number 1000. This means you need four binary digits or bits in the subnet mask.

3. Place the number of binary digits needed at the beginning of the octet, and then fill the remaining eight digits in the octet with 0s.

4. Convert the subnet mask back to decimal format. This value replaces the first 0 octet in the subnet mask.

Suppose, for example, that you are assigned a Class B network ID of 168.20, and you need to create 5 subnets. Following the preceding steps, converting 5 into binary gives 00000101, or simply 101.

This means you need three bits to give enough combinations for 5 networks. Therefore, you need to add three bits to the default subnet mask. The default subnet mask for a Class B network is 255.255.0.0, or in binary is:

Default subnet mask
11111111.11111111.00000000.00000000

Adding the three bits creates the custom subnet mask:

Custom subnet mask
11111111.11111111.11100000.00000000

If you convert this to decimal, you will see the subnet mask is 255.255.224.0.

Step 4: Determine the Network IDs to Use

The next step is to determine the subnet IDs that are created, by applying the new subnet mask to the original assigned network ID. Any or all of the resulting subnet network IDs are used in the internetwork.

Three methods for determining the network IDs are given in this chapter. The first is a manual computation; the second is a short-cut for the first method; and the third uses tables with the values already calculated. As noted previously, you should become familiar with the manual calculations to understand the fundamentals of subnetting. All three methods are described in the following sections.

Defining the Network IDs Manually

For an exercise covering this information, see end of chapter.

The network ID for each subnet is determined using the same number of bits as were added to the default subnet mask in the previous step. Use the following steps to define each subnet network ID:

1. List all possible binary combinations of the additional bits added to the default subnet mask.

2. Discard the combinations with all 1s or all 0s. All 1s or all 0s are not valid as network IDs, because all 1s represents the broadcast address for the subnet and all 0s implies "this network only" as a destination.

3. Convert the remaining values to decimal notation. Remember you must use the full 8 bits of the octet for the binary number that is converted to decimal.

4. Finally, each value is appended to the original assigned network ID to produce a subnet network ID.

If you were assigned a Class B network ID of 168.20.0.0 and need to create at least 5 subnets. You need an additional 3 bits added to the default subnet mask to create the subnets. The new subnet mask is then 255.255.224.0, or in binary:

11111111   11111111   11100000   00000000

Listing all combinations of the additional bits gives the following:

000

001

010

011

100

101

110

111

Discarding the values 000 and 111, and converting the remaining combinations to decimal format, you have the following:

.32.	00100000
.64.	01000000
.96.	01100000
.128.	10000000
.160.	10100000
.192.	11000000

Appending the preceding values to the original assigned network ID gives the following new subnet network IDs:

168.20.32.0

168.20.64.0

168.20.96.0

168.20.128.0

168.20.160.0

168.20.192.0

All the new subnet network IDs use the subnet mask of 255.255.224.0.

A Shortcut for Defining the Network IDs

Defining the network IDs manually becomes tedious when more than three additional bits are added to the default subnet mask, because it requires listing and converting many bit combinations. The following is a shortcut method for defining the subnet network IDs:

1. After determining the new subnet mask you calculated for the required number of subnets and host IDs, list the additional octet added to the default subnet mask in decimal notation.

2. Convert the rightmost 1-bit of this value to decimal notation. This is the lowest order 1-bit in the octet you calculated. This decimal value is the incremental value between each subnet value, known as "Delta."

3. The maximum number of subnet network IDs that can be used with this subnet is 2 less than 2 to the power of n, where n is the number of bits you determined were needed for your subnet (# of subnets = $(2^n)-2$).

4. Append "Delta" as an octet to the original network ID to give the first subnet network ID.

5. Repeat Step 4 for each subnet network ID, incrementing each successive value by "Delta."

Again if you are assigned a Class B network ID of 168.20.0.0 and need to create at least 5 subnets. You needed an additional 3 bits added to the default subnet mask to create the subnets.

The additional bits added to the default subnet mask are 11100000.

The rightmost bit converted to decimal (00100000) is 32. Thus, the incremental value is 32. There will be $(2^3)-2 = 6$ subnets created.

The subnets created are as follows:

168.20.0.0 and 32 = 168.20.32.0

168.20.32.0 and 32 = 168.20.64.0

168.20.64.0 and 32 = 168.20.96.0

168.20.96.0 and 32 = 168.20.128.0

168.20.128.0 and 32 = 168.20.160.0

168.20.160.0 and 32 = 168.20.192.0

If you increment the last subnet network ID once more, the last octet matches the last octet of the subnet mask (224), which is considered a broadcast address and thus is an invalid network ID.

Defining the Network ID Using a Table

After you understand the previous two methods of defining subnet network IDs, you may want to instead use the tables found at the end of this chapter that have the appropriate values already calculated.

Step 5: Determine the Host IDs to Use

The final step in subnetting a network is to determine the valid host IDs and assign IP addresses to the hosts.

The host IDs for each subnet start with the value .001 in the last octet, and continue up to one less than the subnet ID of the next subnet. Keep in mind that the last octet cannot be .000 or .255, as these are reserved for broadcast addresses.

Finally, the valid IP addresses for each subnet are created by combining the subnet network ID with the host ID.

If once again you use the assigned address of 168.20.0.0 with five subnets, the range of IP addresses for each subnet is as follows:

Subnet	First IP Address	Last IP Address
168.20.32.0	168.20.32.1	168.20.63.254
168.20.64.0	168.20.64.1	168.20.95.254
168.20.96.0	168.20.96.1	168.20.127.254
168.20.128.0	168.20.128.1	168.20.159.254
168.20.160.0	168.20.160.1	168.20.191.254
168.20.192.0	168.20.192.1	168.20.223.254

Note in this example that the value of the third octet in the IP address can differ from the value calculated for the subnet. For example, the address 168.20.33.1 specifies a network ID of 168.20, a subnet of 32 (with a combined network address of 168.20.32), and a host ID of 1.1. The 1 in the third octet is added to the 32 to give a total value of 33 (binary 00100001). However, the subnet mask determines that the network portion of the address is 32, as indicated by the upper 3 bits, and the host ID is 1, as indicated by the lower 5 bits.

Using the Network Subnetting Tables

As mentioned earlier, after you understand how to use the previous manual calculations for subnetting a network, you may want to use the tables provided to avoid the lengthy calculations.

Tables 4.9, 4.10, and 4.11 show the number of subnets that are used with a given subnet mask for each of the Class A, B, or C addressing types.

Table 4.9

Class A Subnetting			
Additional Bits Required (n)	Maximum Subnets (2^n-2)	Maximum Number Number of Hosts per Subnet (2^(24-n)-2)	Subnet Mask
0	0	16,777,214	255.0.0.0
1	invalid	invalid	invalid
2	2	4,194,302	255.192.0.0
3	6	2,097,150	255.224.0.0
4	14	1,048,574	255.240.0.0
5	30	524,286	255.248.0.0
6	62	262,142	255.252.0.0
7	126	131,070	255.254.0.0
8	254	65,534	255.255.0.0

Table 4.10

Class B Subnetting			
Additional Bits Required (n)	Maximum Subnets (2^n-2)	Maximum Number Number of Hosts per Subnet (2^(16-n)-2)	Subnet Mask
0	0	65,534	255.255.0.0
1	invalid	invalid	invalid
2	2	16,382	255.255.192.0
3	6	8,190	255.255.224.0
4	14	4,094	255.255.240.0
5	30	2,046	255.255.248.0
6	62	1,022	255.255.252.0
7	126	510	255.255.254.0
8	254	254	255.255.255.0

Table 4.11

Class C Subnetting

Additional Bits Required (n)	Maximum Subnets (2^n-2)	Maximum Number Number of Hosts per Subnet (2^(16-n)-2)	Subnet Mask
0	0	254	255.255.255.0
1	invalid	invalid	invalid
2	2	62	255.255.255.192
3	6	30	255.255.255.224
4	14	14	255.255.255.240
5	30	6	255.255.255.248
6	62	2	255.255.255.252
7	invalid	invalid	255.255.255.254
8	invalid	invalid	255.255.255.255

In the preceding tables, the Additional Bits Required is the number of higher-order bits required to be added to the default subnet mask to achieve the required number of subnets and hosts per subnet. For convenience, the resulting subnet mask is shown in decimal notation rather than in binary.

As an example, suppose you are assigned a Class B network ID of 168.20 that must be subdivided into 3 subnets with a maximum of 500 hosts on any given subnet. Adding three bits to the subnet mask allows for 6 subnets with 8,190 hosts on each subnet. However, this subnet mask does not allow for much growth in the number of subnets, while allowing for more than ample growth in the number of hosts on each subnet. On the other extreme, adding 7 bits to the subnet allows 126 subnets with only 510 hosts on each subnet. This subnet mask allows for a great deal of growth in the number of subnets but very little growth in the number of hosts on each subnet. A more appropriate subnet mask is somewhere in the middle. A subnet mask with 4 additional bits allows 14 subnets with 4,094 hosts on each subnet. A subnet mask with 5 additional bits allows 30 subnets with 2,046 hosts on each subnet. Either of these choices is good. You can lean toward one or the other depending on whether you anticipate greater fragmentation on your network in the future, thus requiring more subnets, or greater growth on existing network segments, thus requiring more hosts on each subnet.

Exercises

Exercise 4.1: Calculating Subnets

This exercise helps you use the Windows Calculator to calculate a custom subnet mask. You have been assigned a network address of 149.3.0.0. You want to set up a network with 45 subnets, and you expect no more than 1,000 hosts on each subnet.

1. Open the Windows Calculator (located under Programs, Accessories).

2. From the View menu, choose Scientific. Note the default numbering scheme is decimal, denoted by the Dec button.

3. Enter the number of subnets required plus 1.

4. Convert the number to binary by selecting the Bin button.

5. Write the number of bits required to express this number in binary.

6. Write an 8-bit binary number, with 1s for the upper digits and 0s for the lower digits. Use the number of 1s as determined in step 5 and the number of 0s remaining to make it an 8-bit number.

7. In the Windows Calculator, make sure the Bin button is selected.

8. Enter the 8-bit binary number.

9. Convert the number to decimal by selecting the Dec button.

10. Write down the decimal result.

11. Use this decimal result to specify a custom subnet mask for this network.

12. To determine the number of hosts possible for this network, in the Windows Calculator, enter 2, select x^y, then enter the number of bits remaining for the host IDs. Select = to calculate the result and subtract 2 to determine the total number of hosts possible on each subnet with this subnet mask.

Answers for Exercise 4.1:

4. The binary equivalent of 47 decimal is 101111.

5. This requires 6 bits.

6. The subnet mask for this octet is 11111100.

10. The decimal equivalent of 11111100 is 252.

11. The resulting subnet mask for a class B network is 255.255.252.0.

12. The number of hosts on each subnet is 1022, $2^{10} - 2$.

Exercise 4.2: Viewing Default Subnet Masks

This exercise notes the default subnet mask assigned to each TCP/IP address. You should have installed TCP/IP on your Windows NT computer.

1. Open the Network Properties by right-clicking Network Neighborhood and selecting Properties from the resulting menu.

2. Select the Protocols tab.

3. Select TCP/IP and then select Properties.

4. Write down any existing IP address so that you can restore this address when the exercise is over.

5. Select the Specify an IP Address button.

6. Type a Class A address in the IP address field, such as 9.36.108.45.

7. Note the subnet mask that appears by default.

8. Select Close to exit the Network Properties dialog box.

9. Repeat steps 1–3 to open the TCP/IP properties.

10. Type a Class B address in the IP address field, such as 131.107.2.200.

11. Note the subnet mask that appears by default.

12. Select Close to exit the Network Properties dialog box.

13. Repeat steps 1–3 to open the TCP/IP properties.

14. Type a Class C address in the IP address field, such as 200.20.5.16.

15. Note the subnet mask that appears by default.

16. Type your original IP address as noted in step 4.

17. Select Close to exit the Network Properties dialog box.

Review Questions

1. A default subnet mask allows for _____.

   A. The maximum number of network IDs

   B. The maximum number of host IDs

   C. A balance between the number of host IDs and network IDs

   D. 254 subnets

2. What devices require a unique host ID on a TCP/IP network?

   A. Each router

   B. Each PC

   C. Each network card

   D. Each network printer

3. What is the default subnet mask used for a Class B network?

   A. 255.0.0.0

   B. 255.255.0.0

   C. 255.255.255.0

   D. 255.255.255.255

4. How many different Class A networks are in the world?

   A. 126

   B. 128

   C. 254

   D. 256

5. How many hosts are on a Class C network with a default subnet mask?

   A. 126

   B. 128

C. 254

D. 256

6. A company is assigned the network ID 150.134.0.0 by InterNIC. The company wants to have 15 subnets and up to 1,000 hosts per subnet. How many bits are needed for the custom subnet mask?

   A. 4

   B. 5

   C. 6

   D. 7

7. In question 6, what should the company use for the subnet mask?

   A. 255.255.0.0

   B. 255.255.5.0

   C. 255.255.31.0

   D. 255.255.248.0

8. An organization is assigned the network ID 114.0.0.0 by Inter-NIC. The organization currently has 5 subnets with about 100,000 hosts per subnet. The management wants to divide the subnets into 25 new subnets to make each subnet more manageable. How many bits are used for the custom subnet mask?

   A. 4

   B. 5

   C. 6

   D. 7

9. In question 8, what should the organization use for the subnet mask?

   A. 252.0.0.0

   B. 255.0.0.0

   C. 255.252.0.0

   D. 255.255.252.0

Review Answers

1. B

2. C, D

3. B

4. A

5. C

6. B

7. D

8. C

9. C

Answers to the Test Yourself Questions at the Beginning of the Chapter

1. A TCP/IP address specifies the address of the network, the address of the host, and the subnet address. There may or not be a subnet address specified.

2. The portion of the subnet mask that converts to binary 1s shows the part of the IP address that is the network ID. The rest of the subnet mask, binary 0s, specifies which bits of the IP address designate the host address. If the subnet mask differs from the default for that class of network, then the binary 1s after the default 1s specify the subnet.

3. A class A address uses the first octet to specify the network ID. A subnet mask of 255.0.0.0 masks the first octet as the network ID and the remaining octets as the host ID.

4. If the subnet mask indicates that the host is local, the packet is not routed. However, if the host is remote and in incorrect subnet mask is used, the packet never reaches the remote host because IP will attempt to send it locally. At the other extreme, IP may attempt to route packets for a local host if the subnet mask is wrong.

5. By default, each network ID specifies only one network. The default subnet mask only designates this one network ID, leaving the remainder of the bits to indicate the host ID. By using additional bits to designate the network ID, a subnet mask can allow more than one network ID in the address. However, this results in a reduction in the number of hosts than can be on each subnet.

Chapter 5

Implementing IP Routing

This chapter helps you prepare for the exam by covering the following objective:

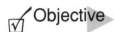 Objective

▶ Configure a Windows NT Server computer to function as an IP router

Test Yourself! Before reading this chapter, test yourself to determine how much study time you will need to devote to this section.

1. When implementing TCP/IP on your wide area network, a user calls and asks why he cannot access the network. What are the three pieces of information a machine must have in a wide area network before it can communicate with other TCP/IP machines/hosts?

2. To update routing tables with an NT multihomed router, which dynamic routing protocol would have to be installed?

3. By default, does a static router know how to route packets to networks other than the ones to which it is physically connected?

4. During a test, you are asked which protocol in the TCP/IP suite is responsible for the routing and delivery of datagrams on the network. Which protocol would you say provided this function?

5. If network communications suddenly stopped between you and a remote network, what utility would best indicate whether a remote router had shut down or was non-functional?

6. You have been told that RIP is really good for small to mid-sized networks, but your network is very large. Does NT support the OSPF protocol as well as the RIP protocol, to help you scale up to enterprise network sizes?

Answers are located at the end of the chapter.

Introduction

Amazingly enough, many chapters and even whole books are dedicated to the concept of routing—discussing the types of routing, how routing works, different kinds of routers, problems encountered with routing, streamlining route tables, and so on. But very few discuss the most fundamentally important question of all: Why do you have to route in the first place? To help you fully understand routing, this chapter begins with a continuation of some of the networking concepts learned in Chapter 2. After the basics are covered, this chapter discusses the reasons for routing, and the benefits of doing so.

Recall from Chapter 2 on the architecture of networks that protocols are written to a standard networking model. Also recall that each layer of the networking model serves as an intermediary to higher layers of the model. Therefore, each layer knows how to communicate with another layer of its type, but has no idea what's going on in layers more than one level removed, either above or below it. In the mail example, the mailman has no clue what kind of message was written, what kind of paper was used, or whether the message was written in English. The only interface between the two layers is the address on the outside of the envelope, which is all the mailman needs. Looking at the networking model then, a frame at the network interface layer would look something like figure 5.1.

Figure 5.1

What the network interface layer sees.

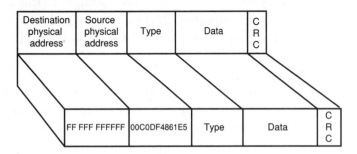

Notice in this example that the network interface layer can identify the destination hardware address, the source hardware address, the type of frame (802.3 ethernet, 802.5 token ring, and so on), and then data. The Network Interface layer has no idea what is in the data layer; it just knows that it's supposed to send the data to the destination hardware address indicated at the front of the packet. Based on the type of communication initiated, the destination address may be all FFs or an actual unique 6-byte physical address.

All this presupposes that the voltage including this information reaches its destination. Recall from Chapter 3 that on an ethernet network each machine transmits on a network segment to communicate. The number of machines that can communicate on a network segment is limited by the machines' capability to sense collisions and retransmit data. Networks are said to reach, or be close to, *bandwidth saturation*, when the machines are unable to avoid collisions while trying to communicate. The best way to avoid bandwidth saturation is to design your ethernet network so that traffic, in the form of voltage, is as segmented and isolated from other traffic as possible. Physical grouping of computers with devices such as bridges and routers minimizes the number of machines within a *collision domain*, or the physical part of the network that machines have to share to send and receive data.

Many network devices have been created to help in this process, to extend network segments and to isolate network traffic. To strengthen your understanding of these concepts, a review of each type of device follows. The author encourages those who are already familiar with these devices and how they work to feel free to skip these sections and move straight to the section titled "Understanding Routing." If these devices still raise some questions in your mind, the summary is provided to fill in conceptual gaps that may exist.

As this is a chapter devoted to IP routing, an in-depth discussion of routers as devices is reserved for later in the chapter, beginning with the "Understanding Routing" section.

Network Review

Discussions of networks to this point have been primarily focused on how they should be put together. In this following section, the review furthers this line of discussion on networks. Instead of covering the theory of network design, however, it provides an overview of the connection devices themselves.

Repeaters, Bridges, and Switches

How do repeaters, bridges, and switches factor into the networking equation? If you're installing a TCP/IP network, why do you have to understand these devices? Mostly because it's extraordinarily rare to run a network using one protocol and because these devices probably already exist on the network you work on. You need to understand how TCP/IP interacts or doesn't interact with these devices to fully understand the protocol suite. First, consider exactly what each device is designed to do.

Repeaters

Copper wire can carry voltage only so far before the integrity of that voltage begins to deteriorate. This deterioration of a voltage signal is referred to as *attenuation*. It more or less means that the difference between a clean 1 (voltage on) and a clean 0 (voltage off) becomes muddled. Figure 5.2 shows the distinction between fresh, clean signals and what the signals look like as the distance increases from where the voltage was applied. The big problem is that this seems to occur after only a couple of hundred feet, certainly not the distance that is necessary for very large networks to successfully communicate. Something had to be done to extend the length of a network segment.

Figure 5.02

Attenuation over distance.

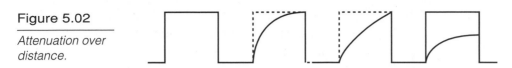

Extending the length of a network segment is difficult because distance is not the only factor that affects voltage. Other sources of interference can alter voltage on a wire. For instance, a copper wire can pick up voltage just from being in the same proximity as a magnetic or electrical source. This means that if a machine wants to communicate a "0" on the wire, but somewhere along the path of the wire it crosses another source of voltage, it picks up that voltage, resonating to that same frequency. Depending on the strength of that secondary source, this could make the "0" look like a "1" to the receiving machine(s). It may be easiest to think of the copper wire as a rambunctious partier who really likes to dance. If the wire hears music anywhere in the neighborhood, it picks up the beat and starts to dance. Imagine how chaotic it would seem to see a dancer try to do the waltz, the cha-cha, ballet, and disco all at the same time.

This troubled the engineers who were trying to design ethernet specifications; they had to figure out how to make sure only one dance was interpreted, while still being able to extend network segments. The network cards with which they were experimenting could transmit and interpret voltage very quickly (approx. 10 MB/sec, an enormous amount of data) and sat around idle most of the time, so speed didn't seem to be the problem. Interpreting whether the voltage was real, on the other hand, was much more difficult.

They experimented with twisting the copper wiring and shielding it from outside interference. They also wrote software to try to make the network devices "pseudo-smart" Along this line, special algorithms were written in the network card logic that basically stated, "If the voltage is close to a 1, make it a 1; if it's close to a 0, make it a 0. We'll have to perform some error checking afterward." After these algorithms were written and the wiring seemed fairly safe, engineers could finally turn to the task of extending the network.

This was fairly simple: design a piece of hardware between two wire segments; if the hardware hears voltage on one side, clean it up and retransmit it on the other side. String as many of these together as you want and you can extend a network for miles and miles, right? Well, no. Machines can't wait forever for a reply to figure out whether a machine receives the voltage; remember, the sending machine has no idea repeaters are on the network. So, after a certain time-out period, the network card just says, "Hey, forget it," or worse, "Hey let's retransmit!"

So, how many repeaters can be strung together, repeating voltage from one segment to another, before the time elapses for a response? The general networking rule is the 5-4-3 rule. This rule states that you can connect up to five network segments with four repeaters where only three of the segments are populated with machines. Standard rules for segment lengths of 100 feet or more, depending on the type of cable, such as coax or UTP, also had to be followed.

All this developed out of the necessity to weed garbage from the data. *Repeaters* were simply designed and implemented to freshen up the voltage on a network segment and retransmit it, all nice and clean again. This type of conditioning of the line occurs at the first layer of the networking model. Although no true error-correction and retransmission utilities are running here, algorithms determine how degraded a signal is, how best to boost the signal that will be rebroadcast, or whether to simply ignore the signal that's been received. Figure 5.3 illustrates at what layer of the networking model a repeater operates.

Figure 5.3

The repeater's role in the networking model.

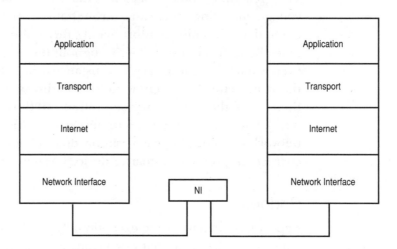

Given how low the repeater works in the networking model, it should be fairly clear that the TCP/IP protocol suite is not terribly concerned about whether there are repeaters in your networking environment—assuming of course, they're working. IP and ARP, the lowest working protocols in the suite, don't even care whether you're on an ethernet, token ring, or other type of network, so long as the underlying network infrastructure is functioning. The one important disadvantage of repeaters occurs when two machines are on the same network segment. When they need to communicate with each other, there is no need for every other segment to receive the same voltage. Figure 5.4 illustrates where repeaters fall a little short.

Figure 5.4

The repeater's shortcomings.

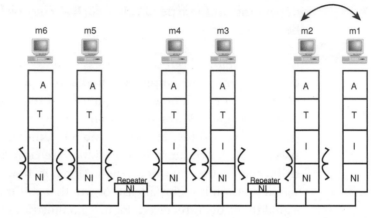

The great thing about repeaters is that they retransmit any kind of voltage, including broadcasts, throughout the network to any machine that is listening. Unfortunately, this is also one of their flaws. Repeaters retransmit—throughout the entire network— even when it is unnecessary. For instance, when two machines on the same network segment want to send directed packets between themselves, the repeater will still retransmit those signals throughout the network. This creates unnecessary traffic on the other network segments. Repeaters simply do not know any better. To correct this problem, a smarter device was needed.

Bridges

Repeaters ended up being exceptionally good at retransmitting data. So good, in fact, that when using a broadcast protocol like NetBEUI, the same bandwidth considerations discussed earlier became a problem again. Machines had a hard time trying to transmit data because they continued to collide with other machines trying to transmit data. This meant that the functional size of an ethernet network was really only a little over 100 machines or so. Numbers greater than this, and sometimes numbers even less than 100, on any segment or extended segment resulted in so many collisions that it usually hung up the entire network. The result was that you, as the network administrator, had to tell everyone to reboot—but please, not all at once! Repeaters were not going to be the only device necessary to make networking feasible.

Bridges were designed to be smarter than repeaters, transmitting data from one network segment to another only if absolutely necessary. Repeaters cannot serve this function because they simply regurgitate anything they see on one segment onto the other segment. Although useful, this is not always a terribly bright idea, as figure 5.5 demonstrates. The repeater correctly identifies that broadcasts are important to retransmit. In fact, most networking protocols provide for some way to implement a broadcast on the network, whether its purpose is to identify a server resource or find a physical address to initiate communication between two machines (even TCP/IP). Even though protocols typically use some form of broadcast to begin communicating with another machine, they are not broadcasting all the time. Besides announcing services, broadcasting is used usually only when you don't know the physical address of the machine with which you're trying to communicate, and have to ask the whole network. After both parties know each other's physical addresses, the machines no longer need broadcasts at this level to communicate. Designers needed a way to isolate the traffic to only the segments necessary for two machines to communicate after they knew the source and destination addresses. In this way, the previous downside to the repeater could be overcome, by only allowing traffic to be transmitted on the network segments where it was necessary, keeping unnecessary traffic to a minimum.

To understand how a bridge works, consider what you would have to know to pass broadcasts. For that matter, what information do you already have at your disposal? When you first turn on a bridge, it is basically blind. The bridge has no idea which machines are on the network and has to figure out which ports it is listening to. But it has memory and a set of rules by which it lives. A bridge only passes data from one segment or port to another based on the following conditions:

▶ If the destination physical address is on the same port as the source physical address, simply retransmit the request onto the same network segment.

▶ If the destination physical address is on a different port than the source physical address, transmit that packet to the port on which the destination physical address resides.

▶ If the destination physical address is unknown (not in the table) or it is a broadcast, pass the broadcast to the other ports, make a note of the source's physical address, and indicate in memory the port on which it resides.

Every time a packet is sent and received on a port, the bridge is responsible for identifying the port on which the source address lives. After this has been determined, that physical address is mapped to the port in the bridge's internal tables.

The advantage of being able to do this is that the number of machines on a network can essentially be doubled, tripled, and so on, depending on where the traffic patterns are and which machines communicate most with each other. Obviously, on some networks in which resources are centralized, this is not much help, but on networks in which resources are distributed in functional groups, it makes a great deal of difference.

Recall from the discussions on broadcasts that when a machine broadcasts a question, it also includes its source MAC address, or physical address. This is true regardless of the communications protocol being utilized. Why would NetBEUI or TCP/IP care about a source address if it is sending a broadcast? The initiator of the communication sends their physical address so that the receiver does not have to broadcast back. In terms of broadcast frames, bridges do not initially help much, because they simply retransmit the broadcast onto the segments and networks to which they are connected. They do come in handy after the source and destination addresses have been discovered. Bridges use the source addresses to build tables in memory of which addresses correspond to its ports. Look at the example shown in figure 5.5 to see how this works.

Figure 5.5

The bridge at work.

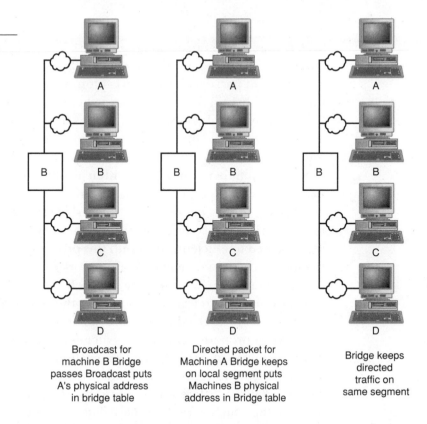

Broadcast for
machine B Bridge
passes Broadcast puts
A's physical address
in bridge table

Directed packet for
Machine A Bridge keeps
on local segment puts
Machines B physical
address in Bridge table

Bridge keeps
directed
traffic on
same segment

As the example indicates, the bridge senses the voltage on the wire and decides whether it will rebroadcast the message based on its table. Bridges rebroadcast broadcasts by default; however, after they find source and destination addresses are on the same segment, they simply retransmit on that segment. If machine A tries to communicate with machine D, the router would mark machine D's physical address in network 2 and would know to pass any frames destined for physical address 5 to network 2. In this way, you can isolate local traffic from other segments, but when machines need to communicate with machines on another segment, they can do that as well. The tables that the bridges keep make them smart enough to look at the frames and determine where they are supposed to go. Different types of bridges learn their tables in different ways, but they all perform essentially the same task. Bridges are typically associated with bus-based and ring-based networks, and can serve as primitive gateways between these networks, reformatting frames from one and placing them on the network of the other.

Switches

Switches are devices that can be configured as bridges or routers and have a far more sophisticated means by which they approach movement of packets on a network. Most readily identified with the star and hybrid star networks, switches are designed to establish virtual circuits between two machines trying to communicate, so that the two machines see the traffic of only one, or at least only a few other, machines. Switches are primarily designed to reduce the number of machines within a collision domain. A *collision domain* is the logical grouping of machines that cannot avoid seeing each other's packets at the network interface layer. Ethernet networks using collision avoidance and detection techniques are designed to efficiently deal with this problem. Remember that the more machines on a particular network segment, the harder it is to communicate. Repeaters are not useful in restricting collisions because they retransmit everything they see. Bridges are more useful for directed packets, but still must transmit broadcasts. When properly configured, switches can establish point-to-point communications between two machines so that collision avoidance is no longer even necessary. Traffic between two machines will not interfere with other traffic that may be passing through the switch because the switch is sophisticated enough to isolate the traffic being transmitted from one port to another. Naturally, more than one machine can be added to a switch's port through the use of hubs. Figure 5.6 illustrates how a switch operates.

Figure 5.6

A look at a switch.

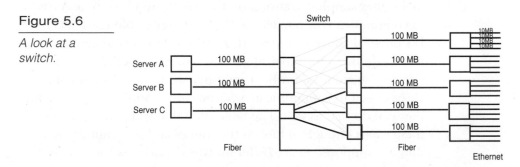

In this hybrid star configuration, the collision domain includes just the machines attached to that hub, not to any other ports. A full-scale discussion of switches is beyond the scope of this chapter. The important point to take away from this summary on switches is this: Although some switches can be configured to perform standard routing functions, most work at the Network Interface layer where IP is not involved yet. This means that if you have a digitally switched network, you may not need to break down your network IDs with subnet masks. The primary role of switches is to reduce the number of machines in your collision domains, thereby providing more sustained bandwidth to each machine on a network segment.

Looking at Broadcast Protocols

Before you can fully appreciate TCP/IP, you need to understand how each protocol in the suite works together. To gain this understanding, you need to spend some time looking at how broadcast protocols work. This section uses NetBEUI as an example protocol on a standard ethernet network. From this review of broadcast protocols, or non-routeable protocols, the discussion extends to the function of protocols that are point-to-point, or routeable protocols. You may be surprised to discover that although there are some significant differences between broadcast and point-to-point protocols, there are probably more similarities than differences.

A great deal of discussion on the networking model has focused up to this point on how each layer of the networking model on a sending machine needs to be able to communicate with its corresponding layer on the receiving machine. For instance, the Application layer knows how to communicate with the Application layer of another machine and the Session layer knows how to communicate with the Session layer of another machine. This function is fundamental to network architecture. At the bottom of the networking model is the Network Interface layer, and it necessarily follows that the Network Interface layer needs to communicate with the Network Interface layer, just as with each of the other layers. Part of the Network Interface layer includes the physical address of a machine, the 6-byte (48-bit) unique hexadecimal address assigned to a network card by the manufacturer.

NetBEUI is a broadcast protocol, but complies with the standard rules for networking in that NetBEUI's first task when trying to establish communication with another machine is to discover the physical address of the destination machine. With NetBEUI, each machine is uniquely identified by a name, called the NetBIOS name. This is the name of the machine given to it during installation of any Windows operating system using the NetBIOS interface. Even if the NetBEUI protocol is not loaded, the name is still a NetBIOS name and any protocol installed will have to support the NetBIOS interface. This is why Microsoft includes the NetBT (NetBIOS over TCP/IP) API in the protocol suite.

But back to NetBEUI; observe figure 5.7. This figure shows two machines in the state in which they would exist if they had never communicated with each other and the application on machine B wanted to communicate with machine A. The real conceptual bridge to cross here is that even though these machines may be sitting next to each other on the same piece of wire, they may not have a clue about how to communicate with each other. Remember that each layer of the networking model must be able to communicate or the whole process breaks down. So, even if the application layer of machine B knows it wants to speak to machine A, the lower layers may have no idea what the application layer is talking about.

Figure 5.7

Two machines that have not communicated before.

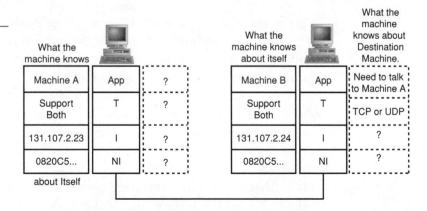

At this point, the lower layers have a choice. They can either report that they don't have a clue, or they can go out on the network and try find a machine with the appropriate name. In this case, machine B initiates a broadcast on the network using an ethernet frame in which the destination address is represented by 6 bytes of all FFs, as in figure 5.1. Recall that a broadcast utilizing all FFs indicates to every network interface card that it must pass this data up to the higher layers of the networking model. But, just as someone screaming incoherently does not tend to facilitate communication, it would behoove machine B to broadcast a meaningful question to those higher layers. In this case, the question is put very simply: "If you are machine A, what is your physical address?" This question also contains information about the sending machine, including the NetBIOS name and physical address. With NetBEUI, this question is sent all the way up to the Session layer of every machine on this network before the question is understood and possibly responded to. After a machine interprets the question and decides the message was intended for it, it sends back a directed message indicating its physical address. After these two machines have figured out each other's physical addresses, they can communicate with directed packets, meaning that they no longer need to use broadcasts that every machine listens to; they can place the physical addresses in the frames just as with a point-to-point protocol. Figure 5.8 illustrates the communication process between two machines using a broadcast protocol.

Figure 5.8

Communication with a broadcast protocol.

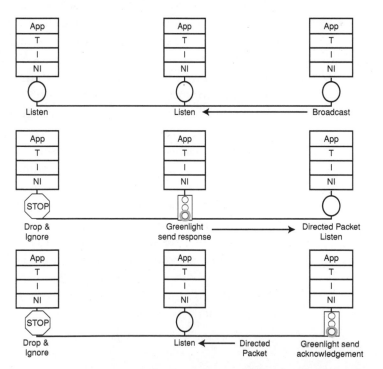

This is true any time a machine using a broadcast protocol attempts to communicate with another machine on the network. Part of the response given to any broadcast message is the destination machine's physical address. After a reply is sent, including the destination machine's physical address, broadcasts between the two machines are no longer necessary, and the actual physical address is placed in its appropriate location during data transfer.

So, if this is the case, what's the problem with NetBEUI? Why can't you use it on the Internet, too? In order to answer this question you need to look much further into the conceptual barriers imposed by this protocol. After you have uncovered and dissected the barriers, it should be fairly clear when NetBEUI is, and is not, useful as a protocol in the networking world.

First, NetBEUI was originally designed to be used on local area networks. This means that NetBEUI doesn't use an individual addressing scheme based on the important assumption that there is more than one network to worry about. This basic and fundamental design assumption lead to simple choices. For instance, as Chapter 2 discussed, it's important to be able to uniquely identify machines on a network. When using NetBEUI, a machine's uniqueness is defined by its physical address and its unique NetBIOS name, the name it received during installation of the operating system. Since its inception as a protocol, NetBEUI never had to worry about whether there was more than one network; it was not designed to worry about how to uniquely identify one network over another or how to move packets from one network to another, because it assumes there is only one network. That is why the question it asks during the broadcast for a physical address is somewhat simple: "If you're machine X, what is your physical address?" Notice the hidden assumption. Nowhere in the question does it ask what network the machine is on, because to NetBEUI, that is a meaningless question; of course we're all on the same network. Without the additional overhead of worrying about having to route packets, it has the advantage of being quick and efficient. It is not, however, routeable because it has no way to identify different networks, and requires each machine on the network segment to dedicate more resources due to its broadcast nature. Consider how far up the networking model a machine has to pass a random frame on the network before determining whether the frame was destined for it, during a broadcast. Figure 5.9 illustrates that process.

Figure 5.9

Session layer processing.

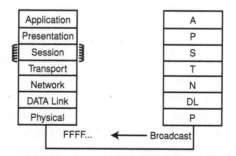

Using a broadcast protocol such as NetBEUI, the only fundamental restrictions in terms of networking are that multiple networks don't exist (remember, to a protocol such as NetBEUI, there's only one network, or LAN), and the functional number of computers you can put on that network is limited.

If you use the TCP/IP protocol, however, the destination for this data could be identified by the physical address assigned to the network card of that machine or the IP address given to that machine. As Chapter 3 indicated, the IP address has a lot of information. Not only does it contain the unique network identifier for that machine on a network, but it also has the unique host identifier as well. The capability to uniquely identify different network IDs is what makes TCP/IP a wide area network protocol, and is what separates it from broadcast protocols. Because IP recognizes the difference between unique machines and unique networks, the protocol had to be written with the capability to move data from one network to another by "routing" them from one network to another. This function is built into the IP protocol. In the case of a routed protocol, machines do not have to pass frames as high up in the networking model to determine if the packet is directed at them. Figure 5.10 illustrates the difference between a broadcast protocol and a directed, or routed, protocol.

Figure 5.10

Broadcast versus directed protocols.

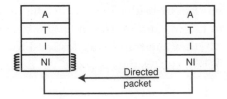

Because the network interface layer is responsible for checking the destination of frames, the determination of whether the data is for that machine occurs at a much lower layer on the networking model. TCP/IP was designed for use on a WAN in which multiple network segments are connected through devices called *routers*. Because TCP/IP uses several addressing schemes—IP addresses and physical addresses—it has the additional overhead of sorting through these and requires the administrator to have more knowledge of the protocol to implement it. However, this added overhead allows TCP/IP to be extraordinarily robust, routeable, and flexible. Figure 5.11 illustrates the addressing levels that TCP/IP uses, including physical address, IP address, and host naming conventions.

Figure 5.11

Unique addressing characteristics.

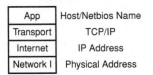

How did the source machine get the destination IP address in the first place? Recall from Chapter 2, that ARP (the detective) is the protocol responsible for going out and finding physical addresses of machines based on the IP address. ARP uses a small broadcast of its own on the network, somewhat similar to what NetBEUI does, except the packet is smaller. The ARP request frame is shown in figure 5.12.

Figure 5.12

Example of the ARP broadcast.

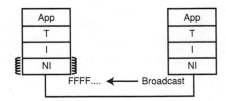

So you can see that even TCP/IP must use some sort of a broadcast to gain physical addresses, much like NetBEUI. These broadcasts just occur in a separate stage of communication. After ARP has negotiated the physical address between the two machines, it passes the physical address to IP so that it can create the directed frame necessary for communication. You can configure the TCP/IP suite with manual entries in the ARP cache so that ARP does not use broadcasts, but this adds a substantial amount of maintenance overhead on the administrator's part.

Refer to figure 5.10. Notice that each machine on the network in these examples still receives the initial frame and has to check it. Both examples in figures 5.9 and 5.10 use a standard ethernet network design using CSMA/CA, but they use a different protocol. Does this mean that a network has to be concerned with bandwidth issues regardless of which protocol is being used? Unfortunately, the answer is yes. Both examples indicate that on an ethernet network, frames (voltage) are applied to the wire segment that these machines are on, regardless of which protocol is being used. In fact, at this layer, the network cards have no idea which protocol is being used. All the network cards know at this level is that they listen and pass broadcasts up to the next layer and drop any packets that aren't broadcasts or aren't specifically addressed to them.

Now that the essential differences between broadcast and directed protocols has been covered, a more formal discussion of TCP/IP routing can be undertaken. The next section discusses what routing is, what a router is, and the routing process as a whole.

Understanding Routing

Recall from the IP addressing and subnetting sections that the first thing a machine does when initiating communication with another machine is try to figure out whether the destination address is local or remote. It carries out calculations on the source and destination address based on the given subnet mask and then compares the two results. If the results are the same, the destination address is on the local network and ARP is then asked to get the physical address of the destination machine. If, however, the results do not match, the destination host is remote, and ARP is asked to get the physical address of a router or the default gateway.

Routers are devices that work at the Internet layer of the TCP/IP protocol suite, and have been designed to transfer or forward packets of data to their destinations, even when the routers themselves are not the destination. Consider for a moment that during a broadcast at the Network Interface layer (for example, ARP broadcast) for an IP address, presumably all the machines except one ignore the broadcast. This is because only one machine has that unique IP address. All other machines pass this data up to IP and then silently discard the data because the data is not intended for them. Routers are special machines that are told not to silently discard these kinds of packets, but to try to find the correct route or path to send messages when they receive messages not destined for them. In this way, packets can traverse one network to another through a router, and because this routing process occurs at the Internet layer, it doesn't matter what kind of network you're running on, be it token ring, ethernet, or FDDI. Most machines are not designed to do this; only routers and gateways are. Figure 5.13 illustrates a simple routed network design with one router and three networks.

Figure 5.13

A simple routed network.

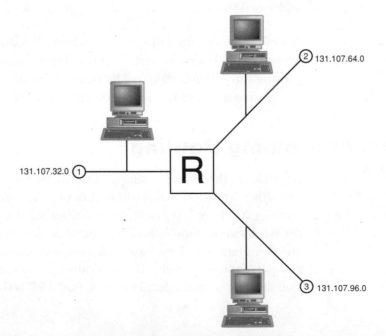

In this figure, the router separates the three network segments and keeps traffic on those network segments isolated from each other. Routers do not inherently support the passing of broadcasts, and must be specifically configured to do so on a network. This means that any machine broadcasting on network 1 will not be seen by machines on network 2 or 3. If a machine needs to communicate with a machine on the other side of a router, it needs to directly identify that machine and send those packets to the router to be forwarded.

How did this machine know the address of the router or default gateway? Host machines gain the IP address of the router in one of two ways. It is either manually configured in the network configuration of the machine, or the machine discovers the router address through a DHCP scope option. This information is stored in the registry and also appears in the machines internal route table.

This route table resides in memory and keeps track of networks and the physical interfaces that give access to those networks. On a local machine, the route table is fairly simple and usually contains no more than a few default entries, including the loopback address, the network on which the machine currently resides, and entries for various broadcasts. Figure 5.14 illustrates a common route table for a local machine.

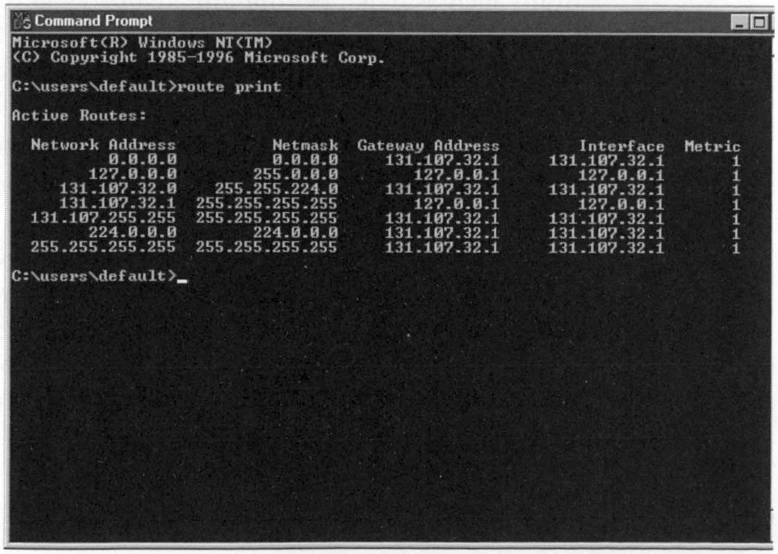

Figure 5.14

A sample route table.

```
  Command Prompt                                                    _ □ ×
Microsoft(R) Windows NT(TM)
(C) Copyright 1985-1996 Microsoft Corp.

C:\users\default>route print

Active Routes:

   Network Address          Netmask  Gateway Address        Interface  Metric
         0.0.0.0          0.0.0.0     131.107.32.1      131.107.32.1       1
       127.0.0.0          255.0.0.0       127.0.0.1         127.0.0.1       1
    131.107.32.0    255.255.224.0     131.107.32.1      131.107.32.1       1
    131.107.32.1  255.255.255.255       127.0.0.1         127.0.0.1       1
  131.107.255.255  255.255.255.255     131.107.32.1      131.107.32.1       1
       224.0.0.0        224.0.0.0     131.107.32.1      131.107.32.1       1
  255.255.255.255  255.255.255.255     131.107.32.1      131.107.32.1       1

C:\users\default>_
```

Every machine on a TCP/IP network consults its route table to determine what to do with addresses that are destined either locally or remotely. If a destination is on the local network, the route table informs IP to send the data to the local machine. If, however, the destination address is remote, IP consults the route table for an entry specific to that network. If an entry specific to that network exists, the packet is sent to the network interface identified by that route table entry. If no entry exists for that specific network and a default gateway has not been identified, the packet is dropped. It is only in the case that an entry does not exist and a default gateway for the machine has been configured, that IP will use the 0.0.0.0 route table entry (default gateway) to find a network interface address to send the data. Figure 5.15 has no specific networks identified and would therefore use the 0.0.0.0 entry, sending data destined for a remote network to 131.107.2.1 to be routed.

Dead Gateway Detection

Microsoft NT supports dead gateway detection when using TCP/IP. This means a machine can have more than one default gateway defined in its IP configuration. If, for some reason, the first default gateway is not responding, TCP/IP can switch to other default gateways to try to find a path to a particular destination. Dead gateway detection works only through the TCP protocol, so a utility such as ping does not initiate dead gateway detection when trying to communicate. A utility such as FTP, on the other hand, tries to establish a TCP connection and detects dead gateways. When TCP sends out data and no acknowledgments are received, it retransmits this data. But it only tries to retransmit data so many times before giving up on the connection. This number of times is defined by the registry entry called *TcpMaxData-Retransmissions*. When TCP reaches half of this value (default = 5), it asks IP to switch from the original default gateway, and to try to establish communication using the next default gateway configured on the machine. Dead gateway detection does not have to be turned on by the user; it is on automatically. After multiple default gateways are configured, dead gateway detection is initiated for any TCP connection, and the entries for the default gateways are placed in the routing table. The registry where you can configure this manually is as follows:

```
HKEY_LOCAL_MACHINE\SYSTEM\CurrentControlSet\Services\Tcpip\Parameters
```

Remember that by default, this selection is on. The only reason to edit this parameter would be if you do not want to use dead gateway detection. For more information on the exact registry entries and parameters, see Microsoft's online knowledge base.

After a machine determines where to send a packet destined for either a local or remote address, all other networking processes discussed earlier have to take place. Take a closer look at the packets that are created during these two processes, local and remote. The first example illustrates a command issued to a local machine and the second example illustrates the same for a remote machine. Both examples use figure 5.15, and the route table in figure 5.14 is the default route table for machine A on the network.

Figure 5.15

Example 1: From machine A, ping the address 131.107.32.20.

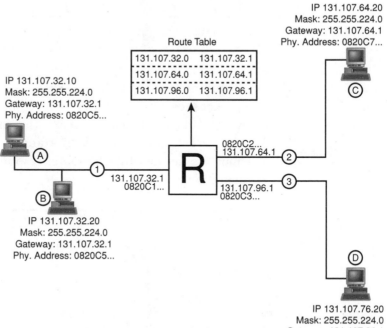

The first step is for machine A to use its subnet mask to determine whether this IP address is local or remote. After determining that the IP address is local, it consults the route table. Even though the destination is local, the machine still needs to figure out what interface to use to send out the data. Although this may seem somewhat trivial, keep in mind that a machine may have more than one IP address bound to a network card, or more than one network card attached to two networks. Either scenario provides a machine with more than one local interface to physical network segments. After the machine establishes the IP address of the interface, ARP is instructed to find the physical address of the local machine. A sample ARP broadcast for this address is shown in figure 5.16.

Figure 5.16

A sample ARP broadcast.

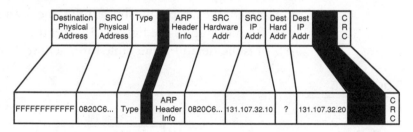

Once the destination address responds with its physical address, ARP relays this information to IP so that IP can formulate the directed packet shown in figure 5.17. Notice both the destination's physical address and IP address are used in the creation of this directed packet. After this packet is transmitted on the wire, only machine B's Network Interface layer responds to the physical address identified.

Figure 5.17

The completed frame.

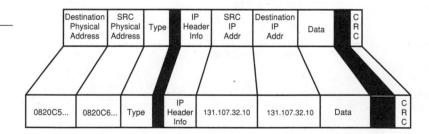

In this way, local communications are initiated. Observe the subtle differences between communicating with a local machine versus a remote machine.

The first step is for machine A to use its subnet mask to determine whether this IP address is local or remote. After determining that the IP address is remote, it consults the route table to determine where to send packets destined for this IP address. After consulting the default table, the machine does not find any entries specific to network 3. It does, however, have a default gateway defined at 131.107.32.1. Therefore, any packets destined for networks this machine does not know about should be sent to the default gateway at 131.107.32.1. IP asks ARP to find the physical address of the default gateway because that is where this packet will have to be sent. ARP consults the ARP cache and either returns a physical address stored in memory or initiates an ARP broadcast for the router. Figure 5.18 illustrates this ARP packet. There does not appear to be anything special about this packet except for the address that ARP is looking for.

Figure 5.18

An ARP broadcast for the router.

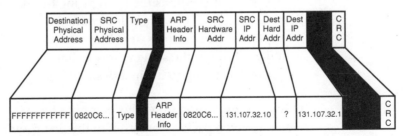

Once ARP locates the physical address of the router, it returns this physical address to IP so that IP can formulate the packet that will be sent. Figure 5.19 illustrates the packet that IP formulates. Take a close look at the destination physical address and the destination IP address.

Figure 5.19

A packet addressed to the router, but destined to a remote address.

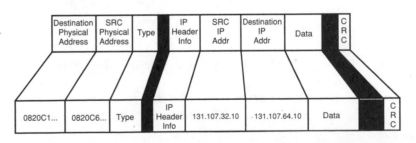

Notice how cleverly IP handles the routing of the packet. IP has to keep the destination IP address the same as that issued by the ping command, but send the packet in such a way that it can be forwarded by the router. It does this by creating a packet destined for the original IP address at the Internet layer, but sending the packet to the physical address of the router at the network interface layer. IP knows that the router is the only machine that will respond to a packet destined for this physical address, but that once the router passes this packet up to the IP layer, the router will be responsible for forwarding this packet to its destination.

After the packet resides on the router, the router has to go through the same process as any other host or machine on the network. The router must use its subnet mask to determine whether the packet's IP address is local or remote, access its route table to find the best possible route to the destination, and utilize ARP to find physical addresses to send the packet(s) to.

If this example had more routers and network segments, the first router would be responsible for figuring out the best route to the destination network. After it determined the best route, it would forward this data on to its next hop or router. This second router would go through the same motions, figuring out the best path to send the data along to its final destination.

Of course, discussion up to this point has focused on how the local machine gets a packet from itself to the first router along the path to a packet's destination. Both routers and machines keep a routing table. On a machine, this table is usually relatively short and simply defines the network that the machine is currently on and the machine's interface (IP address) to that network. On routers, these tables can be long and complex, but by default, a router knows only about the networks to which it has a physical interface. For instance, in figure 5.16, the router only knows about networks 1, 2, and 3, because it has a physical interface to each.

Static and Dynamic Routers

As the previous section discussed, routers have built-in tables used to determine where to send a packet destined for a particular network. By default, routers know only about networks to which they are physically attached. This section discusses how routers find out about networks to which they are not physically attached —either through manual configuration or dynamic configuration.

Static routers are routers that are not able to discover networks other than those to which they have a physical interface. If this type of router is to be able to route packets to any other network, it has to be told manually what to do, through either the assignment of a default gateway on the router, or by manually editing the route table. Microsoft NT enables the user to build a static router, or multihomed router, using multiple network cards and IP addresses. In a static router environment, new changes are not reflected in the routing tables on these routers.

Dynamic routers, on the other hand, utilize inter-routing protocols. These protocols simply provide a language for routers to communicate changes to their route tables to other routers in their environment. In this way, routing tables are built dynamically and the administrator does not have to manually edit route tables to bring up a new network segment.

Dynamic routers cannot provide this function without routing protocols, though. The most popular routing protocols are the Routing Information Protocol (RIP) and Open Shortest Path First protocol (OSPF). RIP is a broadcast-based protocol used primarily on small- to medium-sized networks. The more sophisticated OSPF protocol is used for medium to large networks.

Microsoft NT 4.0 supports the installation and use of RIP to provide dynamic routing for multihomed computers using NT as the operating system. In this way, routing tables can be updated whenever any additions to a network occur. If RIP or OSPF is used in a routed environment, it should help eliminate the need to have to manually edit route tables in your environment.

The Static Routing Environment

Take a look at how static routing works in an environment. Figure 5.20 shows a typical small network environment with two routers dividing three subnets. Each router has a standard routing table consisting of the networks to which they are attached. In the figure, router A is connected to subnet 1 and 2 and has a routing table that reflects this information. Router B is connected to subnet 2 and 3 and its routing table also reflects the networks on which it is currently configured. Take a look at what happens to a ping (echo request) packet when it is initiated by a machine on subnet 1.

Figure 5.20

A typical small network.

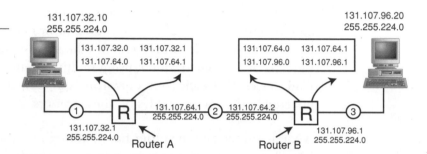

Combine everything you have learned from the previous chapters to isolate exactly how this ping request would flow. From the command prompt, or possibly a specific application on subnet 1, a ping command is issued to an IP address on subnet 3; let's say from IP address 131.107.32.10 to 131.107.96.20. First, IP takes the destination address and compares it to the source address using the subnet mask of that machine. After the comparison is done, IP determines that this destination address is on a remote network. IP checks its internal route table to determine where it's supposed to send packets destined for a remote network. Whenever a destination address is remote, IP knows to ask ARP for the physical address of the default gateway specified in the internal route table. ARP then either returns the physical address from the ARP cache or does a local ARP broadcast for the router's physical address. At this point, the ping request has not yet left the sending machine. IP gathers the physical address of the router, inserts the destination address into the ping packet and finally transmits the packet onto the wire of subnet 1.

Because IP very smartly sends the packet on the wire in such a way that only the router would not discard the packet, the packet safely arrives at the router. The network interface on the router passes the data up its network stack to IP, where IP discovers that this packet is not destined for it. Normally, IP on a machine would discard the packet. But this is a special kind of machine, a router, which has additional responsibilities including trying to forward packets it receives to the necessary network. Router A reads the IP address of the destination and compares this destination to its own source address using its subnet mask. At this point, IP determines the network to which this packet is supposed to be sent and checks its internal route table to see what to do with packets destined for the 131.107.96.0 network. Unfortunately, this router has no entries for this network and therefore drops this packet. ICMP reports an error to the machine on subnet 1, indicating that the destination address cannot be reached.

This seems like an awful lot of work to get an error message, especially if you know that the destination machine is working. There are two ways to get around this kind of scenario.

▶ Add a default gateway to the router's configuration

▶ Add a manual entry in the router's internal table

See what happens if you utilize one or both of these solutions on router A, picking up right where router A decided to drop the packet. Figure 5.21 illustrates the new routing table and default gateway assignment.

Figure 5.21

Adding a default gateway address.

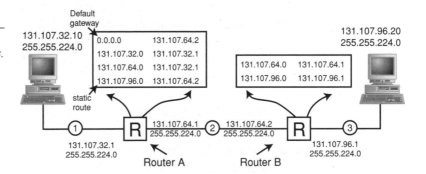

Router A has just figured out that the packet's destination address does not match its own IP address. It therefore checks its route table, looking for either a path to the 131.107.96.0 network or for the IP address of its default gateway. By configuring a default gateway, an administrator indicates to the router that if it handles a packet destined for a network that it has no idea about, the router should send it to the default gateway specified and hope for the best. This can be useful if you don't want to configure 37 route table entries on a network. Merely specifying default gateways can minimize the size of your route tables and minimize the number of manual entries you have to maintain. This, of course, comes with the possibility of making your network a little more inefficient. There are always tradeoffs when configuring a network.

Router A now figures out that it needs to send the ping request to the IP address of the other router based on its route table, in this case 131.107.64.2. Here is yet another conceptual gap. Router A really doesn't know whether the IP address represents a router or just another machine on the network. For that matter, it might be sending this packet into bit-space. Router A trusts that the administrator was wise enough to specify an IP address of a device that will help get the packet to its final destination. As an aside, this means that if you enter a route table entry incorrectly, the router just merrily starts sending packets to wherever you specified.

IP on router A now asks ARP to find the physical address of the next router in line. Just as on another machine, ARP either already has the physical address in cache or initiates an ARP broadcast to get it. After IP has the physical address, it reformulates the packet, addressing it to router B's physical address but leaving the original source address intact. It does not insert its own IP address as the source. If it did this, the destination address would never respond back to the original machine. The packet is transmitted onto the wire destined for router B.

Router B hears the transmission, goes through basically the same process, determines the destination address and discovers that it can send the packet directly to the destination machine. Utilizing the same ARP and IP procedures, the packet finally arrives at the destination machine on subnet 3. The ICMP echo request is acknowledged and ICMP formulates the ICMP echo response packet that must be sent back. Remember that up to this point, the original sending machine is just patiently waiting for a response.

The destination machine looks at the source address (131.107.32.10), figures out that it's remote, finds the physical address of router B to send the message back and transmits it onto the wire.

 Note

In order for routing to work in a static routing environment, be sure that each router is aware of all relevant networks. Otherwise, packets will be dropped unexpectedly on their return to a destination.

Router B receives the packet, breaks it down and tries to figure out what to do with a packet destined for the 131.107.32.0 subnet. And, after all this work, router B drops the packet. Why? We made all our changes to router A in terms of a default gateway and route table entries, but we didn't do anything to router B. To make static routing work, each router has to be updated and configured to know about other networks in the environment. It will only be after a default gateway or manual entry in router B's route table is configured, that the packets will successfully be transmitted between these two networks. Figure 5.22 illustrates the final network configuration for the routers that enables successful communication between these subnets.

Figure 5.22

The final network routing tables.

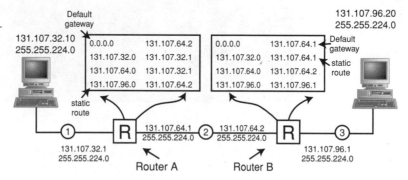

Default Gateways

You can easily identify default gateways on a machine. The two easiest ways to identify default gateways for a machine or multihomed router is through manual configuration through the IP properties sheet, or as a DHCP option. You can specify more than one default gateway on a machine. Remember, however, that dead gateway detection will work only for machines initiating a TCP connection. In a routing table, the default gateway(s) is identified by the entry 0.0.0.0.

Route Tables

Route tables are used by machines/hosts on the network and by routers to determine where packets should be sent to reach their final destination. Each router builds an internal route table every time IP is loaded during system initialization. Take a closer look at a route table. Figure 5.23 illustrates an example of a route table built during the initialization of a machine configured to be a router.

Figure 5.23

Router's route table.

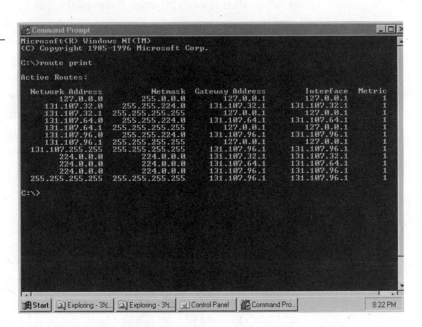

Notice the five columns of information provided within the route table.

▶ **Network Address.** This column represents all networks that this machine or router knows about, including entries for the default gateway, subnet and network broadcasts, the universal loopback address, and the default multicast address. In a route table, you can use names instead of IP addresses to identify networks. If you use names instead of

IP addresses, the names are resolved using the networks file found in the \%system drive%\system32\drivers\etc directory. While you can configure this option, the author strongly recommends against using such names, purely from a troubleshooting perspective. If, for some reason, the networks file was deleted or corrupted, name resolution would not be your only problem. Your router would suddenly find it difficult to route packets to these networks without knowing which IP addresses represented those network IDs.

▶ **Netmask.** This column simply identifies the subnet mask used for a particular network entry.

▶ **Gateway Address.** This is the IP address to which packets should be sent in order to route packets to their final destination. Each network address may specify a different gateway address in which to send packets. This may be particularly true if more than one router is connected to one network segment. This column may also have self-referential entries indicating the IP address to which broadcasts should be sent, as well as the local loopback entries. You can also use names to identify these IP addresses. Any names used here will be resolved using the local hosts file on the machine. Again, while this option is supplied, the author does not recommend introducing another source of possible error by using names in route tables.

▶ **Interface.** This IP address is used primarily to identify the IP address of the machine and to identify this IP address as the interface to the network. On a machine with one network card, only two entries appear. For any network address that is self-referential, the interface is 127.0.0.1, meaning that packets are not even sent onto the network. For all other communications, the IP address represents the network card interface used to communicate out onto the network. For multihomed machines, the interface IP address changes depending on which network address is configured on each network card. In this case, the interface identifies the IP address of the card connected to a particular network segment.

▶ **Metric.** The metric indicates the cost or hops associated with a particular network route. The router's job is to find the path representing the least cost or effort to get the packet to its destination. The lower the cost or hop count, the better or more efficient a particular route. On a static router, the metric for any network address will be one, indicating that the router thinks every network is only one router hop away. This is obviously not true, indicating that on static routers, this column is fairly meaningless. On dynamic routers, however, this column indicates to a router the best possible route to send packets.

Viewing the Route Table

To view the route table of an NT machine/router, two utilities can be used: the netstat utility and the route utility. To view the route table through netstat, go to the command prompt and type **netstat -r**.

This brings up the route table on your machine. However, all you can do is view the table. To view and manage the route table, including adding or changing entries, use the route utility. To view the route table using the route command, type **route print**.

This shows you the same table as before. When you type "route print" from the command prompt, the same table that displays with netstat -r appears. In both cases, the route table appears similar to the example shown in figure 5.22.

The entries that are in a route table on NT 40 by default include the following:

▶ **0.0.0.0.** Assuming, of course, that a default gateway is specified, this entry identifies the IP address of the default gateway, or the IP address to which packets will be sent if no other specific route table entry exists for a destination network. If multiple gateways are defined on an NT machine, you may notice more than one entry that looks like this, specifying each of the default gateways that is defined.

▶ **127.0.0.1.** This is the local loopback address used for diagnostic purposes, to make sure that the IP stack on a machine is properly installed and running.

▶ **Local network.** This is the identifier indicating the local network address. It indicates the gateway and interface, such as the machine's IP address, that is used whenever a packet needs to be transmitted to a local destination.

▶ **Local host.** This is used for self-referential purposes and points to the local loopback address as the gateway and interface.

▶ **Subnet broadcast.** This is a directed broadcast and is treated as a directed packet by routers. Routers support the transmission of directed broadcasts to the network that is defined by the broadcast. The packet is forwarded to the network, where it is broadcast to the machines on that network. In this case, the default entry specifies the IP address of the current machine for sending out subnet broadcasts to the network this machine is on.

▶ **224.0.0.0.** This is the default multicast address. If this machine is a member of any multicast groups, this and other multicast entries indicate to IP the interface used to communicate with the multicast network.

▶ **255.255.255.255.** This is a limited broadcast address for broadcasts destined for any machine on the local network. Routers that receive packets destined for this address may listen to the packet as a normal host, but do not support transmission of these types of broadcasts to other networks.

When a router looks for where to send a particular packet, it searches through the route table. After a route has been determined, meaning that an IP address has been found to send the data to, IP asks ARP for the physical address of that IP address. As soon as ARP replies, the frame can be constructed and transmitted onto the wire.

Building a Static Routing Table

The route command has a number of other switches that can be used to manage a route table statically. Up to this point, the print command is the only parameter that has been used. To manage a route table, however, an administrator must be able to add, delete, change, and clear route table entries. Each of these options is available; the following table shows each respective command:

To Add or Modify a Static Route	Function
route add [net id] mask [netmask] [gateway]	Adds a route
route -p add [net id] mask [netmask] [gateway]	Adds a persistent route
route delete [net id] [gateway]	Deletes a route
route change [net id] [gateway]	Modifies a route
route print	Displays route table
route –f	Clears all routes

For an exercise covering this information, see end of chapter.

Notice the entry that utilizes a -p (persistent) before the add parameter. By default, route table entries are kept only in memory. After a machine is rebooted, any entries that were manually added are gone and must be reentered. You can use batch files, startup scripts—or the persistent switch—to reenter static routes. The persistent entry switch writes route entries into the registry so that they survive a reboot of the machine. Naturally, this removes the need to create batch files or scripts, but requires manual deletion of the routes if they should change.

Note

Route table entries are kept only in memory and will not survive a reboot unless the -p switch is used.

The TRACERT Utility

Windows NT includes the TRACERT utility, which is used to verify the route a packet takes to reach its destination. To use the this utility, simply go to the command prompt and type **tracert <*IP address*>**.

The result of running this utility for a destination address will probably look similar to the following output :

```
C:\>tracert www.learnix.com

Tracing route to www.learnix.com [199.45.92.97]
over a maximum of 30 hops:

  1    156 ms    156 ms    141 ms   annex.intranet.ca [206.51.251.5]
  2    157 ms    156 ms    156 ms   cisco2.intranet.ca
[206.51.251.10]
  3    172 ms    156 ms    172 ms   spc-tor-6-Serial3-3.Sprint-
Canada.Net [206.186.248.85]
  4    156 ms    172 ms    187 ms   204.50.128.17
  5    171 ms    172 ms    157 ms   205.150.206.97
  6    172 ms    172 ms    297 ms   h5.bb1.tor2.h4.bb1.ott1.uunet.ca
[205.150.242.70]
  7    172 ms    171 ms    172 ms   max1.ott1.uunet.ca
[205.150.233.2]
  8    188 ms    203 ms    218 ms   router.learnix.ca
[199.71.122.193]
  9    203 ms    218 ms    235 ms   sparky [199.45.92.97]

Trace complete.
```

The result shows each router traversed to get to a destination as well as how long it took to get through each particular router. The time it takes to get through a particular router is calculated using three algorithms, which are displayed for each router hop. The IP address of each router traversed also displays. If a FQDN is available, this displays as well.

The TRACERT utility is useful for two primary diagnostic purposes.

▶ It detects whether a particular router is not functioning along a known path. For instance, say a user knows that packets on a network always go through Texas to get from Florida to California, but communication seems to be dead. A tracert to a California address shows all the hops up to the point where the router in Texas should respond. If it does not respond, the time values are marked with "*"s, indicating a non-functioning path.

▶ This utility also determines whether a router is slow and possibly needs to be upgraded or helped by adding additional routes on the network. You can determine this simply by looking at the time it takes for a packet to get through a particular router. If a particular router is deluged by packets, its return time may be significantly higher than that of any of the other hops, indicating it should be upgraded or helped in some way.

Dynamic Routing

For an exercise covering this information, see end of chapter.

The discussion to this point has focused on how to manually edit the route table to notify routers of the existence of networks to which they are not physically connected. This would be an enormously difficult task on large networks, where routes and networks may change on a frequent basis. It also makes redundant pathways horribly complex to manage, because you have to rely on each host to manage multiple default gateways and utilize dead gateway detection. Even utilizing these features on the client side does not guarantee timely reactions to the failure of links between routers.

These problems led to the development of routing protocols used specifically by routers to dynamically update each other's tables. Two of the most common protocols used by dynamic routers are RIP and OSPF. These protocols notify other routers that support these protocols of the networks they are attached to and of any changes that occur due to links being disconnected or becoming too congested to efficiently pass traffic. The standard rule of thumb when considering the use of either protocol is that RIP works well for small- to medium-sized networks, and OSPF works well for medium- to large-sized networks. The characteristics of RIP are discussed here because NT supports RIP on its multihomed routers. The characteristics of OSPF are left to other reference sources. NT multihomed routers do not support the OSPF protocol out of the box.

Routing Internet Protocol

To understand RIP better on routers, first consider figure 5.22 (static routing), where routing tables had to be built manually. To pass packets from one network to another, each router had to be told where to send packets destined for a specific network (route table entry) or where to send packets it had no idea what to do with (default gateway). By default, routers know about the networks to which they are physically attached because their IP addresses on each of those networks give them the necessary information. The problem of remote networks is encountered almost immediately, though. For this reason, it became apparent that as networks grew in size, a more sophisticated way to update route tables would be necessary. From this need arose routing protocols, which enable routers to communicate with each other. The protocols enable one router to send information about the networks it knows about to any other router physically connected to the wire, and enable the router to receive information about other networks dynamically from other routers that also are able to communicate.

The RIP procedure for communicating between routers is through broadcasts over UDP port 520. RIP routers broadcast their route tables over this port and listen on this port for broadcasts from other routers that may be connected to the network. In this way, eventually all routers that are physically connected have up-to-date route tables and know where to send data for any network in the environment.

Not only do routers communicate the networks to which they are attached, but they also communicate how far away remote networks are from their particular location. This distance to another network is called a *hop*, or metric, and each router keeps track of this value within the route table. Each router along the path to a destination network represents a hop. For this reason, RIP is considered a distance-vector routing protocol. In this fashion, RIP can determine the route with the least number of hops necessary to get a packet to its final destination. Figure 5.24 illustrates how each hop count may be different within route tables on a network.

Figure 5.24

Hop counts in network route tables.

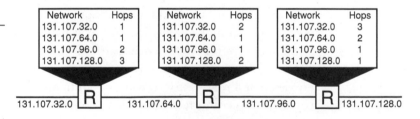

Network	Hops
131.107.32.0	1
131.107.64.0	1
131.107.96.0	2
131.107.128.0	3

Network	Hops
131.107.32.0	2
131.107.64.0	1
131.107.96.0	1
131.107.128.0	2

Network	Hops
131.107.32.0	3
131.107.64.0	2
131.107.96.0	1
131.107.128.0	1

131.107.32.0   R   131.107.64.0   R   131.107.96.0   R   131.107.128.0

As RIP was being developed, it was decided that routers would need to keep track of a maximum of 15 hops between networks. Therefore, any network address that had a hop count of 16 is considered unreachable. If a router's route table has two different hop counts for a particular network, the router sends the data to the route that has the least number of hops to the destination network.

Initially, it doesn't seem to make sense to limit the number of hops to a destination address, but this limitation is based primarily on how the RIP protocol works. Because RIP routers broadcast the networks they know about and how far away they are from those networks, certain precautions must be made in case any of these connections fail. After a router determines that a connection has failed, it must find a better route to that network from other route tables. This could create circular and upward-spiraling loops between routers, where the hop count continues to increase, ad infinitum.

If a redundant connection to that network exists with a higher hop count, eventually each router's tables increase to the point that the redundant route is chosen over the connection that died. But if no redundant route is available, the hop count could continue to increase indefinitely. To reduce this risk, several algorithms have been written to successfully react to connection failures, including the maximum hop count of 16, indicating an unreachable network. Administrators also have the ability to alter the hop count between routers, to encourage the use of some network routers over others that may be used purely for redundancy.

Broadcasts between routers occur every 30 seconds, whether the route table has changed or not. Figure 5.24 shows the original network in figure 5.22, but with dynamic tables instead of manual tables. In figure 5.24, router A sends a broadcast every 30 seconds, indicating the networks it knows about and how many hops it takes to get to those networks. Router B listens to this broadcast and checks router A's broadcast with its current route table. It enters any new information in its table and double-checks any entries that already exist. If router A indicates that it has a better route or hop count to a network, router B updates its table to reflect the better path. Router B initiates the same kind of broadcast to the networks to which it is attached, indicating its route table information as well.

Because RIP is the oldest routing protocol on the block and is widely used throughout the industry, several well-known problems exist when trying to implement this protocol in larger networks. These protocol deficiencies result in RIP being useful only in small to medium networks. RIP falls short in the following basic categories:

▶ Because RIP keeps track of every route table entry, including multiple paths to a particular network, routing tables can become large rather quickly. This can result in multiple RIP packets having to be broadcast in order to send a complete route table to other routers.

▶ Because RIP can allow hop counts only up to 15, with 16 representing an unreachable network, the size of networks on which RIP can be successfully implemented is necessarily restricted. Any large enterprise may need to achieve hop counts over and above this value.

▶ Broadcasts are sent by default every 30 seconds. This results in two fundamental problems. First, significant time delays occur between the times when a route goes down and all routers in the environment are notified of this change in the network. If a network goes down nine routers (hops) away, it can take up to $4\,^1/_2$ minutes before that change makes it to the other end of the network. Meanwhile, packets sent in that direction can be lost and connections dropped. Second, while on a LAN, these broadcasts may not be significant in terms of bandwidth; but on an expensive WAN connection, these broadcasts may become bothersome, especially if the network is stable and the route tables are large. These broadcasts transmit redundant route table entries every 30 seconds without regard to whether it is necessary.

But these problems should not discourage the administrator of a small to medium network from using the RIP protocol. As long as you understand the benefits and limitations of the protocol, you should be able to use it quite successfully on a network.

Static and Dynamic Router Integration

Figure 5.25 illustrates a possible scenario in which a network consists of static routers and dynamic routers.

Figure 5.25

Integrating static and dynamic routers.

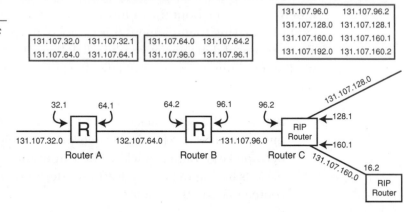

The best way to picture the integration of these two types of routers in an environment is to think of static routers as being dumb as a wall and dynamic routers as being a particularly chatty person. Think about it. Walls don't talk, thankfully, and no matter how much you talk to a wall, it's not going to respond. Now imagine a very chatty person standing in front of a wall, communicating a mile a minute about everything under the sun. The wall, no matter what incentives this person provides or promises, will simply return silence. Now extend this example to figure 5.25, which illustrates the default route tables for each of the routers.

Follow the path of a packet originating from the 131.107.32.0 network as it tries to reach the 131.107.128.0 network. By remembering our earlier example, it is fairly clear that router A will simply drop any packets destined for the 128 network. So, that fails, but you have come to expect that from static routers.

Therefore, you add static route table entries to router A. After you add the route table entries, the packet is again resent. Things seem to be running smoothly until router B gets hold of the packet and drops it. Oops, forgot! You must make static route table entries on all static routers in the environment. So, now, you add the appropriate route table entries on the static routers and the packet is ready to be sent again. Figure 5.26 illustrates the new route tables that have been created.

Figure 5.29

Static route table additions to the network.

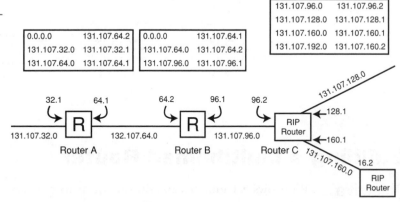

The packet is resent and makes it to Router B. Router B knows to send all packets destined for the 131.107.128.0 network to 131.107.96.1 and does so. However, the process of sending the packet does not result in router C having any idea where this packet comes from; the packet just lands on router C's doorstep. router C moves the packet to the 131.107.128.0 network. The machine that receives the packet tries to send a response to network 131.107.32.0 and sends its response to router C. Even though router C is a new RIP-enabled router, it has received no information about a 131.107.32.0 network from any of its friends. The packet gets dropped. So, when combining static and dynamic routers on a network, you have to enter static entries into the route table of your dynamic routers. Elegant, no; necessary, yes. To make matters worse, some dynamic routers do not propagate static route table entries, requiring all dynamic routers to have static route table entries added to them. Figure 5.27 illustrates the final route tables necessary to fulfill the communications requirements on the network.

Figure 5.27

Static route table additions to all routers on the network.

131.107.96.0	131.107.96.2
131.107.128.0	131.107.128.1
131.107.160.0	131.107.160.1
131.107.192.0	131.107.160.2
131.107.32.0	131.107.96.1
131.107.64.0	131.107.96.1

0.0.0.0	131.107.64.2
131.107.32.0	131.107.32.1
131.107.64.0	131.107.64.1

0.0.0.0	131.107.64.1
131.107.64.0	131.107.64.2
131.107.96.0	131.107.96.1

32.1   64.1   64.2   96.1   96.2

131.107.32.0   132.107.64.0   131.107.96.0

Router A   Router B   Router C

RIP Router

131.107.128.0 ← 128.1
← 160.1
131.107.160.0   16.2

RIP Router

Building a Multihomed Router

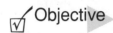 **Objective**

Windows NT enables an administrator to convert a machine into either a static or dynamic IP router. Static routers work well for extending a small network segment; dynamic routers using RIP work well on small to medium networks. A multihomed computer would probably not work well on large networks, however, based on RIP's limitations and the significant overhead associated with maintaining large route tables. Other considerations aside, however, building an NT router is fairly simple and easy to do.

Before continuing, let's define a or multihomed router. A multihomed router is simply a computer with more than one network card that has been configured to route packets from one network segment to another. The defining characteristic between a hardware router and a multihomed router is that on a multihomed computer, the operating system is the one that performs the routing. A hardware router is a device that is specifically manufactured and designed for routing only. You could think about it in more simple terms. For instance, you can run any Windows application, including Freecell, on a multihomed router; you cannot on a hardware router.

The first step toward building an NT router is to install two or more network cards in the machine. Anyone who has ever tried to do so will tell you this can often sound much easier than it is.

Each network card has to have its own IRQ and I/O address to use on the machine. These must be independent of other hardware cards you may be using in your machine, including video cards, sound cards, modems, hard disk controller cards, and so on. Basically, the machine needs to be stripped of any bells and whistles and other functions so that enough resources are available. Any resource conflicts result in significant headaches as your network cards don't appear and protocol drivers fail to load. The typical machine built for NT seminars and classes utilizes an NT router with three network cards and little else. After the machine successfully identifies the network cards, be careful of installing any additional third-party utilities. Sometimes they decide to steal the I/O addresses your network cards are using. The bottom line is that once this machine is built, try to leave it alone. Getting your machine stable will be the toughest part. Afterward, everything else is easy.

 Note

Be careful when installing third-party utilities after the router is configured. Sometimes they steal I/O addresses that may conflict with your network cards and cause routing problems.

After installing the network cards, make sure to assign separate IP addresses to each card, as follows:

1. In the network section of Control Panel under the protocol tab. Select TCP/IP and choose properties. Notice that where the network card is identified, the drop-down box reveals all the network cards you have installed, enabling you to choose a different IP address scheme for each network card.

2. After you give each network card its own IP address, indicating which network it is on, the machine can respond to packets coming from the networks to which it is attached. However, the machine is still not a router.

3. To turn the machine into a router, go back to TCP/IP properties and choose the routing Tab. Select the Enable IP Forwarding check box. After you select this box and have chosen OK to exit this configuration and the network configuration, you are asked to reboot your machine.

4. Reboot the machine. After the machine is rebooted, it is officially a router that can pass packets from one network to another.

The administrator then needs to decide whether the router will be static or dynamic. After IP forwarding is enabled, the router is a static router. If this is what is desired, no more configuration is necessary. If the administrator want to make this a dynamic router, then the RIP protocol needs to be installed.

This can be installed in the Services Tab through the network icon. After RIP is installed, this router listens for other RIP broadcasts, and broadcasts its own route table entries.

Although Windows NT supports the capability to create a static or dynamic router, the most important consideration for an administrator is probably whether he or she should spend the money to upgrade a machine for occasional routing of packets or spend the money for a hardware router. If the administrator plans to spend over $1,000 for a machine to route packets on a network, he may be better off spending it on hardware optimized for that purpose. Think of Windows NT routing versus hardware routing in much the same way as you would think about Windows NT RAID versus hardware RAID. Hardware implementation is usually a little more expensive, but is optimized for that specific task, whereas Windows NT implementations work well and are cheaper, but are not designed for constant pounding by a large network.

Exercises

Exercise 5.1:   Viewing the Route Table

Follow these steps to view your NT machines route table:

1. From the Start menu, select Command Prompt.

2. Type **route print**.

Exercise 5.2:   Adding an Entry to Your Route Table

Follow these steps to add a network to your route table:

1. From the Start menu, select Command Prompt.

2. Type **route add 131.107.64.0 mask 255.255.224.0** *IP address of your current gateway.*

3. Type **route print** to observe the addition.

Exercise 5.3:   Using the TRACERT Utility

1. From the Start menu, select Command Prompt.

2. Type **tracert** *ip_address* at the command prompt. For IP_address, chose a site that doesn't mind you hitting their server. Most sites won't mind an occasional hit, but it's bad form to continually do so.

3. Observe the results.

Review Questions

The following questions will test your knowledge of the information in this chapter:

1. In your environment, you have an NT machine that seems to not be responding to ping requests using an IP address. You would like to make sure that the machine's configuration is appropriate for the network. Which of the following options would you need to check?

   A. IP address

   B. Subnet mask

   C. Default gateway

   D. DNS

2. You've noticed a significant increase in the amount of time it takes to reach your remote offices. You think one of your routers may not be functioning. Which utility would you use to find the pathway a packet takes to reach its destination?

   A. WINS

   B. DNS

   C. TRACERT

   D. Network monitor

3. You have a machine that seems to be capable of communicating with other machines on its same local subnet, but whenever you try to reach destinations on a remote network, the communications fail. You run IPCONFIG /ALL and receive the information shown in figure 5.28. What is the problem?

   A. IP address

   B. Subnet mask

   C. Default gateway

   D. WINS

Figure 5.28

4. Your network is laid out like the one in figure 5.29. You seem to be having trouble with machine B in this environment. Although it seems to be able to communicate with machines on the same subnet, it can't communicate with machines on remote subnets. What seems to be the problem?

Figure 5.29

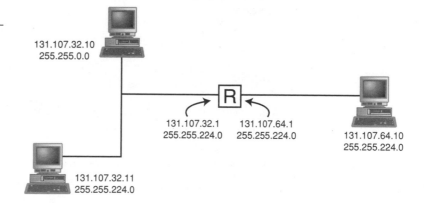

A. IP address

B. Subnet mask

C. Default gateway

D. DNS

5. You have set up a simple routed environment in which one router is central to three subnets, meaning that the router can see each of the three segments. No default gateway has been assigned because there does not seem to be any reason to do so. If a router does not know where to send a packet and no default gateway has been assigned, what will the router do with the packet?

   A. Drop the packet

   B. Store the packet for later processing

   C. Broadcast on the local network

   D. Use ARP to locate another pathway

6. Given the network shown in figure 5.30, will a packet from network 131.107.32.0 be able to reach network 131.107.96.0?

Figure 5.30

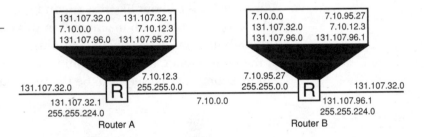

   A. Yes

   B. No

7. What would you have to change on the network in question 6 to make this scenario work?

   A. Change the default gateway address on router B

   B. Add a static ARP cache entry for 131.107.95.27 on router A

   C. Change the subnet mask for the 7.10 network to 255.255.255.0

   D. Change the gateway address for 131.107.96.0 on router A to 7.10.95.27

8. You want to have your NT routers share information on the network so that you don't have to continually update the route tables manually. What protocol do you need to install to allow this to happen?

    A. DNS

    B. RIP

    C. OSPF

    D. WINS

9. Ten machines on your network have stopped communicating with other machines on remote network segments. The router seems to be working properly, but you want to make sure the route table itself has not been modified. What utilities can you use to view the route table on your NT router?

    A. route

    B. netstat

    C. ping

    D. rttable

10. You set up an NT multihomed computer to be a router between two networks. You added multiple adapter cards and multiple IP addresses to the router. Because you are connecting only two subnets, you don't need to have a default gateway on your router. You do configure default gateways on all your clients to point to either side of the router based on what network they are on. You set up your network to look like the one in figure 5.31, but for some reason things are still not quite right. You can communicate on either side of the router, but not through the router. You must determine why machines on the 131.107.32.0 subnet seem to be having problems communicating with the 222.13.23.0 network. After you have figured out why your machines seem to be having trouble, what would you do to fix the problem?

Figure 5.31

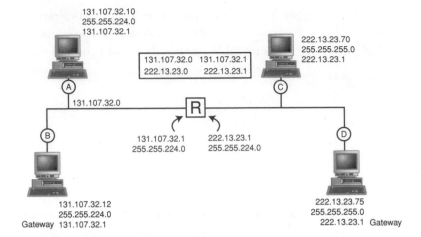

A. Change the subnet masks so that they are all the same

B. Add a default gateway to the router for the 222.13.23.0 network

C. Reconfigure the network so that both sides are on the 131.107.32.0 network

D. Enable IP forwarding on the router

11. Your environment consists of both LAN and WAN connections spread out over five continents. You've begun an expansion that has added a number of routers to your already large organization. Your network currently uses RIP as the routing protocol, but as new network segments are being added, routers on either end of your network insist that they cannot see each other and that they are unreachable. What seems to be the problem?

A. The routers were not made by Microsoft.

B. The RIP protocol cannot share route table information.

C. The RIP protocol cannot support more than 15 hops.

D. Routers are not designed for WAN connections.

12. When installing and testing a brand new NT router, you notice that the router routes packets to any network that it is physically attached to but drops packets to networks it is not attached to. There are seven of these networks that it cannot seem to route packets to. What would be the easiest way to make sure the router performs its function for those other networks?

    A. Disable IP routing

    B. Enable IP filtering on all ports

    C. Change the IP address bindings

    D. Add a default gateway

13. After adding a network segment (131.107.7.0) for a new wing, you discover that your route tables need to be altered. In this case, you simply need to add a new entry for this segment, but you want to make sure that the entry survives a reboot. What command would you choose for the addition?

    A. route change 131.107.2.0 131.107.7.0

    B. route add 131.107.7.0 mask 255.255.255.0 131.107.2.1

    C. route -p add 131.107.2.1 mask 255.255.255.0 131.107.7.0

    D. route -p add 131.107.7.0 mask 255.255.255.0 131.107.2.1

14. Last year, one of the big problems you encountered was a connectivity problem associated with only having one router in your environment that could route packets between subnets. This year your budget allowed you to add a second router to provide some backup for your primary router. Windows NT is smart enough to utilize dead gateway detection, but during your test of this feature it did not work at all. What might you have forgotten to configure for dead gateway detection to work?

A. Dead gateway detection must utilize RIP; therefore, RIP must be installed on each router.

B. Each host machine must be configured with the IP addresses of both routers before dead gateway detection is utilized.

C. Static route table entries must be configured on the routers so that they can communicate with each other.

D. Because they are initiating the communication, every application must be individually tailored to perform dead gateway detection.

15. After checking a route table, you notice that it is missing a very important route to one of your network segments. Before you can add the route to your routers table, however, you need to know what pieces of information to use the route utility?

A. Network ID

B. Netmask

C. MAC address

D. Gateway address

Review Answers

1. A, B, C

2. C

3. C

4. B

5. A

6. B

7. D

8. B

9. A, B

10. D

11. C

12. D

13. D

14. B

15. A, B, D

Answers to the Test Yourself Questions at the Beginning of the Chapter

1. IP address, subnet mask, and default gateway. The IP address, subnet mask, and default gateway are critical for a machine to know who it is, where it is, and how to send data to other networks.

2. RIP. RIP is the only routing protocol currently supported on Microsoft NT routers.

3. No, only the networks to which it is attached. To route to other networks, a static router would need to have manual entries placed in its routing table.

4. IP. This protocol is responsible for routing and delivering packets.

5. Tracert. The tracert utility is provided for troubleshooting slow or non-functioning routers.

6. No, NT routers do not support OSPF.

C h a p t e r

Dynamic Host Configuration Protocol

6

This chapter will help you prepare for the exam by covering the following objectives:

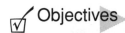 Objectives

▶ Configure scopes by using DHCP Manager

▶ Install and configure the DHCP relay agent

Test Yourself! Before reading this chapter, test yourself to determine how much study time you will need to devote to this section.

1. Which fields in the TCP/IP configuration will DHCP overwrite on a DHCP client that previously had TCP/IP manually configured?

2. What are three benefits of using DHCP to automatically configure a client for TCP/IP?

3. What extra steps should you take after installing two DHCP servers on a subnet?

4. What are the router requirements on an internetwork for enabling a DHCP client to communicate with a DHCP server on a remote subnet?

5. What steps should you take to ensure that DHCP does not assign an IP address that is already in use by a non-DHCP client?

6. Is it possible for two DHCP clients on an internetwork lease the same IP address at a given time? Why or why not?

7. A DHCP client is having difficulty communicating with hosts on an adjacent subnet. You do some troubleshooting and determine that the DHCP client is not using the default gateway that is set in the scope option for that subnet. What could be causing this problem?

8. How many DHCP servers are required on an internetwork of 10 subnets, each with 200 hosts and with BOOTP forwarding routers connecting the subnets? How many would you recommend and why?

9. Through which two methods can a DHCP client be configured to use DHCP for automatic TCP/IP configuration?

Answers are located at the end of the chapter.

Understanding DHCP

The configuration of Microsoft TCP/IP involves you knowing the correct values for several fields for each TCP/IP host and entering them manually. At the minimum, the host IP address, and subnet mask need to be configured. In most cases other parameters, such as WINS and DNS server addresses, also need to be configured on each host. DHCP relieves the need for manual configuration and provides a method of configuring and reconfiguring all the TCP/IP related parameters.

It is critical that the correct TCP/IP address is configured on each host; otherwise, hosts on the internetwork might:

▶ Fail to communicate

▶ Fail to initialize

▶ Cause other hosts on the internetwork to hang

The Dynamic Host Configuration protocol is an open industry standard that enables the automatic TCP/IP configuration of DHCP client computers. The use of Microsoft's DHCP server greatly reduces the administrative overhead of managing TCP/IP client computers by eliminating the need to manually configure clients. The DHCP server also allows for greater flexibility and mobility of clients on a TCP/IP network without administrator intervention. If used correctly, DHCP can eliminate nearly all the problems associated with TCP/IP. The administrator enters the valid IP addresses or ranges of IP addresses (called a scope) in the DHCP server database, which then assigns (or leases) the IP addresses to the DHCP client hosts.

Having all the TCP/IP configuration parameters stored on the DHCP server provides the following benefits:

▶ The administrator can quickly verify the IP address and other configuration parameters without having to go to each host. Also, reconfiguration of the DHCP database is accomplished at one central location, thereby eliminating the need to manually each host.

▶ DHCP does not lease the same IP address from a scope to two hosts at the same time; this can prevent duplicate IP addresses if used properly.

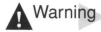 **Warning**

DHCP cannot detect which IP addresses are already being used by non-DHCP clients. If a host has a manually configured IP address and a DHCP scope is configured with that same address, the DHCP server may lease the address to a DHCP client, creating a duplicate IP address on the network. To prevent this situation, you must exclude all manually configured IP addresses from any scopes configured on the DHCP server.

▶ The DHCP administrator controls which IP addresses are used by which hosts. DHCP uses local network broadcasts to lease IP addresses to client hosts. If a second DHCP server resides on the same local network segment, the DHCP client can communicate with either server and may receive an IP address lease from the unintended DHCP server. See "Using Multiple DHCP Servers" later in this chapter for the ways to detect and prevent this situation.

▶ The chance of clerical and typing errors is reduced because the TCP/IP configuration parameters are entered in one place; the DHCP server database.

▶ Several options can be set for each DHCP scope (or globally for all scopes) that are configured on the client along with the IP address, for example, default gateway, WINS server addresses, and so on.

▶ An IP address may be leased for a limited time, which requires the DHCP client periodically to renew its lease before the lease expires. If the host is no longer using the IP address (is no longer running TCP/IP or is powered off), the lease expires and can then be assigned to another TCP/IP host. This feature is useful if the number of hosts requesting IP addresses is larger than the number of available valid IP addresses (such as when the network is part of the Internet).

▶ If a host is physically moved to a different subnet, the DHCP server on that subnet automatically reconfigures the host with the proper TCP/IP configuration information for that subnet.

What DHCP Servers Can Do

To enable automatic TCP/IP configuration by using DHCP, the DHCP administrator first enters the valid IP addresses as a scope in the DHCP server database and then activates the scope. The DHCP administrator now enters other TCP/IP configuration information that will be given to the clients. The administrator or user then selects the Enable Automatic DHCP Configuration option on the client (found in their network configuration).

When a DHCP client host starts up, TCP/IP initializes and the client requests an IP address from a DHCP server by issuing a Dhcpdiscover packet. The Dhcpdiscover packet represents the client's IP lease request.

After a DHCP server receives the Dhcpdiscover packet, the DHCP server offers (Dhcpoffer) one of the unassigned IP addresses from the scope of addresses that are valid for that host. This ensures that no two DHCP clients on that subnet have the same IP address. This Dhcpoffer information is sent back to the host. If your network contains more than one DHCP server, the host may receive several Dhcpoffers. In most cases, the host or client computer accepts the first Dhcpoffer that it receives. The client then sends a Dhcprequest packet containing the IP address offered by the DHCP server.

The DHCP server then sends the client an acknowledgment (Dhcpack) that contains the IP address originally sent and a lease for that address. The DHCP server leases the IP address to the DHCP client host for the specified period. The DHCP client must renew its lease before the lease expires. During the life of the lease, the client attempts to renew the lease.

The renewal request is sent automatically if the host still has TCP/IP initialized, can communicate with the DHCP server, and is still on the same subnet or network. After 50 percent of the lease time expires, the client attempts to renew its lease with the DHCP server that assigned its TCP/IP configuration. At 87.5 percent of the active lease period, the client, if unable to contact and renew the lease with the original DHCP server, attempts to communicate with any DHCP server to renew its configuration information. If the client cannot make contact with a DHCP server and consequently fails to maintain its lease, the client must discontinue use of the IP address and begin the entire process again by issuing a Dhcpdiscover packet.

Limitations of DHCP

Although DHCP can substantially reduce the headaches and time required to administer IP addresses, you should note a few limiting characteristics of DHCP:

▶ DHCP does not detect IP addresses already in use on a network by non-DHCP clients. These addresses should be excluded from any scopes configured on the DHCP server. This problem was fixed in service pack 2 for NT4.0.

▶ A DHCP server does not communicate with other DHCP servers and cannot detect IP addresses leased by other DHCP servers. Therefore, two DHCP servers should not use the same IP addresses in their respective scopes.

▶ DHCP servers cannot communicate with clients across routers unless BOOTP forwarding is enabled on the router, or the DHCP relay agent is enabled on the subnet.

▶ As with manually configured TCP/IP, incorrect values configured for a DHCP scope can cause unexpected and potentially disastrous results on the internetwork.

Other than the IP address and subnet mask, any values configured manually through the Network Control Panel Applet or Registry Editor of a DHCP client override the DHCP server scope settings. If you intend to use the server configured values, be sure to clear the values from the host TCP/IP configuration dialog boxes. Enabling DHCP on the client host does not automatically clear any preexisting values, although DHCP clears the IP address and subnet mask.

Planning a DHCP Implementation

As with all network services that you will use, you should plan the implementation of DHCP. There are a few conditions that must be met that will be covered in the next few sections.

Network Requirements

The following requirements must be met to implement Microsoft TCP/IP using DHCP:

▶ The DHCP server service must be running on a Windows NT server.

▶ The DHCP server must have a manually configured IP address.

▶ A DHCP server must be located on the same subnet as the DHCP clients, or the clients subnet must have a DHCP relay agent running, or the routers connecting the two subnets involved must be able to forward DHCP (BOOTP) datagrams.

▶ Pools of IP addresses known as *scopes* must be configured on the DHCP server.

It is easiest to implement DHCP with only one DHCP server on a subnet (local network segment). If more than one DHCP server is configured to provide addresses for a subnet then either could provide the address—there is no way to specify with server to use such as you can in WINS (Windows Internet Name Service). Because DHCP servers do not communicate with each other, a DHCP server has no way of knowing if an IP address is leased to a client from another DHCP server.

To prevent two DHCP servers from assigning the same IP address to two clients, you must ensure that each IP address is made available in a scope on only one DHCP server on the internetwork. In other words, the IP address scopes cannot overlap or contain the same IP addresses.

If no DHCP server is available to lease an IP address to a DHCP client—due to hardware problems, for example—the client cannot initialize. For this reason, you may want to have a second DHCP server, with unique IP address scopes, on the network. This scenario works best when the second DHCP server is on a different subnet connected by a router that forwards DHCP datagrams.

A DHCP client accepts the first IP address offer it receives from a DHCP server. This address would normally be from the DHCP server on the local network because the IP address request broadcast would reach the local DHCP server first. However, if the local DHCP server is not responding, and if the DHCP broadcasts were forwarded by the router, the DHCP client could accept a lease offer from a DHCP server on a remote network.

Finally, the DHCP server must have one or more scopes created by using the DHCP Server Manager application (Start, Programs, Administrative Tools, DHCP Manager). A *scope* is a range of IP addresses available for lease by DHCP clients; for example, 200.20.5.1 through 200.20.5.20 may be a scope for a given subnet, and 200.20.6.1 through 200.20.6.50 may be a scope for another subnet.

Installing the DHCP Relay Agent

√ Objective ▶ Essentially, the job of the DHCP relay agent is to forward DHCP broadcast messages between DHCP enabled clients and DHCP servers, across IP routers. The relay agent can be configure on any NT Server computer and adds very little load. The section deals with installing and configuring the DHCP relay agent.

 Note ▶ The DCHP relay agent that comes with NT 4.0 is a new service that will listen for DHCP broadcasts and forward them to one or more configured DHCP servers. This is different from an RFC1542 compliant router in that the system running the relay agent is not a router. The DHCP relay agent is similar to a WINS proxy agent—discussed in Chapter 9.

1. Open the Network configuration dialog box and select the Services tab.

2. Select Add and from the list that appears, select the DHCP relay agent. Click OK and when prompted, enter the path to the distribution files.

3. Click the Protocols tab and double-click the TCP/IP protocol.

4. On the DHCP Relay tab enter the IP address of a DHCP server and the maximum number of hops and seconds that the relay can take.

5. Close the TCP/IP configuration dialog box and the Network configuration dialog box.

6. Restart the computer when prompted.

Client Requirements

A Microsoft TCP/IP DHCP client can be any of the following Microsoft TCP/IP clients:

▶ Windows NT server 3.5 or later that is not a DHCP server

▶ Windows NT Workstation 3.5 or later

▶ Windows 95

▶ Windows for Workgroups 3.11 running the Microsoft TCP/IP-32 software from the Windows NT Server CD-ROM

▶ Microsoft Network Client for MS-DOS 3.0 from the Windows NT Server CD-ROM

▶ LAN Manager server for MS-DOS 2.2c from the Windows NT server CD-ROM

If some clients on the network do not use DHCP for IP address configuration—because they do not support DHCP or otherwise need to have TCP/IP manually configured—the IP addresses of these non-DHCP clients must not be made available for lease to the DHCP clients. Non-DHCP clients can include clients that do not support Microsoft DHCP (see the preceding list), and clients that must always use the same IP address, such as Windows Internet Name Service (WINS) servers, Domain Name Service (DNS) servers, and other DHCP servers.

 **Warning**

> You should not assign the addresses of servers (file and print, DNS, WINS, and so forth) by DHCP as the address could change. If you do you have to reconfigure the scope options every time one of these servers restarts.

Although you can use DHCP Manager to reserve an IP address for use by only a specific WINS or DNS server, this technique is not recommended. If a DHCP server with the proper address for these servers is not available on the network for some reason, the client is not assigned an IP address and cannot initialize TCP/IP.

 Tip

> WINS servers, DNS servers, DHCP servers, multihomed IP routers, and any other computer that has its IP address specified in another host's TCP/IP configuration should have a static IP address. This method ensures that they always use the same IP address and that they can initialize even if the DHCP server is down.
>
> The DHCP client must have DHCP enabled. For Windows NT and Windows 95, DHCP is enabled in the TCP/IP configuration dialog box by selecting "Obtain address automatically."

Using Multiple DHCP Servers

It is not recommended to have more than one DHCP server on a subnet because there is no way to control from which DHCP server a client receives an IP address lease. Any DHCP server that receives a client's DHCP request broadcast can send a DHCP offer to that client. The client accepts the first lease offer it receives from a DHCP server.

If more than one subnet exists on a network, it is generally recommended to have a DHCP server on each subnet. However, if the DHCP relay agent or routers that support the forwarding of BOOTP braodcasts are used then request for DHCP addresses can be handled by a single DHCP server.

A DHCP server has an IP address scope configured for each subnet to which it sends DHCP offers. If the DHCP server receives a relayed DHCP request from a remote subnet, it offers an IP address lease from the scope for that subnet. To ensure that a DHCP client can receive an IP address lease even if a DHCP server is not functioning, you should configure an IP address scope for a given subnet on more than one DHCP server. Thus, if a DHCP client cannot obtain a lease from the local DHCP server, the DHCP relay agent or router passes the request to a DHCP server on a remote network that can offer a DHCP lease to the client.

For example, consider a network with two subnets, each with a DHCP server, joined by a RFC 1542-compliant router. For this scenario, Microsoft recommends that each DHCP server contain approximately 75 percent of the available IP addresses for the subnet the DHCP server is on, and 25 percent of the available IP addresses for the remote subnet. Most of the IP addresses available for a subnet can be obtained from the local DHCP server. If the local DHCP server is unavailable, the remote DHCP server can offer a lease from the smaller range of IP addresses available from the scope on the remote DHCP server.

If the range of IP addresses available are 120.50.7.10 through 120.50.7.110 for Subnet A and 120.50.8.10 through 120.50.8.110 for Subnet B, you could configure the scopes on each DHCP server as follows:

Subnet	DHCP Server A	DHCP Server B
A	120.50.7.10 - 120.50.7.84	120.50.7.85 - 120.50.7.110
B	120.50.8.10 - 120.50.8.34	120.50.8.35 - 120.50.8.110

 **Warning**
You must ensure that no IP address is duplicated on another DHCP server. If two DHCP servers contain the same IP address, that IP address could potentially be leased to two DHCP clients at the same time. Therefore, IP address ranges must be split between multiple DHCP servers, as shown in the preceding example.

Using Scope Options

Each time a DHCP client initializes, it requests an IP address and subnet mask from the DHCP server. The server is configured with one or more scopes, each containing a range of valid IP addresses, the subnet mask for the internetwork, and additional optional DHCP client configuration information, known as scope options. For example, the default gateway for a subnet is often configured as a scope option for a given subnet. If any scope options are configured on the DHCP server, these are given to the DHCP client along with the IP address and subnet mask to be used by the client. The common scope options supported by Microsoft DHCP clients are shown in table 6.1.

Table 6.1

Scope Options Supported by Microsoft DHCP Clients

Scope Option	Option Number
Router	3
DNS server	6
DNS Domain Name	15
NetBIOS Name server (e.g. WINS)	44
NetBIOS Node Type	46
NetBIOS Scope ID	47

The Scope Options Configuration dialog box in the DHCP Manager application contains many other scope options (such as Time server) that can be sent to the clients along with the other TCP/IP configuration information. The Microsoft DHCP clients, however, ignore and discard all the scope option information except for the options listed in table 6.1.

Note

It is possible to lease addresses to non-Microsoft clients, in this case you may have to add a client reservation. Then you will be able configure options for that single client.

How DHCP Works

DHCP client configuration is a four-part process, as follows:

1. When the DHCP client initializes, it broadcasts a request for an IP lease from a DHCP server called a DHCPDISCOVER.

2. All DHCP servers that receive the IP lease request respond to the DHCP client with an IP lease offer known as a DHCPOFFER. This includes DHCP servers on the local network and on remote networks when the relay agent is used or a router that passes BOOTP requests.

3. The DHCP client selects the first offer it receives and broadcasts an IP lease selection message specifying the IP address it has selected. This message is known as a DHCPREQUEST.

4. The DHCP server that offered the selected lease responds with a DHCP lease acknowledgment message known as a DHCPACK. The DHCP server then updates its DHCP database to show that the lease can no longer be offered to other DHCP clients. The DHCP servers offering leases that were not selected can offer those IP addresses in future lease offers.

DHCPACK Phase

After the server that offered the lease receives the DHCPREQUEST message, it checks its DHCP database to ensure that the IP address is still available. If the requested lease remains available, the DHCP server marks that IP address as being leased in its DHCP database and broadcasts a DHCPACK to acknowledge that the IP address has been leased to the DHCP client. The DHCPACK contains the same information as the DHCPOFFER sent, plus any optional DHCP information that has been configured for that scope as a scope option. If the requested lease is no longer available, the DHCP server broadcasts a DHCP negative acknowledgment (DHCPNACK) containing the DHCP client's hardware address. When the DHCP client receives a DHCPNACK, it must start the lease request process over with a DHCPDISCOVER message. After receiving a DHCPACK, the DHCP client can continue to initialize TCP/IP, and it updates its registry with the IP addressing information included with the lease. The client continues to use the leased IP address information until the command ipconfig/release is typed from a command prompt, or it receives a DHCPNACK from the DHCP server after unsuccessfully renewing its lease.

DHCP Lease Renewal

The DHCP client attempts to renew its IP address lease after 50 percent of its lease time has expired (or when manually requested to renew the lease by the ipconfig/renew command from a command prompt). To renew the lease, a DHCP client sends a DHCPREQUEST directly to the DHCP server that gave it the original lease. Again, the DHCPREQUEST contains the hardware address of the client and the requested IP address, but this time uses the DHCP server IP address for the destination and the DHCP client IP address for the source IP address in the datagram. If the DHCP server is available and the requested IP address is still available (has not been removed from the scope), the DHCP server responds by sending a DHCPACK directly to the DHCP client. If the server is available but the requested IP address is no longer in the configured scopes, a DHCPNACK is sent to the DHCP client, which then must start the lease process over with a DHCPDISCOVER. A DHCPNACK can be sent because of the following reasons.

▶ The IP address requested is no longer available because the lease has been manually expired on the server and has been given to another client.

▶ The IP address requested has been removed from the available scopes on the DHCP server.

▶ The DHCP client has been physically moved to another subnet that will use a different scope on the DHCP server for that subnet. Hence, the IP address changes to a valid IP address for the new subnet. If the server does not respond to the DHCPREQUEST sent after the lease is 50 percent expired, the DHCP client continues to use the original lease until it is seven-eighths expired (87.5 percent of the lease time has expired). Because this DHCPREQUEST is broadcast rather than directed to a particular DHCP server, any DHCP server can respond with a DHCPACK or DHCPNACK to renew or deny the lease.

Installing the DHCP Server Service

For an exercise covering this information, see end of chapter.

The DHCP server service can be installed on a computer running Microsoft TCP/IP and Windows NT Server version 3.5 or later. Exercise 6.1 demonstrates how to install the DHCP server service on a Windows NT Server 4.0 computer.

1. Open the Control Panel and double-click the Network icon.

2. From the Network settings dialog box, choose the services tab, click Add.

3. Choose the Microsoft DHCP Service from the list that appears and click OK. When prompted, enter the directory for the NT source files.

4. Click close on the Network settings dialog box and when prompted restart your computer.

The DHCP server must have a manually configured IP address, subnet mask, and default gateway. It cannot be assigned an address from another DHCP server, even if an address is reserved for the DHCP server.

Configuring the DHCP Server

After a DHCP server has been installed on an internetwork, you need to configure the following items:

▶ One or more IP address scopes (ranges of IP addresses to be leased) must be defined on the DHCP server.

▶ Non-DHCP client IP addresses must be excluded from the defined scopes.

▶ The options for the scope must be configured, for example, the default gateway for a subnet.

▶ IP address reservations for DHCP clients requiring a specific IP address to be assigned must be created.

▶ The DHCP clients must have automatic DHCP configuration enabled and should have unwanted manually configured TCP/IP parameters deleted.

Each of these is discussed in the following sections.

Creating Scopes

 **Objective**

For an exercise covering this information, see end of chapter.

For a DHCP server to lease IP addresses to the DHCP clients, a range of valid IP addresses for those clients must be configured on the DHCP server. Each range of IP addresses is called a *scope*. One scope must be configured on the server for each subnet the DHCP server provides IP address leases to. The DHCP server is normally configured with a scope for the local subnet (the subnet the DHCP server is on) and, optionally, with a scope for each remote subnet that it will provide addresses for. The benefits of configuring scopes for remote subnets on a DHCP server are as follows:

▶ **The DHCP server can provide IP address leases to clients on remote subnets.** This feature is especially useful as a backup in case another DHCP server is not available. If no DHCP server is available with an IP address lease for a DHCP client, the client cannot initialize TCP/IP. To prevent this, you may want to have more than one DHCP server that can provide a DHCP client with a lease. You must ensure, however, that the scopes on each DHCP server have unique IP address ranges so that no duplicate IP addresses are on the internetwork.

▶ **You can create separate scope options for each subnet.** For example, each subnet would have a different default gateway that can be configured individually for each scope. After installing the DHCP server and restarting the computer, you must create an IP address scope. The following list demonstrates the creation of a scope. To perform this exercise, you must have the DHCP server service installed and running as shown in above. You should also know a range of IP addresses that you can use to create a DHCP scope, as well as the IP addresses that should be excluded out of that range.

The following list provides the steps that are required to configure a scope on the DHCP server.

1. Start the DHCP Manager (Start, Programs, Administrative Tools, DHCP Manager).

2. Select the local DHCP server "Local Machine" by clicking the entry, and then choose Create from the Scope menu item. The Create Scope dialog box is displayed. (Note: This will happen automatically the first time you run the DHCP Manager).

3. Type the starting and ending IP addresses for the first subnet in the Start Address and the End Address fields of the IP Address Pool.

4. Type the Subnet Mask for this scope in the Subnet Mask field.

5. If required, type a single IP address or a range of IP addresses to be excluded from the IP. The IP address that is not used in the Address Pool in the Exclusion Range Start Address scope is added to the Excluded Addresses list. Choose Add. Repeat if required.

 **Warning**

If any hosts are not using DHCP but have an IP address that falls within the IP address pool, the IP addresses of these hosts must be excluded from the scope. If the IP address is not excluded, DHCP does not know that the IP address is already in use and might assign the IP address to a DHCP client, causing a duplicate IP address on the network. If you want certain DHCP clients to use a specific IP address out of the scope, you can assign this address from the Add Reservations dialog box as described later in this section.

6. If you do not want the IP address leases to expire, select the Unlimited option under Lease Duration (if you do this then the configuration of the client will never be updated). If you want to force the DHCP clients to renew their leases periodically (to ensure that the client is still using the IP address), choose the Limited To: option and type the lease duration in days, hours, and minutes. By default, the Lease Duration is three days. If you have a large ratio of available IP addresses to hosts on the network, you may want to use a longer lease duration to reduce broadcast traffic. If hosts are regularly coming and going and changing subnets on the network,

such as with laptops and docking stations, you want a relatively short lease duration so the DHCP server recovers previously used IP addresses fairly quickly.

7. In the Name field, type the name to be used for referring to the scope in the DHCP Manager, for example, **subnet 200.20.1.0**.

8. In the Comment field, type an optional descriptive comment for the scope, for example, **Third floor – west side**.

Scope Options

For an exercise covering this information, see end of chapter.

Each DHCP scope can have several options set that are configured on the client along with the IP address, such as default gateway and WINS server addresses. DHCP Manager includes many scope options that can be configured and sent to the DHCP clients; it should be noted that if TCP/IP configuration has been manually entered, then the options (other than IP address and subnet mask) will be ignored by the client.

Two types of DHCP scope options are available:

▶ Global options, which are set for all scopes in the DHCP Manager

▶ Scope options, which are set for a selected scope in the DHCP Manager

The value set in a scope option overrides a value set for the same DHCP option in a global option. Any values manually configured on the DHCP client—through the Network Control Panel applet Microsoft TCP/IP Configuration dialog box, for example—override any DHCP configured options.

The following list outlines how to view and define global options for a DHCP server.

1. Start the DHCP Manager tool.

2. Choose either Scope or Global from the DHCP Options menu.

3. Configure the DHCP options required following these steps.

1. From the unused Options list, select an option and click Add. The option is added to the Active Options list.

2. Choose Value, the value for the option will now be displayed.

3. You can now edit the value. There are three types of values that can be edited. Strings (such as Domain name), which you can simply enter. Hexadecimal values (such as NetBIOS node type), which you can enter. And finally IP address ranges—for these you click Edit Array and another dialog box appears allowing you to enter one or more IP addresses.

4. When all the required options are entered, click OK and exit the DHCP manager.

Address Reservations

For an exercise covering this information, see end of chapter.

If a DHCP client requires a specific IP address to be assigned to it each time it renews its IP address lease, that IP address can be reserved for the DHCP client through the DHCP Manager tool. Following are examples of clients that should have an IP address reservation:

▶ Servers on a network with non-WINS-enabled clients. If a server on such a network does not always lease the same IP address, the non-WINS clients might not be able to connect to the servers using NetBIOS over TCP/IP (NetBT).

▶ Any other host that is expected to have a specific IP address that hosts use to connect to.

The following list outlines how to reserve an IP address from a scope for a specific DHCP client.

1. Determine the hardware address for the DHCP client with the IP address to be reserved from the scope. This can be done by typing **ipconfig/all** at a client's command prompt. A sample ipconfig/all output is shown here:

```
Ethernet adapter NDISLoop1:
        Description . . . . . . . . : MS LoopBack Driver
        Physical Address. . . . . . : 20-4C-4F-4F-50-20
        DHCP Enabled. . . . . . . . : No
        IP Address. . . . . . . . . : 200.20.1.30
        Subnet Mask . . . . . . . . : 255.255.255.0
        Default Gateway . . . . . . : 200.20.1.1
```

2. Start the DHCP Manager, and select the DHCP server to be configured.

3. Select the scope containing the IP address to be reserved.

4. Choose Add Reservations from the Scope menu. The Add Reserved Clients dialog box is displayed.

5. In the IP Address field, type the IP address to be reserved for the DHCP client.

6. In the Unique Identifier field, type the hardware address of the network card for the IP address used. The hardware address should be typed without hyphens (-).

7. In the Client Name field, type a name for the client to be used only in DHCP Manager. This value is purely descriptive and does not affect the client in any way.

8. In the Client Comments field, optionally type any comments for the client reservation.

9. Choose Add. The reservation is enabled.

10. Choose Active Leases from the Scope menu of DHCP Manager. The Active Leases dialog box is displayed and the reservations are shown.

DHCP Clients

For a client to use DHCP to obtain IP address information, automatic DHCP configuration must be enabled at the client. The procedure is slightly different for Windows NT and Windows for Workgroups clients.

Windows NT and Windows 95 as DHCP Clients

You can enable Automatic DHCP configuration either before or after Microsoft TCP/IP is installed. To ensure that the DHCP TCP/IP parameters are used instead of any configured manually on the host, you should preferably enable automatic DHCP configuration before Microsoft TCP/IP is installed. To enable automatic DHCP configuration after TCP/IP is installed, follow these steps.

1. Double-click the Network icon in Control Panel. The Network settings dialog box will be displayed.

2. Select the Protocols tab. From the list of installed protocols, select TCP/IP and choose the Properties button. The TCP/IP configuration dialog box appears.

3. Select the Enable Automatic DHCP Configuration check box. The previous IP address and subnet mask values disappear. Ensure that all other configuration parameters you want DHCP to supply are cleared.

4. Close the TCP/IP configuration dialog box and the Network setting dialog box. Restart the system when prompted.

Windows for Workgroups as a DHCP Client

Configuring Windows for Workgroups as a DHCP client is simple.

1. Double-click the Network Setup icon in the Network program group of the Windows for Workgroups client.

2. Choose the Drivers button, select Microsoft TCP/IP- and choose the Setup button. The TCP/IP Configuration dialog box is displayed.

3. Select the Enable Automatic DHCP Configuration check box, and choose Continue. The dialog box closes and you are prompted to restart the computer.

4. Do not configure any other parameters, unless you want to override the options set in the DHCP scope, which is not recommended.

Using the IPCONFIG Utility

The IPCONFIG command-line utility is installed with Microsoft TCP/IP for Windows NT and Windows for Workgroups clients. This command-line utility and diagnostic tool can be used to

▶ Display detailed information about a computer

▶ Renew a DHCP IP address lease

▶ Release a DHCP IP address lease

Displaying Information

To display concise TCP/IP information about the local host, type **ipconfig** at a command prompt. This entry displays the IP address, subnet mask, and default gateway for each network interface card on the local host that uses TCP/IP. The following is an example of output displayed after ipconfig is typed from a command prompt:

```
C:\>ipconfig

Windows NT IP Configuration
Ethernet adapter NDISLoop1:
        IP Address. . . . . . . . : 200.20.1.30
        Subnet Mask . . . . . . . : 255.255.255.0
        Default Gateway . . . . . : 200.20.1.1
```

For more detailed information, you can run the ipconfig/all command from a command prompt. The ipconfig/all command lists the following bits of information for each network interface card on the local host that is bound to TCP/IP:

▶ The Domain Name Service (DNS) host name, appended to the DNS domain name if one is configured

▶ The IP address of any DNS servers configured

▶ The NetBIOS name resolution node type, such as broadcast (b-node), hybrid (h-node), peer-to-peer (p-node), or mixed (m-node)

▶ The NetBIOS scope ID

▶ Whether IP Routing is enabled between two network interface cards, if on a multihomed computer

▶ Whether this host acts as a WINS proxy agent for non-WINS
clients

▶ Whether NetBT on this host uses DNS for NetBIOS name
resolution

Also, for each network interface card bound to TCP/IP on the
host, ipconfig/all displays the following:

▶ A description of the type or model of network card

▶ The hardware or physical address of the network card

▶ Whether DHCP is enabled for automatic IP address configuration for the network card

▶ The IP address of the network card

▶ The subnet mask for the network card

▶ The default gateway for the network card

▶ The IP address for the primary WINS server for the network
card, if configured

▶ The IP address for the secondary WINS server for the network card, if configured

The following example shows output after you type **ipconfig/all** at
a command prompt:

```
C:\>ipconfig/all

Windows NT IP Configuration
        Host Name . . . . . . . . . : binky.gopherit.com
        DNS servers . . . . . . . . : 200.20.16.122
        Node Type . . . . . . . . . : Hybrid
        NetBIOS Scope ID. . . . . . :
        IP Routing Enabled. . . . . : No
```

```
        WINS Proxy Enabled. . . . . : No
        NetBIOS Resolution Uses DNS : Yes
Ethernet adapter NDISLoop1:
        Description . . . . . . . . : MS LoopBack Driver
        Physical Address. . . . . . : 20-4C-4F-4F-50-20
        DHCP Enabled. . . . . . . . : No
        IP Address. . . . . . . . . : 200.20.1.30
        Subnet Mask . . . . . . . . : 255.255.255.0
        Default Gateway . . . . . . : 200.20.1.1
        Primary WINS server . . . . : 16.255.1.50
```

Renewing a Lease

The ipconfig/renew command, typed at a command prompt, causes the DHCP client immediately to attempt to renew its IP address lease with a DHCP server. The DHCP client sends a DHCPREQUEST message to the DHCP server to receive a new lease duration and any options that have been updated or added to the scope. If a DHCP server does not respond, the DHCP client continues to use the current lease information.

The ipconfig/renew command is usually performed after scope options or scope address information has been changed on the DHCP server and you want the DHCP client to have these changes immediately.

By default, the ipconfig/renew command renews all leases for each network adapter on a multihomed computer. To renew the lease for only a specific network adapter, type **ipconfig/renew <adapter>**, where <adapter> is the specific adapter name.

Releasing a Lease

You can type the ipconfig/release command at a command prompt to have the DHCP client advise the DHCP server that it no longer needs the IP address lease. The DHCP client sends a DHCPRELEASE message to the DHCP server to have the lease marked as released in the DHCP database.

The ipconfig/release command is usually performed when the administrator wants the DHCP client to give up its lease, and possibly use a different lease. For example, the DHCP client's IP address can be reserved for another host or deleted from the DHCP database scope, and then the ipconfig/release command can be run to have the DHCP client give up that IP address lease and be forced to receive a different lease.

By default, the ipconfig/release command releases all leases for each network adapter on a multihomed computer. To release the lease for only a specific network adapter, type the **ipconfig/release <adapter>** command, where <adapter> is the specific adapter name.

Compacting the DHCP Database

Entries in the DHCP database are continually being added, modified, and deleted throughout the IP address leasing process. When entries are deleted, the space is not always completely filled with a new entry, due to the different sizes of each entry. After some time, the database contains unused space that can be recovered by compacting the database. This process is analogous to defragmenting a disk drive.

Microsoft recommends compacting the DHCP database from once every month to once every week, depending on the size of the internetwork. This compaction increases transaction speed and reduces the disk space used by the database.

The jetpack utility compacts the DHCP database (DHCP.mdb) into a temporary database, which is then automatically copied to DHCP.mdb and deleted. The command used is jetpack DHCP.mdb temp_name.mdb, where temp_name.mdb is any file name specified by the user, with extension .mdb.

The following shows how to compact the DHCP database:

1. Stop the DHCP server service by using the Control Panel, Server Manager, or a command prompt.

2. To stop the service from a command prompt, type **net stop dhcpserver service**. This stops the DHCP server.

3. Type **cd \systemroot\system32\dhcp**, where systemroot is WINNT35. This changes to the DHCP directory.

4. Type **jetpack dhcp.mdb temp.mdb**. This compacts dhcp.mdb into temp.mdb, then copies it back to dhcp.mdb, and automatically deletes temp.mdb.

5. Type **net start dhcpserver**. This restarts the DHCP server service.

Backing Up the DHCP Database

By default, the DHCP database is automatically backed up at a specific interval. You can change the default interval by editing the DHCP server BackupInterval parameter value contained in the Registry.

```
SYSTEM\current\currentcontrolset\services\DHCPServer\Parameters
```

Backing up the DHCP database enables recovery from a system crash or DHCP database corruption.

You can change the default backup interval of 15 minutes by performing the following steps:

1. Stop the DHCP server service from a command prompt by typing **net stop dhcpserver**.

2. Start the Registry Editor (REGEDT32.EXE).

3. Open the HKEY_LOCAL_MACHINE\SYSTEM\ CurrentControlSet\Services\DHCPserver\Parameters key, and select BackupInterval.

4. In the Radix, make a selection, and configure the entry to the desired value. Close the Registry Editor.

5. Restart the DHCP server service from a command prompt by typing **net start dhcpserver**.

Restoring a Corrupt DHCP Database

If the DHCP database becomes corrupt, it can be restored from a backup in one of the following ways:

► It can be restored automatically.

► You can use the RestoreFlag key in the Registry.

► You can manually replace the corrupt database file.

Automatic Restoration

The DHCP server service automatically restores the backed-up copy of the database if it detects a corrupt database. If the database has become corrupt, stop and restart the DHCP server service. You can do this by typing **net stop dhcpserver** and then **net start dhcpserver** at a command prompt.

Registry RestoreFlag

If a corrupt DHCP database is not automatically restored from a backup when the DHCP server service is started, you can force the database to be restored by setting the RestoreFlag key in the Registry. To do this, perform the following tasks:

1. Stop the DHCP server service from a command prompt by typing **net stop dhcpserver**.

2. Start the Registry Editor (REGEDT32.EXE).

3. Open the HKEY_LOCAL_MACHINE\SYSTEM\ CurrentControlSet\Services\DHCPserver\Parameters key, and select RestoreFlag.

4. Change the value to 1 in the data field, and choose OK. Close the Registry Editor.

5. Restart the DHCP server service from a command prompt by typing **net start dhcpserver**. The database is restored from the backup, and the RestoreFlag entry in the Registry automatically resets to 0.

Copying from the Backup Directory

You can manually replace the corrupt database file with a backed-up version by performing the following tasks:

1. Stop the DHCP server service from a command by typing **net stop dhcpserver**.

2. Change to the DHCP directory by typing **cd \systemroot\ system32\dhcp\backup\jet**, where systemroot is WINNT, for example.

3. Copy the contents of the directory to the \systemroot\ system32\DHCP directory.

4. Type **net start dhcpserver** from a command prompt to re-start the DHCP server service.

Exercises

Exercise 6.1:   Installing the DHCP Server

In this exercise, you will install the DHCP service.

1. Open the Networking Setting dialog box, and choose Add from the Services tab.

2. Select Microsoft DHCP Server and click OK.

3. Enter the path for your Windows NT source files. Close the Network Setting dialog box and restart your computer.

4. From the Start menu, choose Programs, Administrative Tools. Verify that the DHCP Manager is installed.

Exercise 6.2:   Configuring a DHCP Scope

In this exercise, you will configure a scope on the DHCP server.

1. Start the DHCP Manager. Double-click the Local Machine to ensure you are connected to it.

2. Choose Scope, Create from the menu. The Create Scope dialog box appears.

3. Enter the following information for the IP Address Pool:

   Start Address   148.53.66.1

   End Address   148.53.127.254

   Subnet Mask   255.255.192.0

4. To add an Exclusion enter 148.53.90.0 into the Start Address and 148.53.90.255 in to the End Address. Click the Add button.

5. Leave the duration at default, and enter "Test Subnet 1" as the Name. Click OK.

6. You will be prompted to activate the scope; choose Yes.

Exercise 6.3: Adding Scope and Global Options in the DHCP Server

Now you will add options to the scope you configured.

1. Click the scope that was create in the previous exercise.

Note

> If you get an error click OK to continue, this is an undocumented feature (a bug). Close the DHCP Manager and reopen it to stop this.

2. From the menu choose DHCP Options, Scope.

3. From the list of Unused Options, choose 003 Router and click Add.

4. Click on the Values button to see the rest of the dialog box. Currently there is no router listed.

5. Choose Edit Array. In the dialog box that appears, enter 148.53.64.1 in the IP Address field. Click Add to add the address to the list.

6. Choose OK to close the IP Address Array Editor, and then choose OK to close the DHCP Options: Scope dialog box.

   The router option should appear in the Options Configuration panel.

7. Choose DHCP Options, Global from the menu, and add the following options:

   006 DNS Servers

   015 Domain Name

   044 WINS/NBNS Servers (You will get a message when you add this one.)

   046 WINS/NBT Node Type

8. Add the configuration for these options, using the following values:

DNS Server   148.53.64.8

Domain Name   scrimtech.com

WINS/NBNS Servers   198.53.64.8

WINS/NBT Node Type   0x8

9. Click OK.

Exercise 6.4:   Configuring a Second DHCP Scope

In this exercise, you will configure a second scope of addresses.

1. Add anther DHCP scope using the following values:

IP Address Pool

Start Address   148.53.140.0

End Address   148.53.191.255

Subnet Mask   255.255.192.0

2. Set the lease duration for 14 days, and the name the scope "Test Subnet 2."

There should be a number listed for each scope in the DHCP Manager. The number given is the subnet ID for the scope. This scenario used a Class B address, which is split into two subnets: 148.53.64.0 and 148.53.128.0.

3. Set the default gateway for this scope to 148.53.128.1.

4. This scope will not be used immediately, therefore you will deactivate it by choosing Scope, Deactivate.

Exercise 6.5: Adding Client Reservations

Finally, you will add a client reservation.

1. Highlight the first subnet (148.53.64.0).

2. Choose Scope, Add Reservations from the menu.

3. In the Add Reserved Clients dialog box, change the IP address to 148.53.66.7.

4. Enter the unique identifier, 0000DE7342FA, and enter the client name as Rob.

5. Click Add.

6. Enter the IP address 148.53.66.9, with the unique identifier 00D4C9C57D34. The client name is Judy. Click add.

7. Choose Done.

Review Questions

1. Which of the following is not one of the five possible broadcasts in the DHCP process?

    A. DHCPNACK

    B. DHCPOFFER

    C. DHCPDISCOVER

    D. DHCPLEASE

2. Before a client can receive a DHCP address, what must be configured on the DHCP server?

    A. The DHCP relay agent

    B. A scope for the clients subnet

    C. A scope for the servers subnet

    D. A host name

3. What must a router support in order to pass DHCP broadcasts?

    A. RFC 1543

    B. BOOTP Relay

    C. RFC 1544

    D. This cannot be done

4. What is the recommended method of providing backup to the DHCP server?

    A. Configure two DHCP servers with the same scope

    B. Configure a BOOTP server

    C. Replicate the database using directory replication

    D. Configure two DHCP servers with different sections of the scope

5. What is the effect of a lease duration of unlimited?

    A. DHCP configuration options will never be update.

    B. There is no effect.

    C. There will be an increase in network traffic.

    D. Addresses cannot be shared dynamically.

6. In what environment is it advisable to have a short lease duration?

    A. In static environments where addresses don't change often

    B. When you have fewer hosts than IP addresses

    C. In environments where you have hosts moving and many changes to IP addresses

    D. When you have more hosts than IP addresses

7. What portions of the DHCP process are initiated by the server?

    A. Lease acquisition

    B. Lease renewal

    C. Lease release

    D. No processes are initiated by the server

8. How must an NT Server be configured before you install a DHCP server?

    A. The WINS server must be installed.

    B. The server requires a static IP configuration.

    C. TCP/IP must not be installed.

    D. None of the above.

9. What information is required to define a scope?

    A. Starting and ending address and the subnet mask

    B. Subnet ID and the number of addresses to lease

C. Number of hosts to be leased

D. The name of the scope

10. Which clients cannot use a DHCP server?

   A. MS LAN Manager for DOS 2.2c

   B. Windows NT Workstation

   C. MS LAN Manager for OS/2 2.2c

   D. Windows 95

11. How do you configure a client to use DHCP?

   A. Install the DHCP client service

   B. Select automatic configuration icon from the Control Panel

   C. DHCP automatically configures all clients

   D. Select Obtain IP address automatically in the TCP/IP configuration

12. What is the difference between a global and a scope option?

   A. Global options affect all system on the network whether DHCP clients or not.

   B. Scope options are set in the DHCP manager for individual scopes.

   C. Global options affect the clients on scopes where no scope options are configured.

   D. There is no difference in the options, just in how they are entered.

13. Why would you use a client reservation?

   A. To provide dynamic configuration of TCP/IP options with a static IP address.

   B. To be able to control all the IP addresses.

    C. This is required for any host that that cannot be a
       DHCP client but that uses an address in the scopes
       range.

    D. You cannot reserve addresses.

14. What is required for a client reservation?

    A. The NetBIOS name of the client

    B. The host name of the client

    C. The MAC address of the client

15. What happens to the client if you delete their lease?

    A. They immediately stop using the address.

    B. The will not be able to initialize at next startup.

    C. Nothing until they attempt to renew the address.

    D. The host will stop working.

Review Answers

1. D

2. B

3. B

4. D

5. A

6. C

7. D

8. B

9. A

10. C

11. D

12. B

13. A

14. C

15. C

Answers to the Test Yourself Questions at the Beginning of the Chapter

1. The IP address and subnet mask are no longer used when the Enable Automatic DHCP Configuration check box is selected.

2. The following are benefits of using DHCP:

   ▶ The administrator can quickly verify the IP address and other configuration parameters without having to check each host individually.

   ▶ DHCP does not lease the same IP address from a scope to two different hosts at the same time.

   ▶ The DHCP administrator controls which IP addresses are used by which hosts.

   ▶ Clerical and typing errors can be reduced.

   ▶ Multiple scope options can be set reducing the amount of manual configuration.

   ▶ An IP address may be leased for a limited time.

   ▶ A host can be automatically reconfigured when it moves to a different subnet.

3. These are the extra steps that should be taken after two DHCP servers have been installed on a subnet:

   ▶ You must ensure that the IP address ranges on each DHCP do not overlap. A given IP address must not be in a scope on more than one DHCP server in an internetwork.

   ▶ You should consider having the DHCP servers on separate subnets connected by a router configured as a DHCP relay agent.

4. To use a router on an internetwork that will enable a DHCP client to communicate with a DHCP server on a remote subnet, the router must possess the following characteristics:

   ▶ It must support RFC 1542.

   ▶ It must be configured to forward BOOTP packets between the subnets.

5. To ensure that DHCP does not assign an IP address that is already in use by a non-DHCP client, the non-DHCP client IP address should be excluded from that subnet's scope.

6. Yes, it is possible for two DHCP clients on an internetwork to lease the same IP address—if each received its lease from a different DHCP server and the DHCP server scopes contained overlapping IP addresses.

7. The DHCP client might still have a manually configured default gateway that is no longer correct.

8. Only one DHCP server is required, although it is usually recommended that each subnet have a DHCP server. Having one DHCP server on each subnet reduces DHCP lease broadcasts that have to be broadcast on a remote subnet. The DHCP servers can also be configured with ranges of unallocated IP addresses for each other's subnets so that another DHCP server can lease a DHCP client an IP address if the DHCP server on that client's subnet is unavailable. You must, however, ensure that the IP address scopes do not overlap so that any given IP address is found in only one scope on the internetwork.

9. You can select the Enable Automatic DHCP Configuration check box before or after Microsoft TCP/IP is installed and configured.

Chapter

NetBIOS Over TCP/IP

7

This chapter will help you prepare for the exam by covering the following objectives:

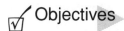 Objectives

- ▶ Configure HOSTS and LMHOSTS

- ▶ Diagnose and resolve name resolution problems

Test Yourself! Before reading this chapter, test yourself to determine how much study time you will need to devote to this section.

1. What Winsock ports are used for NetBIOS communications?

2. Which node type(s) use a NetBIOS Name Server as the primary means of name resolution?

3. In all NetBIOS name resolution node types, which method of name resolution is first tried?

4. Describe the three main functions of NetBIOS.

5. What is an SMB?

6. Assuming Hybrid node resolution, in what order are the methods of name resolution attempted?

7. For what is the 16th character of the NetBIOS name used?

8. What is the use of the #BEGIN ALTERNATE tag in the LMHOSTS file?

9. In what scenario are you required to use the #DOM tag in an LMHOSTS file?

10. In what two ways can you configure a client to use a NetBIOS Name Server?

Answers are located at the end of the chapter.

Defining NetBIOS

Microsoft has been using NetBIOS for the upper layers of their networking architecture for years. This chapter looks at the NetBIOS standard and how it communicates. Mapping of NetBIOS functions to those found in TCP/IP also is discussed. This mapping is required for TCP/IP and any other network protocol installed in Windows NT so that the internal NetBIOS commands can traverse the network.

Although there are three main functions that need to be supported for NetBIOS to function—Name Management, Session Management and Data Transfer—there will be much emphasis given to the Name Management in this chapter. This is the key issue in using NetBIOS over TCP/IP because TCP/IP uses IP addressing, whereas NetBIOS uses computer names. The other functions present in NetBIOS are already present in TCP/IP.

NetBIOS is a networking standard based on the OSI (Open System Interconnect) model—also known as the seven-layer model. When referencing the OSI model, NetBIOS as implemented in Windows NT provides the services required for the top three layers: application, presentation, and session.

The application layer interacts with user programs (for example, Windows NT Explorer or Microsoft Word) and handles network access for those programs. When the application layer receives a request for network access, it turns the request into an SMB (Server Message Block). An SMB is a unit of work that tells the system at the other end what the user on this system wants to do (for example, read a file from the network). SMBs are considered Protocol Data Units (PDUs) and as such perform the work of moving requests and data between systems. All the other layers in the protocol stack simply serve to move the SMB from one system to another system.

After the SMB has been generated, the presentation layer prepares to deliver the information to the correct computer. This requires the services of the session layer, which creates or uses a session with the remote computer to deliver the information. In some cases (broadcasts), a session is not required. The presentation layer checks to see whether a session is required for the transmission—and, if a session is required, whether one already exists. If a session does not exist, the presentation layer uses the services of the session layer to create a session with the remote host. The presentation layer can then generate an NCB (Network Control Block) that tells the underlying layer what to do with the SMB (which is now the data to be transferred).

The session layer receives the NCB and acts on it normally by sending the data to the remote host. As already mentioned, the session layer is responsible for creating and terminating sessions with other hosts, as well as for controlling the flow of data. By using sessions, Windows NT adds a layer of security because the user's credentials (access token) are checked and verified when the session is created. In addition, sessions enables extra checking of the information flowing across the network to verify that it has arrived in good order.

NetBIOS Over TCP/IP (NBT)

When the OSI networking model, of which NetBIOS is a part, is compared to the TCP/IP networking model, it is essential to understand that the first layer in the TCP/IP stack is also the application layer. However, it encompasses the functions of the top three layers of the OSI model (see fig. 7.1). Because this is also where NetBIOS resides in the OSI model, some method is required to map the NetBIOS functions to the TCP/IP functions. Sitting between the TCP/IP application layer and the Transport layer is the Winsock interface. Winsock provides end points for communications. For example, to connect to a Web site, you call an IP address, protocol, and port number (for instance, 199.45.92.97:TCP:80 is a Web page address). The port number is the Winsock port on which the requested service lives.

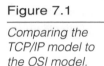

Figure 7.1

*Comparing the
TCP/IP model to
the OSI model.*

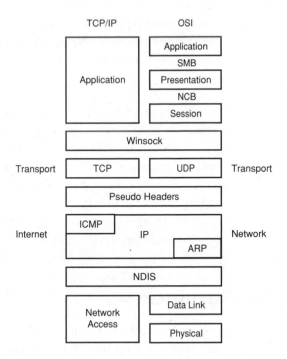

Therefore, for NetBIOS to function over TCP/IP, NetBIOS needs
to use ports. Three ports have been assigned to NetBIOS on
which to send information and listen for incoming traffic. Table
7.1 lists the three NetBIOS ports that are used.

Table 7.1

NetBIOS Port Numbers and Protocols

Service	Nickname	Port	Protocol
NetBIOS Name Service	nbname	137	UDP
NetBIOS Datagram Service	Nbdatagram	138	UDP
NetBIOS Session Service	Nbsession	139	TCP

As shown in table 7.1, the ports for the NetBIOS Name Service
and the NetBIOS Datagram Service use UDP (User Datagram
Protocol). This means that no session is required to transmit information. NetBIOS is based heavily on broadcasts. This system
dates to the time when NetBIOS was developed; the networks

were smaller and typically only one segment, so broadcasts worked well. As this discussion on NetBIOS continues, you will discover that using broadcasts now represents a major problem.

 Note

> Most routers are configured not to forward broadcasts on ports 137 and 138 (although they can pass directed transmissions). NetBIOS uses broadcasts for many functions and the amount of broadcast traffic can congest routers. This can cause problems because functions such as domain validation and browser services require the use of broadcasts. These problems are addressed in Chapter 10, "IP Internetwork Browsing and Domain Functions."

NetBIOS Services

As previously established, Windows NT uses NetBIOS internally, and any protocol (not just TCP/IP) that works with NT must have some means of translating NetBIOS to a native format. You have already seen that three ports are used: 137, 138, and 139. This section looks at the NetBIOS services and maps them to TCP/IP services and the port numbers indicated.

Three main services need to be handled by the protocol to enable communications over the network. There is a requirement to find the remote computer, because NetBIOS uses computer names rather than IP addresses; this is probably the most critical service in enabling NetBIOS to function over TCP/IP. Name resolution is handled on port 137, which is the NetBIOS Name Service port.

Another function that needs to be handled by an underlying protocol (such as TCP/IP) is Session Management. NetBIOS creates a session with a remote computer when it wants to communicate. As previously noted, this provides better security because the user has to be identified, and also enables extra checking in the transfer of large files. TCP also has the capability to create a session (by use of the three-way handshake). Creating a NetBIOS session, therefore, first creates a TCP session that provides base-level communications. This requires TCP and therefore uses the Net-BIOS Session port, which is TCP port 139, as listed in table 7.1.

The last—and for users, most important—function is the capability to transfer data from one system to another (whether it is a print job going to the printer, or a file being saved on the network). Two types of Data Transfer are available to NetBIOS and therefore must be available in the underlying protocol: connection-oriented (for transferring files, and so on) and connectionless (for broadcasts, logon requests, and so forth). The first uses the services of a session, and therefore uses TCP and the NetBIOS session port (139). Connectionless transfer simply sends the information and doesn't care if the information is received; this suits the UDP transport protocol. As you may have guessed, connectionless transfers use the NetBIOS Datagram Service on UDP port 138.

As you can see, most of the functions map out easily. Session Management is a natural for TCP. Data Transfer is a basic network function, and TCP/IP already has connection-oriented and connectionless transfer methods available. The only function of NetBIOS that does not translate well is Name Management. Unfortunately, neither of the other functions works without the capability to resolve a NetBIOS name to a TCP/IP address.

Name Management

When a system is going to communicate with another computer on the network, some method of identifying the other computer is required. The identification is, of course, handled in the Net-BIOS world by the computer name (which can be up to 15 characters in length). When IBM and Microsoft developed the NetBIOS standard, fewer wide area networks (WANs) existed, and generally the local area networks (LANs) were small enough that they did not require the capability to be segmented. Generally, main frame and mini-computers were used when segmenting was required. Looking at other networking technologies, such as TCP/IP, that required computers to have numeric addresses, Microsoft and IBM decided that NetBIOS should use computer names to put a friendly face on the network because these could be resolved using broadcasts.

Because the identity of the system is the name, each name that you use for a computer must be unique on the network. However, as time has passed, networks became larger and it became desirable to group computers on the network and to be able to send information (messages) to users working on the computers. This lead to the requirement for multiple NetBIOS names. Currently, Windows NT enables you to register up to 250 NetBIOS names for any given computer. The common names that Windows NT registers are as follows:

▶ **Computer name.** This is the name that the computer uses on the network,; in all cases, this name must be unique. When a system starts and the name is already on the network, the networking portion of the system cannot initialize. (It is possible to duplicate a name in some multi-segment networks; however, the hosts can never communicate. This is because the name is checked on the local segment or on a NetBIOS Name Server).

▶ **User name.** The user name also is registered on the network. This enables the user to receive messages (such as printer notifications) that are sent to the user name. More than one instance of a user name can exist. However, only the first person to register the name receives messages; all other attempts to register that name fail until the person currently using the name shuts down. (The system continues to function correctly, but the user does not receive any messages.)

▶ **Workgroup or domain name.** This is a group name, and many different systems can register the name. This name is used to group computers into a single management area (a set of computers that are managed together).

Being as there are several different types of names, you may have more than one name registered on your computer. This is further complicated by the need to find a service that is running on a computer (for example, if you are trying to access network resources, the Workstation service in your system needs to communicate with the Server service on the remote system). If you think about sending a letter, simply addressing the letter to an apartment building does not get it to the person to whom you are writing. In the same way, sending an SMB to a computer does not guarantee that it reaches the correct service on the computer. Many services can use NetBIOS. The three most common services in Windows NT are as follows:

▶ **Server Service.** Provides the resources of your system for the other computers on the network to use

▶ **Workstation Service.** Enables you to use the services of another computer that is running the Server Service

▶ **Messenger Service.** Receives and displays messages for the names that are registered on your computer

As you can see, getting the information to the computer is half the battle. To make the network function, you need to connect to the correct service (end point). This means you require not only the name of the computer, but also the name that the service registered.

Thankfully, this is easy. When I noted previously that the names are 15 characters, I was referring to the portion you can enter. NetBIOS names are, in fact, 16 characters long; the last character identifies the service. Each service adds a 1-byte identifier to the end of the name when it is registered. The following is a list of some of the names that are registered and the services that they represent. (Note that the number the service uses is given in hexadecimal format—it is hard to see a space or a null in print.)

▶ **Computername[0x00].** The Workstation service on the computer being registered.

▶ **Computername[0x03].** The Messenger service registering on the computer.

▶ **Username[0x03].** The Messenger service registering the logged-on user on the network.

- ▶ **Computername[0x20].** The Server service registering the computer on the network.

- ▶ **Domainname[0x00].** Registers the computer as a member of the domain (or workgroup, as the case may be).

- ▶ **Domainname[0x1E].** Facilitates browser elections (also used in workgroup environments—browsing is covered in Chapter 10, "IP Internetwork Browsing and Domain Functions").

- ▶ **Domainname[0x1B].** Registers the computer as the Domain Master browser (covered in Chapter 9, "Administering a WINS Environment").

- ▶ **Domainname[0x1C].** Registers the computer as a domain controller, which enables your system to find a domain controller for logon validation.

- ▶ **Domainname[0x1d].** Registers the system as the local subnet's Master Browser.

Suppose, for example, that you are on a computer called WKS2399 and want to retrieve a file called exprep.xls from a server on a network called NTS94. In this case, an SMB is created by the application layer with a request to get the file, and your workstation service uses the NCB to get to a computer called NTS94[0x20]. After the server receives the SMB and wants to send the information back, it sends it to WKS2399[0x00].

Obviously, your system must have some way to find the server—that is, to resolve the name from NTS94[0x20] to a MAC address where it can send the information.

Name Resolution

Now that the naming of computers has been discussed, hopefully you can see the need for the system that has evolved. Up to this point, however, this chapter has discussed only theory. You now need to learn what happens with NetBIOS names. You can work with NetBIOS names in one of two ways: using broadcasts, or using the services of a NetBIOS Name Server. Either method can handle the four main functions required by the NetBIOS Name Service. The functions are as follows:

▶ **Name Registration.** As previously discussed, this is the process of registering a name for every service on the system on which you are working.

▶ **Name Query.** When your want to connect to another computer across the network, your system has to be able to find that computer's MAC address. This requires, in the case of TCP/IP, that you have the IP address (which TCP/IP resolves to a MAC address—the hardware address discussed in Chapter 2, "Architectural Overview of the TCP/IP Suite"). The Name Query is sent on the network (like the Address Resolution Protocol packet that follows) and requests a response from the computer that has this name registered.

▶ **Name Release.** As you shut down your system, a Name Release broadcast is sent on the wire. This informs hosts you are communicating with that you are shutting down. Notably, though, this releases your user name, which also is registered. By doing this, no problem with duplicate names arises if you log on at a different workstation.

▶ **Positive Name Query Response.** As implied, this is the response to the Name Query. Note that every host on the local network receives and accepts the Name Query packet that is sent as a broadcast packet. Each passes the packet to IP, which passes it to UDP, which passes it to the NetBIOS Name Service port. This means that every computer needs to spend CPU time checking whether the queried name is one of theirs.

Previously, it was mentioned that name services can be done using either a broadcast or a NetBIOS Name Server (NBNS). You should note that if a broadcast is used, the services are usable only on the local segment; in most multi-segment networks, an NBNS should be used to provide enterprise-wide name registration and resolution services. Name registration is handled using a local broadcast (actually a Name Query), and the name is registered if no local system responds with a Positive Name Query Response.

Windows NT has six methods for name resolution. The next few sections provide details of each of the methods and the order in which they are used. The six methods are as follows:

- ▶ NetBIOS Name Cache

- ▶ LMHOSTS file

- ▶ Broadcast

- ▶ NetBIOS Name Server

- ▶ HOSTS file

- ▶ DNS Server

NetBIOS Name Cache

The NetBIOS Name Cache is an area of memory containing a list of NetBIOS computer names and the associated IP address. An address in the Name Cache can get there in one of two ways: you have resolved that address or the address was preloaded from the LMHOSTS file (see "The LMHOSTS File"). The Name Cache provides a quick reference to frequently used IP addresses.

The NetBIOS Name Cache, however, cannot keep every address on your network. The cache (like ARP) only keeps entries for a short period of time—ten minutes by default. The exceptions are preloaded entries, which remain in cache.

You cannot directly modify the NetBIOS Name Cache. However, you can add preloaded entries in the LMHOSTS file. If you do this (or if you want to clear the Name Cache), use nbtstat -R. This purges and reloads the Name Cache. If you want to view the re-solved names, you can use nbtstat -r (the switches for nbtstat are, as you might have guessed, case sensitive).

A couple of registry entries affect the way the Name Cache works. The entries are found under the following registry key:

`HKEY_LOCAL_MACHINE\SYSTEM\CurrentControlSet\Services\NetBT\Parameters`

The entries are as follows:

▶ **Size: Small/Medium/Large.** The number of names kept in the Name Cache. The settings are Small (1—maintains only 16 names), Medium (2—maintains 64 names), and Large (3—maintains 128 names). The default is 1, which is sufficient for most client stations.

▶ **CacheTimeout.** The time in milliseconds that an entry remains in cache. The default is 927c0 (hex) or 600,000, which is ten minutes.

Broadcast

If the name cannot be found in the NetBIOS Name Cache, the system attempts to find the name using a broadcast on the local network. A broadcast is a necessary evil. It takes up bandwidth, but in many cases is the simplest way to find a system.

NetBIOS uses UDP (port 137) to send a Name Query to every computer on the local network. Every computer must then take the packet and pass it all the way up the protocol stack to NetBIOS so the name can be checked against the local name table. Two problems with using a broadcast are increased network traffic, and wasted CPU time on all the systems as the request is passed to NetBIOS to check names that don't exist.

You are going to see two methods that enable you to resolve names without broadcast traffic. You should note that broadcasts are a throwback to the early days of networks when computers were slower, networks tended to be single segments, and the bandwidth of networks was more than enough to cover the occasional broadcast.

You can use a couple of registry entries to customize the broadcast function. These are under the following registry key:

```
HKEY_LOCAL_MACHINE\SYSTEM\CurrentControlSet\Services\NetBT\Parameters
```

The entries are as follows:

▶ **BcastNameQueryCount.** The number of times the system retries the broadcast for the name. The default is three times.

▶ **BcastQueryTimeout.** The amount of time to wait before retrying the Name Query broadcast. The default is 7.5 seconds.

The LMHOSTS File

For an exercise covering this information, see end of chapter.

Microsoft has been building network operating systems for a long time. Before Windows NT, Microsoft put out a product called LAN Manager. LAN Manager was based internally on NetBIOS and used NetBEUI as a protocol, which you may recall has one major problem—it cannot be routed from network to network. Microsoft choose NetBEUI in the first place because the NetBEUI protocol was compatible with the NetBIOS networking model that they were using.

To make LAN Manager more acceptable as a network operating system, Microsoft included TCP/IP as an alternate protocol for medium-to-large organizations wanting to use their product (which was based on Microsoft OS/2 version 1.3). But there was a problem: How do you resolve NetBIOS names using TCP/IP on a routed network? On the local network, the system could use the NetBIOS Name Service port and broadcast a request for the local name.

Note

Windows NT only checks the LMHOSTS file if a broadcast on the local network fails to resolve the address.

The solution was relatively easy: create a list of the systems to which the computer would have to talk. Given peer-to-peer networking had not become in vogue, only a limited number existed, anyway. In this file, you could put the IP address and the NetBIOS name of an systems you need to talk to. It was an obvious solution that does work. However, in some situations, the client would not be talking to a single machine, but rather searching for any machine with a particular service (the Netlogon service is a good example).

The list is the file LMHOSTS (no extension), which is located in the \%winroot%\system32\drivers\etc directory. A sample LMHOSTS file also was added during installation; this file is called lmhosts.sam. (If you use Notepad to create or edit the file, ensure that the file is saved as text and not as Unicode.)

 Note

All the hosts on the Internet used to be listed in a single file at Stanford Research Institute's Network Information Center (SRI-NIC.) Whenever you tried to connect to another host, your system had to consult this file on the SRI-NIC server to find the IP address. The file was called hosts.txt.

The solution to the problem of finding a system running a particular service (such as Netlogon) rather than a particular computer was solved by including tags. Microsoft introduced several tags that enabled systems to send a request to all the computers that had a particular service running (for example, the #DOM tag tells your system that a particular system should be running the Netlogon service).

The result was a system that could communicate across routers even though it internally used NetBIOS. A workable compromise —sort of. As time went on, the amount of time that was spent updating the LMHOSTS file increased. In addition, because this file needs to be located on every host, the task became even more difficult.

Tags were a good solution once, and again proved to be able to resolve the issue. Microsoft added new tags that enabled computers to read a central LMHOSTS file. The client computer still needed a local LMHOSTS file so the system would know where and how to find the central one, however; this reduced the required number of lines from 70 or 80 or more, to 5 or 6.

Windows NT supports and uses several tags. Table 7.2 describes the tags available.

Table 7.2

Tags Available for Use by Windows NT	
Tag	Use
#PRE	Tells the computer to preload the entry to the cache during initialization or after the nbtstat -R command has been issued. Entries with the #PRE tag have a life of −1 (static), meaning they are always in cache.
#DOM:domain_name	Indicates to the system that the computer is a domain controller and the domain that it controls. This enables Windows NT to handle domain functions, domain logon, and browsing services, among other things.
#NOFNR	Prevents the use of NetBIOS-directed name queries in the LAN Manager for a Unix environment.
#INCLUDE	Tells the computer the location of a central LMHOSTS file. The file is specified using a UNC (Universal Naming Convention)-type name such as \\MIS\Information\LMHOSTS. It is important that the computer name must be resolved to an IP address and must be included in the local LMHOSTS file as a preloaded entry.
#BEGIN_ALTERNATE	Used in conjunction with the #INCLUDE tag. Marks the beginning of a list of alternate locations for the centralized LMHOSTS file that can be used if the first entry is not available. Only one central LMHOSTS is used.

Tag	Use
#END_ALTERNATE	Ends the list of alternate locations for a central LMHOSTS file. Between the two entries, add as many alternates as you like. Windows NT tries each in sequence (remember, the names must resolve to IP addresses).
#MH	Multihomed computers may appear in the LMHOSTS file more that once. This tag lets the system know that this is a cases where it should not ignore the other entries in the list.

 The LMHOSTS file is scanned from top to bottom. Therefore, your most frequently used servers should be listed first. Any entries to preload a server address should be at the bottom because they will already be in the NetBIOS Name Cache.

The following is an example of what an LMHOSTS file might contain:

```
152.42.35.2      victoria1    #DOM:MYCORP   #PRE
152.42.9.255     london2      #DOM:MYCORP
152.42.160.45    ottawa8      #PRE
152.42.97.56     houston4     #PRE
#INCLUDE \\victoria1\INFO\LMHOSTS
#BEGIN_ALTERNATE
#INCLUDE \\ottawa8\INFO\LMHOSTS
#INCLUDE \\houston4\INFO\LMHOSTS
#END_ALTERNATE
152.42.193.5     capetown4    #PRE #DOM:MYCORP
152.42.194.255   capetown8    #PRE #DOM:MYCORP
```

 Use nbtstat -R to flush the NetBIOS Name Cache and reload from the LMHOSTS file. This enables you to test an LMHOSTS file as you create it.

Of course, nothing in this world is perfect, so you need to keep the following facts in mind when using the LMHOSTS file:

▶ If the IP address is wrong, then your system resolves the address. However, you cannot connect. Normally this shows up as a "Network Name not Found" error.

▶ Windows NT is good; however, if the NetBIOS name is spelled wrong in the LMHOSTS file, Windows NT can do nothing to resolve it. (Note the names are not case sensitive.)

▶ If the LMHOSTS file has multiple entries, the address for the first one is returned. If that entry is wrong, the result is the same as have a wrong IP address.

Only one registry entry affects LMHOSTS; however, you can easily change the entry in the Network Settings dialog box. The entry is Enable LMHOSTS, and if it is not selected, the system ignores the LMHOSTS file. This is selected by default in Windows NT and Windows 95, but deselected in Windows for Workgroups.

To change the Enable LMHOSTS setting, perform the following steps:

1. Open the Network Settings dialog box.

2. Select the Protocol tab and open the Properties for TPC/IP.

3. On the WINS Addressing tab, ensure there is a check in the Enable LMHOSTS Lookup check box to turn this on. Clear the check box to turn it off.

4. Close the TCP/IP Settings dialog box and the Network Settings dialog box.

5. Restart your computer.

NetBIOS Name Server

The LMHOSTS file has some limitations; even using a central LMHOSTS file requires a great deal of updating. If you don't use a central LMHOSTS file, and you attempt to update a host's address, you must visit every station on your network. In addition, the LMHOSTS file does not reduce broadcast traffic unless every entry is preloaded (meaning the system never has to perform a NetBIOS Name Query broadcast).

As the size of networks around the world began to increase, another method of name resolution had to be found. The method had to be able to reduce broadcast traffic and to update itself without intervention. TCP/IP already had a simple DNS service that computers could query to find the IP address for a given host name. The problem with DNS is it only resolves the basic host name; you are not be able to find services (such as Netlogon) that you sometimes seek.

In addition, DNS required a large—but, at least, centralized—file to be kept with a listing of all the IP-address-to-host name mappings. Of the three functions of NetBIOS naming—registration, resolution and release—the DNS service fit only one of the criteria.

So, a new type of name service had to be built that would enable systems to register their own IP addresses and that could respond to these systems' queries about the IP addresses of others. The system that emerged was the NetBIOS Name Server (NBNS). Windows NT implements this in the form of the WINS (Windows Internet Name Service) server discussed in Chapter 8, "Implementing Windows Internet Name Service."

Just as TCP/IP hosts had always had a DNS server entry, the NetBIOS world could now use an NBNS (such as WINS) server entry. The process was aided by the capability of the available routers to pass directed transmission over UDP port 137. A set of three basic commands was established, and NetBIOS networking was now capable of talking to the world.

You enter the WINS server address and a secondary WINS server address in the TCP/IP Settings page. This is all you need to do to use a WINS server as your NBNS.

The available commands include:

- ▶ **Name Registration.** The transmission registers a computer name with the NBNS. In this way, the NBNS is a dynamic system requiring little or no maintenance by the network administrators.

- ▶ **Name Query.** Normally, all the systems in an organization use the same NBNS. (Chapter 9 discusses replication, which makes a group of NBNS act as a single unit.) Then, it is easy to resolve a name—send the NetBIOS Name Query to the NBNS. The server responds with the IP address if the system has registered it.

- ▶ **Name Release.** Some names, such as user names, can move from one computer to another and, therefore, from one IP address to another. By including the capability to release a registered name, conflicts in the database are avoided.

Using an NBNS such as WINS has some major advantages if you use TCP/IP as your networking protocol with Windows products. The advantages include the following:

- ▶ Reduces broadcast traffic

- ▶ Reduces administrative overhead for maintenance

- ▶ Facilitates domain activity over a WAN

- ▶ Provides browsing services across multiple subnets

You can customize a couple of registry entries for the NBNS. These are under the following subkeys:

`HKEY_LOCAL_MACHINE\SYSTEM\CurrentControlSet\Services\NetBT\Parameters`

- ▶ **NameServerPort.** The UDP port used for NetBIOS Name Queries going to the NBNS. The default is 137 (89 hex).

- ▶ **NameSrvQueryCount.** Indicates the number of times your system should try each NBNS. The default is three times.

> ▶ **NameSrvQueryTimeout.** Indicates how long your computer
> should wait for a response from the NBNS. Default is 15
> seconds (5dc hex milliseconds).

The HOSTS File

Because you are looking at NetBIOS name resolution, including
the HOSTS file here might seem out of place. The HOSTS file is
primarily associated with host name resolution. However, Windows NT uses the HOSTS file if all other methods of NetBIOS
name resolution fail.

Host names are the TCP/IP names given to the computer. Usually, the host name is the same as the NetBIOS name (without the
16th character). However, it does not have to be. The host name
may also include the Internet domain name; these parts together
are the Fully Qualified Domain Name (FQDN). The host name
can be any length. For example, thisisawebserver.mycorp.com is a
valid FQDN; however, it is not a valid NetBIOS name. (More on
this in Chapter 12, "Domain Name System.")

The HOSTS file that is located in the \%winroot%\system32\
drivers\etc directory is similar in makeup to the LMHOSTS file
discussed earlier. The difference is that the HOSTS file is simpler
in the following ways:

> ▶ No tags are in the HOSTS file.

> ▶ You can associate more than one name with a host by enter-
> ing all the names on the same line, separated by spaces.

A sample HOSTS file might look like the following:

```
160.16.5.3      www www.scrimtech.com   # corporate web server
38.25.63.10     www.NTworld.com         # NT associate page
127.0.0.1       localhost
```

As noted, the first entry resolves www as well as www.scrimtech.com to
the IP address 160.16.5.3. You may have noticed the # signs. These
indicate comments in the HOSTS file that are always placed at the
end of the line.

The entry for localhost at 127.0.0.1 is a default entry that Windows NT adds. This enables you to ping your computer by name to ensure the HOSTS file is working. (Ping is discussed in detail in Chapter 14, "Connectivity in Heterogeneous Environments.")

DNS

Just like using the HOSTS file, using DNS to resolve NetBIOS names may seem a little out of place. However, Windows NT can use a DNS server to resolve a host name. In environments that are working with the Internet almost exclusively, having a DNS server makes sense, and you can use it instead of WINS. If you want to do this, simply check the Enable DNS for Windows Resolution check box shown in figure 7.2.

Figure 7.2

The WINS Address tab in the TCP/IP Properties dialog box.

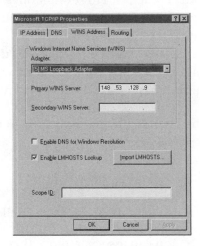

Configuring Windows NT to use a DNS server is simple, as you are shown in Chapter 9. All you need to do is enter a DNS server address in the DNS tab of the TCP/IP Properties dialog box (see fig. 7.3).

Order of Resolution

For an exercise covering this information, see end of chapter.

As you have just seen, there are six ways that Windows NT can resolve a NetBIOS name to an IP address. As discussed, each way works although some have limitations that make them impractical for a large-scale WAN. Thankfully, this does not matter because the methods of resolution back each other up and enable which-ever method that can resolve the name to resolve it.

Figure 7.3

The DNS tab in the TCP/IP Properties dialog box.

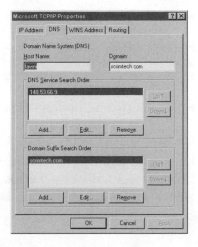

A problem could arise, though, if you are not careful. For instance, it makes sense for you to first read the HOSTS file, then broadcast the NetBIOS Name Query to the local subnet. Perhaps checking with the DNS server should be next. The point is, that the order in which you use the methods of resolution is more important than the resolution. You are fairly well-assured the name will be resolved (if you spelled it right); however, going through the resolution methods in the wrong order could slow down the process.

Remember that this is the resolution order for NetBIOS names only. Resolving host names uses a different method. Chapter 11, "Host Name Resolution," discusses that topic. For now, though, bear in mind that this is NetBIOS name resolution, which occurs when you use the NetBIOS interface instead of the Winsock interface. All the standard Microsoft products—Windows NT Explorer, User Manager, net.exe—use this method of resolution.

The NetBIOS node type sets the order of resolution. This can be set either by editing the registry, or by using the Dynamic Host Configuration Protocol (DHCP) server, if you are using DHCP to allocate IP addresses and services. You should note that the default is b-node (Broadcast)—unless a WINS server address is entered—in which case, it defaults to h-node (Hybrid). The node types that can be set are as follows:

▶ b-node (broadcast node)

▶ p-node (peer-to-peer node)—Uses an NBNS

▶ m-node (mixed node)—First tries b-node, then p-node

▶ h-node (hybrid node)—First tries p-node, then b-node

Microsoft's version of b-node is an enhanced form of the b-node standard. Because Microsoft already had an LMHOSTS file that had been used successfully with LAN Manager, Microsoft included searching this file in the b-node form of resolution.

b-node

The simplest way to resolve a name on the network is to ask everyone on the network if a name is his or her name. Obviously, this has to be done as a broadcast to the network with every host on the network responding to the broadcast.

NetBIOS Name Queries that are broadcast can take up a significant amount of bandwidth from the network, and also take CPU time from every host on the network. This causes the overall network performance to not only seem slower, but to be slower. Windows NT attempts three times to resolve the name using broadcasting, waiting 7.5 seconds between each.

The steps a b-node system goes through to resolve a name are as follows:

1. Checking the NetBIOS Name Cache

2. Broadcasting a NetBIOS Name Query

3. Checking the LMHOSTS file (Microsoft enhanced b-node only)

4. Checking a HOST file

5. Checking with a DNS server

p-node

As you saw, there are better ways to resolve a NetBIOS name. The best way is to ask a central system that has a list of every host's IP address and NetBIOS name, as well as special entries for systems from run services such as Netlogon. p-node does this for us.

p-node still uses a NetBIOS Name Query that is sent on the network. However, rather than being sent as a broadcast, the query is sent directly to an NBNS. In this way, the resolution is made quicker, and no CPU time is taken up on the other hosts on the network. Like the b-node, p-node makes three attempts to contact an NBNS, waiting 15 seconds each time.

The order of resolution for p-node is the following:

1. NetBIOS Name Cache

2. Asking a NetBIOS Name Server

3. HOSTS file

4. DNS

m-node

A Mixed Node system tries every method of resolution. This and h-node are combinations of the b-node and p-node systems. The only difference is the order in which Windows NT resolves the names.

For m-node, the order of resolution is the following:

1. NetBIOS Name Cache

2. Broadcasting a NetBIOS Name Query

3. Checking the LMHOSTS file

4. Asking a NetBIOS Name Server

5. Checking the HOSTS file

6. Consulting the DNS

h-node

The Hybrid Node, as stated, is a combination of the p-node and b-node resolution methods. Unlike m-node, h-node reduces broadcast traffic on your network by first consulting the NBNS before attempting a broadcast.

If you put a WINS address into the TCP/IP configuration, Windows NT automatically uses the h-node. The steps in h-node resolution are as follows:

1. Checking the NetBIOS Name Cache

2. Asking a NetBIOS Name Server

3. Broadcasting a NetBIOS Name Query

4. Checking the LMHOSTS file

5. Checking the HOSTS file

6. Consulting the DNS

Viewing and Setting the Node Type

Because the node type is important to the performance of the system that you are using, you can see the node type you are using and change it if a better method is available.

To check the current node type, you can use the command IP-CONFIG /ALL, which you have seen several times already. In figure 7.4, you can see the output from this command; note that the node type is Hybrid (also note that a WINS server is listed).

Figure 7.4

*Output from the
IPCONFIG /ALL
command.*

You can set your node type manually. By default, you area b-node
system. If you want to become an h-node, simply add the address
of a WINS server into the TCP/IP configuration screen. If you
want to be a different node type, you have to edit the registry. The
entry is under the following subkey:

```
HKEY_LOCAL_MACHINE\SYSTEM\ CurrentControlSet\Services\NetBT\
Parameters
```

The entry is NodeType, which can be set to the following values:

▶ 1 (hex)—b-node

▶ 2 (hex)—p-node

▶ 4 (hex)—M-Mode

▶ 8 (hex)—h-node

On most networks, you automatically set the node type by using
the DHCP server. The DHCP options that you set are 044—
WINS/NBNS Server and 046—WINS/NBT Node Type. This enables an administrator to set the node type for all machines that
use DHCP.

nbtstat

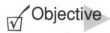 Objective

This chapter has made several references to the nbtstat command, which can be used to work with and diagnose NetBIOS over TCP/IP. This section looks at this command and the functions that you can perform using it. nbtstat is a diagnostic command that displays protocol statistics and current TCP/IP connections using NBT. The syntax is as follows:

```
nbtstat [-a remotename] [-A IP address] [-c] [-n] [-R] [-r] [-S]
[-s] [interval]
```

Although some of the command-line parameters for nbtstat have already been discussed, table 7.3 lists all the available switches.

Table 7.3

Switches for the nbtstat Command	
Switch	Description
-a remotename	Lists the names that another host has registered on the network. Remotename is the computer name of the other host.
-A IP address	Basically the same as the previous command; however, you can specify the IP address rather than the name.
-c	Displays all the names that are in the NetBIOS Name Cache and the IP address to which they map.
-n	Lists all the names that your computer has. If they have been registered, they are marked as such.
-R	Purges and reloads the NetBIOS Name Cache. The cache is reloaded from the LMHOSTS file, if one exists, using the entries marked with #PRE.
-r	Lists all the names that your computer has resolved and the IP address from them. The difference from the -c switch is that preloaded names are not listed.

Switch	Description
-S	Lists all the current sessions that have been established with your computer. This includes both the client and server sessions.
-s	Basically the same as the -S switch; however, the system attempts to resolve the IP addresses to a host name.
Interval	The interval in seconds at which the computer redisplays the information onscreen.

The following an example of the output from the nbtstat command:

```
NetBIOS Connection Table

Local  Name      State     In/Out  Remote Host   Input   Output
---------------------------------------------------------------
TAWNI      <03>  Listening
SCRIM      <03>  Listening
TAWNI      <00>  Connected  Out    198.53.147.2  0B      174B
```

The preceding example does not show all the possible columns, however. The column headings generated by the nbtstat utility listed along with their meanings are as follows:

▶ **Input.** The number of bytes of information that have been received.

▶ **Output.** The number of bytes of information that have been sent.

▶ **In/Out.** The direction in which the connection was made, with OUT to the other computer, or IN from it.

▶ **Life.** The time remaining before the cache entry is purged.

▶ **Local Name.** The local name used for the session.

▶ **Remote Host.** The name on the remote host being used in this session.

▶ **Type.** The type of name that was resolved.

▶ **State.** The state of the connection. Possible states include the following:

> ▶ **Connected.** A NetBIOS session has been established between the two hosts.
>
> ▶ **Associated.** Your system has requested a connection, and has resolved the remote name to an IP address. This is an active open.
>
> ▶ **Listening.** This is a service on your computer that is not being used. This is a passive open.
>
> ▶ **Idle.** The service that opened the port has since paused or hung. No activity is possible until the service resumes.
>
> ▶ **Connecting.** At this point, your system is attempting to create a NetBIOS session. The system is attempting to resolve the name of the remote host to an IP address.
>
> ▶ **Accepting.** A service on your system has been asked to open a session, and is negotiating the session with the remote host.
>
> ▶ **Reconnecting.** After a session has dropped (often due to time-out), your system is trying to reconnect.
>
> ▶ **Outbound.** The TCP three-way handshake is in progress. This establishes the transport layer session that is used to establish the NetBIOS session.
>
> ▶ **Inbound.** Same as outbound; however, this is a connection being made to a service on your system.
>
> ▶ **Disconnecting.** The remote system has requested a session be terminated, so the session is being shut down.
>
> ▶ **Disconnected.** Your system is requesting a session be terminated.

Exercises

Exercise 7.1:   Configuring an LMHOSTS file

This exercise takes you through the configuration of an LM-HOSTS file for a sample network. You then build the LMHOSTS file and verify that the preloaded entries are working.

1. Consider the diagram in figure 7.5.

Figure 7.5

The example network for the LMHOSTS exercise.

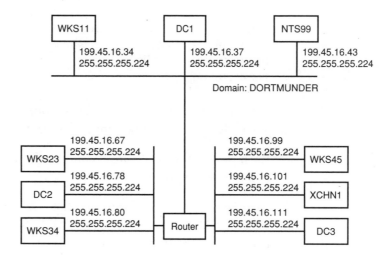

2. If all that is required is the capability to validate logon requests, which systems need to be configured with an LM-HOSTS file?

   None; there is a Domain Controller on each subnet.

3. For WKS23, what entries are required in the LMHOSTS file to enable DC1 or DC3 to validate the logon if DC2 is down?

   The following entries:

   ```
   199.45.16.37      DC1    #DOM:DORTMUNDER
   199.45.16.111     DC3    #DOM:DORTMUNDER
   ```

4. If all systems are required to work with NTS99 and XCHN1, what would be required in the LMHOSTS file? Which systems would need this file?

continues

The address of each server with its name would be required. All systems that are not on the same subnet should have these entries added.

5. To provide WKS11 with all the addresses it requires, what should be in its LMHOSTS file?

   ```
   The LMHOSTS would look like this:
   199.45.16.37     DC1    #DOM:DORTMUNDER
   199.45.16.78     DC2    #DOM:DORTMUNDER
   199.45.16.111    DC3    #DOM:DORTMUNDER
   199.45.16.43     NTS99
   199.45.16.101    XCHN1
   ```

6. If the workstations also provided services to the network, what additions would be required in the LMHOSTS file?

   Each workstation's IP address and computer name would need to be added.

7. Assume each domain controller (DC) keeps a central copy of the LMHOSTS file. Write the LMHOSTS file that should now be on WKS45.

   The file should look like the following.

   ```
   199.45.16.37     DC1    #PRE    #DOM:DORTMUNDER
   199.45.16.78     DC2    #PRE    #DOM:DORTMUNDER
   199.45.16.111    DC3    #PRE    #DOM:DORTMUNDER
   #INCLUDE   \\DC1\public\LMHOSTS
   #BEGIN ALTERNATE
   #INCLUDE   \\DC2\public\LMHOSTS
   #INCLUDE   \\DC3\public\LMHOSTS
   #END ALTERNATE
   ```

8. In the answers for questions 5 and 7, what lines are redundant?

   Any line that includes a host that exists on the local subnet is redundant.

9. Using Notepad (or Edit), create the following file:

```
199.45.16.37     DC1    #PRE   #DOM:DORTMUNDER
199.45.16.78     DC2    #PRE   #DOM:DORTMUNDER
199.45.16.111    DC3    #PRE   #DOM:DORTMUNDER
199.45.16.43     NTS99  #PRE
199.45.16.101    XCHN1  #PRE
```

10. Save the file as %winroot%\SYSTEM32\Drivers\ETC\ LMHOSTS.

    (If one already exists, back it up first so you can return to your original settings.)

11. From a Command Prompt, enter the command nbtstat -c and note the names that are listed.

12. Enter the command nbtstat -R and then repeat step 11.

    The names should change.

13. Attempt to PING DC1. What happens?

    There should be a delay and then the name and address appear. The request should time out, or the host will be unreachable.

Exercise 7.2: Setting Node Types

In this exercise, you set your node type both by modifying the TCP/IP configuration and by editing the registry. (This exercise requires that you have a permanent address.)

1. Open the TCP/IP configuration dialog box (right-click Network Neighborhood, choose Properties. On the Protocols tab, double-click TCP/IP).

2. Select the WINS tab and clear the WINS entry.

3. Choose OK to close the TCP/IP Configuration dialog box and then Close to exit the Network Settings dialog box.

4. Restart your computer.

continues

5. Start a DOS prompt and enter the command IPCONFIG / ALL. You should be set for Broadcast node.

6. Return to the WINS tab (see steps 1 and 2) and enter the IP address of your WINS server (any address will do).

7. Close the TCP/IP and Network configuration dialog boxes and restart your computer.

8. Start a DOS prompt and enter the command IPCONFIG / ALL. You NetBIOS node type should change.

9. Start the Registry Editor (Start, Run REGEDT32, OK).

10. Under HKEY_LOCAL_MACHINE, open the following keys and subkeys: SYSTEM, CurrentControlSet, Services, NetBT, Parameters.

11. NodeType is not listed in this key. Choose Edit, Add Value.

12. Enter NodeType as the name for the value and choose REG_DWORD as the type. Choose OK.

13. Enter 4 as the value. (Hex should be selected.)

14. From a command prompt, type IPCONFIG /ALL. Your node type should be Mixed.

15. Edit the value in the registry, changing NodeType to 0x2.

16. From a command prompt, type IPCONFIG /ALL. Your node type should be "Peer-Peer."

17. Delete the value and reset the network settings to their initial state, and then restart your computer.

Review Questions

1. Which of the following utilities will use NetBIOS name resolution?

   A. FTP

   B. NT Explorer

   C. Internet Explorer

   D. net.exe

2. What settings are available for the size of the NetBIOS Name Cache?

   A. Big

   B. Large

   C. Small

   D. Tiny

3. On a network with one segment, what benefit can be gained by using WINS?

   A. WINS can aid in the resolution of HOST names.

   B. WINS will facilitate Inter-Domain browsing.

   C. WINS will reduce network traffic.

   D. All of the above.

4. What command can you use to verify which sessions exist over NBT?

   A. net sessions

   B. nbtstat

   C. netstat -nbt

   D. netstat

5. In using the #INCLUDE statement, what is required for the server that contains the central LMHOSTS file?

   A. The server is listed in the LMHOSTS file with a #DOM tag.

   B. The server is listed in the LMHOSTS file with a #PRE tag.

   C. The server is listed in the LMHOSTS file.

   D. The server is on the local subnet.

6. Which port does a logon validation use?

   A. 136

   B. 137

   C. 138

   D. 139

7. Which layers in the OSI network model equate to the application layer in the TPC/IP network model?

   A. Application, presentation, and session

   B. Application and presentation

   C. Application only

   D. None of the above

8. What is the purpose of an NCB?

   A. Used for compatibility with NetWare

   B. Contains the request that is being sent to the remote system

   C. Controls where the SMB is sent

   D. An NCB is a Novell data structure

9. What port is used to transfer a file to a remote host?

   A. 136

   B. 137

   C. 138

   D. 139

10. At what point in broadcast node resolution is the LMHOSTS file checked?

    A. Second

    B. Third

    C. Fourth

    D. Fifth

11. What are the three basic names that are registered on a computer?

    A. Computername[0x00], Computername[0x03], Computername[0x1D]

    B. Computername[0x03], Computername[0x20], Computername[0x1D]

    C. Computername[0x00], Computername[0x20], Computername[0x1D]

    D. Computername[0x00], Computername[0x03], Computername[0x20]

12. Which name must be unique for every system on the network?

    A. The computer name

    B. The user name

    C. The workgroup name

    D. The domain name

13. When the messenger service registers a name, what is the value that identifies it with the messenger service?

    A. [0x00]

    B. [0x03]

    C. [0x20]

    D. [0x1D]

14. What two methods can be used to register a name on the network?

    A. Broadcast and the LMHOSTS file

    B. The LMHOSTS file and the HOSTS file

    C. Broadcast and an NBNS server

    D. The name is registered on the network when the computer is installed

15. If your organization uses WINS, how many hosts need to be configured with an LMHOSTS file?

    A. The WINS server only

    B. Domain controllers only

    C. All non-WINS capable workstations

    D. None

16. What are the three main functions of Name Management?

    A. Name resolution, renewal, and release

    B. Name queries, release, and renewal

    C. Name registration, renewal, and release

    D. Name registration, query, and release

17. Why are ports 137 and 138 normally configured not to pass broadcasts on most routers?

    A. For security purposes

    B. To prevent NetBIOS name conflicts

C. To prevent router congestion

D. These ports are not configured this way

18. By default, how long does a NetBIOS name remain in the Name Cache?

A. 2 minutes

B. 5 minutes

C. 10 minutes

D. 1 day

19. Can you change the size of the NetBIOS Name Cache?

A. Yes

B. No

C. Only by reinstalling NT

20. How many names can you register on a single Windows NT computer?

A. 16

B. 64

C. 128

D. 250

Review Answers

1. B, D

2. B, C

3. D

4. B

5. B

6. C

7. A

8. C

9. D

10. B

11. D

12. A

13. B

14. C

15. D

16. D

17. C

18. C

19. A

20. D

Answers to the Test Yourself Questions at the Beginning of the Chapter

1. NetBIOS communications are facilitated over TCP/IP using three ports: 137 (UDP) NetBIOS Name Service port, 138 (UDP) NetBIOS Datagram port, and 139 (TCP) NetBIOS Session Service Port.

2. Two node types use the NetBIOS Name Server as their main source of resolution: Peer-to-Peer node and Hybrid node.

3. For all methods of NetBIOS name resolution, the NetBIOS Name Cache is checked first.

4. The three main functions of NetBIOS are as follows:

   ▶ **Name Management.** Provides the capability to register and resolve names on the network, which provides a means of locating the target computer

   ▶ **Session Management.** Provides a method of communicating with a remote host, and provides security via user validation and error correction in large file transfers

   ▶ **Data Transfer.** Provides the capability to transfer data either using a session that already exists or, in the case of broadcasts, without a session

5. A Server Message Block (SMB) is a Protocol Data Unit; that is, the package that takes the request from the redirector to the server and back again. SMBs are usable only by the application layer in the OSI model, and are the data being transferred to all other layers.

6. In a Hybrid node environment, the order of resolution is as follows:

   NetBIOS Name Cache

   NetBIOS Name Server

   Local broadcast

   LMHOSTS file

   HOSTS file

   DNS server

7. The 16th character of the NetBIOS name identifies the service that is registering the name. For example, a registered name of NTS45[0x20] indicates Server service on a system with the computer name NTS45.

8. The #BEGIN ALTERNATE and #END ALTERNATE tags in the LMHOSTS file enclose a series of alternate locations for a centralized LMHOSTS file. A series of lines start with the #INCLUDE tag.

9. The #DOM tag identifies a domain controller. This tag facilitates the logon validation across a router when there is no local domain controller or the local domain controller is not available.

10. A client workstation can be configured manually by entering the address of a WINS server on the WINS tabs of the TCP/IP configuration dialog box, or it can be configured automatically from a DHCP server using the 044 NBNS server address and 046 NBNS node type options.

C h a p t e r 8

Implementing Windows Internet Name Service

This chapter will help you prepare for the exam by covering the basics of WINS. This information is required to understand the next chapter.

Test Yourself! Before reading this chapter, test yourself to determine how much study time you will need to devote to this section.

1. What does a WINS server do?

2. How does the WINS server add entries to its database?

3. Where does a WINS client send its registration request?

4. What kind of platforms can be WINS clients?

5. How can non-WINS clients register their addresses with a WINS server?

6. How can non-WINS clients resolve addresses using the WINS server?

7. How many WINS servers should you install on a network?

8. How many names does a WINS client register with the WINS server?

9. What are the benefits of using a WINS server?

Answers are located at the end of the chapter.

The Windows Internet Name Service

The Windows Internet Name Service (WINS) provides name registration, renewal, release, and resolution services for NetBIOS names and IP addresses. It is implemented as an extension of RFCs 1001 and 1002.

A WINS server maintains a dynamic database linking NetBIOS names to IP addresses. The database is dynamic because each name registration has a *time to live* value—after its time to live has expired, the record is discarded from the database. The WINS server receives registration, renewal, and release requests from WINS clients, and updates its database based on this information. Name resolution queries from WINS clients are resolved using this database.

Using the WINS server for name registration, renewal, release, and resolution services provides a marked improvement over using broadcast messages or static mappings for these services. In the case of broadcast messages, rather than each computer sending a broadcast to all clients on its subnet for every name registration, each computer sends a unicast message to the WINS server. The same applies for name queries: rather than sending a broadcast message to all clients on its subnet, a WINS client sends a unicast message directly to the WINS server. For networks using static mappings, such as an LMHOSTS file, each computer has a fixed list of NetBIOS names and IP addresses, which can become difficult to manage—and impossible to manage when using dynamic IP address assignments, such as environments using DHCP (Dynamic Host Control Protocol). See Chapter 6 for more information on DHCP.

Note

A broadcast message is a TCP/IP packet sent from one computer to every other computer on a subnet. A unicast message is a TCP/IP packet sent from one computer directly to another computer.

The following section looks at how WINS works, and details the services that a WINS server provides to WINS clients.

How WINS Works

A WINS server provides name registration, renewal, release, and resolution services to client computers configured to use WINS. Just how these services are provided is an interesting combination of client and server processes. The four fundamental services provided by WINS are detailed in the following sections.

Name Registration

Name registration is the process by which the WINS server obtains information from WINS clients. Name registration occurs when a WINS client computer starts. The name registration process enables the WINS database to be maintained dynamically, rather than statically.

When a WINS client starts up, it sends a name registration to its configured WINS server. This registration provides the computer name and IP address of the WINS client to the WINS server. If the WINS server is running, and no other client has the same name registered, the server returns a successful registration message to the client. This message contains the name registration's time to live.

Each computer must have a unique name within the network. Without unique names, network communication would be next to impossible. After WINS clients send name registration requests to the WINS server, the server ensures that the name registration is unique—no other computer may have the same name. The following section looks at how the WINS server handles an attempt to register an existing name.

Note

At name registration, the WINS server detects a client's attempt to register a duplicate name—that is, a NetBIOS name already in use. If the name is already in use, the following occurs:

1. The server challenges the computer already holding the name registration to ensure that it is still active. If the

computer does not answer the challenge, the registration proceeds.

2. If the original host answers the challenge, the request receives a negative acknowledgment, and an error is registered in the System Event Log. The computer attempting to claim an existing name cannot communicate using NetBIOS on that adapter.

Name Renewal

Once a WINS client's name is registered, it is assigned a time to live, after which the name is removed from the WINS server's database. If there were no mechanism to renew leases, this would be an inefficient system, because at the end of each registration's time to live, the client computer would have to go through the entire registration process again. To avoid this, WINS clients can request a renewal to their name registration record.

This process is straightforward and similar to the initial name registration process. After one-eighth of the time to live value has passed, the client attempts to renew its name registration. If no response is received, the WINS client retries its renewal every two minutes, until half of its time to live has passed. The WINS client then tries to renew its lease with the secondary WINS server, as with the primary WINS server—the timer is reset to zero, and after one-eighth of its time to live value has passed, until it succeeds or half of its time to live has passed. If it is unsuccessful after half of its time to live has passed, it reverts to its primary WINS server.

After a name renewal succeeds at any point in the process— whichever WINS server accepts the renewal—the WINS client is provided with a new TTL value for its name registration.

Name renewal is a feature provided to the WINS client by the WINS server. The server does not provide this service to computers that are not WINS clients.

Name Release

WINS clients send a name release request to the WINS server during an orderly shutdown. This release message is a request to remove the IP address and NetBIOS name from the WINS server database. For computers that use broadcast name resolution, it sends a broadcast message indicating the name release to all computers on its subnet.

Upon receipt of the release request, the WINS server verifies that it has the IP address and NetBIOS name in its database. If an error occurs, the server sends a negative response to the WINS client. The following circumstances are possible errors that would cause the WINS server to send a negative response:

- ▶ If another client has a different IP address mapped to the same NetBIOS name

- ▶ If the WINS database is corrupted

- ▶ If the IP address or NetBIOS name specified does not exist within the WINS server's database

Note

If a computer is not shut down correctly, the WINS server does not know that the name has been released, and the name is not released until the WINS name registration record expires.

Name Resolution

WINS clients send name resolution requests to the WINS server. A name resolution request typically occurs when the client computer tries to map a network drive. To connect to a network drive, the user needs to specify two things: a system name and a share name. The system name provided needs to be resolved to an IP address. The basic flow of a name resolution request is as follows:

1. When a client computer wants to resolve a name, it first checks its local NetBIOS name cache. (You can view the cache using the nbtstat command, which is covered in detail in Chapter 7.)

2. If the name is not in the local cache, a name query is sent to the primary WINS server. If the primary WINS server is unavailable, the request is re-sent twice before going to the secondary WINS server. If either WINS server resolves the name, a success message is sent to the client, containing the requested NetBIOS name and IP address.

3. If neither the primary nor secondary WINS server is available, or if neither server can resolve the query, a negative response is sent to the client. The WINS client then attempts to resolve the name using either an LMHOSTS file, a broadcast request, or DNS. Note that WINS clients can be configured to use many name resolution strategies.

 Note

WINS clients can be configured to use various methods of name resolution. These are referred to as b-node, h-node, m-node and p-node. Each method differs slightly.

These name resolution strategies are shown in the following list:

▶ **b-node name resolution** does not use WINS. It relies entirely on broadcast packets for name registration and resolution. This is the type of name resolution used in environments that do not have a WINS server, and can result in a large quantity of broadcast traffic.

▶ **p-node name resolution** uses WINS exclusively. The client does not fall back on broadcast messages when the WINS server cannot resolve the query or is unavailable.

▶ **m-node name resolution** is a combination of b-node and p-node. The client first uses b-node to attempt to resolve a query, and if the query is unsuccessful, the client resorts to p-node. The client computer can use WINS, but primarily uses broadcast messages.

▶ **h-node name resolution** also combines b-node and p-node strategies. Unlike m-node, the client uses p-node first and uses b-node as a last resort. This is the most efficient implementation because it reduces the reliance on broadcast messages, and still provides WINS clients with a backup method of name resolution if the WINS server is unavailable or cannot resolve the query.

 Note

WINS clients can be configured to use either method. Details on how to configure WINS clients are discussed in the "WINS Client Configuration" section of this chapter.

Implementation Considerations

Prior to implementing WINS, you need to examine a number of issues. These issues will largely determine the best implementation for your environment. Due to the scaleable nature of Windows NT networks, your environment could range from a network with one server and three workstations to a worldwide WAN with hundreds of servers and thousands of clients. The following sections examine these issues in more detail.

WINS Server Considerations

WINS servers are the most critical element of a WINS deployment. Determining how many WINS servers you need, where to place them, and how to configure them are important aspects of pre-deployment planning.

At an absolute minimum, you need one WINS server. Two WINS servers provide some degree of fault tolerance if the primary WINS server fails.

WINS servers don't have a built-in limit of the number of clients that can be served. A basic rule of thumb is that one WINS server can handle up to 1,500 name registrations per minute, and about 4,500 name queries per minute. As a good estimate, you would need to implement one primary and one secondary WINS server per 10,000 clients.

The WINS server must be running Windows NT Server; the WINS server cannot be installed on a Windows NT workstation. If the WINS server were a multiple processor system, this would increase performance considerably since the WINS server is a multi-threaded application, and can then run one thread on each processor.

One interesting component of the WINS server is that it supports database logging. *Database logging* is a fault-tolerance feature that maintains a log file in addition to the database. The log contains recent transaction information. If this feature is enabled, the database can be "rolled back" to a known state. However, this also decreases performance because all name registrations are processed twice. The tradeoff is fault tolerance: if logging is disabled, the most recent updates to the WINS database can be lost if the WINS server software crashes.

Finally, if your network spans multiple subnets, client computers can be configured to use WINS servers on the local subnet or on a different subnet. Clearly, this slows performance, and increases traffic through routers. Also, if WINS servers are located on a different subnet than the WINS client computers, the availability of the routers becomes paramount—if they are no longer available, neither arc the WINS services.

Integrating WINS with DHCP

If your network is using DHCP to assign client IP addresses, integrating WINS is quite simple. Within your DHCP scope definitions, you can specify a number of WINS-related configuration parameters for client computers. DHCP client computers can be automatically configured to be WINS clients also. The following WINS-related configuration parameters can be specified within a DHCP scope:

▶ Primary WINS server IP address

▶ Secondary WINS server IP address

▶ Name resolution type (b-node, h-node, m-node, or p-node)

WINS Proxies

WINS servers provide name registration, renewal, release, and resolution services only to WINS clients. In environments with client systems that cannot use WINS, such as UNIX systems, there is a way to configure your network so that the WINS server can provide a subset of these services to non-WINS clients via a WINS proxy. The services that a WINS proxy provides are as follows:

> ▶ **Name registration.** A WINS proxy listens for name registration broadcasts from non-WINS clients and forwards the registration to the WINS server. Note that the name is not registered; it is only checked to ensure that no WINS client has the same name registered.

> ▶ **Name resolution.** WINS proxies also forward name resolution broadcasts to the WINS server for resolution. The WINS server processes the query and sends the information to the WINS proxy, which then forwards the query result to the non-WINS client.

> ▶ **Name renewal and release.** Because the non-WINS client does not have a database entry in the WINS server database, the server does not provide name renewal and release services to non-WINS clients.

Implementing a WINS proxy is straightforward: all you needs to do is modify one registry value on the computer that is to become the WINS proxy. WINS proxies *cannot be WINS servers*, and must be WINS clients. Also, no more than two WINS proxies can reside on one subnet. If your environment requires a WINS proxy, the installation procedure is shown below:

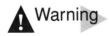 **Warning**

As with any other operations using the Registry Editor, please be careful. Making a recovery disk before using the Registry Editor is a good idea.

Note

To configure a client as a WINS proxy, start the Registry Editor, and change the `HKEY_LOCAL_MACHINE\System\CurrentControlSet\Services\NetBT\Parameters\EnableProxy` parameter to 1 (REG_DWORD value type).

WINS Client Considerations

Each WINS client must be configured to communicate with at least a primary WINS server. WINS client computers can be configured with both a primary and a secondary WINS server. This provides a certain degree of fault tolerance. If the primary WINS server is unavailable, the secondary WINS server can provide the same services.

Implementing WINS

The following two sections provide an overview of the implementation of a WINS server and a WINS client under Windows NT.

Implementing a WINS Server

To install a WINS server on a Windows NT server, simply select the Windows Internet Name Service from the Control Panel/Networks/Services screen, as shown in figure 8.1.

Figure 8.1

Installing a WINS server.

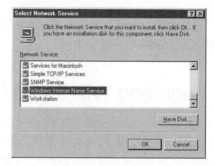

No other configuration information is required. The installation copies the required files for the WINS server, and also copies the WINS Administration utility. The WINS server is installed as a service, and starts after your server is restarted. Because WINS is installed as a service, it can be stopped and started from Control Panel/Services or from the command line using **NET START/ STOP/PAUSE/CONTINUE WINS**.

Configuring WINS Clients

WINS client configuration is equally straightforward. After the TCP/IP protocol has been installed on a client computer, such as a Windows NT computer, all you need to do is supply the address of the primary (and, if desired, secondary) WINS server by selecting Control Panel/Network, and then selecting the TCP/IP protocol's WINS Address tab (see fig. 8.2).

Figure 8.2

WINS client configuration.

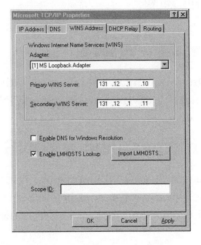

That's all! Next to no information is required to configure a WINS client.

Integrating WINS with DHCP

As would be expected, WINS and DHCP share a high level of integration. By definition, any DHCP client can have a different IP address at any time; this poses no problem for WINS, because both packages are tightly bound.

Within DHCP scope, global, or default settings, several WINS-related parameters can be specified. All of these parameters can be specified within the DHCP Manager; see Chapter 6 for more details. These parameters include the following:

- ▶ **044 WINS/NBNS Servers.** A list of the IP addresses of primary/secondary WINS servers for the DHCP client computers.

- ▶ **046 WINS/NBT Node Type.** Specifies the name resolution node for DHCP clients (see note earlier in this chapter regarding b-node, h-node, m-node, and p-node name resolution).

Note

If a WINS record is marked as released, and a name registration request arrives for the same host name, but with a different IP address, the WINS server registers the new request.

Review Questions

The following questions will test your knowledge of the information in this chapter.

1. What is the role of a WINS proxy?

   A. A WINS proxy is a secondary WINS server.

   B. A WINS proxy is any WINS server configured to provide name registration, renewal, release, and resolution services to non-WINS clients.

   C. A WINS proxy is any WINS client configured to provide name resolution services to non-WINS clients.

   D. A WINS proxy is a WINS server located on a different subnet than a WINS client.

2. Your network has client computers that are not WINS clients, and you have added a WINS proxy. Which services are not provided by the WINS proxy?

   A. Name registration

   B. Name resolution

   C. Name renewal

   D. Name release

3. Your Windows NT network has both a primary and a secondary WINS server. Which statement is accurate?

   A. If the primary WINS server is unavailable, the secondary WINS server can provide the same services to WINS clients.

   B. If the primary WINS server is unavailable, a WINS proxy agent is used to provide name services.

C. If the primary WINS server is unavailable, and the secondary WINS server is also unavailable, a workstation automatically becomes a WINS proxy and provides name services.

D. None of the above.

4. When does name renewal occur?

A. Name renewal occurs when a WINS client is shut down in an orderly fashion.

B. Name renewal occurs when the name registration's time to live expires.

C. Name renewal occurs automatically before the name registration's time to live expires.

D. Name renewal occurs only when initiated by a WINS proxy.

5. When does name registration occur?

A. Name registration occurs whenever a WINS client sends a request to a WINS server to obtain the IP address of a NetBIOS host.

B. Name registration occurs when a non-WINS client starts and sends a broadcast to a WINS proxy.

C. Name registration occurs when a WINS client starts and sends a name registration request to a WINS server.

D. Name registration occurs when a WINS client sends a name registration request to a WINS server, and then the WINS server sends a negative acknowledgment because the name is already registered.

6. Given a WINS client configured to use a primary and a secondary WINS server, if both servers are available, which statement is incorrect?

   A. The WINS client can perform name registration, renewal, release, and resolution operations.

   B. The WINS client cannot obtain the IP address associated with a given NetBIOS name.

   C. The WINS client can act as a WINS proxy.

   D. The WINS client is unable to resolve IP addresses associated with a given NetBIOS name unless broadcast name resolution is used.

7. Which features are not provided directly or indirectly by a WINS server?

   A. Name resolution for WINS clients

   B. Name release for non-WINS clients

   C. Name registration for WINS clients

   D. Name registration for non-WINS clients

   E. Name resolution for non-WINS clients

8. Your network presently has 100 client computers and 4 servers. Name resolution is handled by broadcast. By implementing a primary and a secondary WINS server to your network, and configuring all client computers to use WINS for name resolution, which of the following will not occur?

   A. Broadcast traffic will decrease.

   B. Broadcast traffic will increase.

   C. Non-WINS clients will be able to register their computer names on the WINS server.

   D. Non-WINS clients will be able to resolve name queries from both the primary and secondary WINS servers.

9. Your network has 50 client computers using WINS, and 2 servers acting as primary and secondary WINS servers. You want to add a WINS proxy to your network to provide name services to non-WINS clients. Which of the following statements would satisfy this requirement?

   A. Do nothing; non-WINS clients can use WINS servers directly.

   B. Configure the primary WINS server as a WINS proxy.

   C. Configure the secondary WINS server as a WINS proxy.

   D. Configure one of the WINS client computers as a WINS proxy.

10. Your network has 20 client computers configured as WINS clients using p-node name resolution. If the primary and secondary WINS servers are not available but a WINS proxy is available, how will names be resolved by clients?

    A. Clients will use broadcast name resolution.

    B. Clients will attempt to resolve names from a WINS proxy.

    C. One of the client computers will be promoted to the primary WINS server.

    D. Clients will be unable to resolve names.

11. Your network has 800 client computers configured as WINS clients using m-node name resolution. The client computers are split onto 4 subnets of 200 computers. Each subnet has a primary WINS server. You want to decrease broadcast traffic and increase reliability. Your solution is to add a secondary WINS server to each subnet and to change the client configuration from m-node to h-node. This solution:

    A. Accomplishes both of the objectives

    B. Accomplishes the first objective but not the second

    C. Accomplishes the second objective but not the first

    D. Accomplishes neither objective

12. In an environment having both a primary and a secondary WINS server, with clients configured accordingly, which of the following would be a consequence of the primary WINS server failing?

   A. Clients would be unable to resolve names from the secondary WINS server.

   B. Clients would be able to resolve names from the secondary WINS server.

   C. Name registrations would not be accepted by the secondary WINS server.

   D. Name registrations would be accepted by the secondary WINS server.

13. Which services are not provided by a WINS server?

   A. Resolving name queries sent from WINS clients

   B. Registering names based on name registration requests from WINS clients

   C. Dynamically assigning IP addresses to client computers

   D. Responding to broadcast name registrations

14. Which of the following is likely to occur when you add a WINS server to a network without one, and configure all network clients to use WINS?

   A. Broadcast traffic increases.

   B. Broadcast traffic decreases.

   C. Client computers send name requests to the WINS server.

   D. Client computers continue to send name requests using broadcast messages, but send name registration requests to the WINS server.

15. What is the role of the time-to-live value given to a WINS client after a successful name registration?

   A. The time to live indicates how long the name registration will be valid.

   B. The time to live indicates how long of an interval will pass before the client attempts to renew its name registration.

   C. The time to live indicates when the WINS client will attempt its first name renewal.

   D. The time to live indicates when the WINS server will attempt to renew the client name registration.

16. Which tasks do WINS proxies perform?

   A. WINS proxies act as secondary WINS servers.

   B. WINS proxies handle name renewal requests.

   C. WINS proxies handle name registration requests from non-WINS clients by ensuring the name is not registered in the WINS server.

   D. WINS proxies can forward non-WINS client name resolution requests to a WINS server.

17. What is the purpose of name renewal?

   A. Name renewal ensures no duplicate names exist on the network.

   B. Name renewal resolves NetBIOS names to IP addresses by WINS proxies.

   C. Name renewal reduces traffic generated on the network by allowing WINS clients to renew their name registrations rather than performing a full name registration.

   D. Name renewal removes the name registration from the WINS server's database when the WINS client shuts down.

18. Under what circumstances does name release occur?

   A. When a client sends a name registration for a name that is already registered

   B. When a client sends a name query, which cannot be resolved by the primary or secondary WINS server

   C. When a client computer shuts down

   D. Whenever a client computer sends a name renewal request that is not acknowledged

19. What is the purpose of a secondary WINS server?

   A. A secondary WINS server splits the database of name registrations between two WINS servers.

   B. A secondary WINS server handles only name release requests and name renewal requests; the primary WINS server handles only name registrations.

   C. A secondary WINS server acts as a backup in case the primary WINS server is unavailable for name queries and resolution.

   D. None of the above.

20. When a WINS client issues a request to access a network resource and needs to resolve a NetBIOS name to an IP address, which is the first step in the name resolution process?

   A. The WINS client issues a request directly to the primary WINS server.

   B. The WINS client first checks its local NetBIOS cache.

   C. The WINS client sends a broadcast message to all computers on the subnet.

   D. The WINS client sends its request directly to the secondary WINS server.

Review Answers

1. C

2. A, B, C, D

3. A

4. C

5. C

6. D

7. B, D

8. B, C, D

9. D

10. D

11. A

12. B, D

13. C, D

14. B, C

15. A

16. C, D

17. C

18. C

19. C

20. B

Answers to Test Yourself Questions at Beginning of Chapter

1. A WINS server automatically builds a database to resolve TCP/IP addresses. This database has entries that map TCP/IP addresses to NetBIOS computer names. WINS clients send name registrations to the WINS server. When validated, these registrations are added to the database. WINS clients also query WINS servers to resolve NetBIOS names to TCP/IP addresses. The WINS server uses its database to answer these queries.

2. Each time a WINS client boots, it registers its name with the WINS server. The WINS server verifies that the registration is unique, then sends a successful response to the client. If the mapping already exists, the WINS server queries the host of the original registration to see if the host is still active. If the host is still active, the WINS server sends a negative response to the WINS client requesting registration. If the WINS server doesn't receive a positive response from the existing host, then the WINS client is allowed to register and the WINS server sends the client a successful response.

3. A WINS client can register its NetBIOS name only with the WINS server specified in its TCP/IP settings. A WINS client can have two WINS server addresses, one for a primary WINS server and one for a secondary WINS server. However, only an address for a primary WINS server is required. The client first tries to register its name with its primary WINS server. If the client does not receive a response from the WINS server, it tries again until it has failed to register three times with the primary server. Then, if the WINS client has a secondary WINS server address configured, it also tries three times to register its name with the secondary WINS server. If successful, the client stops. If not, the client sends a broadcast in an attempt to register its name.

4. Basically, any Microsoft client capable of networking with TCP/IP can be a WINS client.

5. Non-WINS clients cannot register their names directly with a WINS server. However, you can manually add static entries to the WINS server for non-WINS clients. You can also import mappings from an LMHOSTS file. These imported mappings also become static entries. After you add static entries for all non-WINS clients, WINS clients should be able to resolve the name of any NetBIOS-based computer on the network.

6. A WINS proxy agent, configured on any Windows-based WINS client, can forward a request from a non-WINS client to the WINS server. Non-WINS clients usually request a name resolution through a broadcast. If a proxy agent is located on the same network segment as the non-WINS client, the proxy agent can hear the broadcast and forward it to the WINS server. The WINS server can be on a remote segment because the proxy agent sends the request directly to the TCP/IP address of the WINS server. The WINS server sends a response to the WINS proxy agent, which then sends a response to the non-WINS client that made the original request.

7. You should have at least two WINS servers. If one server goes down, clients can use the second server to continue to resolve addresses. If you have only one WINS server and that server goes down, WINS clients lose their capability to quickly resolve IP addresses. They may have to resort to broadcasts to resolve addresses, but because most b-node broadcasts are not forwarded, the clients have little chance of resolving addresses beyond their own network segment. As your network grows, you may need to add more WINS servers. Microsoft recommends that you have two WINS servers (one primary and one backup) for every 10,000 WINS clients.

8. A client registers a name for each service that has a networking component. For example, a client registers its own name, a name for the server service, a name for the workstation service, and a name for the messenger service. If additional networking services are installed, they are also registered. A domain controller also registers the name of its domain so domain controllers can be located for logon requests and for network browsing.

9. Because the WINS server builds its database automatically, the administrative burden of maintaining static mappings in an LMHOSTS file is greatly reduced. Also, you eliminate the chance of introducing errors in the LMHOSTS file because the WINS database is built dynamically with the exact TCP/IP addresses and NetBIOS names coming directly from the registering computer. Because WINS clients send their registration requests and address resolution requests directly to the WINS server, broadcast traffic is greatly reduced. Finally, because clients send registrations and queries directly to the server, you do not need to locate a WINS server on each network segment; directed packets can be routed directly to the WINS server.

Chapter

9

Administering a WINS Environment

This chapter will help you prepare for the exam by covering the following objectives:

 Objectives

▶ Install and configure a WINS server

▶ Import LMHOSTS files to WINS

▶ Run WINS on a multihomed computer

▶ Configure WINS replication

▶ Configure static mappings in the WINS database

Test Yourself! Before reading this chapter, test yourself to determine how much study time you will need to devote to this section.

1. How often must WINS clients renew their name registrations with the WINS server?

2. How are entries removed from the WINS database?

3. How can a WINS client resolve addresses that are located in another WINS server's database?

4. How do you configure a WINS server to receive entries from another WINS server's database?

5. How do you configure two WINS servers so they have identical databases?

6. How can you back up a WINS server database?

7. How can you restore a WINS server database? Does this ever happen automatically?

8. On what platform can you install WINS, and how do you install it?

9. When does push replication occur and when does pull replication occur?

10. How is a WINS client configured to use a WINS server?

Answers are located at the end of the chapter.

Installing a WINS Server

Objective

For an exercise covering this information, see end of chapter.

WINS must be installed on a Windows NT Server version 3.5x or 4.0. WINS servers on any version are compatible with the others; that is, you can mix an NT 3.51 WINS Server with an NT 4.0 WINS Server, including using them as replication partners. You can install WINS on any configuration of NT server—a member server, a Backup Domain Controller, or a Primary Domain Controller. The WINS server should have a static TCP/IP address with a subnet mask and default gateway along with any other TCP/IP parameters required for your network (such as a DNS server address). You can assign a DHCP address to the WINS server (the address should be reserved so the WINS server always receives the same address), but using a static address is the recommended option. Also, you should specify a WINS server address; in this case, the address would be the same machine. The exercises show you how to install a WINS server.

Note

Normally the WINS service should not be run on a computer that is multihomed (has two or more network cards). This is because the WINS server always registers its names in the local database. This is a problem if you will run DOS clients as they will always try the first address that they receive from the WINS server. Since the WINS server will register all of its card in order, the DOS client might not be able to reach resources on the WINS server from network other than the one on which the first card is located.

The WINS service is installed as a network service. After it is installed, it is immediately available for use. However, until WINS clients are configured with the TCP/IP address of the WINS server, they cannot register their names nor use the WINS server for name resolution. In fact, if there weren't any clients configured with this WINS server's address, the WINS database would remain empty unless you add static entries or set up replication with another WINS server.

WINS Clients

Any Microsoft client capable of networking can be a WINS client:

▶ Windows NT Server 3.5x, 4.0

▶ Windows NT Workstation 3.5x, 4.0

▶ Windows 95

▶ Windows for Workgroups with TCP/IP-32

▶ Microsoft Network Client 3.0 for MS-DOS

▶ LAN Manager 2.2c for MS-DOS

However, only the Windows-based clients can register their names with the WINS server. The DOS-based clients can use the WINS server for name resolution, but you must add static entries for DOS clients to the WINS server so their names can be resolved.

For an exercise covering this information, see end of chapter.

To enable these clients for WINS, the address of the primary WINS server must be specified on the client. The client can also have the address of a secondary WINS server configured. The client can either have this configuration information manually entered at the client or it can receive the configuration information with its TCP/IP address from a DHCP server. Exercises 11 and 12 at the end of the chapter show how to configure WINS clients manually and through a DHCP server.

Configuring WINS to be Used by Non-WINS Clients

A WINS server interacts in two ways with WINS clients. First, it registers the names of those clients. Second, it answers requests for name resolutions (name queries). You can enable both functions for non-WINS clients through additional configuration.

Registering Non-WINS Clients with Static Entries

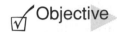

Objective

For an exercise covering this information, see end of chapter.

You can register a non-WINS client with a WINS server by adding a static entry to the WINS database. With entries added for non-WINS clients, a WINS client can resolve more names without resorting to looking up the entries in an LMHOSTS file. In fact, by adding entries for all non-WINS clients, you can eliminate the need for an LMHOSTS file. Static entries are added through the WINS Manager, as described in exercise 9.4 at the end of the chapter.

There are several types of static mappings. Table 9.1 summarizes the types you can add.

Table 9.1

Types of Static Mappings

Type of Mapping	Explanation
Normal Group	Group names don't have an address rather the WINS server returns FFFFFFFF (the broadcast address). This forces the client to broadcasts on the local subnet to resolve the name.
Multihomed	A multihomed name is used to register a computer with more than one network card. It can contain up to 25 addresses.
Domain Name	In Windows NT 3.51, the Domain Name mapping was known as an Internet Group. The domain-name mapping contains up to a maximum of 25 IP addresses for the primary or backup domain controllers in a domain. This enables client computers and servers to locate a domain controller for logon validation and passthru authentication.
Internet Group	An Internet group mapping name is a user-defined mapping used to store addresses for members of a group other than a domain (such as a workgroup).

Adding Entries to WINS from an LMHOSTS File

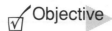

Objective

You also can copy entries from an LMHOSTS file to a WINS server. Any entries copied this way are considered static entries. The exercises show you how to add static entries and how to import entries from an LMHOSTS file.

Resolving Names Through a WINS Server for Non-WINS Clients

For an exercise covering this information, see end of chapter.

You can also allow non-WINS clients to use a WINS server to resolve NetBIOS names by installing a *WINS proxy agent*. By definition, a non-WINS client cannot directly communicate with a WINS server to resolve a name. The non-WINS client resolves names by resorting to a b-node broadcast. If you install a WINS proxy agent, the proxy agent forwards any broadcasts for name resolution onto the WINS server. The proxy agent must be located on the same subnet as non-WINS clients so the proxy agent receives the broadcast for name resolution.

When a non-WINS client broadcasts a name resolution request, a proxy agent that hears the broadcast checks its own NetBIOS name cache to see whether an entry exists for the requested name. If the entry doesn't exist, the proxy agent adds to the cache an entry for that name with the status of pending. The proxy agent then sends a name resolution request for the same name to the WINS server. After the WINS server responds with the name resolution, the proxy agent adds the entry to its cache and then removes the pending status from the entry. The proxy agent does not forward the response to the non-WINS client making the request. When the non-WINS client broadcasts another request for the name resolution, the proxy agent now finds an entry for the name in its cache and the proxy agent can respond to the non-WINS client with a successful name resolution response.

The WINS proxy agent also forwards registration requests to the WINS server. However, registration requests for non-WINS clients are not added to the WINS server's database. The WINS server uses these forwarded registration requests to see whether there are any potential conflicts in its database with the requested name registration. You must still add static entries to the WINS database so names of non-WINS clients can be resolved.

You must place a WINS proxy agent on each subnet where non-WINS clients are located so those clients have access to the WINS server. Because those clients resolve names only by using broadcasts, which are not typically routed, those broadcasts never go beyond the subnet. With a proxy agent on each subnet, broadcasts on each subnet can then be forwarded to the WINS server. You can have two proxy agents on a subnet, but you shouldn't exceed this limit. Even having more than one proxy agent on a subnet can generate excessive work for the WINS server because each proxy agent forwards name resolution and name registration requests to the WINS server. The WINS server has to respond to duplicate messages from proxy agents if more than one proxy agent is on a subnet.

Any Windows-based WINS client can be a WINS proxy agent. To configure an NT server or workstation to be a proxy agent, you must turn on a parameter in the registry. This proxy agent cannot be a WINS server. Windows 95 and Windows for Workgroups computers are more easily configured by turning on a switch in the TCP/IP configuration. Exercise 9.13 at the end of the chapter shows how to configure a Windows NT computer and a Windows 95 computer to be a WINS proxy agent.

 Tip

To make an NT server or workstation into a proxy agent, open

`HKEY_LOCAL_MACHINE\System\CurrentControlSet\Services\NetBT`
`\Parameters`

and change the value of the EnableProxy parameter to 1.

After you configure a WINS client to be a proxy agent, you must reboot the machine for this change to take effect. No other configuration is needed for this proxy agent. This WINS client remains a proxy agent until you turn off the proxy agent parameter and reboot the computer.

Configuring a Client for WINS

To manually configure a WINS client, you specify the WINS server address as part of the TCP/IP configuration. Open the TCP/IP properties in the Protocol tab of the Network Properties dialog (opened with Control Panel, Network). Select the WINS tab in the TCP/IP properties dialog and simply specify the address of a primary WINS server. If you are using a secondary WINS server, you should also type in the IP address of the secondary WINS server.

You can also specify the address of a secondary WINS server. Figure 9.1 shows a client with manually configured WINS addresses.

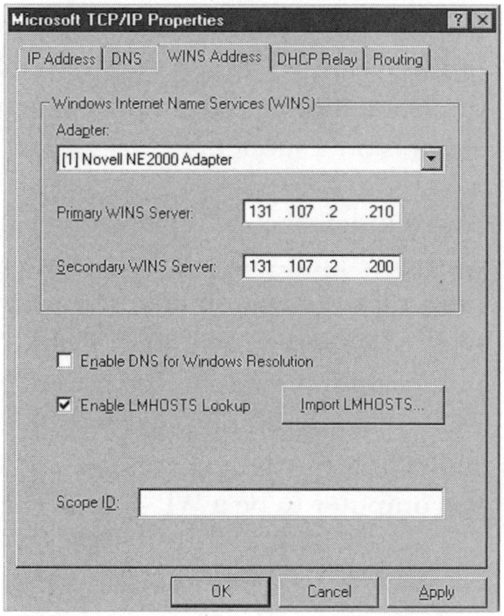

Figure 9.1

Manually configuring a WINS client through TCP/IP properties.

To configure a DHCP client to be a WINS client, you must add two properties to the DHCP scope created on the DHCP server. Installing and configuring DHCP is described in chapter 7. Under the DHCP scope options, add the following parameters:

▶ **044 WINS/NBNS Servers.** Configure this with the address of the primary WINS server and a secondary WINS server, if desired.

▶ **046 WINS/NBT Node.** By default, this is set to 2, a b-node broadcast. WINS clients use h-node broadcasts, so you must change the value of the this parameter to 8. Figure 9.2 shows these options added to a DCHP scope.

Figure 9.2

Configuring a DHCP scope to distribute WINS client configuration with a DHCP address.

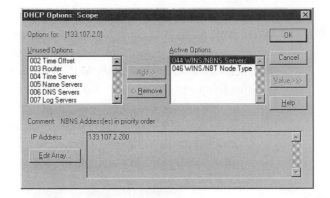

Replication

 Objective

Because WINS clients are configured to communicate only with specified WINS servers, the database on each WINS server may not have entries for all the WINS clients in the network. In fact, many TCP/IP implementations divide WINS clients among different WINS servers to balance the load. Unfortunately, WINS clients cannot resolve addresses registered with another WINS server unless the registrations from that server are somehow copied to the client's WINS server. *WINS replication* is the process used to copy one WINS server's database to another WINS server.

You can configure a WINS server so it replicates its database with another WINS server. This way, clients registered with one WINS server can be added to the database of another server. Static mappings entered on one server are also replicated to replication partners. In fact, you can enter static entries on only one WINS server and yet these entries can be propagated to any number of WINS servers through replication.

After you enable replication, clients seeking name resolution can see not only entries from their server but entries of the replication partners. Remember that clients register their names with the WINS server for which the clients are configured. WINS registrations are not done through broadcasts (in fact, one of main benefits of WINS is the reduction of broadcast traffic). Because one WINS server is collecting registrations just for its clients, the only way for its clients to resolve names registered with another WINS server is for replication to be configured between the servers.

For an exercise covering this information, see end of chapter.

To set up replication, you must configure a WINS server as a push partner or a pull partner. A *push partner* sends its entries to another server, such as if you want to send a copy of the database from this WINS server to the other WINS server. A *pull partner* receives entries from another server, such as if you want this server to receive a copy of the database from another WINS server. You must always configure WINS servers in pairs; otherwise, replication won't work. Figure 9.3 shows a WINS server that is configured to be a push and a pull partner.

Figure 9.3

Configuring a WINS server to be a push-pull partner.

At the very least, one WINS server must be a push partner to send its entries out, while the other WINS server must be a pull partner to receive the entries. Replication does not occur unless both WINS servers are properly configured. If both WINS servers are configured as push and pull partners, then each server ends up with entries from the other server. In theory, the combined database on each WINS server should be the same. However, due to the lag time in replication, this doesn't always happen. Exercise 9.7 at the end of the chapter shows how to configure a WINS server as a replication partner.

Deciding which WINS server will be a push partner and which will be a pull partner is often driven by performance considerations. You often use a pull partner across slow WAN links because you can configure a pull partner to replicate only at certain times, such as at night when the WAN link is not as heavily utilized. In this case, you could make the WINS server on each side of the WAN link a pull partner with the other WINS server. This is known as pull-pull replication.

On faster links, you can use push partners. Push partners replicate when a specified number of changes are made to the database. These updates can happen fairly frequently, but are not too large because you are not waiting to replicate a whole day's worth of changes. If you want two WINS servers to have identical databases, you must configure each WINS server to be a push and a pull partner for the other server.

You can configure a replication partner to start replication in several ways:

1. When the WINS server starts, you can configure this startup replication for either a push or a pull partner.

2. At a specified interval, such as every 24 hours. This applies to pull replication.

3. When a push partner reaches a specified number of changes to the database. These changes include name registrations and name releases. When this threshold is reached, the push partner notifies all its pull partners that it has changes for replications.

4. You can manually force replication from the WINS Manager.

WINS can automatically replicate with other WINS servers if your network supports multicasting. By default, every 40 minutes, each WINS server sends a multicast to the address 224.0.1.24. Any servers found through this multicast are automatically configured as push and pull partners, with replication set to occur every two hours. If the routers on your network do not support multicasting, the WINS servers only see other servers on the same subnet.

You can turn off this multicasting feature by editing the registry in the following location:

`HKEY_LOCAL_MACHINE\System\CurrentControlSet\Services\NetBT\Parameters`

Change the value of UseSelfFndPnrs to 0. Change the value of McastIntvl to a large number.

The Replication Process

A WINS server replicates only its active and extinct entries; released entries are not replicated. A replication partner can have entries that are marked active even though they have been released by its partner. Released entries are not replicated, to reduce the traffic from computers booting and shutting down each day. However, if a registration changes, it is considered a new entry and it is replicated. The following example shows how records are replicated between replication partners.

Using the WINS Manager

As you install WINS, a WINS Manager tool is added to the Administrative Tools group. You can use this tool to manage the local WINS server and remote WINS servers as well. You can use WINS Manager to view the WINS database, add static entries to the database, configure push and pull partners for replication, and back up and restore the WINS database. Figure 9.4 shows the WINS Manager window that appears when you start WINS Manager.

Figure 9.4

The WINS Manager window.

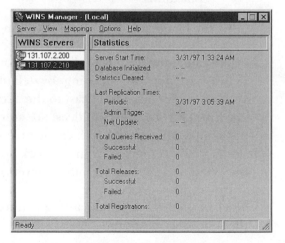

WINS Manager Configuration Dialog

For an exercise covering this information, see end of chapter.

You can use the WINS Server Configuration dialog box to configure how long entries stay in the WINS database. Figure 9.5 shows this dialog. The following four parameters control the life of entries:

Figure 9.5

The WINS Server Configuration dialog box.

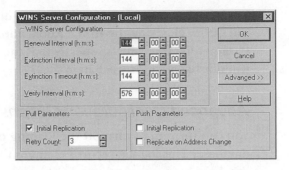

▶ **Renewal Interval.** This is the interval given to a WINS client after it successfully registers its name. The client begins renewing the name registration when half this time has expired. The default is six days.

▶ **Extinction Interval.** This is the amount of time that must pass before the WINS server marks a released entry as extinct. An extinct entry is not immediately deleted. The default is six days. The time until removal is controlled by the following parameter.

▶ **Extinction Timeout.** This is the amount of time WINS waits before removing (scavenging) entries that have been marked extinct. The default is six days.

▶ **Verify Interval.** This parameter applies if WINS servers are set up for replication. This is the interval at which the WINS server verifies that names in its database that came from other servers are still valid. The default is 24 days, and cannot be set below this value.

Initial Replication Configuration

You can configure whether the WINS server replicates with its replication partners it starts. Check the Initial Replication option under Pull Parameters on the WINS Server Configuration dialog to have a pull replication partner replicate on start up. You can also specify the number of times the pull partner tries to contact the other WINS server as the pull partner does the startup replication.

For a push partner, you can also configure it to replicate upon startup by checking the Initial Replication option under Push Parameters. You can also specify that the push partner replicates when it has an address change.

Advanced Configuration Options

You can turn on or turn off the logging of entries to the WINS database. This log file records changes that are made to the WINS database before they are made. By default, logging is on, which gives the WINS server a backup via the log file. If you turn off the logging, the WINS server registers names more quickly, but you lose the backup support of the log file. These settings are configured through the WINS Advanced Configuration dialog box, as shown in figure 9.6.

Figure 9.6

The WINS Advanced Configuration dialog box.

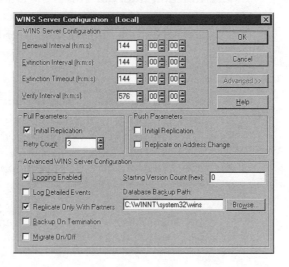

The following are the advanced settings you can configure:

▶ **Log Detailed Events.** If you turn this on, the logging of WINS events in Event Viewer is more verbose. This means that you get more useful troubleshooting information from the log file. However, some performance degradation occurs when verbose logging is turned on.

▶ **Replicate Only With Partners.** By default, WINS replicates only with other WINS servers that are specifically configured as push or pull partners. If you want the WINS server to replicate automatically, you must turn off this setting.

▶ **Backup On Termination.** If you set this option, the WINS database is automatically backed up when the WINS service is stopped. However, the database is not backed up when the NT server is shut down.

▶ **Migrate On/Off.** If this switch is on, static entries that have the same address as a WINS client requesting registration are overwritten. This option is helpful if you are converting a computer from a non-NT machine to an NT machine with the same TCP/IP address. To have addresses resolved for this non-NT machine in the past, you may have added a static entry to the WINS database. With the option on, the new dynamic entry can overwrite the old static entry. It is usually best to turn off this switch after you have migrated (upgraded) the new NT machine. This switch is off by default so static entries are not overwritten.

▶ **Starting Version Count.** This specifies the largest version ID number for the database. Each entry in the database is assigned a version ID. Replication is based on the version ID. A replication partner checks its last replicated entries against the version IDs of the records in the WINS database. The replication partner replicates only records with a later version ID than the last records it replicated from this partner. Usually, you don't need to change this parameter. However, if the database becomes corrupted, you may need to adjust this number so a replication partner replicates the proper entries.

▶ **Database Backup Path.** When the WINS database is backed up, it is copied to a local hard drive. This specifies the path to a directory on a local drive where the WINS backups are stored. This directory can also be used to automatically restore the WINS database. You must specify a local drive path.

Backing Up the WINS Database

For an exercise covering this information, see end of chapter.

The database can be backed up automatically when WINS shuts down. You also can schedule backups or manually start a backup. All these backups are copied to the backup directory specified in the Advanced Configuration options. You can manually start a WINS backup from the Mappings menu in the WINS Manager. To automatically schedule backups, configure the path for a backup directory. After you set this path, the WINS server automatically backs itself up every 24 hours.

You should also back up the WINS subkey in the registry. This subkey has the configuration settings for WINS, but does not contain any entries from the WINS database. The regular backup for WINS makes a copy of the database itself.

 Tip

> To back up the WINS registry subkey, use the NT registry editor, REGEDT32. Then backup the HKEY_LOCAL_MACHINE\ System\CurrentControlSet\Services\WINS subkey. You can save this subkey in the same location you store the WINS database backups.

Restoring the WINS Database

For an exercise covering this information, see end of chapter.

You can restore the WINS database from the backups you made previously. To restore the database, from the Mappings menu in WINS Manager, choose Restore database.

WINS also can automatically restore the database.. If the WINS service starts and detects a corrupted database, it automatically restores a backup from the specified backup directory. If you suspect the database is corrupt, you can stop and start the WINS service from Control Panel, Services to force this automatic restoration.

Files Used for WINS

The WINS database is stored in the path \WINNT\SYSTEM32\
WINS. Several files make up the WINS database:

- ▶ **WINS.MDB.** This is the WINS database itself.

- ▶ **WINSTMP.MDB.** This is a temporary working file used by
  WINS. This file is deleted when the WINS server is shut
  down normally, but a copy could remain in the directory
  after a crash.

- ▶ **J50.LOG.** This is the transaction log of the WINS database.

- ▶ **J50.CHK.** This is a checkpoint file used by the WINS database. This is equivalent to a cache for a disk drive.

Compacting the WINS Database

You can compact the WINS database to reduce its size. However,
WINS under NT 4.0 is designed to automatically compact the
database, so you shouldn't have to compact it. To force manual
compacting of the database, use the JETPACK utility in the
\WINNT\SYSTEM32\WINS directory. (The WINS database is a JET
database, so this utility packs that database.) To pack the database,
you must first stop the WINS service. You cannot pack an open
database. Then type the following command:

jetpack WINS.mdb temp.mdb

This command compacts the database into the file temp.mdb,
then copies the compacted database to WINS.mdb. The temporary file is deleted. After the database is compacted, you can
restart the WINS service from Control Panel, Services.

Exercises

Exercise 9.1: Installing a WINS Server

With this exercise, you install the WINS service and configure your WINS server to use itself as the primary WINS server.

Prerequisites: You have installed Windows NT 4.0 Server with the TCP/IP protocol. The NT server can be a member server, a back-up domain controller, or a primary domain controller.

1. Right-click on Network Neighborhood, and choose properties from the menu. (Network properties can also be accessed from the Network icon in Control Panel.)

2. Select the Services tab, then choose Add. From the Network Service box, select Windows Internet Name Service and then choose OK.

3. Select the Protocols tab, select TCP/IP Protocol, then choose properties.

4. Select the WINS Address tab. Type the TCP/IP address of your Windows NT server as the primary WINS server.

5. Choose OK, then choose Close to close the Network properties dialog.

6. When prompted, choose Yes to reboot your server.

Exercise 9.2: Checking the Windows NT Application Log

With this exercise, you see where WINS writes its error messages.

Prerequisites: You have installed WINS on your Windows NT 4.0 server. You have rebooted the server since you installed WINS.

1. Choose Start, Programs, Administrative Tools.

2. From the Administrative Tools menu, choose Event Viewer.

3. From the Log menu in Event Viewer, choose Application.

4. Double-click on the top message.

5. Select Next to continue scrolling through the messages.

6. Note the messages generated by starting the database engine and checking its integrity upon startup.

7. Choose Close to return to the Application Log window.

8. Note the source of most of the messages, the JET database. WINS is a JET database, which is why WINS messages are recorded in the Application log of Event Viewer.

9. Close Event Viewer.

Exercise 9.3: Viewing the WINS Database Mappings

This exercise enables you to see the database mappings collected by the WINS server.

Prerequisites: You have installed WINS.

1. Choose Start, Programs, Administrative Tools.

2. From the Administrative Tools menu, choose WINS Manager.

3. In the WINS Manager window, note the statistics for your WINS server. The items listed are: the latest starting time of the WINS service (typically the last boot); the last registration time; and the total queries, releases, and registrations.

4. From the Server menu, choose Detailed Information.

5. Note you can see some total statistics about the WINS database from the Detailed Information window.

6. Choose Close.

7. From the Mappings menu in WINS Manager, choose Show Database. Note: If the menu is gray, select your WINS server in the WINS Manager window before choosing Show Database.

8. Note the different numbers registered for each machine name. See if you can find the registration for your computer's name, your computer's server service, your computer's

continues

Exercise 9.3:   Continued

> workstation service, and your user name. Use table 9.1 to find which numbers are used to register each service. Hint: Use the Set Filter button to view only your computer name in the database. When you are finished, use the Clear Filter button to reset the display to see the entire database.

>   9. Try the different sort order options to see how they affect the display.

> 10. Note the time stamp for each entry as well as the version ID. The time stamp specifies when the current status of the entry expires. The version ID is used to determine whether the record is replicated.

> 11. Close the Show Database window.

Exercise 9.4:   Adding Static Entries to a WINS Database

> In this exercise, you add static entries manually to the WINS database through WINS Manager. Figure 9.7 shows the static mappings after exercises 4 and 5 have been completed.

> Prerequisites: You have installed WINS on a Windows NT 4.0 Server.

>   1. Choose Start, Programs, Administrative Tools.

>   2. From the Administrative Tools menu, choose WINS Manager.

>   3. From the Mappings menu in WINS Manager, choose Static Mappings.

>   4. Choose Add Mappings.

>   5. In the computer box, type **ABDCE**.

>   6. In the IP Address box, type **131.107.2.25**.

>   7. In the Type box, select Unique.

>   8. Choose Add to save the entry.

>   9. Add an entry for a computer named FGHIJ with an IP address of 133.107.4.53 and Type Group.

10. Add an entry for a computer named KLMNO with an IP address of 136.107.3.34 and Type Domain Name. Note with the Domain Name mappings you must also move the IP address down with the arrow before you can save it. This is because you can have multiple addresses (for multiple domain controllers) associated with a domain name.

11. Close the Add Static Mappings dialog. Note the mappings you have added in the Static Mappings dialog.

12. Try editing each of the entries. Note the type of each entry differs. Note also the Edit Static Mapping dialog for the domain mapping differs from the dialogs for the unique and group types.

13. Close the Static Mappings dialog box after exploring the Edit Static Mapping dialogs.

14. In the WINS Manager window, choose Show Database from the Mappings menu.

15. Scroll down the mappings database and note the static entries you added. The static mappings are marked with a check in the S column.

16. Sort the database by expiration date. Scroll to the bottom of the database and note the static mappings are there with a time stamp that won't let these entries expire.

17. Close the Show Database window.

Figure 9.7

Static mappings added manually and from an LMHOSTS file.

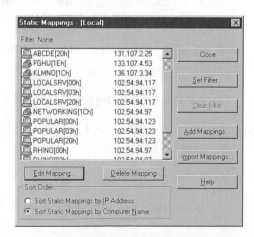

Exercise 9.5: Importing an LMHOSTS File into the WINS Database

In exercise 9.5, you add static mappings to a WINS database from an LMHOSTS file.

Prerequisites: You have installed WINS on a Windows NT 4.0 Server. You do not need an LMHOSTS file, although if you have written one or have one available, you can use it in this exercise.

Note

If you have your own LMHOSTS file you want to import, skip steps 1–4. Figure 9.7 shows the static mappings after labs 4–5 have been completed.

1. From Explorer, locate LMHOSTS.SAM. This file is located in the System32\Drivers\Etc subdirectory of your NT root directory.

2. Edit LMHOSTS.SAM with Notepad.

3. Remove the # comment characters in front of the lines registering IP addresses for rhino, appname, popular, and localsrv.

4. Save this file as LMHOSTS. Now the file is ready for importing.

5. Choose Start, Programs, Administrative Tools.

6. From the Administrative Tools menu, choose WINS Manager.

7. From the Mappings menu in WINS Manager, choose Static Mappings.

8. Choose the Import Mappings Button.

9. Browse to find the LMHOSTS file you modified, then choose that file.

10. Choose Open.

11. Note the names from the LMHOSTS file have been added to the static mappings.

12. Close the Static Mappings dialog.

13. From the Mappings menu, choose Show Database.

14. Note the mappings you added from the LMHOSTS file are now in the WINS database.

Exercise 9.6: Configuring the WINS Server

In this exercise, you see the different configuration options in WINS Manager.

Prerequisites: You have installed WINS on a Windows NT 4.0 Server.

1. Choose Start, Programs, Administrative Tools.

2. From the Administrative Tools menu, choose WINS Manager.

3. From the Server menu, choose Configuration.

4. Note the default times for the Renewal Interval, the Extinction Interval, and the Extinction Timeout. Each of these values is six days (144 hours). These times dictate how quickly a WINS database entry moves from active to released (renewal interval), from released to extinct (extinction interval), and from extinct to being removed from the database (extinction timeout). Note that Microsoft recommends you do not modify these values.

5. Note the default time for the verify interval is 24 days (576 hours). This specifies when a WINS server verifies that entries that it does not own (entries added to the database due to replication) are still active. The minimum value you can set for this parameter is 24 days.

6. Note the check box to do push or pull replication when the WINS server initializes.

7. Choose the Advanced button.

8. Note two of the settings here that can affect WINS performance—Logging Enabled and Log Detailed Events.

continues

Exercise 9.6:   Continued

>   With Logging Enabled, WINS must first write any changes
>   to the WINS database to the JET.LOG file. Then, the chang-
>   es are made to the database. This log file serves as an ongo-
>   ing backup to the database should it crash during the write
>   process. However, if a number of changes are being made
>   to the database simultaneously, logging can slow WINS
>   performance—for example, when everyone powers up their
>   computers in the morning and the clients try to register at
>   the same time. With Log Detailed Events turned on, more
>   detailed messages are written to the Event Log. Note that
>   both settings are turned on by default.

9. Note the default setting for Replicate Only With Partners.
   WINS replicates only with specified partners unless you turn
   this setting off. When turned off, WINS tries to replicate with
   all the WINS servers it can locate through broadcasts.

10. Choose OK to close the Configuration dialog.

Exercise 9.7:   Configuring Replication Partners

In this exercise, you set up replication with another WINS server.

Prerequisites: You have installed WINS on a Windows NT 4.0 Server. Although it is ideal to have another WINS server to do this
exercise, you can go through the steps of setting up replication
without having another WINS server. However, you will not be
able to see the results of replication.

1. Choose Start, Programs, Administrative Tools.

2. From the Administrative Tools menu, choose WINS Manager.

3. If you don't have another WINS server, skip to step 5. If you
   have another WINS server, do step 4.

4. From the Server menu, choose Add server. Type the TCP/IP
   address of the other WINS server, the choose OK.

5. Select your WINS server in the WINS Manager window.

6. From the Server menu, choose Replication Partners.

Note

If you do not have another WINS server, you cannot complete the remaining steps. However, you can see the interface for the remaining steps by referring to the figures in the section on "Replication" earlier in this chapter.

7. From the Replication Partners box, select the other WINS server.

8. In the Replication Options box, select the other WINS server to be both a push and a pull partner.

9. Choose Configuration for a Push Partner. Note that push replication is triggered when an Update Count is reached.

10. Choose Configuration for a Pull Partner. Note that pull replication is started at a specific time and then from an offset time after the initial replication time.

11. Note that in this dialog you can also manually trigger replication by choosing the Push or the Pull button in the Send Replication Trigger Now box.

Exercise 9.8:   Backing Up the WINS Server

In exercise 9.8, you configure the WINS server for automatic backup and to manually back up the WINS server.

Prerequisites: You have installed WINS on a Windows NT 4.0 Server.

1. Choose Start, Programs, Administrative Tools.

2. From the Administrative Tools menu, choose WINS Manager.

3. From the Server menu in the WINS Manager windows, choose Configuration.

4. Choose Advanced.

5. In the Database Backup Path box, browse to find the System32\WINS subdirectory under the root of the NT installation.

continues

Exercise 9.8: Continued

    6. Choose OK. A path similar to C:\WINNT\SYSTEM32\WINS should appear in the Database Backup Path box.

 Note

> With this path set, WINS backs up the database to this directory every 24 hours. This backup can be used for automatic recovery if WINS detects the database is corrupt. You can also restore the database manually from this directory.

    7. Note the Backup On Termination option in the Advanced WINS Server Configuration box. When this option is checked, WINS automatically backs up the WINS database when the WINS service is stopped. However, the WINS server does not back up the database when the Windows NT server is shut down.

    8. Choose OK to close the WINS Server Configuration dialog.

    9. From the Mappings menu of the WINS Manager window, choose Backup Database.

    10. Choose OK to back up the database to the path entered in the Advanced Configuration settings. You can also choose to save the backup in a different directory.

    11. A message appears indicating the backup is successful.

Exercise 9.9: Restoring the WINS Database Backup

In this exercise, you manually restore a WINS database backup.

Prerequisites: You have installed WINS on a Windows NT 4.0 Server. You have completed exercise 9.8.

    1. Choose Start, Settings, Control Panel.

    2. From the Control Panel window, choose Services.

    3. From the Services windows, select Windows Internet Name Service.

    4. Choose Stop.

5. Choose Start, Programs, Administrative Tools.

6. From the Administrative Tools menu, choose WINS Manager.

7. From the Mappings menu in the WINS Manager windows, choose Restore Local Database.

 Note   This option is grayed out if the WINS service is started. The WINS service must be stopped to restore the WINS database.

8. Choose OK to restore a backup from the path specified in the Advanced Configuration settings. You can also choose to restore a backup from a different directory.

9. A message indicating a successful restoration should appear.

10. Choose Start, Settings, Control Panel.

11. From the Control Panel window, choose Services.

12. From the Services dialog, choose Windows Internet Name Service.

13. Choose Start.

14. A message indicating WINS started successfully should appear.

Exercise 9.10:   Scavenging the WINS Database

This exercise initiates scavenging on the WINS server.

Prerequisites: You have installed WINS on a Windows NT 4.0 Server.

1. Choose Start, Programs, Administrative Tools.

2. From the Administrative Tools menu, choose WINS Manager.

3. From the Server menu in the WINS Manager window, choose Detailed Information. Note the last scavenging time, if any.

4. Choose Close.

5. From the Mappings menu, choose Initiate Scavenging.

continues

Exercise 9.10: Continued

    6. A message appears indicating that the scavenging command has been queued.

    7. Later, you can check the Detailed Information to see if scavenging has occurred.

Exercise 9.11: Manually Configuring a WINS Client

With this exercise, you manually configure a TCP/IP client to be a WINS client. You configure the WINS server to be a WINS client, but the same process is used to configure other WINS clients, that is, you specify the address of the primary WINS server in the specified box and if desired, the address of a secondary WINS server in the specified box.

Prerequisites: You have installed WINS on a Windows NT 4.0 Server.

    1. Right-click on Network Neighborhood, then, from the menu, choose Properties. (You also can access the Network Properties dialog from Control Panel, Network.)

    2. Select the Protocols tab.

    3. Select TCP/IP Protocol, then choose Properties.

    4. Select the WINS Address tab.

    5. Type the address of your WINS server in the primary WINS Server box.

    6. Choose OK, then choose Close.

    7. Reboot your computer when prompted. You have now configured your computer manually to be a WINS client.

Exercise 9.12: Configuring a DHCP Client to be a WINS Client

The purpose of this exercise is to configure DHCP clients to automatically receive WINS client configuration through the DHCP scope.

Prerequisites: You have installed WINS on a Windows NT 4.0 Server. You have installed a DHCP server with a scope. See Chapter 6 for information on installing a DHCP server and adding a DHCP scope.

1. Choose Start, Programs, Administrative Tools.

2. From the Administrative Tools menu, choose DHCP Manager.

3. In the DHCP Manager window, choose the local machine.

4. Select the scope created under the local machine.

5. From the DHCP Options menu, select Scope.

Note   This option is grayed out unless you have selected the scope.

6. In the Unused Options box, select 044 WINS/NBNS Servers and choose Add.

7. In the Unused Options box, select 046 WINS/NBNS Node Type and choose Add.

8. From the Active Options box, select 044 WINS/NBNS Servers and choose Value.

9. Choose Edit Array, type the address of your WINS server, then choose Add.

10. Choose OK to close the IP Address Array Editor.

11. From the Active Options box, select 046 WINS/NBNS Node Type.

12. In the Byte box, change the value 0x2 (b-node broadcast) to 0x8 (h-node broadcast).

13. Choose OK. The scope options are now set for DHCP clients from this scope to automatically become clients of your WINS server.

Exercise 9.13:   Configuring a WINS Proxy Agent

In exercise 9.13, you configure a Windows NT 4.0 computer to be a WINS proxy agent. In prior versions of Windows NT, configuring a computer to be a proxy agent was done through a check box in the advanced settings of TCP/IP. This is how Windows 95 and Windows for Workgroups machines are configured to be a proxy agent. However, this check box was removed in NT 4.0, so you must now go to the registry to configure a proxy agent.

Prerequisites: You have installed WINS on a Windows NT 4.0 Server.

1. Choose Start, Run.

2. Type **REGEDT32**, then choose OK.

3. In the window, HKEY_LOCAL_MACHINE, walk down the path:

```
HKEY_LOCAL_MACHINE\System\CurrentControlSet\Services\NetBT\Parameters
```

4. Notice the parameter called EnableProxy. To make this NT computer into a WINS proxy agent, you must change the value of this parameter to 1 and reboot the computer. However, because the computer you are working on is most likely your WINS server, and because you shouldn't have a proxy agent and a WINS server on the same machine, don't set the parameter.

5. Close the registry editor.

Review Questions

The following questions test your knowledge of the information in this chapter.

1. How does a WINS server gather entries to add to its database?

   A. It examines each packet sent on the network.

   B. It receives a copy of the browse list from the master browser on each network segment.

   C. WINS clients send a name registration to the WINS server.

   D. It retrieves a copy of the computer accounts in each domain.

2. Where does a client first look to resolve a NetBIOS name?

   A. In the NetBIOS cache on the WINS server

   B. In the NetBIOS cache on the WINS proxy agent

   C. In the NetBIOS cache on the primary Domain Controller

   D. In the NetBIOS cache on the client

3. What type of names are registered by WINS clients (select all that apply)?

   A. The computer name

   B. The domain name of a domain controller

   C. Share names created on that computer

   D. The names of network services

4. How do you configure automatic backup of the WINS database?

   A. Use the AT command to schedule the backup

   B. Specify the name of the backup directory in WINS Manager

    C. Specify the backup interval in WINS Manager

    D. Install a tape device through Control Panel, SCSI Adapters

5. When does a WINS client try to renew its registration?

    A. After three days

    B. One day before the registration expires

    C. Every 24 hours

    D. When one half of the registration life has expired

6. By default, where does the WINS server first write changes to the database?

    A. To the log file

    B. To the database

    C. To the registry

    D. To the temporary database

7. How do you configure replication to occur at specified intervals?

    A. Configure a WINS server to be a pull partner

    B. Use the AT command to schedule replication

    C. Configure a WINS server to be a push partner

    D. Edit the ReplIntrvl parameter in the registry

8. How can you add entries for non-WINS clients to a WINS server's database?

    A. Configure the WINS server to be a pull partner for a DNS server

    B. Import an LMHOSTS file

    C. Install the WINS proxy agent on the segment with non-WINS clients

    D. Add the entries with WINS Manager

9. When is an entry scavenged from the WINS database?

   A. When a WINS client requests a name release

   B. When a name registration expires without renewal

   C. When an entry has been marked extinct

   D. When the extinction interval has elapsed

10. Where can you see a record of WINS server error messages?

    A. In the Windows NT System Event Log

    B. In the ERROR.LOG file in the WINS directory

    C. In the Windows NT Application Event Log

    D. In the error log in WINS Manager

11. What does a WINS server do if it receives a name registration request for a host name already in its database?

    A. It replaces the old entry with the newer one.

    B. It queries the host of the existing registration to see whether the registration is still valid.

    C. It denies the registration request.

    D. It adds the registration as an alternate address for the existing name.

12. How do you install a WINS proxy agent?

    A. From Control Panel, Network, Services

    B. From Control Panel, Add Programs

    C. By changing a registry entry

    D. Running the Network Client Administration tool from the WINS program group

13. How can you configure a WINS server to automatically replicate its database with any other WINS servers?

    A. Specify All Servers as push partners for replication

    B. Turn on the Migrate On/Off switch in WINS Manager

    C. Change the UseSelfFndPnrs parameter in the registry to 0

    D. Turn off the Replicate Only With Partners switch in WINS Manager

14. How does a client decide which WINS server to use?

    A. The first WINS server that responds to a broadcast

    B. The WINS server that WINS an election

    C. The Initial WINS server configured in TCP/IP

    D. The primary WINS server specified in the DHCP scope options

15. What happens to a name registration when the host crashes?

    A. The WINS server marks the record as released after it queries the client at half of TTL

    B. The name is marked as released after three renewal periods are missed

    C. The name is scavenged after the registration expires

    D. The name is released after the TTL is over

16. On which platform can you install a WINS server?

    A. On a Windows NT 3.51 member server

    B. On a Windows NT 4.0 workstation running the WINS proxy agent

    C. On a Windows NT 4.0 Backup Domain Controller

    D. On a Windows NT 4.0 Primary Domain Controller

17. How many WINS servers should be installed?

    A. One primary for each subnet and one secondary for every two subnets

    B. One primary for every 2,000 clients and one secondary for each additional 2,000 clients

    C. One primary and one secondary for every 10,000 clients

    D. One primary and secondary for each domain

18. How do you configure automatic address resolution for DHCP clients?

    A. Specify the Create WINS database option in the DHCP scope

    B. Install a WINS server with an address specified by the DHCP scope

    C. Schedule the active leases to be copied from DCHP manager to an LMHOSTS file

    D. Locate a DHCP relay agent on the same subnet as the WINS server

19. Where should a WINS proxy agent be located?

    A. On the same subnet as non-WINS clients

    B. On the same subnet as the DHCP server

    C. On the same subnet as the DNS server

    D. On the same subnet as the DHCP Relay Agent

20. To configure a DHCP scope to use WINS, the WINS/NBT Node type should be set to _____?

    A. 1

    B. 2

    C. 4

    D. 8

21. How can the WINS clients of one WINS server resolve the addresses of clients registered with another WINS server?

    A. The WINS server can be configured for recursive lookup to the other WINS server.

    B. The WINS server can be a replication partner of the other server.

    C. The client can be configured with the address of the other WINS server as its secondary WINS server.

    D. The WINS servers automatically synchronize their databases.

22. How can you remove entries from a WINS database that have been replicated from another WINS server?

    A. Select Delete Owner in WINS Manager.

    B. Stop WINS, restore the database backup, then start WINS.

    C. Remove the other WINS server as a replication partner.

    D. You must manually delete the entries.

23. How can you remove obsolete entries from the WINS database?

    A. Shorten the Extinction Timeout interval to 0

    B. Sort the entries by TTL and delete entries with TTL of 0.

    C. Select Initiate Scavenging from WINS Manager

    D. Set the Filter in WINS Manager to display only registrations with TTL > 0

24. Where is WINS configuration information stored?

    A. In the \WINNT\SYSTEM32\WINS directory

    B. In the registry

    C. In the WINS.CFG file in the WINNT directory

    D. In the J50.CHK file in the WINS directory

25. Which replication option is best for WINS servers separated by a slow WAN link?

    A. Pull replication configured to replicate after 100 changes

    B. Push replication configured to replicate after 100 changes

    C. Pull replication configured to replicate at 6 a.m. and 6 p.m.

    D. Push replication configured to replicate at 6 a.m. and 6 p.m.

Review Answers

1. C

2. D

3. A, B, D

4. B

5. D

6. A

7. A

8. B, D

9. D

10. C

11. B

12. C

13. D

14. D

15. D

16. A, C, D

17. C

18. B

19. A

20. D

21. B

22. A

23. C

24. B

25. C

Answers to Test Yourself Questions at Beginning of Chapter

1. Clients first register their names with the WINS server when they boot. Upon successful registration, they receive a time to live for their registration from the WINS server. Clients try to renew the registration when half this time has elapsed. The default time to live is six days, so the WINS client tries to renew its registration after three days. After the client renews its registration, the new time to live is, again, six days, so in another three days the client renews its registration.

2. Entries can be removed either when a client requests a release or when the registration expires. A client sends a registration release request when it shuts down normally. The WINS server marks released entries as inactive. If the client has not renewed its registration when its time to live expires (assuming the client has not released the registration), the WINS server marks the entry as released. After the specified extinction interval (the default is six days), the entry is marked extinct. The entry is not removed from the database until the extinction timeout interval is reached, which is also six days by default. In total, then, a client's address can remain in the WINS server database for 18 days after the initial registration, even if the client never renews its registration (six days for the time to live, six days for extinction interval, and six days for the extinction timeout).

3. A WINS client queries only WINS servers that are specified as its primary or secondary WINS servers. However, you can have a number of WINS servers on the network, with each server servicing a different set of clients. You can configure the WINS servers to copy their entries to another server through replication.

4. Configure the target WINS server as a replication partner of the source WINS server. To receive entries from another server, the WINS server must be a pull partner. You must also configure the source WINS server as a replication partner. To send entries to another WINS server, the local WINS server must be a push partner. You must configure both servers as replication partners of the other WINS server or replication does not happen.

5. You must configure each server as both a push and a pull replication partner for the other WINS server. Being a push partner sends a WINS server's entries to its partner. Being a pull partner lets a WINS server receive entries from its partner.

6. You must specify a backup directory path in WINS Manager. When the WINS server starts, it automatically backs up this directory. Every 24 hours after startup, it also automatically does a backup. You can also manually back up a WINS server through WINS Manager.

7. You can restore a WINS database backup manually through WINS Manager. A WINS server attempts to automatically restore a backup when it detects a corrupt database upon startup. You can force this automatic restoration when you suspect a corrupt database by stopping and starting the WINS service.

8. You can install a WINS server on an NT server, version 3.5x or 4.0. It can be on any variety of server—a member server, a backup domain controller, or a primary domain controller. You can install the WINS service during installation, but normally you install it later by configuring the network properties of the server through Control Panel, Network.

9. Push replication is configured to occur after a certain number of changes are made to the WINS database. This is usually used for replication partners on the same subnet, so replication can occur fairly often with only a small amount of traffic transmitted with each replication attempt.

   Pull replication is configured to take place at certain time intervals. Pull replication first occurs at a specified starting time and then at specified intervals after the starting time. Using the time setting for pull replication, you can schedule replication during hours when network traffic is at its lowest. This type of replication is typically used when a slow WAN link separates replication partners. During heavy traffic times on a WAN link, it is not usually desirable to have fairly constant traffic between servers, such as the traffic generated by push replication.

10. If the client is manually configured with a TCP/IP address, the address of a primary WINS server must also be configured. Although not required, you can also configure the address of a secondary WINS server.

    If the client receives its TCP/IP address from the WINS server, you must configure the options of the DHCP scope to include the address of a primary WINS server. You can also specify the address of a secondary WINS server. One additional parameter you must configure in the DHCP scope is the type of broadcasts used for WINS as h-node broadcasts.

C h a p t e r

10

IP Internetwork Browsing and Domain Functions

This chapter helps you prepare for the exam by covering the following objectives:

 Objectives

▶ Configure HOSTS and LMHOSTS file

▶ Configure and support browsing in a multiple-domain route environment

Test Yourself! Before reading this chapter, test yourself to determine how much study time you will need to devote to this section.

1. What is Windows NT internetwork browsing and what does it provide?

2. When is a WINS server not an adequate browsing solution?

3. What other browsing-related Windows NT services cause broadcasts?

Answers are located at the end of the chapter.

Browsing in Windows NT

The sharing of resources is the key to networking. For what other purpose does networking exist? Therefore, it is of utmost importance that there be an easy way of not only sharing a resource but of knowing what resources on the network are accessible. Figure 10.1 shows multiple networks, each with resources that need to be accessible by the other networks.

Figure 10.1

Browsing over-view.

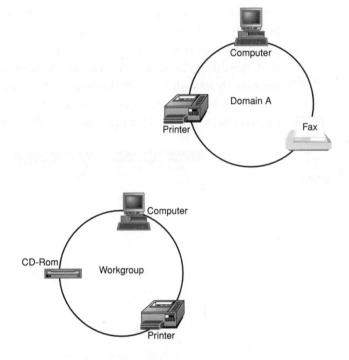

Microsoft has made this process of viewing network resources available through what may be referred to as *browsers*.

What these browsers do is actually collect a list (called the *browse list*) of the resources available on the network and pass this list out to requesting clients. One main computer is designated to collect and update the browse list. Having one computer keep track of the browse list frees the other systems to continue processing without the added overhead of constantly finding where everything is. It also cuts down on the network traffic by having a single source for this list of information rather than everyone needing a separate copy.

Browsing Tools

The next question you may ask is, "How do I browse and what am I browsing for?" The answer is easier than you might think and you have probably already used this browsing technique. One very simple example of browsing is the Network Neighborhood icon on your desktop. When you open up Network Neighborhood it provides a list of the network resources available in your local workgroup or domain. These network resources include but are not limited to: printers, fax, CD-ROM, and other drives or applications available on the network. This is the default list you should see when you first open it. The top icon, Entire Network, refers to just that, anything else that may be available on your network but not necessarily in your local workgroup or domain. This implies that there may be multiple workgroups and or domains in your network environment. Figure 10.2 illustrates the domain grouping.

Figure 10.2

Domain listing.

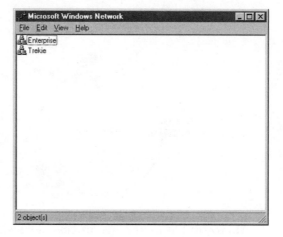

When you start opening up some of these remote domains or workgroups, you are in the process of browsing. This is much like window shopping. You go to the mall not knowing exactly what you need and so you browse through the shops until you find what you want.

The same applies to the network, but now you are browsing network resources—remote files, printers, CD-ROMs. Anything you need access to can be considered a resource. After you find the resource you want, you can utilize it—such as by printing a document to a network printer or by changing to a server-based database. By using the Network Neighborhood for browsing network resources, you are using the graphical view method or GUI (Graphical User Interface). You may also browse network resources from the command prompt by using the Net View command. After you specify the server name, a list appears showing the resources available on that specific server. Notice that you must use the correct Universal Naming Convention with the two backslashes (\\Server\Share).

For example

```
C:\users\default>net view \\instructor
```

results in the following:

```
Shared resources at \\instructor


Share name   Type          Used as  Comment

_____

cdrom        Disk
MSDOS        Disk
NETLOGON     Disk                   Logon server share
Public       Disk
SQLSETUP     Disk
WGPO         Disk
The command completed successfully.
```

System Roles

Certain predefined roles must be addressed with certain names. The computer that has the resource you are trying to access may be referred to as the *host computer*. While you are trying to access its resources, this computer is also playing the role of a server because it is providing a service: the sharing of its resources. The person trying to access the host computer is in the role of a *client*.

Remember, a computer may play the roles of both client and server at once. If, for example, you are trying to access a printer on a remote computer while someone is utilizing your shared CD-ROM, you are then both client and server, because you are both sharing a resource and accessing a remote one.

Any time a resource—drive, printer, and so forth—is shared, it will appear on the browse list, which is available to everyone. Even if you have not been given permission to use the resource, it will still appear on the list you see. This is because it is an overall list of what network resources are available, not just the network resources that are available to you. There are ways of limiting access to the resource to the specific clients that you want, but there is not a way to just have the resources you have access to appear in your list, because your list is not specific to you, it is the entire list for either your workgroup, domain, or network. You limit access by setting permissions directly on the resource you are sharing.

You may have noticed that sometimes the browse list appears incomplete, or things are on the list that you cannot access, and have been given the correct permissions. If you do not have enough permissions to access this network resource, even though it appears in your browse list, you will still be denied access. The issues of proper permissions but no access and not appearing on the browse list at all happen because there is a delay on updating the browse list you are accessing. What happens is the resource you attempt to access is either not available anymore (which results in you being denied access to a resource you had previously been allowed to access), or does not appear in the browse list. Browse list timing issues are covered later in this section.

The Direct Approach

There is, however, a way around this problem of the browse list delay. One way is the direct approach, but this requires you to know the exact name of the network host that has the resource you desire to obtain, but not the resource itself. This is similar to the net view command but with a graphical interface.

The following steps show how to use the direct approach to access a computer:

1. Click the Start button.

2. Click Find.

3. Click Computer.

4. Type in the name of the server you are trying to find.

5. Click Find Now.

You should then see a list of resources that system has available (see fig. 10.3).

Figure 10.3

Computer browsing.

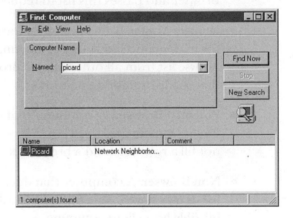

The direct approach bypasses browsing and does a broadcast for that host computer. It is especially helpful when a new resource has been made available but may not have appeared on any browse list, or when you want to see whether a resource to which you are getting denied access is really currently available on the network. You can also utilize the Net Use command at the command prompt to specify the remote resource you are going to access. The Net Use command is usually used in conjunction with the previously described Net View command (which just lists that servers shared resources), whereas the Net Use command actually attaches you to the resource.

Browsing Roles

Now that you understand what browsing itself is and what it can do for you, the next stage is to discuss the different browsing processes and the defined roles for browsing. The following are the browsing roles available. Figure 10.4 illustrates their placement and usage.

▶ **Master Browser.** Collects and maintains the master list of available resources in its domain or workgroup, and the list of names, not resources, in other domains and workgroups. Distributes the browse list to backup browsers.

▶ **Backup Browser.** Obtains its browse list from the Master Browser and passes this list to requesting clients.

▶ **Domain Master Browser.** Fulfills the role of a Master Browser for its domain as well as coordinating and synchronizing the browse list from all other Master Browsers for the domains that reside on remote networks.

▶ **Potential Browser.** A computer that could be a Master, Backup, or Domain Master Browser if needed, but currently does not fill a role nor hold a browse list.

▶ **Non-Browser.** A computer that does not maintain a browse list. It may have been configured not to participate, or it may possibly be a client computer.

Figure 10.4

Browsing roles.

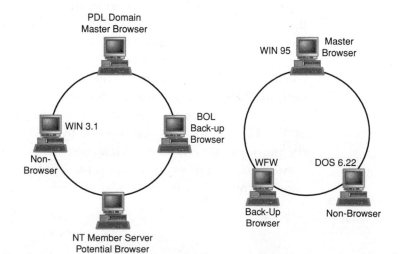

Filling Roles

Now that browsing roles are defined, who can fill them? Windows NT Workstation, Windows NT Server, Windows for Workgroups, and Windows 95 all can perform these browsing roles. However, only a Windows NT Server acting as a Primary Domain Controller (PDC) may occupy the role of the domain Master Browser. In a LAN, the Domain Master Browser is also the Master Browser.

Windows NT Workstation and Windows NT Member Servers can become backup browsers if there are at least three Windows NT server-based computers not already filling these roles for the workgroup or domain. Figure 10.5 shows how the browse list is distributed.

Figure 10.5

Distribution of the browse list.

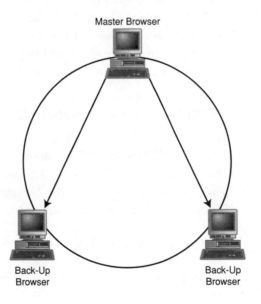

Master Browser

Back-Up
Browser

Back-Up
Browser

How do you know and control in which roles your computers are participating? Unfortunately, there is not a way to see what browsing role the computer is filling without looking in the Registry. By understanding some default rules and by a little user intervention, however, you can control the browsing environment to a certain extent. The first default to grasp is that Windows NT and Windows 95 are set to auto—meaning it potentially can fill a browsing role. The Master Browser is chosen through what is called an *election process*, which is based on the following criteria:

▶ A Windows NT-based computer takes precedence over a Windows 95 or Windows for Workgroups computer. Windows 95 will take priority over Windows for Workgroups. This is at any time. If a Windows 95 machine has been on for two years as soon as a Windows NT computer comes online an election will be held and the Windows NT computer will win because of its higher priority rating.

▶ The computer that has been turned on the longest wins the election and will become the new Master Browser. The idea behind this is that if it has been on the longest it has the most potential to not go down frequently, thus providing a more accurate and current browse list.

▶ If none of the preceding criteria fit, the server with a NetBIOS name of lowest alphabetical lettering will win the election race of Master Browser. For example: a server with the name of Argyle will become the next Master Browser over a server with the name of Zot.

Controlling Your Browser Role

To control the browser role that your computer is playing for a Windows NT Server and Windows NT Workstation, you can change the IsDomainMaster Registry setting to a *true* or *yes* to force your computer to be the Master Browser This setting is found in the following Registry subkey:

`\HKEY_LOCAL_MACHINE\SYSTEM\CurrentControlSet\Services\Browser\Parameters`

To control your browser role for Windows 95, perform the following steps:

1. Right-click Network Neighborhood.

2. Choose Properties.

3. Select the File and Print Sharing for Microsoft Networks service if you have it installed. If it is not installed, you are not currently participating in browsing. You can install it by clicking on the Add button, selecting Microsoft, and then adding File and Print Sharing for Microsoft Networks.

4. Choose Properties.

5. Select Browse Master. This is set to Automatic by default; you can either enable or disable it (see fig. 10.6).

Figure 10.6

Windows 95 browsing control.

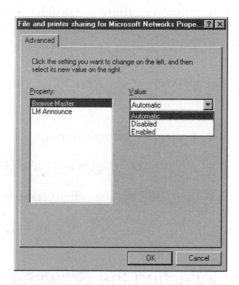

These are the only controls you have for configuring the browser roles of your computers. So you could turn it off on all but the specific machines that you want to participate in browsing, allowing you to at least narrow the possibilities. If one of those goes down, however, there goes your browsing. You cannot directly control backup browsers, only set them to auto with one set to IsDomainMaster.

Understanding the Cost of Browsing

Does being a Browse Master affect a computer's performance? Yes, it affects system performance. This performance degradation may be noticeable on slower systems, such as 486/66, but not as noticeable on most newer machines, such as a P5/100. Anything the computer does in some way affects its performance, but remember that being a Browse Master means keeping an updated list of network resources. The number of network resources with which the Browse Master needs to keep up obviously affects that computer's performance accordingly. The best you can do to minimize this performance degradation is to keep the amount of computers sharing network resources to a minimum. Doing so allows the Browse List to be short, relieving the strain on the Master Browser.

Windows NT Browsing Services

A lot is involved with browsing to make it do what it does—most of which happens automatically without any intervention. Sometimes, however, there are problems and it can help to understand the process involved to better understand the possible solutions to the problem.

The browsing services have three main break points, or sections, in Windows NT:

▶ Collecting information for the browse list

▶ Distributing the browse list itself

▶ Servicing browser client requests for the list

Each of these break points is discussed in the following sections.

Collecting the Browse List

The first important part of being able to browse network resources is the collection of the browse list itself. The Master Browser continually updates its browse list to include the current network resources available. This update process is continual, in that it is constantly having to revise its browse list as network resources appear and disappear. This process happens every time a computer is turned on that has something to share and every time one that is sharing resources is turned off. The Master Browser obtains a list of servers in its own domain or workgroup, as well as a list of other domains and workgroups and updates these servers with network resources to the browse list as changes are made. Much of this process has to do with browser announcements. Figure 10.7 shows the browser collection process.

When a computer that is running a server service is turned on, it announces itself to the Master Browser, which then adds this new resource to its browse list. This happens regardless of whether the computer has resources to share or not. When a computer is shut down properly, it announces to the Master Browser that it is leaving and again the Master Browser updates its list accordingly. If a Master Browser has an empty list, it can force domains to announce themselves so that it can add them to its list.

Figure 10.7

Browser collection.

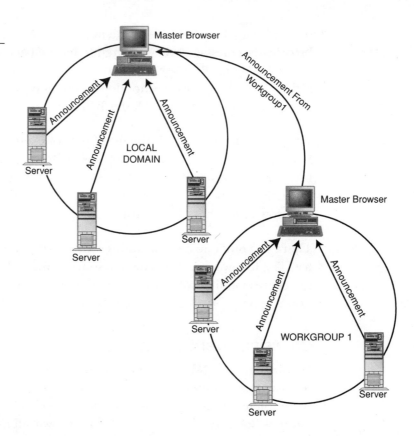

Master Browsers also receive what are called DomainAnnouncement packets that come from other domains and place these packets in their own local browse lists. These DomainAnnouncement packets contain the following information:

▶ The name of the domain.

▶ The name of the Master Browser for that domain.

▶ Whether the Browser is a Windows NT Server or Windows NT Workstation computer.

▶ If the Browser is a Windows NT Server computer, it is the Primary Domain Controller for that domain.

Distributing the Browse List

The next important part of browsing is the distribution of the previously collected browse list. The extent of this distribution depends largely on the size of the network. A Master Browser broadcasts a message every so often to let the backup browsers know the Master Browser is still around. This is important because if the Master Browser does not do this the network holds an election process to elect a new Master Browser.

The Master Browser holds the list of network resources. It is the Backup Browser that contacts the Master Browser and copies the list from the Master Browser. Therefore, the Backup Browsers are the active component, intermittently contacting the passive Master Browser for the updated list.

There can often be complications with distributing this browse list. The following sections discuss some of these difficulties and the corresponding solutions, such as browsing over subnets, announcement period timings, and Domain Master Browser failure.

Browsing Over Subnets

Within Windows NT, every local subnet, a collection of computers separated by a router, is its own browsing area. This browsing area is complete with its own Master Browser and Backup Browsers. Subnets hold Browser elections, for their own subnet, which demonstrates the need for a Domain Master Browser if you have multiple subnets on your internetwork to allow for browsing over more than just one subnet. Additionally, each subnet needs at least one Windows NT controller in each subnet to register with the Domain Master Browser. This allows for multi-subnet browsing.

Generally, broadcasts do not go through a router; the router needs to be BOOTP-enabled to allow passing of broadcasts. If a domain has multiple subnets, each Master Browser for each subnet uses a directed datagram called a MasterBrowserAnnouncement. The MasterBrowserAnnouncement lets the Domain Master Browser know it is available and what it has on its subnet list. These datagrams pass through the routers enabling these updates to occur. The Domain Master Browser adds all the subnet Master Browser lists to its own browse list, providing a complete browse list of the entire domain, including all subnets. This process occurs every 15 minutes to ensure regular list updates. The timing is not adjustable. Windows NT workgroups and Windows for

Workgroups are not able to send a MasterBrowserAnnouncement packet and therefore cannot span these multiple subnets or have a complete list—thus the need for Windows NT domain controllers to allow for multiple subnet browsing. Figure 10.8 illustrates what browsing over subnets might look like in a network design.

Figure 10.8

Browsing over subnets.

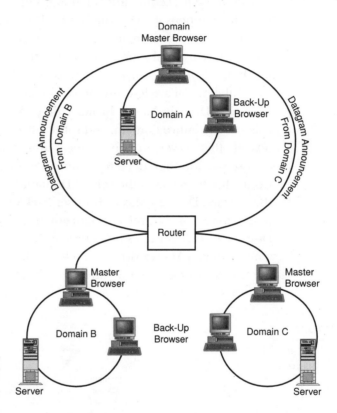

Announcement Periods

When the Master Browser first comes online it sends out a Domain-Announcement once a minute for the first 5 minutes and then only once every 15 minutes. If the domain does not respond by sending out its own DomainAnnouncement for three successive announcement periods, the domain is removed from the Master Browser list. A resource, therefore, might appear on your browse list but actually be unavailable, because it remains on the browse list until three full announcement periods have passed. It is then possible for a domain to appear up to 45 minutes after it is originally unavailable, which may be due to the Primary Domain Controller being off or having physical connectivity problems, such as a bad network card and or cable. You cannot change these announcement times or removal periods.

Domain Master Browser Failure

Based on the preceding information on browsers and subnets, notice what happens if a Domain Master Browser fails (see fig. 10.9). In the event of a failure, users on the entire network are limited to their own individual subnets, assuming they have a Master Browser for their subnet, of course. If there is not a Master Browser within your subnet, you are left with no browsing capabilities whatsoever. Without a Domain Master Browser, no complete overall browse list exists of the entire domain, and within three announcement periods all other servers not on the local subnet are removed from the browse list. You then need to either promote a Backup Domain Controller to perform the role of Domain Master Browser, or bring the downed Domain Master Browser back online before the time limit expires for its three announcements. Remember the Backup Domain Controller does not automatically promote itself, and once a new Domain Master Browser is elected it will take time to collect the browse list from all the different subnets. There is no way you can force the browse list.

Figure 10.9

Domain Master Browser failure.

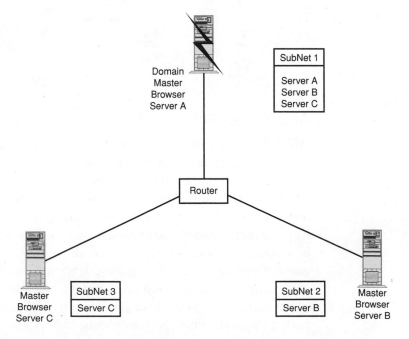

Servicing Client Requests

The final browsing service process is the actual servicing of client requests. Now that a browse list exists and has been distributed, clients have something to access. Figure 10.10 illustrates what happens from the point when a client requests a resource to the actual connection of that resource.

Figure 10.10

Servicing clients.

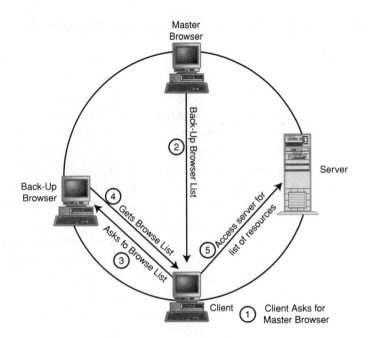

The process follows these steps:

1. The client tries to access a domain or workgroup using Explorer. In doing so, it contacts the Master Browser of the domain or workgroup that it is trying to access.

2. The Master Browser gives the client a list of three backup browsers.

3. The client then asks for the network resource from one of the backup browsers.

4. The Backup Browser gives the list of servers in that domain or workgroup for which the client is asking.

5. The client chooses a server and obtains a list of that server's shared resources.

This process can occasionally cause some conflict if the Master Browser has a resource in its list, but the Backup Browser has not updated itself yet, and the client connects to that Backup Browser and looks for the current list. The resource is not listed in the Backup Browse list yet. This is another reason why items that are not available may appear on the list, or may not be on the list at all.

Browsing in an IP Internetwork

 Now that you've learned about browsing itself and know how it works, you are ready to learn about browsing in an IP internetwork, meaning browsing over multiple subnets. This is not as easy as it sounds. Some has already been explained through the process of domain announcement. But this only allows for Master Browsers to talk to the Domain Master Browser. This requires a Windows NT domain controller to be in each subnet. It may not be feasible to put a domain controller at each subnet, thus, no browsing. The first major obstacle is that browsing relies on broadcast packets, which means they are actually sent to everyone on the network segment. However, routers do not generally forward these broadcast packets, creating a browsing problem for collecting, distributing, and servicing the client request for browse lists. If these packets are not forwarded, you are unable to browse in an internetwork environment without a local domain controller.

If the browse list cannot get distributed properly, then you have no browsing capability.

Solutions

There are a few possible solutions to the problem of being able to browse in an IP internetwork. There is the use of a BOOTP enabled router and an LMHOSTS file. The following section discusses the usefulness of the IP router.

IP Router

You can use a few solutions to get around the problem of routers and multiple subnets, not being able to browse without a Windows NT controller on each subnet. The first solution is to have a specific router that can forward these NetBIOS name broadcasts. This makes all the broadcasts and network resource requests appear to all client computers as if the broadcasts are all on the same subnet. Master browsers have their own lists as well as those of the other domains and workgroups, so when a client makes an inquiry for a browse list, the list can be provided for any domain or workgroup.

Having a BOOTP-enabled router, of course, fixes the browsing problem across routers. But this solution may not be perfect for every network layout and size. The reason having this BOOTP-enabled router is not the perfect solution is because if you do have the BOOTP-enabled router, all NetBIOS traffic is broadcast over the entire network, rather than limited to each subnet. This adds extremely high overhead to all the nodes of the network, degrading overall performance. The subnets are no longer isolated to their own specific areas, which causes a higher potential for browser election conflicts and excessive network traffic. Therefore, even though it does fix the problem of routers and multiple subnets, other problems, such as the excessive traffic that is generated, should be anticipated.

Directed Traffic

Additional solutions to the problem of browsing an IP internetwork without using a BOOTP-enabled router are available. The following section explains how to use directed IP traffic to service the client's browsing requests.

LMHOSTS File

 An LMHOSTS file helps distribute the browsing information and service client requests. You can also use WINS to collect the browse lists and service client requests.

In the LMHOSTS file, the LM stands for LAN Manager; HOSTS is for the host computer. Its job is to resolve NetBIOS names to the corresponding IP address of remote hosts on different subnets. The purpose is to allow for communication between Master Browsers on remote subnets and the domain Master Browser. This sets up direct communication, enabling an updated list to be developed across a subnet. The one thing to remember about an LMHOSTS file is that it is your responsibility to create and maintain the file. Figure 10.11 illustrates using an LMHOSTS file in a network. A WINS service can dynamically provide this resolution for you.

Figure 10.11

Browsing using LMHOSTS.

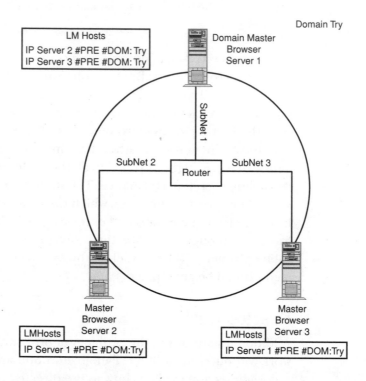

Using an LMHOSTS file is a workable solution, but be aware of some considerations. The LMHOSTS file must be on each and every subnet's Master Browser with an entry to the domain Master Browser to work. It must also be updated manually any time there are changes to the LMHOSTS list. The LMHOSTS file needs to be placed in the winntroot\system32\drivers\etc directory. There are sample TCP/IP files already you can use to reference. It is just a regular text file that can be created using any text editor. There is no file extension, and Windows NT will look and reference the file in this location whenever it needs to. The two items needed in the LMHOSTS file for it to work across a subnet are as follows:

▶ IP address and computer name of the domain Master Browser

▶ The domain name preceded by #PRE and #DOM:

For example:

```
129.62.101.5     server1        #PRE #DOM:try
129.62.101.17    server2        #PRE
129.62.101.25    server3        #PRE
```

The #PRE statement preloads the specific line it is on into memory as a permanent entry in the name cache making it easily available without having to first access the domain.

#DOM:<domain_name> allows for login validation over a router, account synchronization, and, in this case, browsing. Every time the computer sends a broadcast to a domain it also sends it to every computer that has a #DOM: in its LMHOSTS file. These types of broadcasts do go across routers, but are not sent to workgroups. There are many difficulties to watch out for, each of which shall be discussed in the following subsections.

Domain Master Browser

For the domain Master Browser you need an LMHOSTS file that is set up with entries pointing to each of the remote subnet Master Browsers. You should also have a #DOM: statement in each of the Master Browsers' LMHOSTS files pointing to each of the other subnet Master Browsers. If any of them gets promoted to the domain Master Browser, you then do not have to change all your LMHOSTS files.

Duplicate Names

If it finds duplicate LMHOSTS entries for a single domain, the Master Browser decides which relates to the domain Master Browser by querying each IP address for each entry it has. None of the Master Browser respond; only the domain Master Browser does that. Therefore it narrows down the list of duplicates and because only the real one responds it communicates with the one that responds and proceeds to exchange browse lists.

LMHOSTS File Placement

The placement of the LMHOSTS file is in the \etc directory of the client, as mentioned previously. For Windows NT, for example, it is placed in \systemroot\system32\drivers\etc. For Windows 95 and Windows for Workgroups, it is placed in \system_root (c:\windows).

LMHOSTS File Problems

The following are the most common problems you might have with the LMHOSTS file:

▶ The NetBIOS name is misspelled.

▶ The IP address is incorrect.

▶ An entry is not listed for that host.

▶ There are too many entries for a host whereas only the first entry is used. For example, if there are multiple entries in the LMHOSTS file for the same host computer, only the first one listed will be used.

▶ The LMHOSTS file is in the incorrect location and is not being read.

The LMHOSTS file certainly has its place in IP internetwork browsing, but it is certainly not the ultimate solution.

The WINS Solution

WINS (Windows Internet Naming Service) helps fix the problem of NetBIOS broadcast difficulties by dynamically registering the IP address and NetBIOS name, and keeping track of them in a database. Keeping these computer names in its database greatly enhances the network performance. Whenever they need to find a server, clients access the WINS server rather than broadcast on the network. Accessing the WINS server directly allows for a more direct approach when looking for network resources. Plus, it makes updating much easier, because you do not have to manually configure anything. Using a WINS server also provides easier browsing capability because you can freely use NetBIOS names in the place of IP address. The following is an example of using the PING utility with the NetBIOS name rather than specifying the entire IP address.

```
ping Server2
```

rather than

```
ping 207.0.58.33
```

See figure 10.12 for an example of the WINS implementation.

Figure 10.12

*Browsing using
WINS.*

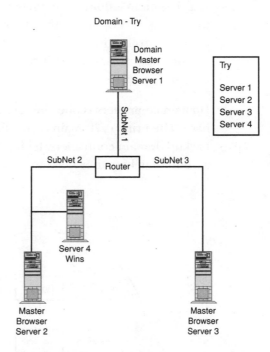

Domain Browser

If the computer is made a WINS client, the domain Master Browser periodically queries the WINS server to update its database of all the domains listed in the WINS database, thereby providing a complete list of all the domains and subnets including remote ones. This list has only domain names and their IP address, not the names of the Master Browsers of each particular subnet as before.

Client Access

When a client needs access to a network resource it calls up the WINS server directly and asks for a list of domain controllers in the domain. WINS provides a list of servers of up to 25 domain controllers, referred to as an *Internet group*. The client is then able to quickly access the domain controller it needs without a complete network broadcast.

Login and Domain Database Replication

Windows NT network services also performs other tasks that initiate broadcasts to all computers in the domain (see fig. 10.13). Two of these tasks are described as follows:

▶ **Logging on to a domain and password changes.** A broadcast message is sent out from the client computer to find a domain controller that can provide authentication of the login or find the primary domain controller to allow changing of the user's password.

▶ **Domain controllers replicating the domain user account database.** The primary domain controller sends a broadcast to the backup domain controllers, telling them it has changes to the account database they need to update to themselves.

Figure 10.13

Login and domain database replication.

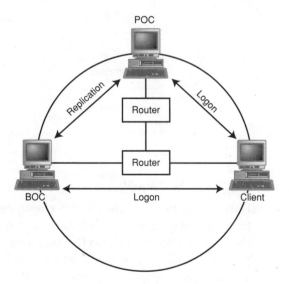

The preceding items are important to understand because they are broadcasts and therefore do not cross IP routers on their own. You have to utilize directed traffic instead. A broadcast initiated to perform these jobs is also given to the remote domain controllers. The list of remote domain controllers is decided by what is listed in either the LMHOSTS file or the WINS database.

When the client needs to access a domain controller, it broadcasts the message directly to the domain and looks for any #DOM:

entries in its LMHOSTS file that matches the domain name. If it finds an identical entry it sends the message specifically to that computer.

It is probably a good idea to add remote domain controller #DOM: entries into the LMHOSTS file with an identical domain name to each client. If the domain controller ever goes down, the users are still able to access remote domains and log on. This is also useful if there are no local domain controllers to enable users to log in to a domain controller on a remote subnet.

 Note

LMHOSTS files are generally for non-WINS clients. You can still reference these non-WINS clients by using a WINS proxy agent, enabling a WINS server to add a non-WINS client to its database through the use of an additional machine that updates the WINS server in place of the non-WINS client. Proxy servers are covered lightly in the following section but are not mentioned anymore as they are a topic all their own and not tested in this exam.

All the backup domain controllers should have #DOM: entries for the primary domain controller, as well as all other backup domain controllers. This way, if one gets promoted to the primary domain controller the backup domain controllers still have mappings to the new primary domain controller.

Overall, WINS provides the better solution for accessing multiple domains and workgroups over different subnets, provided, of course, that all systems are WINS-compliant: Windows 95, Windows NT, Windows for Workgroups with TCP/IP 32 add on.

WINS Proxy Agent

WINS proxy agents are Windows-based WINS clients, not WINS servers, that help non-WINS clients get NetBIOS name resolution. A non-WINS client cannot use a WINS server for its NetBIOS name resolution, so it sends out a name resolution broadcast. The WINS proxy agent listens for such broadcasts and, if it has the information needed, responds itself. If it doesn't have the resolution, it queries the WINS server to get the information and then pass it back to the non-WINS client, acting as a go-between.

Exercises

Exercise 10.1: Implementing WINS

The following exercise shows how WINS works across routers. You need a network with a router and at least one Master Browser on each side of the router, a few WINS-capable clients on each side of the router, and one WINS server on one side (see fig. 10.14).

Figure 10.14

WINS lab layout.

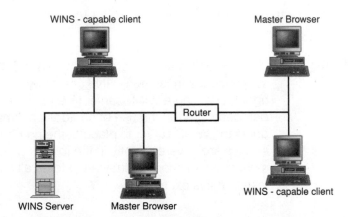

 Note Don't worry if you currently do not have WINS set up or enabled; the first thing to do in the exercises is to disable WINS.

The first thing you need to do is disable the WINS server. This does not mean, however, to de-install it. Figure 10.15 shows using a manual implementation of WINS. Use the following steps:

1. Go to Control Panel and double-click on the Services icon.

2. Click Windows Internet Name service.

3. Click Startup and then select Manual.

4. Click OK and close all windows.

Figure 10.15

*Starting WINS
manually.*

The next thing you need to do is make certain the clients are not enabled to access WINS. Use the following steps:

1. Go to Control Panel and double-click the Network icon.

2. Select Protocols, TCP/IP, Properties.

3. Click WINS Address.

4. Remove any WINS server address by highlighting the address listed and pressing the delete key.

5. Close the windows by clicking OK and then reboot.

6. After Windows NT reboots, use the Windows NT Explorer and find out who you see on the network.

With WINS disabled, no LMHOSTS, HOSTS, DNS, or an IP-enabled router can pass NetBIOS broadcasts, and you should only see what is on your local subnet. It may help to draw a diagram of your network design so that you can identify what systems you should be able to see. It may take a few minutes of updating before everyone appears on the browsing list in your subnet; have patience and keep refreshing or do a direct search.

Now that you have isolated your subnets, the next step is to set up WINS and watch it work.

continues

Exercise 10.1: Continued

If you had WINS set up prior to beginning this exercise and disabled it, all you need to do now is go back into the Services and tab enable the WINS service.

If you did not have WINS previously installed, don't worry. Now is a good time to install WINS.

With WINS newly enabled or installed, go to Network Neighborhood and browse the network. With WINS enabled, you should now see resources on both sides of the router. Figure 10.16 shows an example of what you might see in a WINS database. Sometimes WINS takes a minute to update its database so again keep refreshing before assuming you did something wrong.

Figure 10.16

WINS database.

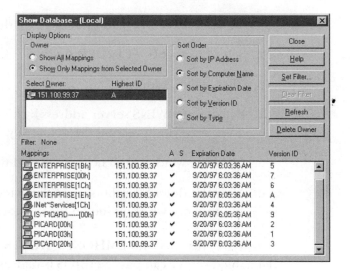

Exercise 10.2: Using an LMHOSTS File

In this exercise, you want to show how you can use an LMHOSTS file to browse across a router. You need the same configuration as in the previous exercise, except that this time you need to make certain that WINS is disabled. Figure 10.17 shows a diagram of the lab layout.

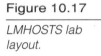

Figure 10.17

*LMHOSTS lab
layout.*

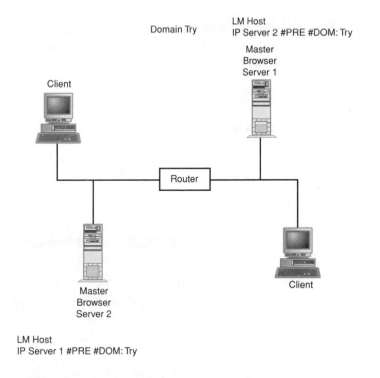

First, you should browse using Network Neighborhood and notice what you see available. With everything disabled, you should only be able to see what is currently on your local subnet. If this is true, you can go on to create an LMHOSTS file. If this is not true, you will continue to be able to see other domains and workgroups in other subnets, which means that even if you implement the LMHOSTS file you will not be able to guarantee that it is actually the LMHOSTS file providing your resolution. This is why you need to check that there is no access before setting up the LMHOSTS file so that after you set it up you can prove the access to a remote subnet is provided by the LMHOSTS file and not some other means of resolution.

You now need to create an LMHOSTS file on each of the Master Browsers on each subnet, pointing specifically to the Master Browser on the other side of the subnet. Make sure you put the LMHOSTS file in the correct location. On Windows NT systems it goes in the \system_root\system32\drivers\etc directory. On Windows 95 and WFW it goes in the \system_root (c:\windows). Don't forget the #PRE and #DOM: statements.

continues

Exercise 10.2: Continued

After you have the files set up in the correct location, you need to enable LMHOSTS to be read by following these steps:

1. Go into the Windows NT Network Properties.

2. Select Protocols, TCP/IP, Properties.

3. Go to WINS address and click on Enable LMHOSTS lookup (see fig. 10.18).

4. Click OK and close all screens.

Figure 10.18

Enabling LMHOSTS lookup.

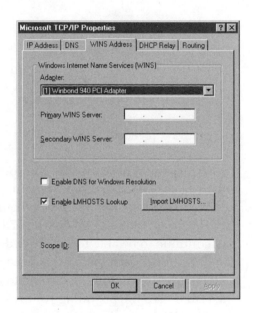

Now you should have LMHOSTS enabled. Go to Network Neighborhood and try exploring. You should see resources on both sides of the router now that you have enabled the usage of an LMHOSTS file. Again when browsing these remote resources through Network Neighborhood the browse list does take a few minutes to update.

Review Questions

The following questions test your knowledge of the information in this chapter.

1. What enables users to search for availability of network resources without knowing the exact location of the resources?

    A. Browsing through Network Neighborhood

    B. The Net Use command

    C. The Net View command

2. If a server name doesn't appear on the browse list, what are some possible causes?

    A. The server is on a different domain.

    B. The master domain hasn't updated the backup domain.

    C. The master domain hasn't updated the server.

3. If you are printing a file on your Windows NT workstation to a network printer and using your A: drive for a disk copy, while sharing your CD-ROM and writing a histogram report using performance monitor, can a remote system access your resources as a client to server?

4. Is there a way to access a network resource without browsing for the resource?

5. You are running a Windows NT 4.0 Server that is currently the primary domain controller, and you have a multiple domain network. What browser role(s) does the server have?

    A. Backup browser

    B. Master browser

    C. Potential browser

    D. Domain Master browser

    E. Potential browser

6. Which one of these situations is true regarding Master Browser to backup browser synchronization?

   A. The Master Browser copies the updates to the backup.

   B. The backup browser copies the updates to the master.

   C. The Master Browser copies the updates from the backup.

   D. The backup browser copies the updates from the master.

7. If I have a domain set up with two Windows 95 computers, three Windows NT workstations computers, three Windows NT server computers, and four Windows for Workgroup computers, who is the third backup browser for this domain?

   A. Windows 95

   B. Windows for Workgroups

   C. Windows NT workstation

   D. No one can fill this role

8. Who is in charge of continually updating the browse list and managing the database of network resources of domains and workgroups?

   A. Backup browser

   B. Master browser

   C. Potential browser

   D. Browser browser

9. Which of these statements is not true about the Domain-Announcement packet?

   A. It has the name of a domain.

   B. It has the name of the Master Browser for that domain.

   C. It specifies whether the Master Browser is a Windows NT server or workstation.

   D. If it is a Windows NT server it specifies the version number of the server.

10. You have a network with five different subnets, each with its own Master Browser. The network administrator wants to be able to see resources of each subnet at the same time. Which process allows for this?

   A. Directed datagram

   B. Directed telegram

   C. Replication

   D. Synchronization

11. If a domain announcement is sent out to a domain and the domain does not respond, how long is it before the remote domain is removed from the browse list?

   A. 4 announcement periods and 45 min

   B. 3 announcement periods and 45 min

   C. 4 announcement periods and 35 min

   D. 3 announcement periods and 35 min

12. You have a network with three subnets: Subnet A, Subnet B, and Subnet C. What happens if the domain Master Browser on Subnet A goes down?

   A. Browsing is restricted to each subnet.

   B. Subnet B can see C but not A.

   C. Subnet C can see B but not A.

   D. All subnets continue browsing normally.

13. How is it possible to browse across routers without the use of WINS, DNS, HOSTS, or LMHOSTS?

   A. You can browse using Network Neighborhood.

   B. You can use an IP-enabled router.

   C. You can use a bootp-enabled router.

14. The LMHOSTS file is mainly used on a network with non-WINS clients specifically for the job of _____.

    A. Resolving a NetBIOS name to MAC-level address.

    B. Resolving an IP address to NetBIOS name.

    C. Resolving an IP address to Internet names.

15. What does the #PRE statement in an LMHOSTS file do?

    A. Prepares a name to load into memory.

    B. Preloads an entry into cache.

    C. Permanently caches a preloaded file.

16. When should you put the other Master Browsers' domains into the LMHOSTS file as well as the domain Master Browser?

    A. If the Domain Master Browser is busy you have to change your LMHOSTS file to access the new Domain Master Browser.

    B. If the Domain Master Browser goes down you do not have to change your LMHOSTS file to access the new Domain Master Browser.

    C. If your LMHOSTS file is unavailable you have to update your Domain Master Browser list.

17. WINS can take the place of an LMHOSTS file over a network by _____ updating across routers?

    A. Dynamically

    B. Statically

18. If the Domain Master Browser is a WINS client, it can get automatic updates of remote domains.

    A. This is a true statement.

    B. This statement is false.

    C. This statement has nothing to do with the Master Browser and WINS.

19. What are two additional Windows NT network services that initiate a broadcast in a domain but not across routers?

    A. Logging in and passwords, PDC to PDC replication

    B. Directory replication and authentication

    C. Logging in and passwords, PDC to BDC replication

20. What is the purpose of a WINS proxy agent?

    A. To take the place of a WINS server

    B. To provide NetBIOS name resolution to non-WINS clients

    C. To provide host name resolution to non-WINS clients

Review Answers

1. A

2. B

3. Yes. The key is that you are sharing your CD-ROM, thus acting in the role of a server as well as a client while you are accessing other resources.

4. Yes, with either the Net View command or by choosing Start, Find, Computer.

5. B, D

6. D

7. C

8. B

9. D

10. A

11. B

12. A

13. C

14. B

15. B

16. B

17. A

18. A

19. C

20. B

Answers to the Test Yourself Questions at the Beginning of the Chapter

1. Windows NT internetwork browsing is a service that enables users to obtain a list of network resources available in their network environment. With internetwork browsing, users do not have to search for resources, nor does every machine need to maintain its own list. See "Browsing in Windows NT."

2. A WINS server does not provide an adequate browsing solution when there are clients that are unable to utilize the WINS services. These clients are commonly called *non-WINS clients*. The appropriate solution for these non-WINS clients is the use of an LMHOSTS file or a WINS proxy agent. See "Browsing in an IP Internetwork."

3. Browsing in an internetwork also contributes to the action of logging on to a domain, for authentication, and Domain controller replication. See "Login and Domain Database Replication."

Chapter 11

Host Name Resolution

This chapter will help you prepare for the exam by covering the following objectives:

 **Objectives**

- ▶ Configure HOSTS and LMHOSTS files
- ▶ Diagnose and resolve name resolution problems

Test Yourself! Before reading this chapter, test yourself to determine how much study time you will need to devote to this section.

1. The HOSTS file is an ASCII text file that statically maps _____.

    A. Host names and IP addresses

    B. NetBIOS names and IP addresses

    C. MAC addresses to IP addresses

    D. Fully Qualified Domain Names

2. The following entry is in the HOSTS file:

    ```
    197.197.197.5    MADONNA    rita
    ```

    When the command **PING MADONNA** is given, 197.197.197.5 responds successfully. When the command **PING RITA** is given, the host is not found. What is causing this problem?

    A. The line is not read after the MADONNA entry.

    B. An invalid IP address is used.

    C. Rita is not a valid server name.

    D. The file is case-sensitive.

Answers are located at the end of the chapter.

Host Names

Names are stored, and referenced, in many formats in TCP/IP. Although a host name is but one of many, it is one of the easiest to use. Problems, however, stem from the fact that Windows NT does not reference host names in the same manner as other operating systems.

In Unix, the host name is mapped directly to an IP address, and the IP address is mapped to a hardware address. Because NT uses NetBIOS internally, there is a stronger reliance on NetBIOS names than anything else. When a command is issued referencing a server, the NetBIOS name is resolved to an IP address, and then to a hardware address. For more information on this, please refer to Chapter 7, "NetBIOS over TCP/IP."

The primary advantage of using host names is that they are easy to remember and bound only by the limitation that they be under 255 characters in length. You can use more than one host name for a host.

 Note

The host name used does not have to match the NetBIOS name of the Windows NT machine.

Host name resolution, quite simply, is the process by which host names are mapped to IP addresses. You can do this in a number of ways, including:

▶ Local host name

▶ HOSTS files

▶ DNS (Domain Name System) servers

In the same way we saw that NetBIOS name resolution used host name resolution as a backup, NT uses NetBIOS name resolution to back up host name resolution. This means there are another three ways to resolve host names:

▶ WINS servers

▶ Local broadcast

▶ LMHOSTS file

Each of these methods, and corresponding utilities, is examined in the following pages.

Configure HOSTS Files

 Objective

The HOSTS file is an ASCII text file that statically maps local and remote host names and IP addresses. It is located in *systemroot*\ System32\Drivers\etc.

The HOSTS file is not case sensitive, however, some utilities that you will use may be. Entries in the HOSTS file are limited to 255 characters per entry. The HOSTS file is used by PING and other Winsock utilities to resolve host names locally and remotely. One HOSTS file must reside on each host, and the file is read from top to bottom. As soon as a match is found for a host name, the file stops being read. For that reason, when there are duplicate entries, the latter ones are always ignored, and the most commonly used names should be near the top of the file.

The following is an example of the default HOSTS file:

```
# Copyright (c) 1993-1995 Microsoft Corp.
#
# This is a sample HOSTS file used by Microsoft TCP/IP for Win-
dows NT.
#
# This file contains the mappings of IP addresses to host names.
Each entry should be kept on an individual line. The IP address
should be placed in the first column followed by the correspond-
ing host name.
# The IP address and the host name should be separated by at
least one space.
#
# Additionally, comments (such as these) may be inserted on indi-
vidual lines or following the machine name denoted by a '#' sym-
bol.
#
# For example:
#
```

```
#       102.54.94.97    rhino.acme.com      # source server
#        38.25.63.10    x.acme.com          # x client host

127.0.0.1       localhost
```

You should notice several things in this file. First, the pound sign (#) indicates a comment. When the system reads the file, every line beginning with a comment is ignored. When a # appears in the middle of a line, the line is read only up to the sign. If this file were in use on a live system, you would delete the first 17 lines or move them to the end of the file to keep them from being read every time the file is referenced.

The second thing to note is the entry:

```
127.0.0.1       localhost
```

This is a *loopback* address in every host. It references the internal card, regardless of the host address, and can be used for diagnostics to verify that connections are working properly internally, before testing that they are working properly down the wire.

Within the HOSTS file, fields are separated by white space that can be tabs or spaces. As mentioned earlier, a host can be referred to by more than one name—to do so, separate the entries on the same line with white space, as shown in the following example:

```
127.0.0.1       me loopback localhost
199.9.200.7     SALES7 victor
199.9.200.4     SALES4 nikki
199.9.200.3     SALES3 cole
199.9.200.2     SALES2 victoria
199.9.200.1     SALES1 nicholas
199.9.200.5     SALES5 jack
199.9.200.11    ACCT1
199.9.200.12    ACCT2
199.9.200.13    ACCT3
199.9.200.14    ACCT4
199.9.200.15    ACCT5
199.9.200.17    ACCT7
```

The aliases are other names by which the system can be referred. Here, "me" and "loopback" do the same as "localhost," and "nicholas" is the same as "SALES1." If an alias is used more than once, the search stops at the first match because the file is searched sequentially.

Exercise 11.2 allows you to practice editing this file.

Configure LMHOSTS File

 Whereas the HOSTS file contains the mappings of IP addresses to host names, the LMHOSTS file contains the mappings of IP addresses to Windows NT computer names. When speaking of Windows NT computer names, the inference is to NetBIOS names, or the names that would be used in conjunction with NET USE statements.

An example of the default version of this file follows:

```
# Copyright (c) 1993-1995 Microsoft Corp.
#
# This is a sample LMHOSTS file used by the Microsoft TCP/IP for
Windows NT.
#
# This file contains the mappings of IP addresses to NT computer
names # (NetBIOS) names.  Each entry should be kept on an indi-
vidual line.
# The IP address should be placed in the first column followed by
the # corresponding computername. The address and the comptername
# should be separated by at least one space or tab. The "#" char-
acter # is generally used to denote the start of a comment (see
the exceptions below).
#
# This file is compatible with Microsoft LAN Manager 2.x TCP/IP
lmhosts # files and offers the following extensions:
#
#       #PRE
#       #DOM:<domain>
#       #INCLUDE <filename>
```

```
#       #BEGIN_ALTERNATE
#       #END_ALTERNATE
#       \0xnn (non-printing character support)
#
# Following any entry in the file with the characters "#PRE" will
cause # the entry to be preloaded into the name cache. By de-
fault, entries are # not preloaded, but are parsed only after
dynamic name resolution fails.
#
# Following an entry with the "#DOM:<domain>" tag will associate
the # entry with the domain specified by <domain>. This affects
how the # browser and logon services behave in TCP/IP environ-
ments. To preload # the host name associated with #DOM entry, it
is necessary to also add a #PRE to the line. The <domain> is al-
ways preloaded although it will not be shown when the name cache
is viewed.
#
# Specifying "#INCLUDE <filename>" will force the RFC NetBIOS
(NBT) # software to seek the specified <filename> and parse it as
if it were local. <filename> is generally a UNC-based name, al-
lowing a # centralized lmhosts file to be maintained on a server.
# It is ALWAYS necessary to provide a mapping for the IP address
of the # server prior to the #INCLUDE. This mapping must use the
#PRE directive.
# In addition the share "public" in the example below must be in
the # LanManServer list of "NullSessionShares" in order for cli-
ent machines to # be able to read the lmhosts file successfully.
This key is under # \machine\system\currentcontrolset\services\
lanmanserver\ parameters\nullsessionshares # in the registry.
Simply add "public" to the list found there.
#
# The #BEGIN_ and #END_ALTERNATE keywords allow multiple #INCLUDE
# statements to be grouped together. Any single successful in-
clude will cause the group to succeed.
```

```
#
# Finally, non-printing characters can be embedded in mappings by
# first surrounding the NetBIOS name in quotations, then using
the \0xnn notation to specify a hex value for a non-printing
character.
#
# The following example illustrates all of these extensions:
#
# 102.54.94.97      rhino          #PRE #DOM:networking  #net
group's DC
# 102.54.94.102     "appname  \0x14"                     #special
app server
# 102.54.94.123     popular             #PRE             #source
server
# 102.54.94.117     localsrv            #PRE             #needed
for the include
#
# #BEGIN_ALTERNATE
# #INCLUDE \\localsrv\public\lmhosts
# #INCLUDE \\rhino\public\lmhosts
# #END_ALTERNATE
#
# In the above example, the "appname" server contains a special
# character in its name, the "popular" and "localsrv" server
names are preloaded, and the "rhino" server name is specified so
it can be used to later #INCLUDE a centrally maintained lmhosts
file if the "localsrv" system is unavailable.
#
# Note that the whole file is parsed including comments on each
lookup, so keeping the number of comments to a minimum will im-
prove performance.
# Therefore it is not advisable to simply add lmhosts file en-
tries onto the end of this file.
```

Once more, the pound sign (#) indicates comments, and the file is read sequentially on each lookup, so limiting the size of the comment lines at the beginning of the file is highly recommended.

You can use a number of special commands in the file to load entries into a name cache that is scanned on each lookup prior to referencing the file. (By default, entries are not preloaded, but are parsed only after dynamic name resolution fails). Using these commands decreases your lookup time and increases system efficiency.

Other Files to Be Aware Of

While the exam objectives specifically speak of the HOSTS and LMHOSTS files, these work in conjunction with other files copied to *systemroot*\System32\Drivers\etc, namely the following:

▶ SERVICES

▶ NETWORKS

▶ PROTOCOL

A copy of each of these files is included for reference. Although you need not memorize them for the exam, be familiar with them for the real world.

SERVICES

The SERVICES file is used to identify the port numbers on which services operate. The following listing is the system default.

```
# Copyright (c) 1993-1995 Microsoft Corp.
#
# This file contains port numbers for well-known services as de-
fined by RFC 1060 (Assigned Numbers).
#
# Format:
#
# <service name>  <port number>/<protocol>  [aliases...]
[#<comment>]
#

echo            7/tcp
echo            7/udp
discard         9/tcp    sink null
discard         9/udp    sink null
```

```
systat        11/tcp
systat        11/tcp      users
daytime       13/tcp
daytime       13/udp
netstat       15/tcp
qotd          17/tcp      quote
qotd          17/udp      quote
chargen       19/tcp      ttytst source
chargen       19/udp      ttytst source
ftp-data      20/tcp
ftp           21/tcp
telnet        23/tcp
smtp          25/tcp      mail
time          37/tcp      timserver
time          37/udp      timserver
rlp           39/udp      resource       # resource location
name          42/tcp      nameserver
name          42/udp      nameserver
whois         43/tcp      nicname        # usually to sri-nic
domain        53/tcp      nameserver     # name-domain server
domain        53/udp      nameserver
nameserver    53/tcp      domain         # name-domain server
nameserver    53/udp      domain
mtp           57/tcp                     # deprecated
bootp         67/udp                     # boot program server
tftp          69/udp
rje           77/tcp      netrjs
finger        79/tcp
link          87/tcp      ttylink
supdup        95/tcp
hostnames     101/tcp     hostname       # usually from sri-nic
iso-tsap      102/tcp
dictionary    103/tcp     webster
x400          103/tcp                    # ISO Mail
x400-snd      104/tcp
csnet-ns      105/tcp
pop           109/tcp     postoffice
pop2          109/tcp                    # Post Office
pop3          110/tcp     postoffice
portmap       111/tcp
portmap       111/udp
sunrpc        111/tcp
```

```
sunrpc          111/udp
auth            113/tcp     authentication
sftp            115/tcp
path            117/tcp
uucp-path       117/tcp
nntp            119/tcp     usenet        # Network News Transfer
ntp             123/udp     ntpd ntp      # network time protocol (exp)
nbname          137/udp
nbdatagram      138/udp
nbsession       139/tcp
NeWS            144/tcp     news
sgmp            153/udp     sgmp
tcprepo         158/tcp     repository    # PCMAIL
snmp            161/udp     snmp
snmp-trap       162/udp     snmp
print-srv       170/tcp                   # network PostScript
vmnet           175/tcp
load            315/udp
vmnet0          400/tcp
sytek           500/udp
biff            512/udp     comsat
exec            512/tcp
login           513/tcp
who             513/udp     whod
shell           514/tcp     cmd           # no passwords used
syslog          514/udp
printer         515/tcp     spooler       # line printer spooler
talk            517/udp
ntalk           518/udp
efs             520/tcp                   # for LucasFilm
route           520/udp     router routed
timed           525/udp     timeserver
tempo           526/tcp     newdate
courier         530/tcp     rpc
conference      531/tcp     chat
rvd-control     531/udp     MIT disk
netnews         532/tcp     readnews
netwall         533/udp                   # -for emergency broadcasts
uucp            540/tcp     uucpd         # uucp daemon
klogin          543/tcp                   # Kerberos authenticated
rlogin
kshell          544/tcp     cmd           # and remote shell
new-rwho        550/udp     new-who       # experimental
```

```
remotefs          556/tcp    rfs_server rfs# Brunhoff remote filesystem
rmonitor          560/udp    rmonitord   # experimental
monitor           561/udp                # experimental
garcon            600/tcp
maitrd            601/tcp
busboy            602/tcp
acctmaster        700/udp
acctslave         701/udp
acct              702/udp
acctlogin         703/udp
acctprinter       704/udp
elcsd             704/udp                # errlog
acctinfo          705/udp
acctslave2        706/udp
acctdisk          707/udp
kerberos          750/tcp    kdc         # Kerberos authentication—tcp
kerberos          750/udp    kdc         # Kerberos authentication—udp
kerberos_master   751/tcp                # Kerberos authentication
kerberos_master   751/udp                # Kerberos authentication
passwd_server     752/udp                # Kerberos passwd server
userreg_server    753/udp                # Kerberos userreg server
krb_prop          754/tcp                # Kerberos slave propagation
erlogin           888/tcp                # Login and environment pass-
ing
kpop              1109/tcp               # Pop with Kerberos
phone             1167/udp
ingreslock        1524/tcp
maze              1666/udp
nfs               2049/udp               # sun nfs
knetd             2053/tcp               # Kerberos de-multiplexor
eklogin           2105/tcp               # Kerberos encrypted rlogin
rmt               5555/tcp    rmtd
mtb               5556/tcp    mtbd        # mtb backup
man               9535/tcp               # remote man server
w                 9536/tcp
mantst            9537/tcp               # remote man server, testing
bnews             10000/tcp
rscs0             10000/udp
queue             10001/tcp
```

```
rscs1           10001/udp
poker           10002/tcp
rscs2           10002/udp
gateway         10003/tcp
rscs3           10003/udp
remp            10004/tcp
rscs4           10004/udp
rscs5           10005/udp
rscs6           10006/udp
rscs7           10007/udp
rscs8           10008/udp
rscs9           10009/udp
rscsa           10010/udp
rscsb           10011/udp
qmaster         10012/tcp
qmaster         10012/udp
```

To prevent services from running, or to alter their port assignments, you can edit the SERVICES file.

NETWORKS

The NETWORKS file holds mappings and aliases to network IP addresses. A copy of the default file follows:

```
# Copyright (c) 1993-1995 Microsoft Corp.
#
# This file contains network name/network number mappings for
# local networks. Network numbers are recognized in dotted
  decimal form.
#
# Format:
#
# <network name>  <network number>     [aliases...]  [#<comment>]
#
# For example:
#
#     loopback    127
#     campus      284.122.107
#     london      284.122.108

loopback                  127
```

Notice that the only active listing in the default file is to the loopback address.

PROTOCOL

The PROTOCOL file identifies protocols in the TCP/IP suite that are running and the assigned port number they are running on. A copy of the default file follows:

```
# Copyright (c) 1993-1995 Microsoft Corp.
#
# This file contains the Internet protocols as defined by RFC
1060 (Assigned Numbers).
#
# Format:
#
# <protocol name>  <assigned number>  [aliases...]  [#<comment>]

ip        0    IP       # Internet protocol
icmp      1    ICMP     # Internet control message protocol
ggp       3    GGP      # Gateway-gateway protocol
tcp       6    TCP      # Transmission control protocol
egp       8    EGP      # Exterior gateway protocol
pup       12   PUP      # PARC universal packet protocol
udp       17   UDP      # User datagram protocol
hmp       20   HMP      # Host monitoring protocol
xns-idp   22   XNS-IDP  # Xerox NS IDP
rdp       27   RDP      # "reliable datagram" protocol
rvd       66   RVD      # MIT remote virtual disk
```

The protocols listed along the left column should be very familiar to you from other chapters in this book.

DNS Servers

DNS (Domain Name System) servers can also be used by Windows NT 4.0 to resolve Fully Qualified Domain Names (FQDNs) to IP addresses. Although much more common in the Unix world, Windows NT utilizes the resolution in a two-step solution:

1. A DNS server is called to look up the FQDN supplied by the user.

2. ARP (Address Resolution Protocol) is used to find the hardware address or the address of the router that can deliver the request.

FQDNs are best exemplified by user addresses. For example, suppose that edulaney@iquest.net decides to use Internet Explorer to connect to www.mcp.com, which is running on Internet Information Server. The request is made at the application layer using information a user has entered.

The application layer sends it to the transport layer, which uses known ports (16-bit port addresses). The transport layer passes the data (request and information) to the network layer, which uses DNS lookup to find the addresses in 32-bit dotted decimal format.

Lastly, the interface (assume ethernet on both machines for simplicity) layer does an ARP broadcast to find the unique 48-bit hex address stamped into the NIC card.

The connection is now established and the two parties communicate—an immensely complicated procedure made possible by the DNS servers.

Diagnose and Resolve Name Resolution Problems

 Objective

Name resolution problems are easily identified as such with the PING utility. If you can ping a host using its IP address, but cannot ping it by its host name, then you have a resolution problem. If you cannot ping the host at all, then the problem lies elsewhere.

Problems that can occur with name resolution and their solutions fit into the following generalities:

1. The entry is misspelled. Examine the HOSTS or LMHOSTS file to verify that the host name is correctly spelled. If you are using the HOSTS file, capitalization is important because this file is case-sensitive whereas LMHOSTS is not case sensitive.

2. Comment characters prevent the entry from being read. Verify that a pound sign is not at the beginning of the line, or anywhere on the line prior to the host name.

3. There are duplicate entries in the file. Because the files are read in linear fashion, only the first entry is read and all others are ignored when duplication exists. Verify that all host names are unique.

4. A host other than the one you want is contacted. Verify that the IP address entered in the file(s) is valid and corresponds to the host name.

5. The wrong file is used. While similar in nature, HOSTS and LMHOSTS are quite different, and not all that interchangeable. HOSTS is used to map IP addresses to host names, and LMHOSTS is used to map NetBIOS names to IP addresses.

In addition to PING, the all-purpose TCP/IP troubleshooting tool, useful name resolution utilities include:

▶ nbtstat

▶ hostname

NBTSTAT

The nbtstat utility (NetBIOS over TCP/IP) displays protocol statistics and current TCP/IP connections. It is useful for troubleshooting NetBIOS name resolution problems, and has a number of parameters and options that can be used with it:

▶ **-a (adapter status).** Lists the remote machine's name table given its name.

▶ **-A (Adapter status).** Lists the remote machine's name table given its IP address.

▶ **-c (cache).** Lists the remote name cache including the IP addresses.

▶ **-n (names).** Lists local NetBIOS names.

▶ **-r (resolved).** Lists names resolved by broadcast and via WINS.

- ▶ **-R (Reload).** Purges and reloads the remote cache name table.

- ▶ **-S (Sessions).** Lists sessions table with the destination IP addresses.

- ▶ **-s (sessions).** Lists sessions table converting destination IP addresses to host names via the hosts file.

Hostname

The hostname.exe utility, located in *systemroot*\\System32 returns the name of the local host. This is used only to view the name, and cannot be used to change the name. You can change the host name from the Network Control Panel applet. Exercise 11.1 tests this utility.

Exercises

Exercise 11.1: Finding and Testing the Local Host Name

The following exercise shows you how to find the local host name and verify that you can ping it.

1. From the Start menu, choose Programs, MS-DOS prompt.

2. Type **HOSTNAME** to see the local host's name.

3. Type **PING {HOSTNAME}** where the {HOSTNAME} is the value returned in step two.

In this exercise, you found the local host name and were able to ping it.

Exercise 11.2: Editing the HOSTS File

This exercise shows you how to find and edit the HOSTS file.

1. From the Start menu, choose Programs, MS-DOS prompt.

2. Change directory to the appropriate location by typing **cd *systemroot*\\System32\\Drivers\\etc**. *Systemroot* is your Windows NT directory (normally \\WINNT).

3. Type **PING ME** and notice the error that comes back because the host is not found.

4. Type **EDIT HOSTS**.

   The last line of the file should read:

   `"127.0.0.1     localhost"`

5. Move one space to the right of the last character and type **ME**. The line now reads:

   `"127.0.0.1        localhost ME"`

6. Exit the editor and save the changes.

7. Type **PING ME** and notice the successful results.

In this exercise, you edited the HOSTS file and added an alias.

Review Questions

The following questions will test your knowledge of the information in this chapter. Questions 1–3 refer to the following HOSTS file:

```
127.0.0.1       localhost
192.200.2.4     karen     Kristin      #Evan
192.200.2.5     Spencer   Sales
192.200.2.6     #Lorraine Buis
192.200.2.7     Sales
```

1. Kristin, a user in the Finance department, calls to say that she is having trouble connecting to the host called Lorraine. When she pings 192.200.2.6, the result is successful, but when she pings Lorraine, the error message says the host is not found. What is causing this problem?

    A. Invalid IP address

    B. Duplicate entry

    C. Comment character in the wrong position

    D. Improper spelling of host name

2. Evan, in Accounting, needs to get into 192.200.2.7. He can ping the IP address, but if he tries to ping Sales, the results come back telling him that 192.200.2.5 is responding. What is causing this problem?

    A. Invalid IP address

    B. Duplicate entry

    C. Comment character in the wrong position

    D. Improper spelling of host name

3. Spencer, in Sales, needs to connect to the host, Karen. He can ping the IP address successfully, but if he attempts to ping Karen, the host is not found. What is causing this problem?

    A. Invalid IP address

    B. Duplicate entry

    C. Comment character in the wrong position

    D. Improper spelling of host name

4. Which utility is useful for troubleshooting NetBIOS name resolution problems?

    A. Nbtstat

    B. Netstat

    C. Ping

    D. Hostname

5. Which utility is useful for finding the local host name?

    A. Nbtstat

    B. Netstat

    C. Ping

    D. Hostname

6. Which utility is an all-purpose tool for troubleshooting TCP/IP problems?

    A. Nbtstat

    B. Netstat

    C. Ping

    D. Hostname

7. HOSTS file entries are limited to how many characters?

    A. 8

    B. 255

    C. 500

    D. Unlimited

8. The number of entries in the HOSTS file is limited to _____.

    A. 8

    B. 255

    C. 500

    D. Unlimited

9. Which file is used for host name resolution?

    A. HOSTS

    B. LMHOSTS

    C. ARP

    D. FQDN

10. Which file is used for NetBIOS name resolution?

    A. HOSTS

    B. LMHOSTS

    C. ARP

    D. FQDN

11. Which address is the loopback address?

    A. 0.0.0.1

    B. 127.0.0.0

    C. 127.0.0.1

    D. 255.255.255.255

12. HOSTS and LMHOSTS work in conjunction with what other files (select all correct answers)?

    A. NETWORKS

    B. PROTOCOL

    C. SERVICES

    D. RESL

Review Answers

1. C

2. B

3. D

4. A

5. D

6. C

7. B

8. D

9. A

10. B

11. C

12. A, B, C

Answers to the Test Yourself Questions at the Beginning of the Chapter

1. A. See "Configure HOSTS Files."
2. D. See "Diagnose and Resolve Name Resolution Problems."

Chapter 12

The Domain Name System

This chapter will help you prepare for the exam by covering the following objectives:

 Objectives

▶ Connect a DNS Server to a DNS root server

▶ Configure DNS Server roles

Test Yourself! Before reading this chapter, test yourself to determine how much study time you will need to devote to this section.

1. What is DNS?

2. How does DNS differ from other host resolution systems like WINS or HOSTS files?

3. Where are the records that make up the domain name space stored?

4. How does DNS on a Windows NT server differ from other implementations of DNS, such as on a Unix DNS Server?

5. How are DNS host names structured?

6. What are some of the top-level domains on the Internet, and what organization maintains zone files for these domains?

7. Should the DNS entries for one NT domain be in one zone file or placed in several zone files? Why?

8. What type of zone files are needed for DNS?

9. Can you register more than one host to the same name? Why would you want to do this?

10. Can a Windows NT DNS Server be used as a secondary server for a non-Microsoft primary server?

Answers are located at the end of the chapter.

History of DNS

The Domain Name System is one way to resolve host names in a TCP/IP environment. In non-Microsoft environments, host names are typically resolved through host files or DNS. In a Microsoft environment, WINS and broadcasts are also used. DNS is the primary system used to resolve host names on the Internet. In fact, DNS had its beginning in the early days of the Internet.

In its early days, the Internet was a small network established by the Department of Defense for research purposes. This network linked computers at several government agencies with a few universities. The host names of the computers in this network were registered in a single HOSTS file located on a centrally administered server. Each site that needed to resolve host names downloaded this file. Few computers were being added to this network, so the HOSTS file wasn't updated too often and the different sites only had to download this file periodically to update their own copies. As the number of hosts on the Internet grew, it became more and more difficult to manage all the names through a central HOSTS file. The number of entries was increasing rapidly, changes were being made frequently, and the server with the central HOSTS file was being accessed more and more often by the different Internet sites trying to download a new copy.

DNS was introduced in 1984 as a way to resolve host names without relying on one central HOSTS file. With DNS, the host names reside in a database that can be distributed among multiple servers, decreasing the load on any one server and also allowing more than one point of administration for this naming system. The name system is based on hierarchical names in a tree-type directory structure. DNS allows more types of registration than the simple host-name-to-TCP/IP-address mapping used in HOSTS files and allows room for future defined types. Because the database is distributed, it can support a much larger database than can be stored in a single HOSTS file. In fact, the database size is virtually unlimited because more servers can be added to handle additional parts of the database. The Domain Name System was first introduced in 1984.

History of Microsoft DNS

DNS was first introduced in the Microsoft environment as part of the Resource Kit for NT Server 3.51. It was not available as part of the NT source files. With version 4.0, DNS is now integrated with the NT source files. Although DNS is not installed by default as part of an NT 4.0 Server installation, you can specify DNS be included as part of an NT installation or you can add DNS later just as you would any other networking service that is part of NT.

Microsoft DNS is based on RFCs 974, 1034, and 1035. A popular implementation of DNS is called BIND (Berkeley Internet Name Domain), developed at UC Berkeley for their version of Unix. However BIND is not totally compliant with the DNS RFCs. Microsoft's DNS does support some features of BIND, but Microsoft DNS is based on the RFCs, not on BIND.

 Tip

You can read these RFCs, or any other RFC, by going to the InterNIC Web site at `http://ds.internic.net/ds/rfc-index.html`.

 Note

Microsoft is planning major enhancements to DNS for NT 5.0. Microsoft is planning to introduce an X.500-type directory structure for their networks in version 5.0. This directory structure will use DNS as the means to organize and control the network architecture. In current versions of NT, the only way to link domains together is through trust relationships. However, even though the domains are linked, you cannot easily manage all the domains. In NT 5.0, Microsoft is planning to keep trusts but manage them through DNS. In DNS an administrator will be able to see all the servers in the network in a hierarchy that brings all the resources in the network together in a more logical manner than the current interface for trust relationships provides.

Microsoft is planning a migration path to move existing trust relationships into DNS. Although administrators have been using DNS mostly to manage Internet or intranet connections, in the future administrators will use DNS to manage their entire network, both for local access and for Internet access.

The Structure of DNS

Some host-name systems, like NetBIOS names, use a flat database. With a flat database, all names exist at the same level, so there can't be any duplicate names. These names are like Social Security numbers: every participant in the Social Security program must have a unique number. The Social Security System is a national system that encompasses all workers in the United States, so it must use an identification system to distinguish between all the individuals in the United States.

DNS names are located in a hierarchical paths, like a directory structure. As figure 12.1 illustrates, you can have a file called TEST.TXT in C:\ and another file called TEST.TXT in C:\ASCII. In a network using DNS, you can have more than one server with the same name, as long as each is located in a different path.

Figure 12.1

Names in DNS are part of a logical tree structure called the domain name space. Each node in the space is called a domain and it can have subdomains.

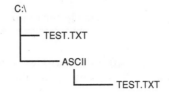

DNS Domains

The Internet Network Information Center (InterNIC) controls
the top-level domains. These have names like "com" (for businesses), "edu" (for educational institutions like universities), "gov"
(for government organizations), and "org" (for non-profit organizations). There are also domains for countries. You can visit the
InterNIC web site at http://www.internic.com/. Table 12.1 summarizes common Internet domains.

Table 12.1

Common Internet Domains

Name	Type of Organization
com	Commercial organizations
edu	Educational institutions
org	Non-profit organizations
net	Networks (the backbone of the Internet)
gov	Non-military government organizations
mil	Military government organizations
num	Phone numbers
arpa	Reverse DNS
xx	Two-letter country code

Figure 12.2 shows the top-level domains on the Internet with
some subdomains illustrated as well.

Figure 12.2

*Domains of the
Internet.*

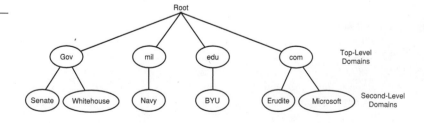

DNS Host Names

To refer to a host in a domain, use a fully qualified domain name (FQDN), which completely specifies the location of the host. An FQDN specifies the host name, the domain or subdomain the host belongs to, and any domains above that in the hierarchy until the root domain in the organization is specified. On the Internet, the root domain in the path is something like "com," but on a private network the top-level domains may be named according to some internal naming convention. The FQDN is read from left to right, with each host name or domain name specified by a period. The syntax of an FQDN follows:

```
host name.subdomain. … .domain
```

An example of an FQDN is www.microsoft.com, which refers to a server called "www" located in the subdomain called "microsoft" in the domain called "com." Referring to a host by its FQDN is similar to referring to a file by its complete directory path. However, a complete file name goes from general to specific, with the file name at the rightmost part of the path. An FQDN goes from specific to general, with the host name at the leftmost part of the name. Fully qualified domain names are more like addresses, as shown in figure 12.3. An address starts with the most specific information: who is to receive the letter. Then address specifies the house number in which the recipient lives, the street on which the house is located, the city where the street is located, and finally the most general location, the state where that city is located.

Figure 12.3

Addresses use a generic to specific naming scheme.

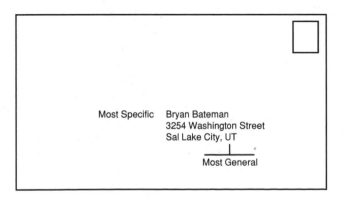

Most Specific   Bryan Bateman
                 3254 Washington Street
                 Sal Lake City, UT

                 Most General

Zone Files

The DNS database is stored in files called *zones*. It's possible, even desirable, to break the DNS database in a number of zones. Breaking the DNS database into zones was part of the original design goals of DNS. With multiple zones, the load of providing access to the database is spread among a number of servers. Also, the administrative burden of managing the database is spread out, because different administrators manage only the parts of the DNS database stored in their own zones. A zone can be any portion of the domain name space; it doesn't have to contain all the subdomains for that part of the DNS tree. Zones can be copied to other name servers through replication. With multiple zones, smaller amounts of information are copied when zone files are replicated than would be if the entire domain was located in one zone file.

Figure 12.4 shows a DNS domain, erudite.com, that is broken into several zones. Because this domain could be very large, splitting it into zones enables the administrators to manage smaller zone files that are located where the administrators work instead of in some central location. Also, because the files are smaller, less network traffic is generated as the zone files are copied from server to server. In fact, if the entire domain is located in one zone file, each time a change is made to the zone file the entire file must be copied to other DNS Servers that are configured to received a copy.

Figure 12.4

The domain erudite.com and its zones.

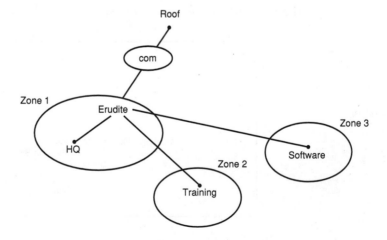

Types of DNS Servers

 Objective ▶

A DNS Server has information about the domain name space that it has already obtained either from a local copy of a zone file or by making a query of another DNS Server. A name server can have more than one zone file installed on it. A name server can have the original copy of a zone, or it can receive a copy of a zone file from another name server. If a name server has any copy of a zone file, it has authority for that zone.

There are three types of name servers: Primary, Secondary, and Master.

A *primary server* has the original copy of a zone file. Any changes made to the zone file are made to the file on the primary server. When a primary server receives a query about a host name in its own zone, it retrieves the host resolution locally from its own zone files.

A *secondary server* gets a copy of zone files from another server. This secondary zone file is a read-only copy of the file; any changes made to the zone are made at the originating zone file. Then the changes are copied down to the secondary server through replication. When zone files are copied from another server it is called a zone transfer.

There are several reasons you should have a secondary server for each zone. A secondary server provides redundancy, enabling host names in the zone to be resolved even if the primary server goes down. A secondary server can also reduce the load on a primary server or reduce network traffic. For example, placing a secondary server on a remote site can reduce network traffic generated when clients cross the WAN link to resolve host names. With a secondary server at this remote site, client queries can be handled locally. The only traffic from DNS is generated when the zone file on the primary server changes and the secondary server downloads a new copy. Also, the primary server sees less activity because it communicates with only one host at the remote site (the secondary server) rather than resolve queries from all the clients at the site.

A server can have any number of zone files stored on it. The primary and secondary designation applies to each zone file rather than to the server itself. A server can be the primary for one zone (it has the master copy of that zone) and a secondary for another zone (it gets a read-only copy of the zone file through a zone transfer).

The server from which a secondary server receives a zone transfer is called the *Master Name Server*. The TCP/IP address of the Master Name Server is configured at the secondary server. The master server can be a primary or a secondary server. If the master is a primary, then the zone transfer comes directly from the source. If the master name server is a secondary server, the file received from the master server via a zone transfer is a copy of the read-only zone file. In this scenario, there can be a delay in receiving changes made to the zone file because the file must first be transferred to the master server and then transferred again to the next server in line.

As figure 12.5 illustrates, however, using secondary servers as master servers can reduce the load on a primary server by limiting the number of secondary servers to which the primary server must send zone transfers. In this figure, the primary server sends a copy of the zone to three servers in total while only communicating directly with one server. The master server for Secondary2 and Secondary3 is on the same side of a slow WAN link. The zone file is transferred once over the slow link to Secondary1, and then is transferred to the other servers on the same LAN.

Both primary and secondary servers are considered authoritative for their zones because they have the zone information. In other words, either the primary or the secondary can respond to a request for information about the part of the domain that is stored in that zone file.

A DNS Server doesn't have to have any zone files, either as a primary or a secondary server. If it has no zone files, the DNS Server is known as a *caching-only server*. The only responsibility of a caching server is to make DNS queries, return the results, and cache any results it obtains. Caching servers are not authoritative for any domains because they don't store copies of any zone files locally. When a caching-only server first starts, it does not have any DNS information stored. A caching server builds information only when it caches results of queries made after the server starts. However, installing DNS as a caching-only server may be a good choice across a slow WAN link, because entire zone files don't need to be transferred. The caching server can make a query across the link, but only one record is transmitted, not the full zone file. After the server has resolved a query, a future query for the same information can be resolved locally from the cache. Resolving locally eliminates the need to communicate across the WAN link (at least until the cached entry expires). The time to live of cached entries is determined by the server that answered the query. It returns a time to live for the query along with the name resolution.

Figure 12.5

Using a secondary server as a master server to reduce network traffic on a slow WAN link.

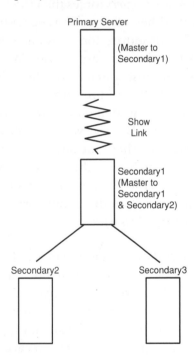

Resolving DNS Queries

A client querying a DNS Server is called a *resolver*, while a DNS Server is generically called a *name server*. DNS works at the Application layer of the OSI model, which is the top or seventh layer.

By working at this layer, DNS can more easily communicate with the client applications needing to resolve a host name. DNS can use either UDP or TCP for its communications. DNS tries to use UDP—which is more efficient—for better performance, but DNS resorts to TCP if can't communicate properly through UDP. TCP and UDP are discussed more completely in Chapter 2.

Three types of queries can be made to a DNS Server: recursive, iterative, and inverse. Some examples of queries include a web browser—such as Internet Explorer—requesting the IP address for a web site, a Microsoft client requesting a browse list, another DNS Server requesting a name query, or a WINS server unable to resolve a name from its own database.

A *recursive query* forces the DNS Server to respond to the request with either a failure or a successful response that includes the TCP/IP address for the domain name requested. Resolvers typically make recursive queries. With a recursive query, the DNS Server must contact any other DNS Servers it needs to resolve the request. When it receives a response from the other DNS Server(s), it then sends a response to the client. With a recursive query, the DNS Server is not allowed to pass the buck by simply giving the client the address of another DNS Server that might be able to handle the request. This type of query is made from a resolver to a name server, and also from a name server to its forwarder (another name server configured to handle requests forwarded to it).

An *iterative query* is one in which the name server is expected to provide the best information based on what the server knows from local zone files or from caching. If the name server doesn't have any information to answer the query, it simply sends a negative response. This is like playing the game, Go Fish. A player asks another player for a certain card: "Do you have any Jacks?" The player either answers yes and supplies the requested information (Jacks) or answers no and says, "Go Fish." In other words, I don't have what you're looking for; go try someone else. A forwarder makes this type of query as it tries to find names outside its local domain. It may have to query a number of outside DNS Servers in an attempt to resolve the name.

Figure 12.6 shows the entire query process, with a DNS client making an initial query of a DNS Server to resolve the name www.erudite.com. The client makes a recursive query; it expects to receive an answer without being referred to another server. The DNS Server receiving the query can't resolve the host name with its own information (cached or from zone files), so it makes an iterative query to a root name server. The root server sends back the address of the name server for the com domain. The DNS Server then sends an iterative query to the com name server. This server sends back the address of the name server authoritative for the erudite.com domain. The DNS Server then sends a query for www.erudite.com to this server, and the erudite.com name server finds a resolution for www and returns a reply. The local DNS Server can finally respond to the client that made the original request for the name resolution. The client was kept on hold while the DNS Server worked to find a response. Because the client sent a recursive query, the DNS Server was forced to go to this extra work until it could obtain an answer.

Figure 12.6

A resolver makes a recursive query, which forces the DNS Server to make several iterative queries so that it can return an answer to the client.

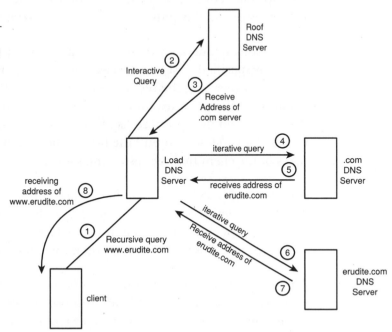

The third type of query , an *inverse query*, is used when the client wants to know the host name of a specified TCP/IP address. A special domain in the DNS name space resolves this type of query. Otherwise, a DNS Server would have to completely search all the DNS domains to make sure it found the correct name. This special domain is called in-addr.arpa. Nodes in this space are named after TCP/IP addresses rather than alphabetic host names. However, these node names have the TCP/IP names in reverse order.

Remember that TCP/IP addresses move from general to specific. The first octet(s) refers to the network; additional octets or portions of octets may be dedicated to defining a subnet as specified by the subnet mask; the remaining octets or parts of octets specify the host address of a specific computer. With DNS, however, host names are read from right to left, with the name of the domain on the right, the name of any subdomains moving from right to left, and finally the name of the host on the leftmost part of the fully qualified name. In order to make the node names of the inverse lookup zones compatible with DNS, the zone files are named with IP addresses, but the addresses are written in reverse order.

Inverse lookup queries are used when a client requests a service that only specified host names have been given permission to use. The server receiving the request only knows the IP address of the client, so the server must find out the host name to see whether the client is on the approved list. In this case, the server issues an inverse lookup query to find the host name matching the IP address of the client that requested the service.

A number of DNS Servers also have zones for inverse lookups. The highest levels of zone files, for Class A, B, and C networks, are maintained by InterNIC. Then individual network address owners can have zone files for subnets on their own networks.

A name server can return three types of responses to a query: a successful response with the IP address for the requested host name (or the host name for an inverse lookup), a pointer to another name server (only in an iterative query), or a failure message.

Time to Live for Queries

A name server caches all the information it receives when it re-solves queries outside its own zone files. These cached responses can then be used to answer queries for the same information in the future. These cached entries don't stay on the DNS Server forever, however. There is a *time to live* (TTL) for the responses to make sure the DNS Server doesn't keep information for so long that it becomes out-of-date. The time to live for the cache can be set on each DNS Server.

There are two competing factors to consider when setting the time to live. One is the accuracy of the cached information. If the TTL is short, then the likelihood of having old information goes down considerably. If the TTL is long, then the cached responses could become outdated, meaning the DNS Server could give false answers to queries. The accuracy of the responses is also depen-dent on how stable your environment is. If names change often, then a short TTL is necessary. It is important, however, to consid-er the load on the server and the network. If the TTL is large, the server can answer more queries from cache and doesn't use local resources or network bandwidth to send out additional queries.

If a query is answered with an entry from cache, the TTL of the entry is also passed with the response. This way other DNS Servers that receive the response know how long the entry is valid. Other DNS Servers honor the TTL from the responding server; they don't set it again based on their own TTL. Thus entries truly ex-pire rather than live in perpetuity as they move from server to server with an updated TTL. Resolvers (clients) also have a cache, and honor the TTL received from a name server that answered a query from the name server's cache.

Forwarders and Slaves

When a client contacts a DNS Server for name resolution, the DNS Server first looks in its local files to resolve the request. If the DNS Server is not authoritative for the zone pertaining to that request, it must look to another name server to resolve the re-quest. When you are browsing the World Wide Web, resolving a domain name involves either making a request of a name server maintained by your ISP or going on the Internet to contact a name server there.

You may not want all DNS Servers to forward these requests. Thus DNS enables you to designate specific DNS Servers as forwarders. In general, only forwarders can communicate on the Internet or beyond the local network. The other DNS Servers are configured with the address of the forwarder. The forwarder is much like a gatekeeper, to which all outside requests are funneled. You can put some firewall software or other protective measures on the forwarder without having to do so to all the DNS Servers in your organization. An entire server is designated as a forwarder; this is not done on a zone-by-zone basis.

When a forwarder receives a request to resolve a name, it accesses outside resources and returns the response to the DNS Server that originated the request. If the forwarder can't answer the request, then the originating DNS Server can resort to other means to resolve the request.

Slaves are DNS Servers configured to use forwarders and also configured to return a failure message if the forwarder can't resolve the request. A slave does not try to contact other DNS Servers if its designated forwarder can't handle the request. In other words, a slave makes a recursive query to a forwarder.

Structure of Zone Files

Non-Microsoft name servers usually require manual editing of text files to create the zone files that comprise the domain name space. These files must be created with a specific syntax that can be read by DNS. Microsoft's DNS Server includes DNS Manager, a GUI interface that displays the settings from these files and enables you to make entries in these files via the interface rather than in the files themselves. DNS Manager also enables you to manage more than one DNS Server from one location. Although you can use DNS Manager to create or modify zone files even when you do not know their syntax, understanding the content and structure of the zone files is essential to your understanding of DNS. In fact, DNS Manager refers to many of the records in the zone file by their syntax name. So whether you use a text editor to modify zone files or do it through DNS Manager, you must still understand what the different records are used for.

The zone file is also known as the *database file*. It contains the resource records for the part of domain covered by the zone. These files are stored in the NT file structure, in the path \WINNT\SYSTEM32\dns. A DNS Server uses three types of zone files: database file (zone), cache, and reverse lookup. You can also have a boot file, which is used to initialize the DNS Server. However, a Microsoft DNS Server is usually initialized from values stored in the registry. The capability to initialize from a boot file is included in Microsoft DNS for compatibility with other types of DNS Servers.

Zone Files

Zone files have a .dns extension, like microsoft.com.dns. A sample zone file called place.dns in the dns\samples directory can be manually edited and used as a zone file. Of course, you can use DNS Manager with its windows interface to create zone files and the records within zone. On non-Microsoft DNS Servers, zone files are typically called db.zone.

You can use DNS Manager to create zone entries even when you do not know the syntax of the records. However, DNS Manager makes entries in zone files according to the syntax. It's important to know what each record is used for and what its parameters specify. The following sections examine the records that are usually found in a zone file.

SOA Record

For an exercise covering this information, see end of chapter.

Each database file starts with an SOA record, stating the *start of authority* for the file. This record specifies the primary server for this zone—the server that maintains the read/write copy of this file. The syntax of this record follows:

```
IN SOA <source host><contact e-mail><ser. No.><refresh
time><retry time><expiration time><TTL>
```

An example of the syntax follows:

```
@ IN SOA ns1.erudite.com kwolford.erudite.com. (
     101     ; serial number
     10800   ; refresh [3 hours]
     3600    ; retry [1 hour]
     604800  ; expire [7 days]
     86400 ) ; time to live [1 day]
```

The "@" symbol in this example indicates the local server; "IN" indicates an Internet record. The fully qualified name for the name server NS1 must end in a period. Note that the e-mail name for the administrator must have a period instead of the "@" symbol in the e-mail address. If the SOA record is on more than one line, an open parenthesis must end the first line and a close parenthesis must end the last line.

The following list explains the other parameters:

▶ **Source host.** The name of the host with the read/write copy of the file.

▶ **Contact e-mail.** The Internet e-mail address of the person who maintains this file. This address must be expressed with a period instead of the "@" that is usually found in e-mail addresses, such as `kwolford.erudite.com` instead of `kwolford@erudite.com`.

▶ **Serial number.** The version number of the database. This number should be changed each time the database changes. This number changes automatically if you use DNS Manager to change the zone file. If you use a text editor to modify the zone file, you must change this number yourself.

▶ **Refresh time.** The time a secondary server waits before checking the master server for changes to the database file. If the file has changed, the secondary server requests a zone transfer. This value is expressed in seconds.

▶ **Retry time.** The time a secondary server waits before trying again if a zone transfer fails. This value is expressed in seconds.

▶ **Expiration time.** The time a secondary server keeps trying to transfer a zone. After the expiration time passes, the old zone information is deleted. This value is expressed in seconds.

▶ **Time to live.** The time a server can cache resource records from this database file. The time to live is sent as part of the response for any queries that are answered from this database file. An individual resource record can have a TTL that overrides this value. This value is expressed in seconds.

If a resource record uses more than one line in a database file, you must end the first line with an open parenthesis and the last line with a close parenthesis.

Figure 12.7 shows the dialog box used in DNS Manager to modify the SOA record.

Figure 12.7

Editing the SOA record.

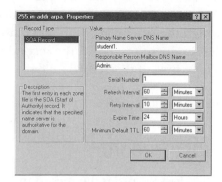

Name Server Record

The Name Server record specifies the other name servers for the specified domain. The syntax for a Name Server record follows:

```
<domain> IN NS <nameserver host>
```

An example of a Name Server record follows:

```
@ IN NS ns1.erudite.com
```

The "@" symbol indicates the local domain. The server NS1 in the domain erudite.com is the name server.

Figure 12.8 shows the interface used in DNS Manager to modify or add a Name Server record.

Figure 12.8

Adding a Name Server record.

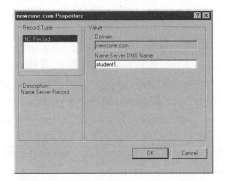

Mail Exchange Record

The Mail Exchange record specifies the name of the host that processes mail for this domain. If you list multiple mail servers, you can specify a preference number that specifies the order in which the mail servers should be used. If the first preferred mail server doesn't respond, the second one is contacted, and so on. The syntax of this record follows:

```
<domain> IN MX <preference><mailserver host>
```

Host Record

For an exercise covering this information, see end of chapter.

The Host Record is the record that actually specifies the TCP/IP address for a specified host. All hosts that have static TCP/IP addresses should have an entry in this database. Clients with dynamic addresses are resolved in other ways, such as through a WINS server. Most of the entries in a database file are host records. The syntax of this record follows:

```
<host name> IN A <ip address of host>
```

An example of some host records follows:

```
arthur      IN A 136.104.3.92
thomas      IN A 136.104.4.85
kathleen    IN A 136.104.1.38
```

In this example, three servers called "arthur," "thomas," and "kathleen" are registered with their corresponding IP addresses.

Figure 12.9 shows the dialog box used in DNS Manager to add a host record. Note that you can also create the corresponding PTR record at the same time. PTR or pointer records are used for reverse lookups, which are described later in this chapter.

Figure 12.9

Adding a Host record.

Local Host Record

The Local Host Record is simply a regular host record using a special host name and the normal TCP/IP loopback address (the address used to direct or "loop back" TCP/IP traffic back to the host generating the traffic). For example, the following record maps the name localhost to the loopback address of 127.0.0.1:

```
localhost IN A 127.0.0.1
```

This record enables a client to query for localhost.erudite.com and receive the normal loopback address.

CNAME Record

The CNAME record is an alias, enabling you to specify more than one name for each TCP/IP address. CNAME stands for *canonical name*. The syntax of a CNAME record follows:

```
<alias name> CNAME <host name>
```

Using CNAME records, you can combine an ftp and a web server on the same host, for example. The following example maps a server called InetServer to a TCP/IP address. Then the names FTP and WWW are aliased to this server.

```
InetServer IN A 136.107.3.43
FTP CNAME InetServer
WWW CNAME InetServer
```

These records illustrate how easy it is to change the server on which services are provided while still allowing access to the new server for clients that refer to its original name. For example, if you want move the Web server to another machine called New-Inet, you can modify the zone files to read as follows:

```
InetServer IN A 136.107.3.43
FTP CNAME InetServer
NewInet IN A 136.107.1.107
WWW CNAME NewInet
```

The only change required for access to the new server was to make entries at the DNS Server; changes do not have to be made at the clients. Any clients querying the DNS Server receive the updated address automatically in response to the query.

Figure 12.10 shows the dialog box used in DNS Manager to add or modify a CNAME record.

Figure 12.10

Adding a CNAME record.

Using the Cache File to Connect to Root-Level Servers

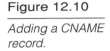 Objective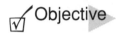

There is a cache file included with DNS that has entries for top-level servers of the Internet domains. If a host name can not be resolved from local zone files, DNS uses the cache file to look for a higher-level DNS Server to resolve the name. If your organization only has an intranet without any Internet access, you should replace this file with one that lists the top-level DNS Servers in your organization. This file is called cache.dns and is located at `\winnt\system32\dns`.

The latest version of this file can be downloaded from InterNIC at `ftp://rs.internic.net/domain/named.cache`.

Reverse Lookup File

The reverse lookup file has entries that enable IP addresses to be resolved to host names. Normally DNS is used to resolve host names to IP addresses, so the opposite process is called *reverse lookup*. The files are named according the Class of network, but with the octets in reverse order. Remember, a Class A network uses the first octet of the IP address for the network address, a Class B address uses the first 2 octets, and a Class C address uses the first 3 octets. The following examples are zone files for a Class A, Class B, and Class C network.

Network ID	Zone File Name
36.x.x.x	36.in-addr.arpa
138.107.x.x	107.138.in-addr.arpa
242.23.108.x	108.23.242.in-addr-arpa

Pointer Record

For an exercise covering this information, see end of chapter.

Pointer records are the reverse lookup entries. They specify the IP address in reverse order (like a DNS name with the most specific information first) and the corresponding host name. The syntax for a PTR record follows:

```
<ip reverse domain name> IN PTR <host name>
```

An example of this record follows:

```
43.3.107.136.in-addr.arpa. IN PTR InetServer.microsoft.com
```

This example is an entry for the server called InetServer with the IP address of 136.107.3.43.

Figure 12.11 shows a reverse lookup zone that includes DNS Server a PTR record as viewed in DNS Manager.

Figure 12.11

A reverse lookup zone with its PTR record.

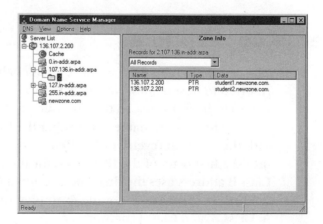

Arpa-127.rev File

The Arpa-127.rev file is included with every DNS Server. It provides reverse lookup for the local host, which is known as the loopback.

BIND Boot File

The BIND boot file is used if you do not plan to administer the DNS Server through windows interface but plan to edit text files instead. This file controls the startup of the DNS Server. The capability to use a BIND boot file is mainly provided for compatibility with BIND versions of DNS, which use boot files for startup. You can copy the files from these servers and with some editing use them to boot an NT DNS Server.

The commands that control the boot process in this file follow.

Directory Command

The directory command specifies the directory where the DNS files are found, including the files referenced by the boot file. The syntax of the directory command follows:

```
directory <directory>
```

An example of this command follows, showing that the files are located in the normal path of DNS files, which is also where NT is installed on C:\WINNT:

```
directory c:\winnt\system32\dns
```

Cache Command

The cache command specifies the cache file that is used to locate root servers for the domain. This command must be in the file. A cache file is part of Microsoft DNS. The syntax is as follows:

```
Cache . <filename>
```

An example of this command follows, which shows the name of the cache file, which is "cache" by default:

```
cache . cache
```

Remember the path for this file is already specified with the directory command.

Primary Command

The primary command specifies zone files for which this server is authoritative. For example, this server has the primary file for the zone. There can be more than one primary record in a file because a server can be the primary server for any number of zones. The syntax is as follows:

```
Primary <domain> <filename>
```

In the following example, the local server is primary for two zone files, erudite.dns and training.dns.

```
primary erudite.com erudite.dns
primary training.erudite.com training.dns
```

Secondary Command

The secondary command specifies those zones files for which this server is a secondary server. For example, it downloads a copy of the zone file from the primary server for the zone. The command specifies the zone file and also the address of the server where the secondary server is to download the zone file. Remember that a server can download the zone file from the primary server or from another secondary server. The file name specified identifies where the local copy of this file is to be stored. You can have more than one secondary command in a file because a server can be the secondary server for any number of zones. The syntax is as follows:

```
Secondary <domain> <hostlist> <local filename>
```

In this example, the local server is secondary for the zone software.dns, which can be transferred from the DNS Server with an IP address of 158.51.20.1.

```
secondary software.erudite.com 158.51.20.1 software.dns
```

Forwarders Command

For an exercise covering this information, see end of chapter.

The forwarders command specifies a server that can help resolve recursive queries if the local DNS Server cannot resolve them. The syntax is as follows:

```
Forwarders <hostlist>
```

In this example, two servers are configured as forwarders: 158.51.20.100 and 158.51.20.101:

```
forwarders 158.51.20.100 158.51.20.101
```

Slave Command

If a slave command is present, the local DNS Server must use the forwarders to resolve queries, the local server can't resolve the query using its own resources. The slave command must follow a forwarders command.

In this example, the local server is slave to the two servers listed in the forwarders command.

```
forwarders 158.51.20.100 158.51.20.101
slave
```

Review Questions

1. What are the benefits of DNS?

    A. It allows a distributed database that can be administered by a number of administrators.

    B. It allows host names that specify where a host is located.

    C. It allows WINS clients to register with the WINS server.

    D. It allows queries to other servers to resolve host names.

2. With what non-Microsoft DNS platforms is Microsoft DNS compatible?

    A. Only Unix DNS Servers that are based on BIND

    B. Only Unix DNS Servers that are based on the DNS RFCs

    C. Unix DNS Servers that are either BIND-based or RFC-based

    D. Only other Microsoft DNS Servers

3. In the DNS name www.microsoft.com, what does "microsoft" represent?

    A. The last name of the host

    B. The domain in which the host is located

    C. The IP address of the building in which the host is located

    D. The directory in which the host name file is located

4. If you do not specify the host name and domain in the TCP/IP configuration before installing DNS, what happens during the DNS installation?

    A. An NS record is not created on the server.

    B. DNS doesn't install.

    C. Default values are used to create NS and SOA records.

    D. You cannot create any zones on the server.

5. How do you create a Primary DNS Server?

    A. Install DNS on a Primary Domain Controller

    B. Configure the DNS Server to be a primary server in the Server Properties

    C. During DNS installation, specify that it is to be a primary server

    D. Create a primary zone

6. Where can a secondary server receive a copy of the zone file?

    A. Only from the primary server for the zone

    B. From any server that has a copy of the zone file

    C. Only from the master server for the zone

    D. Only from the top-level DNS Server for the domain

7. What record must be added to a zone file to alias a host to another name?

    A. An A record

    B. An SOA record

    C. A CNAME record

    D. A PTR record

8. How do you configure a client to use DNS to resolve a HOST name before using other methods?

    A. Query for a host name longer than 15 characters.

    B. Move DNS up in the Host Resolution Order dialog box.

    C. A client always searches DNS last.

    D. Configure the DNS to advertise itself to DNS clients.

9. How does a caching-only DNS Server build a database of host records?

   A. The caching server downloads a copy of zone files into its cache from master servers when the caching server starts.

   B. Entries from the local cache file are read into cache.

   C. The server captures the results of queries as they are sent across the network.

   D. The server makes queries.

10. What kind of query does a DNS client make to a DNS Server?

    A. A reverse lookup query

    B. An iterative query

    C. A recursive query

    D. A resolver query

11. Which server can be a master server for a Unix DNS Server that is the secondary server for a zone?

    A. Any NT DNS Server with a primary zone

    B. Any Unix server with a primary zone

    C. Any NT DNS Server with a secondary zone

    D. Any NT DNS Server with a zone that doesn't use WINS lookup

12. How can zone files be modified?

    A. With NSLOOKUP

    B. By editing the zone files with a text editor

    C. With DNS Manager

    D. With DNSCnfg

13. What is the use of the cache file on a DNS Server?

    A. It has records for DNS Servers at top-level domains.

    B. It provides initial values to the DNS cache.

    C. It specifies the TTL for cached entries.

    D. It specifies the amount of memory and its location for DNS caching.

14. What would the reverse lookup zone be called for a server with the IP address of 149.56.85.105?

    A. 105.85.56.149.in-addr.arpa

    B. 149.56.85.105.in-addr.arpa

    C. 56.149.in-addr.arpa

    D. 149.56.in-addr.arpa

15. How can you configure a secondary server to receive changes to zone files as soon as they are made?

    A. Decrease the refresh interval on the secondary server

    B. Turn on the Notify feature on the primary server

    C. Configure the primary server with push replication

    D. Make the primary server the master server for the secondary

16. How can you configure a DNS Server to send all queries to another DNS Server?

    A. Configure that server to use recursive queries

    B. Configure that server to be a cache-only server

    C. Configure that server to be a slave

    D. Configure that server to be a forwarder

17. You have several secondary DNS Servers on one side of a slow WAN link. How should you configure the master server for these secondary servers to minimize traffic over this slow WAN link?

    A. Have all the secondary servers on one side of link use one master server on the other side of the link.

    B. Have one secondary server use the primary server on the other side of the link as the master. Other secondary servers use the secondary on their side of the link as the master.

    C. Use a caching-only server as the master.

    D. Configure DNS for pull replication scheduled during low traffic times.

18. Where can you find the files needed to install DNS?

    A. On the NT 4.0 Server Resource Kit

    B. On the Backoffice CD

    C. On the NT 4.0 Server CD

    D. On the DNS CD

19. Which protocol does DNS try to use during its queries in order to minimize network traffic?

    A. UDP

    B. ARP

    C. IP

    D. TCP

Review Answers

1. A, B, D

2. C

3. B

4. A

5. D

6. B

7. C

8. A

9. D

10. C

11. B, D

12. B, C

13. A

14. C

15. B

16. C

17. B

18. C

19. A

Answers to the Test Yourself Questions at the Beginning of the Chapter

1. DNS stands for *Domain Name System*. It is a database that enables host names to be resolved to IP addresses. Entries to the database must be manually added; they are not dynamically built as in WINS.

2. The biggest difference between DNS and the other systems is that DNS uses a hierarchical name system that specifies the complete logical location of the host. With DNS, hosts can have common names, as long as they are located in a different portion of the DNS hierarchy, in much the same way that you can have two files with the same name located on different paths in a directory tree. WINS and HOST files use a flat database that simply registers the host name without any reference to where the host is located.

3. The DNS name space exists on a distributed database, in which different parts of the database are stored on different DNS Servers. These files in which the database records are stored are called *zone files*. DNS Servers are configured to query each other when they are trying to resolve queries that can't be resolved in their own files. A DNS Server can access the entire database for the domain name space through these queries without having all the zone files stored locally. The hierarchical structure of DNS helps a DNS Server know where to send a query so it can resolve a host name.

4. Microsoft's implementation of DNS is based directly on the RFC's that define DNS. Some other versions of DNS are based on prior implementations of DNS, such as BIND, rather than directly on the RFC's. A Windows NT DNS Server is fully compatible with any other DNS Server based on the RFC's. The Microsoft DNS Server is also compatible with a BIND server. Microsoft has added enhancements to DNS to enable DNS and WINS to work together to resolve host names.

5. A DNS name is called a *fully qualified domain name* (FQDN). Reading from left to right, the name specifies the name of the host, the name of the domain or subdomain in which the host is located, the domain in which the subdomain is located, and so on until a top level domain is specified. For example, a FQDN like www.microsoft.com specifies a host named www in a domain called microsoft in a top-level domain called com.

6. InterNIC is the organization that assigns IP addresses for the Internet. InterNIC also maintains the zone files for the top-level domains. Some examples of top-level domains include .com for commercial organizations, .org for non-profit organizations, .edu for educational institutions, and .gov for non-military government organizations.

7. You can have all the records for the domain name space in one zone file. However, breaking a name space into more than one zone can offer several advantages. With multiple zones, different administrators can manage different zone files. Also, using different zones enables you to distribute the zone files to spread the load more evenly among servers and throughout the physical network.

8. A Microsoft DNS Server typically uses three types of zone files. A fourth type of file is typically used for non-Microsoft DNS Servers. A database zone file has the records for the zone, with the host name mappings to IP addresses. A cache file has addresses for top-level zones in the domain. The cache file that comes with DNS has addresses for those DNS Servers maintained by InterNIC that have zone files for the Internet. A reverse lookup file has IP address mappings to host names, so an IP address can be resolved to a host name. A fourth type of zone file is not required by DNS, the boot file. A boot file is used by a non-Microsoft DNS Server to specify the startup values for DNS. DNS on Windows NT starts up using values stored in the registry. However, it is possible to have a Microsoft DNS Server start up from a boot file.

9. Yes. In fact, this is done to spread the load for commonly accessed host names like www. When multiple IP addresses are registered to a single name, DNS uses a round-robin technique to resolve addresses. Each time a client queries the server for this name, the DNS Server gives out a different address in the list, returning to the beginning of the list when the server has given out all the names in the list.

10. Yes. Because Microsoft based its DNS on the RFCs, the NT DNS Server is compatible with other DNS Servers. However, if an NT DNS Server is using WINS lookup in a primary zone, this zone should not be copied to a non-Microsoft DNS Server because it doesn't know how to handle WINS records in a zone file.

C h a p t e r **13**

Implementing Microsoft DNS Servers

This chapter will help you prepare for the exam by covering the following objectives:

 Objectives

- ▶ Install and configure Microsoft DNS Server service on a Windows NT Server

- ▶ Configure DNS Server roles

- ▶ Integrate a DNS Server with other name servers

- ▶ Diagnose and resolve name resolution problems

Test Yourself! Before reading this chapter, test yourself to determine how much study time you will need to devote to this section.

1. What is an FQDN?

2. What is the purpose of a CNAME record?

3. What is the difference between a recursive and iterative query?

4. What purpose does an IP Forwarder serve?

5. For what two main roles can a DNS Server be configured?

6. What four main files are used to configure a DNS Server?

7. What is required to configure a Microsoft DNS Server to act as a Dynamic DNS Server?

8. What does reverse lookup provide?

9. Which type of applications use a DNS Server?

10. How do you configure Windows NT to use DNS to resolve NetBIOS names?

Answers are located at the end of the chapter.

Implementing Microsoft DNS Servers

In Chapter 12 you saw the steps involved in using DNS and looked at the configuration files and the types of configurations available; it is time to see how to implement DNS within Windows NT. This Chapter deals with setting up and configuring DNS within Windows NT.

Installing the DNS Server

Objective

For an exercise covering this information, see end of chapter.

The first item of business is to install the DNS Server. The system on which you install the DNS service must be running Windows NT Server and needs to have a static IP configuration (as seen in Chapter 1). Installing the DNS Server is simple given that, installing it is the same as installing any other network service. The steps are as follows:

1. Open the Network settings dialog box (right-click the Network Neighborhood and choose Properties).

2. On the Services tab, click Add, and select the Microsoft DNS Server (see fig. 13.1).

Figure 13.1

Adding the Microsoft DNS Server.

3. Click OK to add the service. When prompted, enter the directory in which your Windows NT source files are located.

4. Choose Close from the Network settings dialog box and, when prompted, restart your system.

You have now installed the DNS Server. To verify that the service is correctly installed, check the Services icon in Control Panel to ensure the Microsoft DNS Server is listed and has started.

Enabling DNS on the Client

Now that you have a DNS Server, you need to have your clients use the DNS Server. To enable Windows clients to use the DNS Server, you can add the address of the DNS Server to each station (manually), or you can set the DNS Server option on the DHCP server.

For Windows NT, you can use the following procedure to set the DNS Server address. (Setting the address on Windows 95 is the same.)

1. Open the TCP/IP settings dialog box. (Open the Network settings dialog box, and from the Protocol tab, double-click TCP/IP.)

2. On the DNS tab (see fig. 13.2), enter the required information. As a minimum, you need to enter the IP address of a DNS Server. The other options on this tab are described as follows:

   ▶ **Host Name.** This is the name of the local host. This is the same as the NetBIOS name by default; however, you can change it. (If you select a different name, you are warned that if the NetBIOS name is ever changed, the host name is set to the new NetBIOS name. If you use WINS to create a Dynamic DNS, the NetBIOS name and the host name must be the same.)

   ▶ **Domain.** This is the Internet domain to which the system belongs. This is combined with the Host Name to create the FQDN name that this system is known as.

   ▶ **DNS Service Search Order.** This is the IP address of one or more DNS Servers that you use. They are tried in the order given.

▶ **Domain Suffix Search Order.** When you search for another host—for example, if you enter **FTP sparky**—the system first looks for "sparky" as the name in the DNS Server. If "sparky" is not in your current domain, then that system will not be found and you would have to enter **FTP sparky.scrimtech.com**. If you work with servers at scrimtech.com frequently, you can add the domain scrimtech.com into this area, and if the address is not resolved from "sparky," a second query for "sparky.scrimtech.com" is automatically sent.

Figure 13.2

The DNS settings for the TCP/IP protocol.

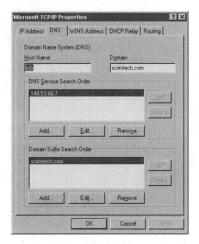

3. Click OK to close the TCP/IP settings. (If you are installing TCP/IP, you will need to enter the path to the Windows NT source files.)

4. Choose Close from the Network settings dialog box and restart your system. (This is not absolutely required, but generally it is recommended to ensure the values are correctly set.)

You can also use the DNS Server in place of the WINS server for resolving NetBIOS names. To do this, you need to change the settings on the WINS tab in the TCP/IP configuration. Specifically, you need to select the option to use DNS to resolve host names (see fig. 13.3).

Figure 13.3

Setting Windows NT to use DNS to resolve NetBIOS host names.

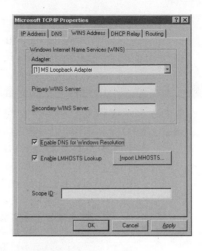

Using Existing BIND Files

If you already have a series of BIND files (as described in Chapter 12) set up on an existing DNS Server, you can use these files to configure the Microsoft DNS Server. The following are the steps you need to follow to configure Microsoft DNS Server to use these files:

1. Install the Microsoft DNS service (see the preceding section for instructions).

2. Stop the DNS service (from the Control Panel, choose the Services icon, click Microsoft DNS, and click the Stop button).

3. Copy the BIND files to the %winroot%\System32\DNS directory.

4. Start the DNS service (from the Control Panel, choose the Services icon, click Microsoft DNS, and click the Start button).

5. Use the DNS Manager to verify that your entries are there. (See "The DNS Administration Tool.")

Reinstalling Microsoft DNS Server

A quick note should be made here in case you need to reinstall the DNS Server. When you start adding zones to a Microsoft DNS Server, it by default switches to starting from the registry rather than the DNS files discussed earlier. It makes a note of this in the boot file. When you remove the server (before you reinstall) it does not remove this file; therefore, when you install the DNS Server again it assumes the boot file is valid and tries to read it. This causes several errors in the Event Log and causes the DNS not to start.

Therefore, if you need to remove the DNS Server, you should remove the boot file from the DNS directory. The original file is in the directory %winroot%\system32\dns\backup and you can copy the files back from there; however, the server continues to boot from the registry.

If you need to enable the system to boot from files, you must use the registry editor to open HKEY_LOCAL_MACHINE\SYSTEM\ CurrentControlSet\Services\DNS\Parameters and delete the value EnableRegistryBoot.

The DNS Administration Tool

Adding the DNS Server adds the DNS administration tool. This tool makes configuring and maintaining the DNS Server very simple. It also provides single-seat administration as you can add several DNS Servers.

First, you need to add the DNS Server that you want to manage, as follows:

1. Start the DNS Manager by choosing Start, Programs, Administrative Tools, DNS Manager.

2. In the left pane of the DNS Manager, right-click Server List (see fig. 13.4).

3. Choose New Server from the menu.

4. In the DNS Server box (see fig. 13.5), enter the name or IP address of the server you wish to add.

Figure 13.4

The context menu from Server List.

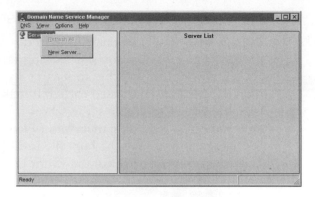

Figure 13.5

Adding a server to the DNS Manager.

Now that you have added the server, you can configure it and add entries. The DNS Server needs to be configured for the role that it plays in the overall system, and you should know what the server you are configuring will be used for.

Roles for a Microsoft DNS Server

The previous chapter discussed the roles that a server can take on Primary and Secondary. Mention also was made of using a DNS Server as a Caching-Only server; that is, a server that can only resolve addresses but which does not host any domains or sub-domains (zones).

The last chapter also discussed a DNS Server that acts as an IP Forwarder. That is, it receives the queries (recursive) from the other hosts on the network, and then attempts to resolve them using a recursive query to another DNS Server. This is useful if you wish to centralize the resolution of addresses at one server (which might be outside your firewall).

In the next few sections this chapter will focus on configuring Microsoft DNS Server for these different roles. The simplest role that a DNS Server has is that of Caching-Only.

Configuring for Caching-Only

There is just about nothing you need to do to run a server as a Caching-Only server. As noted in the previous chapter, the Caching-Only server does not host any zones. If this is all you need, stop here.

Configuring as an IP Forwarder

 An IP Forwarder is also a Caching-Only server; however, you need to configure it with the address of another DNS Server (another Microsoft DNS Server or any other DNS—for example, the one from your ISP). This configuration is fairly simple and the only information you require is the IP address of the server to use. Follow these steps:

1. Right-click the server in the Server List and select Properties.

2. On the Forwarders tab (see fig. 13.6), check the Use Forwarder(s) box.

Figure 13.6

Configuring as an IP Forwarder.

3. If the server is to only use the services of the other system, select Operate As Slave Server. (If you don't select this, the server attempts to resolve through the forwarder; however, it then uses an iterative query if that fails.)

4. Enter the address or addresses of the DNS Servers to which this one should forward queries.

5. If desired, set a time-out for the request.

6. Click OK to close the dialog box.

Creating a Primary DNS Server

For an exercise covering this information, see end of chapter.

The purpose of DNS is to resolve names to IP addresses. There-fore, you need to enter the addresses into the DNS server so other users can find your hosts. You do this by creating a zone in the DNS Server and entering the information that you want to make available to the world. The following list covers the steps required to create a zone:

1. Right-click the server that hosts the zone in the Server List.

2. Choose New Zone.

3. From the dialog box that appears, choose Primary (see fig. 13.7). Then choose Next.

Figure 13.7

Choosing the server's role in the domain.

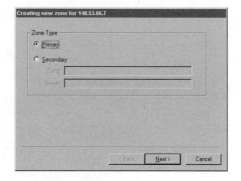

4. Enter the name of the domain (or sub-domain) for which you are creating a zone on the next screen (see fig. 13.8). Then press tab (this automatically enters a zone file name; if you are adding an existing zone file, enter the name of the file that has the information—it must be in the %winroot%\System32\DNS directory). When the informa-tion is in, click Next.

5. On the next screen, choose Finish.

Figure 13.8

Entering the zone name and file information.

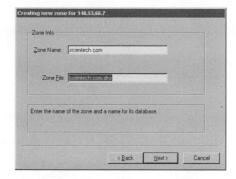

That is all there is to creating a zone. Now you can configure the zone and add the host (and other) records. When you have finished, the DNS Manager should look similar to figure 13.9.

Figure 13.9

The DNS Manager with a zone configured.

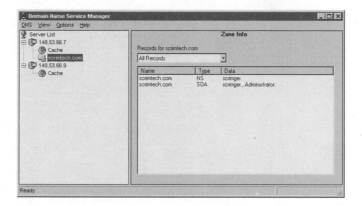

Setting Up and Reviewing the SOA Record

Configuring a zone is straightforward. Essentially, the information that you are entering here includes details for the Start of Authority (SOA) record and information about using WINS.

Setting up the information is easy. The following steps outline the process:

1. Right-click the zone you want to configure. Choose Properties from the menu. The Properties dialog box should appear and present the basic zone information (see fig. 13.10).

Figure 13.10

*The zone proper-
ties with the
General tab.*

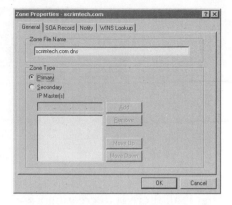

2. Click on the SOA Record tab to bring up the information about the SOA (see fig. 13.11).

Figure 13.11

*The Start of Au-
thority record.*

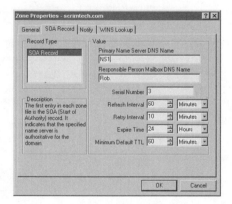

3. Edit the information in the SOA record. The fields that you can change here are as follows:

   ▶ **Primary Name Server DNS Name.** The name of the Primary name server that contains the files for the do-main. Note that only the host name is entered, and then a "." that means this domain (for example, NS1 is NS1.ScrimTech.com.)

   ▶ **Responsible Person Mailbox DNS Name.** The e-mail address of the person who is in charge of the DNS. (Note, as in the Primary Name Server, you need to enter only the e-mail—followed by a period—if the e-mail address is within this domain.)

▶ **Serial Number.** A version ID that is assigned to the zone. The number is updated whenever you make changes to the database, so the secondary servers know that changes were made and can retrieve the new information.

▶ **Refresh Interval.** Tells the Secondary servers how often they should check their version number with the primaries to see if they need to transfer the zone information again.

▶ **Retry Interval.** Tells how long the Secondary server should wait before retrying the Primary server if it could not connect at the time given in Refresh Interval.

▶ **Expire Time.** Sets how long a Secondary server continues to give out information on this zone after not being able to connect with the Primary server.

▶ **Minimum Default TTL.** When a DNS Server performs an iterative query to resolve a name, the name is cached. This value sets how long other DNS Servers are allowed to keep the information about records that your DNS Server resolves for them.

4. Click the Notify tab (see fig. 13.12). (This is not really part of the SOA; however, it is added here because it deals with the Secondary servers.)

Figure 13.12

The Notify tab from the Zone Properties dialog box.

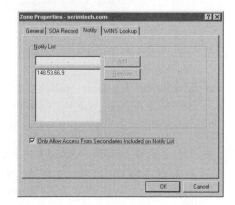

5. Enter the IP addresses of all the Secondary servers that should be notified when a change is made.

6. If desired, you can choose Only Allow Access From Secondaries Included on Notify List, which restricts which servers can retrieve your zone information.

7. Click OK to accept the changes you have made (the WINS tab is covered in the next section).

Integration with WINS

The last tab in the Zone Properties dialog box is the WINS Lookup tab (see fig. 13.13). You can use WINS to resolve DNS queries by telling the server to use the WINS server. Remember, for this to work, the hosts must use the same name for both their NetBIOS name and the host name, and they must register with the WINS server.

Figure 13.13

The WINS Lookup tab is used to configure DNS to use WINS for resolution.

Only a couple of options are available.

▶ **Use WINS Resolution.** Check this box to enable the DNS Server to query the WINS server for queries it receives that it cannot resolve from its own database.

▶ **Settings only affect local server.** Normally a temporary entry is added to the domain when this resolution method is used. Selecting this option only allows the current server to see these entries.

> ▶ **WINS Servers.** Here you need to enter the address of at least one WINS server. This server is queried in the order entered.

From the WINS Lookup tab, you can also open the Advanced Zone Properties dialog box (see fig. 13.14). You may need to use a couple of other settings in this dialog box.

Figure 13.14

The Advanced Zone Properties dialog box.

The options available are described in the following list:

> ▶ **Submit DNS Domain as NetBIOS Scope.** In some organizations, the NetBIOS scope ID is used to limit the number of hosts you can see using NetBIOS. The WINS server only responds with the address if matching scope IDs are used. Therefore, this option enables you to use the domain name as the NetBIOS scope.

> ▶ **Cache Timeout Value.** The length of time the DNS Server keeps the information that it gets from the WINS server.

> ▶ **Lookup Timeout Value.** The length of time the DNS Server waits for a resolution from the WINS server.

Adding HOSTS

Now that the domain has been created, and the WINS resolution is set up, you need to add the records that the WINS resolution cannot handle. Essentially, this is any non-WINS client that you have on your network, as well as any host that has an alias (discussed in the next section).

Adding a host record (or any record) is simple. All you need to do is right-click the domain (or sub-domain) to which you want to add the record. A menu (see fig. 13.15) appears from which you can choose New Host.

Figure 13.15

*The context
menu for a zone.*

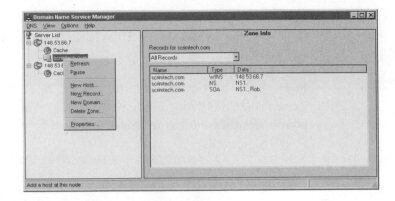

When you choose New Host, you see the dialog box shown in
figure 13.16. Enter the host name and the IP address in this dialog box. You need only the host name because the domain or sub-
domain you clicked on is assumed.

Figure 13.16

*The New Host
dialog box.*

An option to Create Associated PTR Record also exists. This enters the required information for the reverse lookup zone for this
host. You need to create the reverse lookup zone before you can
do this (see "Reverse Lookup").

Adding Other Records

*For an exercise
covering this
information, see
end of chapter.*

The main purpose of a DNS Server is to resolve a host name to an
IP address. There are, however, other types of information that
other organizations may want, such as the address of your mail
server. You can add several types of records to the DNS Server.
The following list describes these other records:

▶ **A.** This is a host entry, exactly the same as was entered in the
previous section.

▶ **AAAA.** This is also a host entry; the difference is that you can
enter an IPng address (the new version of TCP/IP that will
use 128-bit addresses rather than 32-bit).

▶ **AFSDB.** The AFSDB record gives the address of an AFS (Andrew File System) database server, or a DCE (Distributed Computing Environment) authenticated name server.

▶ **CNAME.** The canonical name is an alias that points one name such as WWW to another such as Web (see fig. 13.17). This is one of the most common records that you need to enter.

Figure 13.17

Adding an alias by creating a CNAME record.

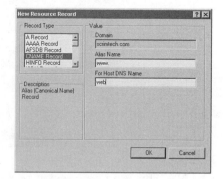

▶ **HINFO.** Enters machine information about a host, which allows other hosts on the network to find out CPU (Central Processing Unit) type and operating system information.

▶ **ISDN.** Integrated Services Digital Network allows you to map an entry to an ISDN phone number rather than an IP address. This is used in conjunction with an RT (Route Through) record to automate routing over dial-up ISDN.

▶ **MB.** This is an experimental record type used to associate an e-mail ID with a particular host *ID*.

▶ **MG.** Like an MB record, the MG is experimental; this associates an MB record with a Mail Group that could be used for mailing lists.

▶ **MINFO.** Another experimental record, MINFO enables you to enter the mail information about the person responsible for a given Mail record.

▶ **MR.** This is another experimental record. This provides for the Mail records the same service that CNAME entries provide for host names—aliases.

▶ **MX.** You need to enter at least one MX record (see fig. 13.18). The MX record takes incoming connections for mail and directs them to a mail server. You may enter more than one MX record. If you do, the system uses the Preference Number to determine the order in which to try them (lowest first).

Figure 13.18

Adding an MX record.

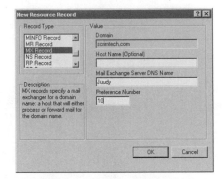

▶ **NS.** This is a name server record. It is used to find the other name servers in the domain.

▶ **PTR.** The Pointer record is part of the reverse lookup zone and is used to point the IP address at the host name.

▶ **RP.** This is where you enter the name (or names) of those people who are responsible for the domain that the server provides resolution for. There can be multiple entries of this type.

▶ **RT.** This points at another record in the DNS database. The Route Through provides information on how to get to a host using dial-up ISDN or X.25.

▶ **SOA.** As already discussed, the Start of Authority record provides the basic configuration for a zone.

▶ **TXT.** The Text record is a way of associating text information with a host. This can provide information about the computer (in addition to the information in an HINFO entry) or other information such as the location.

▶ **WKS.** Provides the capability to indicate which Well Known Services are running on a particular host. These match the service and protocols that are listed in the services file (%winroot%\System32\drivers\etc) below port 256.

▶ **X25.** Similar to the ISDN entry, this provides the capability to map a name to an X.121 name.

Adding these records is similar to adding a host record. Right-click the domain or sub-domain and choose New Record. Figure 13.19 shows a zone with several records defined.

Figure 13.19

A configured zone in the DNS Manager.

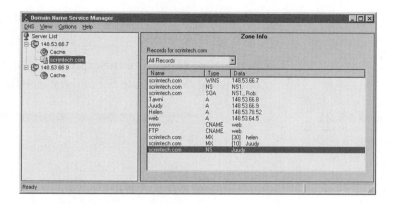

Creating a Sub-Domain

Many organizations are broken down into smaller groups that focus on one area of the business. Or perhaps the organization is dispersed geographically. In either case, the company may decide that they want break down their main domain into sub-domains. This is simple in Microsoft's DNS Server. Choose the parent do-main (scrimtech.com, for example) and then right-click. Choose New Domain and enter the sub-domain name in the dialog box that appears (see fig. 13.20).

If the sub-domain is handled on another server, enter NS records for each of the other servers. If it is handled locally, simply add the records that are required.

Figure 13.20

Adding a Sub-Domain.

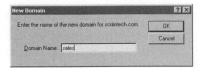

Setting Up the Secondary DNS Server

 **Objective**

After you configure your server, you need to add a Secondary server. Adding this server provides redundancy and also splits the workload among the servers (you can have several Secondary servers if you wish). The following list outlines the steps involved:

1. In the DNS Manager, right-click the server to be configured as a Secondary server.

2. Choose New Zone from the context menu. From the New Zone dialog box, choose Secondary (see fig. 13.21).

Figure 13.21

Creating a Secondary Zone.

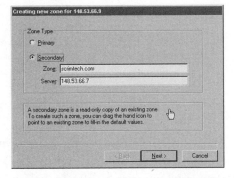

 Note

On this screen, you are asked for the zone name and the server from which to get zone files. A handy option is the ability (as seen here) to drag the hand over another server listed in the DNS Manager to automatically pick up the information.

If the Primary DNS Server is not a Microsoft DNS Server, you will need to enter the information manually.

3. Click the Next button, and you can enter the information for the file. This should already be entered (see fig. 13.22), and you should click Next to accept the defaults.

Figure 13.22

*Enter the zone file
information.*

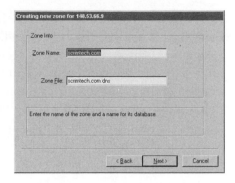

4. The next screen asks you to identify the IP master for the
zone. This should already be filled in for you (see fig. 13.23).

Figure 13.23

*Setting the IP
Master.*

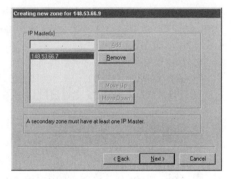

5. The last screen tells you that you are finished. Click Finish to
close this screen.

Reverse Lookup

You should now understand the process of looking up an FQDN
using a DNS Server. Looking up an IP address to find the host
name is exactly the same (only backward). An FQDN starts with
the specific host and then the domain; an IP address starts with
Recall the dialog box used to add a host included an. To do this,
choose DNS from the menu, then Update Server Data Files. This
is done automatically when the server is shut down or when you
exit the DNS Manager.

Now that the IP address is reversed, it is going the same way as an FQDN. Now you can resolve the address using DNS. Just like resolving www.scrimtech.com, you need to create a zone. This zone must have a particular name. To find the name, take the assigned portion of the address—for example, in 148.53.66.7 the portion that was assigned is 148.53, and for 204.12.25.3 it is 204.12.25. Now, create a zone in which these numbers are reversed and to which you add in-addr.arpa—that is, 53.148.in-addr.arpa or 25.12.204.in-addr.arpa, respectively.

Recall the dialog box used to add a host included an option to create a PTR record as you added hosts (refer to fig. 13.15). For this reason, you need to create the reverse lookup zone first, *before the other zones,* so these records can be automatically added. Note that you need to create a reverse lookup zone for each address you are assigned.

Updating DNS Startup Files

After you have added several records to the DNS Server, you need to update the information in the files on the system. Even if the server boots from the registry, the database (zone) files are stored. To do this, choose DNS from the menu, then Update Server Data Files. This is done automatically when the server is shut down or when you exit the DNS Manager.

DNS Manager Preferences

As a final note, you can set three options under Options, Preferences (see fig. 13.24) that affect the way the DNS Manager itself will behave.

These options include:

▶ **Auto Refresh Statistics.** Allows you to configure the statistics screen to automatically update information.

Figure 13.24

The Preferences dialog box.

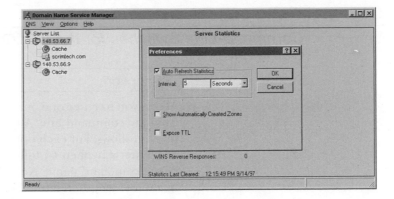

▶ **Show Automatically Created Zones.** Shows the zones that are automatically created. These are used for internal purposes only.

▶ **Expose TTL.** Allows you to expose the TTL for entries in your cache. (You can view these by double-clicking cache and then double-clicking the sub-folders.)

NSLOOKUP

Along with the addition of a DNS Server, Windows NT 4.0 also has a tool that uses the DNS and enables you to verify that it is working. The NSLOOKUP command line is shown as follows:

```
nslookup [-option ...] [computer-to-find ¦ - [server]]
```

You can use NSLOOKUP to query the DNS Server from the command line (see table 13.1 for a list of switches) or you can start an interactive session with the server to enable you to query the database. For our purposes, only look at the command line.

Table 13.1

Command-Line Switches for the NSLOOKUP Command

Switch	Description
-option	Allows you to enter one or more commands from the command line. A list of the commands follows. For each option you wish to add, enter a hyphen (-) followed immediately by the command name. Note that the command line length needs to be less than 256 characters.
Computer-to-find	This is the host or IP address about which you wish to find information. It is processed using the default server, or if given, using the server that is specified.

The following list provides the options that are available with the NSLOOKUP command.

- **-t querytype.** Lists all records of a given type. The record types are listed under querytype.

- **-a.** Lists all the CNAME entries from the DNS Server.

- **-d.** Dumps all records that are in the DNS Server.

- **-h.** Returns information on the DNS Server's CPU and operating system.

- **-s.** Returns the well-known services for hosts in the DNS domain.

Exercises

Now that you have read about the DNS Server, it is time to practice working with the DNS Server and associated files. This section provides you with the steps to create and then test a domain called SunnyDays.com, which has been assigned the address 160.106.

Exercise 13.1:   Installing the Microsoft DNS Server

First, you need to install the DNS Server. This exercise assumes you have a network card in your system. If you do not, install the MS Loopback Adapter. This enables you to do the following exercises. If the system you are working on is running DNS, ensure that you back up the files before you proceed, just in case.

1. Open the Network Settings dialog box. Choose the Protocols tab and double-click the TCP/IP protocol.

2. On the DNS tab, enter your IP address as the DNS Server and click Add. Also add the domain **SunnyDays.com** into the domain field.

3. Click the Services tab and choose Add. From the list that appears, choose the Microsoft DNS Server and click OK.

4. Enter the directory for the Windows NT source files.

5. Close the Network Settings dialog box and restart your computer.

Exercise 13.2:   Configuring a DNS Domain

Now that the server is up and running, you need to create the domains that you will use. The first domain to be created is the reverse lookup domain. After that is in place, you create the SunnyDays.com domain.

1. From the Start menu, choose Programs, Administrative Tools, DNS Manager.

continues

Exercise 13.2: Continued

2. From the menu, choose DNS, New Server. Enter your IP address and click OK.

3. To create the reverse lookup domain, click your system's address. Choose DNS, New Zone.

4. Choose Primary and click Next.

5. For the Zone, enter **106.160.in-addr.arpa** and press tab (the file name is filled in for you).

6. Click Next to continue, then choose Finish.

7. Ensure "106.160.in-addr.arpa" is highlighted, and choose DNS, Properties from the menu.

8. On the WINS Reverse Lookup tab, check the box to Use WINS Reverse Lookup. Enter **SUNNYDAYS.COM** as the host domain, and choose OK. There should now be a new host record.

7. Select your DNS Server's address and select DNS, New Zone from the menu.

8. Select Primary and choose Next. Enter **SUNNYDAYS.COM** as the zone name. Press tab to have the system fill in the file name, then choose Next. Finally, click the Finish button.

9. Right-click the SunnyDays.com domain name. From the context menu that appears, select Properties.

10. Select the WINS Lookup tab.

11. Check the Use WINS Resolution box. Enter your IP address in the WINS server space and choose Add.

12. Choose OK to close the dialog box. A WINS record should be in the SunnyDays.com domain.

Now that you have created the reverse lookup domain and the SunnyDays.com domain, add some records to the database.

1. Right-click the SunnyDays.com and choose Add Host.

2. In the New Host dialog box, add Rob as the Host Name and 160.106.66.7 as the Host IP Address.

3. Check the Create Associated PTR Record to create the reverse lookup record at the same time.

4. Choose Add Host. Now, enter Judy as the Host Name and 160.106.66.9 as the Host IP Address.

5. Click Add Host. Then click the Done button to close the dialog box. You should see the two new records in the DNS Manager.

6. Click on the 106.160.in-addr.arpa domain and press F5 to refresh. Notice there is now a 66 sub-domain.

7. Double-click the 66 sub-domain. What new hosts are there? There should be PTR records for the two hosts you just added.

8. Select the SunnyDays.com domain again. Add the following hosts, ensuring that you add the associated PTR records.

Mail1	160.106.92.14
Mail2	160.106.101.80
Mail3	160.106.127.14
Web1	160.106.65.7
Web2	160.106.72.14
FTP_Pub1	160.106.99.99
FTP_Pub2	160.106.104.255
DEV	160.106.82.7

continues

Exercise 13.3: Continued

9. Close the New Host dialog box. Verify that the records were added to the SunnyDays.com and the reverse lookup domains.

10. Highlight SunnyDays.com, and choose DNS, New Domain from the menu.

11. Enter **DEV** as the Name for the new domain and choose OK.

12. Right click on the DEV sub-domain. Choose New Record. Select CNAME as the record type.

13. Enter **WWW** as the alias, and **web2.SunnyDays.com** as the Host. (This entry sets up WWW.DEV.SUNNYDAYS.COM to point to WEB2.SUNNYDAYS.COM.)

14. Click OK to add the record. (It should appear in the Zone Info window.)

15. Create the following CNAME entries in the SunnyDays.com domain. Right-click SunnyDays.com, each time choosing New Record.

Alias	Host
WWW	web1.SunnyDays.com
FTP	FTP_PUB1.SunnyDays.com
DEV_FTP	FTP_PUB2.SunnyDays.com

16. Create a new record in the SunnyDays.com domain. This time, choose MX as the Record Type.

17. Leave the Host blank for this record, and enter **mail1.SunnyDays.com** as the Mail Exchange Server DNS Name. Enter **10** as the Preference.

18. Choose OK to add the record. Add a second MX record for the SunnyDays.com using **mail2.SunnyDays.com** as the Mail Server and **20** as the Preference.

19. Now add the MX record for dev.SunnyDays.com. To do this, right click on SunnyDays.com and choose New Record; again, this is an MX record.

20. The difference is that you include the Host name. Enter **DEV** as the Host, add **mail3.SunnyDays.com** as the Mail Exchange Server DNS Name, and **10** as the preference.

21. Ensure that all the records appear to be in place, and then close the DNS Manager.

Exercise 13.4: Testing the DNS Server

This exercise gives you a chance to test the information you entered and to check that everything is working correctly.

1. Start a command prompt.

2. Type the command **NSLOOKUP 160.106.101.80** and press enter. What response did you get? (The response should show that 160.106.101.80 is mail2.SunnyDays.com. Here you have done a reverse lookup on the IP address.)

3. Using the **NSLOOKUP** command, find out what responses the following entries give you:

> 160.106.66.7
>
> 160.106.99.99
>
> www.SunnyDays.com
>
> www.dev.SunnyDays.com
>
> ftp.SunnyDays.com

continues

Exercise 13.4: Continued

The results should be:

160.106.66.7	rob.SunnyDays.com
160.106.99.99	ftp_pub1.SunnyDays.com
www.SunnyDays.com	160.106.65.7 (web1.SunnyDays.com)
www.dev.SunnyDays.com	148.55.72.14 (web2.SunnyDays.com)
ftp.SunnyDays.com	160.106.99.99 (ftp_pub1.SunnyDays.com)

4. Start an interactive session with the name server by typing **NSLOOKUP** and pressing enter.

5. Try the following commands:

    ls SunnyDays.com

    ls -t mx SunnyDays.com

    ls -d

    q=soa

    SunnyDays.com

    q=mx

    SunnyDays.com

    Where is the third mail server?

    dev.SunnyDays.com

6. Press Ctrl+C to exit the interactive query.

7. Close the command prompt.

Review Questions

The following questions will test your knowledge of the information in this chapter:

1. Your organization uses primarily Microsoft operating systems; you want to be able to provide reverse DNS lookup for the hosts in your organization for servers on the Internet. Your organization uses DHCP to assign IP addresses. What do you need to do to provide reverse lookup capabilities?

    A. Reserve a DHCP address for each client and enter this information into the DNS server.

    B. Set up the clients to use DNS for WINS resolution.

    C. Add @ IN WINS record in the DNS database.

    D. This is not possible.

2. Your organization wants to be able to control the entries that are in your DNS Server. You currently have a domain registered with the InterNIC and your ISP is providing your DNS resolution. You have a 128Kbps link to your ISP and don't want to use all of the band width resolving DNS queries. Which of the following would best suit your needs?

    A. Increase your line speed to a T1 and set up two DNS Servers.

    B. Set up a DNS Server in your organization and arrange for your ISP to transfer your zone to their servers.

    C. Have your ISP continue to handle DNS for your organization.

    D. Use WINS to handle all name resolution.

3. Which of the following are roles that you can configure your DNS Server for?

   A. Primary

   B. Tertiary

   C. Backup

   D. IP Forwarder

4. You had Microsoft DNS Server installed and had tested the configuration. Later you remove and reinstall the Service in preparation for configuring the DNS Server with the real information. What must you do to make sure the DNS Server starts cleanly?

   A. Remove the files from the %winroot%\system32\dns directory.

   B. Reinstall Windows NT.

   C. Also remove and reinstall the WINS server.

   D. Nothing, the configuration will work fine.

5. Your Organization currently uses a Unix server for DNS. The server is fully configured using BIND files. In which two ways can you configure your Microsoft DNS Server so you will not need to re-enter any information?

   A. Set up Microsoft DNS as the Primary and transfer the zone to the Unix system.

   B. Set up Microsoft DNS as the Secondary and transfer the zone from the Unix system.

   C. Configure the Microsoft DNS server as an IP Forwarder.

   D. Configure the Microsoft DNS server as a Caching Only server.

6. Which of the following statements about DNS are true?

    A. DNS resolves NetBIOS names to TCP/IP addresses.

    B. DNS resolves host names to TCP.IP addresses.

    C. DNS resolves IP addresses to hardware addresses.

    D. DNS resolves IP addresses to host names.

7. You have a computer called WEBSERVER with a TPC/IP address of 148.53.66.45 running Microsoft Internet Information Server. This system provides the HTTP and FTP services for your organization on the Internet. Which of the following sets of entries are correct for your database file?

    A. www IN A 148.53.66.45

       ftp IN A 148.53.66.45

    B. www IN A 148.53.66.45

       ftp IN A 148.53.66.45

       webserver CNAME www

    C. webserver IN A 148.53.66.45

       www CNAME webserver

       ftp CNAME webserver

    D. 45.66.53.148 IN PTR webserver

8. Which of the following is *not* part of a Fully Qualified Domain Name?

    A. Type of Organization

    B. Host name

    C. Company name

    D. CPU type

9. Your organization uses a firewall and inside the firewall, you have five subnets. You intended to provide a DNS Server on each subnet, but want them to query the main DNS server that sits outside the firewall. What configuration should you choose for the DNS Servers that you will put on each subnet?

   A. Configure the DNS Server outside the firewall to use a WINS server on each local subnet, then configure the DNS Servers on the local subnets to use WINS resolution.

   B. Set up the DNS Servers on the local subnets as IP Forwarders to the DNS Server outside the firewall.

   C. Create a Primary zone on each of the DNS Servers inside the firewall and configure the DNS Server outside the firewall to transfer each zone.

   D. This is not possible.

10. When you are configuring your DNS server, where do you configure the length of time that an entry will be cached on your server?

   A. Set the TTL in the DNS Manager properties on your server.

   B. Set the TTL in the Cache file on the remote server.

   C. Set the TTL in the registry under HKEY_LOCAL_MACHINE\SYSTEM\ CurrentControlSet\Services\TCPIP\Parameters.

   D. Set the TTL in the remote server in the SOA record.

11. Which of the following will enable a client computer to use a DNS Server for NetBIOS name resolution?

   A. Configure the WINS Server to use DNS lookup.

   B. Do nothing; this will happen automatically.

    C. On the WINS configuration tab enable DNS for NetBIOS name resolution.

    D. Add a DNS entry in the LMHOSTS file.

12. Which of the following NSLOOKUP commands will provide a list of all the mail servers for the domain nt.com?

    A. NSLOOKUP -t MX nt.com

    B. NSLOOKUP -a MX nt.com

    C. NSLOOKUP -h nt.com

    D. NSLOOKUP -m nt.com

13. In which of the following scenarios will a recursive query *not* be used?

    A. Your system querying the DNS Server

    B. Your DNS Server querying the Root-Level servers

    C. Your DNS Server querying the WINS Server

    D. Your DNS Server querying when configured as an IP forwarder

14. Your user is at a computer called "prod172." The IP address of the computer is 152.63.85.5, and the computer is used to publish to the World Wide Web for the domain "gowest.com." Which entries should you find in the database file?

    A. prod172 IN MX 152.63.85.5

    B. www cname 152.63.85.5

    C. prod172 IN A 152.63.85.5

       www CNAME 152.63.85.5

    D. prod172 IN A 152.63.85.5

       www CNAME prod172

15. What is the purpose of a HINFO record?

    A. Provides host information including the user name

    B. Provides host information including CPU type

    C. Provides host information including BIOS version

    D. Provides host information including hard disk size

16. Which of the following files is *not* required for compliance with the DNS RFCs?

    A. The Cache file

    B. The Database file

    C. The Boot file

    D. The Reverse Lookup file

17. What is the purpose of the Domain Suffix Search Order?

    A. When you look for host name entries, it can be used to complete the FQDN.

    B. When you look for NetBIOS name entries, it can be used as the NetBIOS Scope ID.

    C. Allows your computer to be in more than one domain at a time.

    D. Tells your systems which NT domains to search when looking for a log on server.

18. Which of the following best describes the order in which you should configure the DNS server?

    A. Install the server, create the zone, enter all the records, then create the reverse lookup zone and add the WINS records.

    B. Install the server, create the reverse lookup zone, then add the zone information followed by the WINS lookup records and the other hosts.

C. Create the DNS Server database files using a text editor, install the server, then verify the information.

D. Install the DNS Server and then transfer the zone from the WINS Server.

19. What information is contained in an MX record?

A. A Preference entry.

B. The mail server name.

C. The WWW server name.

D. There is no such record.

20. What is the purpose of the Cache file?

A. Stores the names of hosts that your server has resolved.

B. Allows you to enter commonly used hosts that will be loaded to the cache.

C. Stores the addresses of Root Level servers.

D. Is used to temporarily build the DNS Server information as the server starts.

Review Answers

1. C

2. B

3. A, D

4. A

5. B, C

6. B, D (Note: A is also correct given the fact that NetBIOS name resolution will use host name resolution as a backup.)

7. C

8. D

9. B

10. D

11. C (Note: B is also correct given the fact that NetBIOS name resolution will use host name resolution as a backup.)

12. A

13. B

14. D

15. B

16. C

17. A

18. B

19. A, B

20. C

Answers to the Test Yourself Questions at the Beginning of the Chapter

1. An FQDN is a Fully Qualified Domain Name. This name identifies a TCP/IP host and the domain to which it belongs.

2. A CNAME record or conical name is an alias in a DNS Server that points to a host. Normally this is used to point WWW and/or FTP to the correct server.

3. When a client application is attempting to locate another host, the resolver that is part of the client sends a recursive query to the local DNS Server. If the DNS knows the address, it returns it; otherwise, it queries several servers to find a definitive address for the target host. This series of queries is considered an iterative query.

4. An IP Forwarder is in essence a Caching-Only server; however, rather than doing an iterative query to resolve names it doesn't know, it will perform a recursive query to a central DNS Server. This enables you to have one or two main DNS Servers connected to the Internet and many IP Forwarders that distribute the load or improve performance over slow WAN links.

5. The two main roles for a DNS Server are Primary and Secondary. The Primary maintains the DNS files and the Secondaries retrieve these files from the Primary.

6. The four main files are database file, reverse lookup file, cache file, and boot file.

7. In a Microsoft network, you can configure the DNS Server to use WINS to resolve names. Assuming that NetBIOS names and the host names are the same, this lets the DNS Server dynamically resolve addresses.

8. Reverse lookup provides the capability to look up a host name for a given IP address.

9. DNS is used by applications that work directly with the Winsock interface. This may include Internet Explorer, FTP, or Telnet.

10. On the WINS tab in the TCP/IP configuration, you can select Enable DNS for NetBIOS name resolution. This tells Windows NT to use the DNS Servers to resolve NetBIOS names rather than WINS.

C h a p t e r

14

Connectivity in Heterogeneous Environments

This chapter helps you prepare for the exam by covering the following objectives:

 Objectives

▶ Configure a Windows NT Server computer to support TCP/IP printing

▶ Given a scenario, identify which utility to use to connect to a TCP/IP based Unix host

▶ Use Microsoft TCP/IP utilities to diagnose IP configuration problems

▶ Given a scenario, identify which tool to use to monitor TCP/IP traffic

▶ Identify which Microsoft TCP/IP utility to use to diagnose IP configuration problems

Test Yourself! Before reading this chapter, test yourself to determine how much study time you will need to devote to this section.

1. What must be supported by a remote host system in order to use FTP connect to network resources?

2. What is the role of an SMB server service on a remote host?

3. Which remote execution utility can establish a terminal session with a remote host?

4. Which file transfer utility does not require user authentication?

5. Which utility would be used to send a binary file from a Windows NT computer to a remote host?

6. Which file transfer protocols is not implemented as a server service in Windows NT Server without using a third-party product?

7. Which common winsock utilities use the connection-oriented features of TCP/IP?

Answers are located at the end of the chapter.

Connectivity in Heterogeneous Environments

It is common to have different operating systems and platforms within a network. One way to achieve connectivity between platforms is to use the TCP/IP protocol. TCP/IP is available as a network protocol on most network operating systems, including Windows NT, Novell NetWare, almost all Unix operating systems, and many more. This chapter examines ways to connect different systems using the TCP/IP protocol.

Although you can interconnect different systems without using TCP/IP, TCP/IP provides a large number of utilities and services that are not available when using other protocols. Among others, the following are available:

▶ **Connectivity using Microsoft networking.** Remote host systems that support the requirements of Microsoft networking can easily be accessed by other client computers. This is not strictly provided by TCP/IP, but is supported under TCP/IP.

▶ **Remote execution.** Using standard utilities provided with Windows NT, you can execute commands on remote computers. These utilities such as RSH (Remote Shell) and REXEC (Remote Execute) require TCP/IP.

▶ **File transfer.** When direct connectivity using Microsoft networking is impossible, file transfer utilities are available to transmit and receive files to or from a remote host system. These utilities such as FTP (File Transfer Protocol) and RCP (Remote Copy Protocol) require TCP/IP to operate.

▶ **Printing.** Integration between Microsoft Windows NT and remote host system print sub-systems can be achieved using standard utilities and services available with Windows NT. These utilities LPR (Line Printer Request), and LPQ(Line Printer Query) and the LPD (Line Printer Deamon) service require TCP/IP to operate.

In addition to the preceding list, the TCP/IP protocol supports a large variety of other utilities for troubleshooting and debugging such as netstat and nbtstat.

Varying degrees of connectivity and transparency are possible depending on your requirements and the TCP/IP options your other systems can support.

The remainder of this chapter discusses the options available, depending on your environment.

Communicating Over TCP/IP

You can use standard Microsoft networking commands, such as the **NET USE** command or NT Explorer, to connect to remote hosts if the following requirements are met:

▶ Your computer and the remote host must be using the same transport driver (such as TCP/IP, IPX/SPX, or NBF).

▶ The remote host must provide an SMB server, because the Workstation service in Windows NT communicates with an SMB (server message block—for an overview of SMB communications refer back to Chapter 7) server process.

▶ The remote host must provide the standard suite of NetBIOS services as discussed in Chapter 7 NetBIOS over TCP/IP.

Effectively, connectivity using Microsoft networking is available when the remote host can provide the equivalent to a Windows NT *Server service*. To connect to resources on a remote system, you don't need to change the configuration of the Windows NT system; however the remote computer needs to be configured to act as an SMB server on a protocol used by your Windows NT system.

This option provides the greatest degree of integration between Microsoft client computers and remote host systems. Many systems support connectivity through Microsoft networking. These include LAN Manager for OS/2, LAN Manager for Unix, DEC PATHWORKS and IBM LAN Server for OS/2. In cases where this is impossible, you have other options.

For file services, Windows NT includes several utilities, including an FTP client and server, a TFTP (Trivial File Transfer Protocol) client, and a RCP client. Third-party options also exist, such as

NFS (Network File System) clients for Windows NT. Windows NT does not provide a TFTP server, and cannot accept Telnet sessions without third party utilities.

Printing services can also be provided, using the LPD/LPR print model. The LPD service can be run on Windows NT, and an LPR client is available with Windows NT.

Third-party utilities are available to provide an NFS (Network File System) server via a Windows NT server. These utilities can provide NFS services to PCs, Unix systems, or any other NFS client system. All standard Windows NT file systems are supported.

If the remote host system does not have an SMB client available, a series of TCP/IP utilities are available to connect between a remote host and a Windows NT computer. These utilities are discussed later in this chapter.

Microsoft TCP/IP Utilities

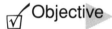

Windows NT includes TCP/IP utilities that provide many options for connecting to foreign systems using the TCP/IP protocol. In cases where it is impossible to connect to remote host systems using Microsoft networking, these utilities provide a variety of network services.

These utilities allow Microsoft clients to perform remote execution, data transfer, printing services, and much more. The following sections examine these utilities in more detail.

Remote Execution Utilities

Windows NT includes a series of remote execution utilities that enable a user to execute commands on a Unix host system. These utilities provide varying degrees of security. Note that varying subsets of these utilities are available with Windows NT Server and Workstation. The resource kit includes all of these utilities.

 Warning

> Any of these utilities that require passwords transmit the password as plain text. Unlike the Windows NT logon sequence, the logon information is not encrypted before being transmitted. Any unscrupulous user with access to network monitoring software could intercept the user name and password for the remote host. If you use the same user name and password on the remote host and on your Windows NT system, your Windows NT account could be compromised.

Windows NT provides three remote execution utilities. Each is discussed in more detail in the following sections.

The REXEC Utility

REXEC enables a user to start a process on a remote host system, using a user name and password for authentication. If the host authenticates the user, REXEC starts the specified process and terminates. Command-line options are as follows:

```
D:\>rexec /?
Runs commands on remote hosts running the REXEC service. REXEC
authenticates the user name on the remote host before executing
the specified command.

REXEC host [-l username] [-n] command

    host          Specifies the remote host on which to run
                  command
    -l username   Specifies the user name on the remote host
    -n            Redirects the input of REXEC to NULL
    command       Specifies the command to run
```

You can specify the remote host as an IP address or as a host name. After REXEC connects to the specified host, it prompts for a password. If the host authenticates the user, the specified command is executed, and the REXEC utility exits. REXEC can be used for command line programs—interactive programs such as text editors would not be usable with REXEC.

This utility provides a reasonable degree of security because the remote host authenticates the user. The down side is that the user name and password are not encrypted prior to transmission.

The RSH Utility

RSH provides much the same function as REXEC, but user authentication is handled differently. Unlike with REXEC, you do not need to specify a user name. The only validation performed by RSH is to verify that the user name is in a hidden file on the Unix system (the .rhosts file). If the remote host is configured to allow any user to use RSH, no user name needs to be provided.

Note

> On Unix systems, the .rhosts and the hosts.equiv files are used for authentication. Because these files can be used to grant access to either all users on a computer or some users on a computer, be careful. Refer to *Internet Firewalls and Network Security*, also by New Riders Publishing, for the formatting and contents of these files and related security issues.

However, because it is extremely unlikely a system would be configured in this way, the RSH utility provides the logged-on user name if no user name is provided. This can be overridden if desired. RSH has the following command-line options:

Runs commands on remote hosts running the RSH service.

```
C:\>rsh /?
rsh: remote terminal session not supported

Runs commands on remote hosts running the RSH service.

RSH host [-l username] [-n] command

   host          Specifies the remote host on which to run
                 command.
   -l username   Specifies the user name to use on the remote
                 host. If omitted, the logged on user name is
                 used.
   -n            Redirects the input of RSH to NULL.
   command       Specifies the command to run.
```

After you start RSH, it connects to the remote system's RSH dae-mon (Unix-speak for a service). The RSH daemon ensures that the user name is in the .rhosts file on the remote host, and if au-thentication succeeds, the specified command is executed.

Like REXEC, RSH provides a certain degree of security insofar as the remote host validates the access.

The Telnet Utility

Telnet is defined in RFC 854 as a remote terminal emulation pro-tocol. It provides terminal emulation for DEC VT100, DEC VT52, and TTY terminals. Telnet uses the connection-oriented services of the TCP/IP protocol for communications.

The remote host system must be running a telnet daemon. After you start telnet, you can connect to a remote host using the Con-nect/Remote system option. You are prompted for the following information (see fig. 14.1):

▶ **Host name.** The IP address or host name of the remote host

▶ **Port.** One of the ports supported by the telnet application—telnet, daytime, echo, quotd, or chargen

▶ **Terminal type.** One of VT100, ANSI (TTY), or VT52

Figure 14.1

The telnet utility.

As with REXEC and RSH, telnet provides some security, insofar as access to the remote system requires a user name and password.

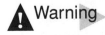 **Warning**

Telnet does not encrypt any information whatsoever. The pass-word and user name are sent as clear text, as is your entire terminal session. If you are using telnet to perform remote administration on a Unix system, your root password could be intercepted by an unscrupulous user.

Data Transfer Utilities

Several utilities are available to allow file transfer between Windows NT systems and remote hosts. As with remote execution utilities, the same caveat applies when dealing with user names and passwords. These utilities are examined in greater detail in the following sections.

RCP

The RCP command copies files from a Windows NT system to a remote host, and handles authentication in much the same way as RSH. To communicate with the RCP daemon on the remote system, the user name provided must be in the remote host's .rhosts file. The following command-line options are available:

```
C:\>rcp ?

Copies files to and from computer running the RCP service.

RCP [-a ¦ -b] [-h] [-r] [host][.user:]source [host][.user:]
path\destination
```

-a	Specifies ASCII transfer mode. This mode converts the EOL characters to a carriage return for Unix and a carriage return/line feed for personal computers. This is the default transfer mode.
-b	Specifies binary image transfer mode.
-h	Transfers hidden files.
-r	Copies the contents of all subdirectories; destination must be a directory.
host	Specifies the local or remote host. If host is specified as an IP address, you must specify the user.
.user:	Specifies a user name to use, rather than the current user name.
source	Specifies the files to copy.
path\destination	Specifies the path relative to the logon

```
directory on the remote host. Use the escape
characters (\ , ", or ') in remote paths to
use wildcard characters on the remote host.
```

As with RSH, RCP provides security by matching the user name provided with a user name in the .rhosts file. Unlike RSH, RCP does not prompt for a password.

FTP

FTP, or the file transfer protocol, provides a simple but robust mechanism for copying files to or from remote hosts using the connection-oriented services of TCP/IP. FTP is a component of the TCP/IP protocol, and is defined in RFC 959. To use FTP to send or receive files, the following requirements must be met:

▶ The client computer must have FTP client software, such as the FTP client included with Windows NT.

▶ The user must have a user name and password on the remote system. In some cases, a user name of *anonymous* with no password suffices.

▶ The remote system must be running an FTP daemon.

▶ Your system and the remote system must be running the TCP/IP protocol.

You can use FTP in either a command line mode or in a command interpreter mode. The following options are available from the command line:

```
Transfers files to and from a computer running an FTP server
service (sometimes called a daemon). FTP can be used
interactively.
```

```
FTP [-v] [-d] [-i] [-n] [-g] [-s:filename] [-a] [-w:windowsize]
[host]

    -v           Suppresses display of remote server responses.
    -n           Suppresses auto-login upon initial connection.
```

```
-i              Turns off interactive prompting during multiple
                file transfers.
-d              Enables debugging.
-g              Disables filename globbing (see GLOB command).
-s:filename     Specifies a text file containing FTP commands;
                the commands will automatically run after FTP
                starts.
-a              Use any local interface when binding data
                connection.
-w:buffersize   Overrides the default transfer buffer size of
                4096.
host            Specifies the host name or IP address of the
                remote host to connect to.
```

If you use FTP in a command interpreter mode, some of the more frequently used options are as follows:

▶ **open.** Specifies the remote system to which you connect.

▶ **close.** Disconnects from a remote system.

▶ **ls.** Obtains a directory listing on a remote system, much like the dir command in DOS. Note that the ls –l command provides file size and time stamps.

▶ **cd.** Changes directories on the remote system. This command functions in much the same way as the DOS cd command.

▶ **lcd.** Changes directories on the local system. This command also functions in much the same way as the DOS cd command.

▶ **binary.** Instructs FTP to treat all files transferred as binary.

▶ **ascii.** Instructs FTP to treat all files transferred as text.

▶ **get.** Copies a file from the remote host to your local computer.

▶ **put.** Copies a file from your local computer to the remote host.

▶ **debug.** Turns on debugging commands that can be useful in diagnosing problems.

Because remote host systems typically are based on Unix, you encounter a number of nuances relating to Unix such as the following:

▶ The Unix operating system uses the forward slash in path references, not the backward slash. In Windows NT, the file name \WINNT40\README.TXT would be /WINNT40/README.TXT.

▶ Unix is case sensitive at all times—the command *get MyFile* and the command *get MYFILE* are not the same. User names and passwords are also case-sensitive.

▶ Unix treats wild card characters, such as the asterisk and the question mark, differently. The glob command within FTP changes how wild card characters in local file names are treated.

You can also install a Windows NT FTP server, which can provide FTP file transfer services to other systems.

TFTP

TFTP provides similar functions as FTP. Unlike FTP, TFTP uses the connectionless communication features of TCP/IP. The features available in FTP are complex; those in TFTP are simpler. Unlike FTP, TFTP can be used only in a command line mode—no command interpreter mode is available. For command-line mode, the following options are available:

```
C:\>tftp /?

Transfers files to and from a remote computer running the TFTP
service.

TFTP [-i] host [GET ¦ PUT] source [destination]

   -i            Specifies binary image transfer mode (also
                 called octet). In binary image mode the file is
                 moved literally, byte by byte. Use this mode
                 when transferring binary files.
   host          Specifies the local or remote host.
```

GET	Transfers the file destination on the remote host to the file source on the local host.
PUT	Transfers the file source on the local host to the file destination on the remote host.
source	Specifies the file to transfer.
destination	Specifies where to transfer the file.

There is no TFTP server included with Windows NT, however third party TFTP servers are available.

Why use TFTP instead of FTP? Some platforms don't support FTP, notably devices that require firmware updates. Routers typically require the use of TFTP to update firmware information, such as micro-kernels.

 Note

> Many network devices such as routers and concentrators use an operating system stored in firmware. As such, upgrades are usually handled using TFTP; the process is known as a firmware update.

HTTP and Web Browsers

The explosive growth of the Internet in recent years is largely due to its flexibility. One of the Internet's building blocks is the HyperText Transfer Protocol, HTTP. It defines a way of transferring hypertext data across TCP/IP networks. The hypertext data is formatted in HTML (HyperText Markup Language). An HTML document can have a link to any other HTML document. This enables Web page designers to include text, audio files, graphics, and video within the same page.

HTTP and HTML are comprehensive standards, and a full discussion is outside the scope of this chapter. However, a discussion of Web browsers is in order. Web browsing software is used to download and view HTML documents using the HTTP protocol, but can also be used to download documents using FTP, gopher, or other protocols.

Unlike the other file transfer utilities mentioned in this section, HTTP does not use a user name or password. Information on the

World Wide Web is typically destined for access by any user, and therefore usually does not require authentication.

Many Web browsers are available; however, they all function in much the same way.

Printing Utilities

 Printing within Windows NT is a remarkably complex process. The same is true of remote host systems, such as Unix platforms. The Windows NT and host system print models can interact to a large extent. The following sections describe how clients and servers on Windows NT and remote host systems can interact.

Windows NT Client Printing to a Remote Host System

You can use two methods to print to a remote host from a Windows NT client: using the LPR command from the Windows NT client computer, or creating an LPR printer on a Windows NT client computer.

Using the LPR Command-Line Utility

One of the utilities included with Microsoft TCP/IP is the LPR utility. This program allows a Windows NT computer to send a print job to a remote host printer. The remote host system must be running the LPD daemon, and you must know the name of the remote host and the printer. This utility has the following command-line options:

```
Sends a print job to a network printerUsage: lpr -S server -P
printer [-C class] [-J job] [-o option] [-x] [-d] filename

Options:
    -S server   Name or IP address of the host providing lpd
                service
    -P printer  Name of the print queue
    -C class    Job classification for use on the burst page
    -J job      Job name to print on the burst page
    -o option   Indicates the type of file (by default assumes a
                text file)
```

```
                          Use "-o l" for binary (for example, postscript)
                          files
        -x                Compatibility with SunOS 4.1.x and prior
                          versions
        -d                Sends data file first
```

Creating an LPR Printer on a Windows NT Computer

By creating an LPR printer on the Windows NT client computer, a higher degree of transparency is provided. If the printer is shared, the Windows NT client can act as a print gateway for other Windows NT computers.

To create an LPR printer under Windows NT, simply follow the procedure shown below:

1. Select Settings/Printers, then click Add Printer. Select My Computer, because you need to add a new printer port, as shown in figure 14.2.

Figure 14.2

Creating an LPR printer on a Windows NT system.

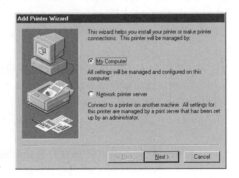

2. At this point, select Add Port, and select LPR port, as shown in figure 14.3.

Figure 14.3

Adding an LPR port.

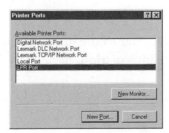

3. You are then prompted to provide the host name (or IP address) of the remote host system, along with the printer name, as shown in figure 14.4.

Figure 14.4

LPR printer infor-mation.

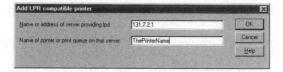

4. If you choose to share the printer, any client computer that can print to your Windows NT computer can also print to the LPR printer on the remote host system.

Remote Host Client Printing to a Windows NT Server

Remote hosts also can print to a Windows NT printer, because Windows NT can provide an LPD service. The LPD service (lpds-vc) provides the same service that an LPD daemon on a Unix host. Because it is implemented as a service, it is controlled through Control Panel, Services. This service automatically installs when you opt to install TCP/IP print services.

Remote host systems use different commands for printing. One command that works on most systems is the LPR command. A sample command line which would work on most systems is as follows:

```
lpr -s NTSYSTEM -p NTPRINTER filename
```

For the lpr command on the remote system, specify the DNS name (or IP address) of your NT system, along with the printer name. Windows NT internally directs the print job to the specified printer.

Please refer to the documentation for your remote host system for more information.

Troubleshooting Utilities

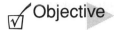

The previously discussed utilities provide basic connectivity services between Windows NT systems and remote host systems. The following utilities are diagnostic and troubleshooting tools for connectivity between heterogeneous systems.

> Most of these utilities are discussed elsewhere in the book. For example, the NBTSTAT utility is discussed in detail in Chapter 7, and NSLOOKUP is discussed in detail in Chapter 13.

These utilities provide debugging and troubleshooting information to determine the cause of a connectivity failure between Microsoft clients and remote host computers. This section does not cover all possible debugging tools—indeed, a separate book could be written on this topic.

In addition to debugging utilities, the following suggestions can be of considerable use when troubleshooting:

▶ If TCP/IP cannot communicate from a Microsoft host to a remote host system, the utilities discussed in this chapter will not work correctly.

▶ If the systems are on different subnets, and cannot communicate, remember that TCP/IP requires routing to communicate between subnets.

▶ If the systems previously were able to communicate, but can no longer communicate, suspect either your router(s) or changes in software configuration.

▶ Utilities that require user names and passwords on the remote host need a user account on the remote system. If you have an account on a Windows NT system, the remote host system does not know or care. Trust relationships are not the same as achieving connectivity.

▶ On Windows NT computers, never forget to consult the Event Viewer. Any messages that are out of the ordinary may provide valuable clues to the cause of the problem.

Although the following tools are not strictly related to connectivity in heterogeneous environments, these tools are useful in troubleshooting almost any TCP/IP network.

PING

The PING command is one of the most useful commands in the TCP/IP protocol. It sends a series of packets to another system, which in turn sends back a response. This utility can be extremely useful in troubleshooting problems with remote hosts.

The PING utility is used as a command-line program, and accepts the following parameters:

```
Usage: ping [-t] [-a] [-n count] [-l size] [-f] [-i TTL] [-v TOS]
            [-r count] [-s count] [[-j host-list] ¦ [-k host-
            list]] [-w timeout] destination-list
Options:
    -t              Pings the specified host until interrupted
    -a              Resolves addresses to host names
    -n count        Number of echo requests to send.
    -l size         Sends buffer size
    -f              Sets Don't Fragment flag in packet
    -i TTL          Time to Live
    -v TOS          Type of Service
    -r count        Records route for count hops
    -s count        Time stamp for count hops
    -j host-list    Loose source route along host-list
    -k host-list    Strict source route along host-list
    -w timeout      Time-out in milliseconds to wait for each reply
```

The PING command indicates whether the host can be reached, and how long it took for the host to send a return packet. On a local area network, the time is indicated as less than 10 milliseconds, but across wide area network links, this value can be much greater.

TRACERT

The TRACERT utility determines the intermediary steps involved in communicating with another IP host. It provides a road map of all the routing an IP packet takes to get from host A to host B.

```
Usage: tracert [-d] [-h maximum_hops] [-j host-list] [-w timeout]
        target_name
```

```
Options:
    -d                      Does not resolve addresses to host names
    -h maximum_hops         Maximum number of hops to search for
                            target
    -j host-list            Loose source route along host-list
    -w timeout              Wait time-out milliseconds for each reply
```

As with the PING command, TRACERT returns the amount of time required for each routing *hop*.

IPCONFIG

One of the key areas that causes problems with TCP/IP is configuration. Windows NT provides a utility that will allow you to view the configuration of a workstation so you can verify the configuration. The following listing provides a summary of the usage of IPCONFIG:

```
C:\>ipconfig /?Windows NT IP Configuration
Usage: ipconfig [/? ¦ /all ¦ /release [adapter] ¦ /renew [adapter]]
Options:
        /?      Display this help message.
        /all    Display full configuration information.
        /release Release the IP address for the specified adapter.
        /renew  Renew the IP address for the specified adapter.
```

The default is to display only the IP address, subnet mask and default gateway for each adapter bound to TCP/IP.

For Release and Renew, if no adapter name is specified, then the IP address leases for all adapters bound to TCP/IP will be released or renewed.

NETSTAT

Once you have determined that your base level communications are working you will need to verify the services on your system. This involves looking at the services that are listening for incoming traffic and/or verifying that you are creating a session with a remote station. The NETSTAT command will allow you to do this.

```
C:\>netstat /?
```

Displays protocol statistics and current TCP/IP network connections.

```
NETSTAT [-a] [-e] [-n] [-s] [-p proto] [-r] [interval]
```

```
-a          Displays all connections and listening ports.
            (Server-side connections are normally not shown).
-e          Displays Ethernet statistics.  This may be
            combined with the -s option.
-n          Displays addresses and port numbers in numerical
            form.
-p proto    Shows connections for the protocol specified by
            proto; proto may be tcp or udp.  If used with the
-s          option to display per-protocol statistics, proto
            may be tcp, udp, or ip.
-r          Displays the contents of the routing table.
-s          Displays per-protocol statistics.  By default,
            statistics are shown for TCP, UDP and IP; the
-p          option may be used to specify a subset of the
            default.
interval    Redisplays selected statistics, pausing interval
            seconds between each display.  Press CTRL+C to
            stop redisplaying statistics.  If omitted,
            netstat will print the current configuration
            information once.
```

NBTSTAT

Whereas NETSTAT deals with all the connections that your system has with other computers, NBTSTAT deals with only the NetBIOS connections. NBTSTAT also allows you to verify that name resolution is taking place by providing a method to view the name cache.

```
C:\>nbtstat /?

Displays protocol statistics and current TCP/IP connections using
NBT (NetBIOS over TCP/IP).

NBTSTAT [-a RemoteName] [-A IP address] [-c] [-n]
        [-r] [-R] [-s] [-S] [interval] ]

  -a    (adapter status) Lists the remote machine's name table
        given its name
  -A    (Adapter status) Lists the remote machine's name table
        given its IP address.
```

```
      -c   (cache)        Lists the remote name cache including the
                          IP addresses
      -n   (names)        Lists local NetBIOS names.
      -r   (resolved)     Lists names resolved by broadcast and via
                          WINS
      -R   (Reload)       Purges and reloads the remote cache name
                          table
      -S   (Sessions)     Lists sessions table with the destination
                          IP addresses
      -s   (sessions)     Lists sessions table converting destina
                          tion IP
                          addresses to host names via the hosts
                          file.


    RemoteName   Remote host machine name.
    IP address   Dotted decimal representation of the IP address.
    interval     Redisplays selected statistics, pausing interval
                 seconds between each display. Press Ctrl+C to stop
                 redisplaying statistics.
```

NSLOOKUP

One of the key issues in using TCP/IP is the capability to resolve a host name to an IP address. This is usually done by a DNS server (see Chapters 12 and 13). In order to test the capability to resolve names, Windows NT comes with a utility called NSLOOKUP.

```
Usage:   nslookup [-opt ...]
     # interactive mode using default server   nslookup [-opt
     ...] - server
     # interactive mode using 'server'   nslookup [-opt ...] host
     # just look up 'host' using default server   nslookup [-opt
     ...] host server
     # just look up 'host' using 'server'
```

ROUTE

Occasionally it is necessary to check how a system will route packets on the network. Normally your system will simply send all packets to the default gateway, however, in cases where your are having problems communicating with a group of computers, the ROUTE command may provide an answer.

```
C:\>route Manipulates network routing tables.ROUTE [-f] [command
[destination] [MASK netmask] [gateway] [METRIC metric]]
   -f           Clears the routing tables of all gateway entries.
                If this is used in conjunction with one of the
                commands, the tables are cleared prior to running
                the command.

   -p           When used with the ADD command, makes a route
                persistent across boots of the system. By default,
                routes are not preserved when the system is
                restarted. When used with the PRINT command,
                displays the list of registered persistent
                routes. Ignored for all other commands, which
                always affect the appropriate persistent routes.

 command        Specifies one of four commands
                PRINT      Prints a route
                ADD        Adds a route
                DELETE     Deletes a route
                CHANGE     Modifies an existing route

 destination    Specifies the host.

 MASK           If the MASK keyword is present, the next parameter
                is interpreted as the netmask parameter.

 netmask        If provided, specifies a sub-net mask value to be
                associated with this route entry.  If not
                specified, it defaults to 255.255.255.255.

 gateway        Specifies gateway.

 METRIC         specifies the metric/cost for the destination
```

All symbolic names used for destination are looked up in the network database file NETWORKS. The symbolic names for gateway are
looked up in the host name database file HOSTS. If the command is
print or delete, wildcards may be used for the destination
and gateway, or the gateway argument may be omitted.

ARP

As has been discussed, once the name has been resolved to an IP
address, you computer must resolve the IP address to a MAC address. This is handled Address Resolution Protocol (ARP). The
ARP utility will allow you to view the addresses that have been
resolved.

```
C:\>arp /?Displays and modifies the IP-to-Physical address trans-
lation tables used by address resolution protocol (ARP).

ARP -s inet_addr eth_addr [if_addr]
ARP -d inet_addr [if_addr]
ARP -a [inet_addr] [-N if_addr]
```

-a	Displays current ARP entries by interrogating the current protocol data. If inet_addr is specified, the IP and Physical addresses for only the speci-fied computer are displayed. If more than one network interface uses ARP, entries for each ARP table are displayed.
-g	Same as -a.
inet_addr	Specifies an internet address.
-N if_addr	Displays the ARP entries for the network interface specified by if_addr.
-d	Deletes the host specified by inet_addr.
-s	Adds the host and associates the Internet address inet_addr with the Physical address eth_addr. The Physical address is given as 6 hexadecimal bytes separated by hyphens. The entry is permanent.

```
eth_addr       Specifies a physical address.
if_addr        If present, this specifies the Internet address of
               the interface whose address translation table
               should be modified. If not present, the first
               applicable interface will be used.
```

Performance Monitor

To tune or optimize Windows NT you will need to be able to look at the performance of the server on many different levels. NT provides an integrated tool that provides information about your system on many different levels. The Performance Monitor will allow you to check not only track the flow of traffic in and out of the system but will also allow you to look at the performance of the various service and programs that are running on your system.

Network Monitor

There are two version of the Network Monitor the basic version that comes with Windows NT and the full version that comes with the SMS (Systems Management Server). Both versions will allow you to capture the packets that are flowing into and out of your computer. The Full version that comes with SMS will also allow you extra functionality such as the capability to capture all packets on the local network or on remote networks, edit those packets, derive statistics about protocols and users on the network.

There are two pieces to the Network Monitor. The Agent which will capture the data. There is also the Monitor Tool which can be used to view the data.

The Network Monitor can be used to diagnose more complex issue with connectivity by allowing you see the actual packets that are flowing on the network verifying which steps are being used to resolve names or which port numbers are being used to connect.

Review Questions

1. Which utility can you use to transfer a file to a remote host using the connection-oriented services of TCP/IP?

    A. TFTP

    B. HTML

    C. FTP

    D. Telnet

2. Which remote execution utility encrypts user names and passwords before transmission?

    A. REXEC

    B. RSH

    C. Telnet

    D. None of the above

3. Which of the following statements about REXEC are incorrect?

    A. REXEC can start processes on Windows NT computers.

    B. REXEC does not require a user name or password.

    C. REXEC can establish terminal sessions on a remote host.

    D. REXEC requires an SMB server on the remote host.

    E. All of the above.

4. Given a remote host system running TCP/IP and having an SMB server service, which of the following provides the most transparent network connectivity for file transfer?

    A. Using an NFS client on a Windows NT computer

    B. Using Microsoft networking functions on a Windows NT computer

C. Using FTP to copy files from the remote host to your local computer

D. Using telnet to establish a remote terminal session with the remote host

5. Which of the following statements about telnet are incorrect?

   A. Telnet can be used to remotely administer Windows NT computers.

   B. Telnet encrypts user names and passwords for enhanced security.

   C. Telnet can be used to provide terminal emulation when connecting to remote host systems.

   D. Telnet can be used to view HTML documents with graphical images.

6. A user on a Windows NT computer wishes to run an interactive text editor on a remote host computer. Which utilities would be suitable for use?

   A. Telnet

   B. FTP

   C. REXEC

   D. RSH

   E. HTTP

   F. LPR

7. A user at a Windows NT computer running the TCP/IP protocol wishes to send a print job to an LPR printer on a remote host system. Which methods enable the user to send the print job to the remote host?

   A. Using the LPD command-line utility from the Windows NT system, specifying the host name, printer name and file name

B. Using the LPR command-line utility from the Windows NT system, specifying the host name, printer name and file name

C. Creating an LPR printer in Control Panel/Printers, specifying the host name and printer name required for the creation of an LPR port

D. Creating an LPR printer in Control Panel/Printers, specifying the host name and printer name required for the creation of an LPD server on the Windows NT computer

8. Which procedure enables a remote computer to send a print job to a Windows NT printer in the fewest steps?

A. Creating an LPR printer on the Windows NT computer, sharing the printer, and running the LPR command from the remote host system specifying the required information

B. Creating the LPR printer on the Windows NT computer, and running the LPR command from the remote host system specifying the required information

C. Running the LPR command on the remote system—Windows NT automatically routes the print job to the printer with no further configuration on the Windows NT computer

D. Running the LPD command from the remote host, because the LPD command spawns a copy of the LPDSVC command on the Windows NT computer whether or not TCP/IP printing support is installed

9. Which of the following allows a Windows NT computer to act as a print gateway to an LPR printer on a remote host?

A. Creating an LPR printer on the Windows NT computer, sharing the printer, and connecting to the newly created printer from any other computer on the network.

B. Creating an LPR printer on the Windows NT computer, and installing an LPR printer on every other computer on the network because Windows NT computers cannot act as print gateways to LPR printers.

C. Creating an LPR printer on the Windows NT computer, and installing the LPDSVC service on every other computer on the network.

D. None of the above—Windows NT automatically routes print jobs to any printer, including LPR, without any configuration.

10. Your network includes a number of NT Servers, workstations and TCP/IP host systems. If you want to establish a secure terminal session to a host system from a Windows NT client, which of the following utilities would be adequate?

A. Telnet

B. FTP

C. TFTP

D. None of the above

11. You have a client computer using TCP/IP on a local subnet, and you want to transfer a file to a remote system overseas. Which of the following utilities would provide the most reliable file transfer?

A. Telnet

B. TFTP

C. TCP

D. FTP

12. In a network which has a mixture of Windows NT and remote host systems, you want to administer remote host systems from a Windows NT computer by running remote

system jobs. Which of the following utilities would allow you to execute a job on a remote system without requiring a log-in password?

   A. TFTP

   B. REXEC

   C. RSH

   D. Telnet

13. Which of the following statements about FTP are INCOR-RECT?

   A. FTP encrypts user names and passwords.

   B. FTP does not encrypt user names and passwords, but uses MD5 and CHAP to encrypt data transfer.

   C. FTP does not perform any encryption whatsoever.

   D. None of the above.

14. Your network provides a Web server to the Internet through a firewall. Which of the following protocols would usually NOT be available to a client on the other side of your fire-wall?

   A. HTTP

   B. FTP

   C. TFTP

   D. Telnet

15. HTML documents are transferred using the HTTP protocol. Of the following statements, which accurately describes the HTTP protocol?

   A. HTTP uses the non-connection-oriented communica-tion features of TCP/IP for data transfer.

   B. HTTP requires a user name and password for all HTML documents.

C. The HTTP protocol uses the connection-oriented communication features of TCP/IP for data transfer.

D. HTTP can only be used for text files.

16. Which parameters are required when using the LPR command on a Windows NT computer to send a print job to a remote host?

A. The remote host name

B. User name and password for the remote system

C. The remote printer name

D. The name of the file to be printed

E. The remote system's SMB server name

17. By creating an LPR printer on a Windows NT computer, and sharing the newly created printer, which of the following statements describes the added functions?

A. Remote host systems can print to the LPR printer, and Windows NT client computers can print to the LPR printer, but only by using the LPR command.

B. Remote host systems can print to the LPR printer, and Windows NT computers can print to the LPR printer using Windows NT printing, but other Windows NT computers cannot print to the LPR printer.

C. Remote host systems can print to the LPR printer, Windows NT computers can print to the LPR printer using Windows NT printing, and other Windows NT computers can print to the LPR printer.

D. Remote host systems cannot print to the LPR printer, Windows NT computers can print to the LPR printer using Windows NT printing, and other Windows NT computers can print to the LPR printer.

Review Answers

1. C

2. D

3. E

4. B

5. A, B, D

6. A, D

7. B, C

8. B

9. A

10. D

11. D

12. C

13. A, B

14. D

15. C

16. A, C, D

17. C

Answers to the Test Yourself Questions at the Beginning of the Chapter

1. The remote host must be using the same transport protocol as the Microsoft client and the remote host must be configured as an FTP server.
2. The SMB server communicates with the workstation service on a Windows NT computer.
3. Telnet can be used to establish a remote terminal session.
4. The only file transfer utility that does not require authentication is HTTP.
5. Files can be transferred to another station using RCP, FTP, and TFTP.
6. The Internet Information Server has FTP, Gopher and HTTP services. This means TFTP and RCP are not implemented as services in NT.
7. FTP, Telnet, and HTTP are the common winsock applications that use TCP (connection oriented) transfers.

Chapter 15

Implementing the Microsoft SNMP Service

This chapter will help you prepare for the exam by covering the following objective:

 Objective

▶ Configure SNMP

Test Yourself! Before reading this chapter, test yourself to determine how much study time you will need to devote to this section.

1. What is the purpose of SNMP?

2. To what extent does SNMP resolve host names?

3. At what level does SNMP fit into the TCP/IP architecture?

4. What levels of security exist for SNMP?

Answers are located at the end of the chapter.

The Usefulness of SNMP

SNMP (Simple Network Management Protocol) is part of the TCP/IP protocol suite. It corresponds to the Application layer in the Internet Protocol Suite.

SNMP enables network administrators to remotely troubleshoot and monitor hubs and routers (see fig. 15.1). Much of SNMP is defined within RFCs 1157 and 1212, though there are many more RFCs on SNMP. SNMP can be found, along with other RFCs, on various web sites, including `http://ds.internic.net`. You can also do a search on SNMP or RFC and find more specific information related to a specific part of SNMP—for example, on just ethernet and SNMP.

Figure 15.1

Hubs and routers.

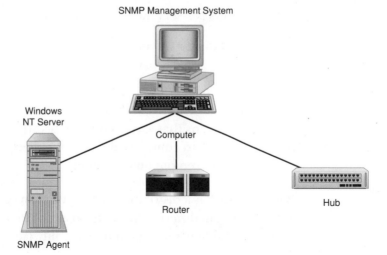

Using SNMP, you can find out information about these remote devices without having to physically be at the device itself. This can be a very useful tool if understood and used properly. You can find a wide variety of information about these devices, depending on the device itself, of course. Some examples include the following:

- ▶ IP address of a router

- ▶ Number of open files

- ▶ Amount of hard drive space available

- ▶ Version number of a Windows NT host

Before you set up SNMP, you need the IP address or host names of the systems that will either be the initiators or those that will respond to the requests. Microsoft's SNMP Service uses the regular Windows NT host name resolution, such as HOSTS, DNS, WINS, and LMHOSTS. Therefore, if you are using one of these resolution methods, add the correct host name to IP address resolution for the computers that you are setting up with SNMP.

The types of systems on which you can find data include the following:

▶ Mainframes

▶ Gateways and routers

▶ Hubs and bridges

▶ Windows NT servers

▶ LAN Manager servers

▶ SNMP agents

SNMP uses a distributed architecture design to facilitate its properties. This means that various parts of SNMP are spread throughout the network to complete the task of collecting and processing data to provide remote management.

Because SNMP is a distributed system, you can spread out the management of it in different locations so as not to overtax any one PC, and for multiple management functionality (see fig. 15.2).

Figure 15.2

SNMP in the works.

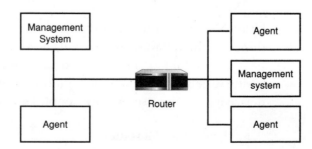

An SNMP Service by Microsoft enables a machine running Windows NT to be able to transfer its current condition to a computer running an SNMP management system. However, this is only the agent side, not the management tools. This chapter's Labs use an SNMPutil.exe that is a basic command prompt utility. Various third-party management utilities are available, including the following:

▶ IBM NetView

▶ Sun Net Manager

▶ Hewlett-Packard OpenView

This chapter focuses primarily on the SNMP protocol rather than the management utilities; the management utilities are a product of their own and not included in Microsoft training material or exam.

SNMP Agents and Management

There are two main parts to SNMP: the agent and the management side.

▶ The management station is the centralized location from which you can manage SNMP.

▶ The agent station is the piece of equipment that you are trying to extract data from.

Each part is discussed in the following sections.

The SNMP Management System

The management system is the key component for obtaining information from the client. You need at least one management system to even be able to use the SNMP Service. The management system is responsible for "asking the questions." As mentioned earlier, there are a certain number of questions it can ask each device, depending upon the type of device. The management system is, of course, a computer running one of the various software components mentioned earlier (see fig. 15.3).

Figure 15.3

Agents and management systems.

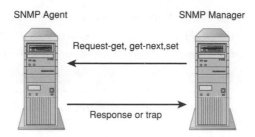

There are also certain commands that can be given specifically at the management system. These are generic commands not specific to any type of management system directly:

▶ **get.** Requests a specific value. For example, it can query how many active sessions are open.

▶ **get-next.** Requests the next object's value. For example, you can query a client's arp cache and then ask for each subsequent value.

▶ **set.** Changes the value on an object that has the properties of read-write. This command is not often used due to security, and the fact that the majority of objects have a read-only attribute.

Usually, you have only one management system running the SNMP Service per group of hosts. This group is known as a *community*. Sometimes, however, you may want to have more. Some of these reasons are discussed in the following list:

▶ You may want to have multiple management systems inquire different queries to the same agents.

▶ There might be different management sites for one community.

▶ As the network grows and becomes more complex, you may need to help differentiate certain aspects of your community.

The SNMP Agent

You have seen so far what the SNMP management side is responsible for and can specifically do. For the most part, the management side is the active component for getting information. The SNMP agent, on the other hand, is responsible for complying with the requests and responding to the SNMP manager accordingly. Generally, the agent is a router, server, or hub. The agent is usually a passive component only responding to a direct query.

In one particular instance, however, the agent is the initiator, acting on its own without a direct query. This special case is called a *trap*. A trap is set up from the management side on the agent. But the management does not need to go to the agent to find out if the trap information has been tripped. The agent sends an alert to the management system telling it that the event has occurred. Most of the time, the agent is passive except in this one occasion. A trap is similar to a father and son fishing with a net on a stream. The dad sets up the net on the stream. The net has certain sized holes in it, just the right size for catching a certain type and size of fish. The dad then goes downstream to set up more, leaving his son to tend to the net. When the fish comes along, it gets caught in the net and the son runs to tell his father.

The stream is the traffic going through the router. The net is the trap set by the management system. The son is the one responding to the trap and running to tell his father they have caught the fish without the father having to go back and check on his trap. The special fish that is caught might be an alert that a particular server's hard drive is full or a duplicate IP address. Although this is a rough analogy, it gets the basic idea across. What happens, however, if a spare tire comes down the stream and gets caught in the trap? Sometimes invalid packets can set off the trap without it being what you are looking for. These are rare events and the traps set are very specific in what they are looking for.

Management Information Base

Now that you've learned a little about the management system and agents, you can delve into the different types of query databases.

The data that the management system requests from an agent is contained in a *Management Information Base* (MIB). This is a list of questions that the management system can ask. The list of questions depends on what type of device it is asking. The MIB is the database of information that can be queried against.

A variety of MIB databases can be established. The MIB is stored on the SNMP agent and is similar to the Windows NT Registry in its hierarchical structure. These MIBs are available to both the agents and management system as a reference that both can pull information from.

The Microsoft SNMP Service supports the following MIB databases:

▶ Internet MIB II

▶ LAN Manager MIB II

▶ DHCP MIB

▶ WINS MIB

These databases are discussed in the following sections.

Internet MIB II

Internet MIB II defines 171 objects for fault troubleshooting on the network and configuration analysis. It is defined in RFC 1212, which adds to, and overwrites, the previous version, Internet MIB I.

LAN Manager MIB II

LAN Manager MIB II defines about 90 objects associated with Microsoft Networking, such as:

- ▶ Shares

- ▶ Users

- ▶ Logon

- ▶ Sessions

- ▶ Statistical

The majority of LAN Manager MIB II's objects are set to read-only mode due to the limited security function of SNMP.

DHCP MIB

The DHCP MIB identifies objects that can monitor the DHCP server's actions. It is set up automatically when a DHCP server service is installed and is called DHCPMIB.DLL. It has 14 objects that can be used for monitoring the DHCP server activity, including items such as the following:

- ▶ The number of active leases

- ▶ The number of failures

- ▶ The number of DHCP discover requests received

WINS MIB

WINS MIB (WINSMIB.DLL) is a Microsoft-specific MIB relating directly to the WINS server service. It is automatically installed when WINS is set up. It monitors WINS server activity and has approximately 70 objects. It checks such items as the number of resolution requests, success and failure, and the date and time of last database replication.

MIB Structure

As mentioned previously, the name space for MIB objects is hierarchical. It is structured in this manner so that each manageable object can be assigned a globally unique name. Certain organizations have the authority to assign the name space for parts of the tree design.

The MIB structure is similar to TCP/IP addresses. You get only one address from the InterNIC and then subnet it according to your needs. You do not have to contact "InterNIC" for each address assignment. The same applies here. Organizations can assign names without consulting an Internet authority for every specific assignment. For example, the name space assigned to Microsoft's LAN Manager is 1.3.6.1.4.1.77. More recently, Microsoft has been assigned 1.3.6.1.4.1.311; any new MIB would then be identified under that branch. Figure 15.4 illustrates the hierarchical name tree.

Figure 15.4

*Hierarchical
name tree.*

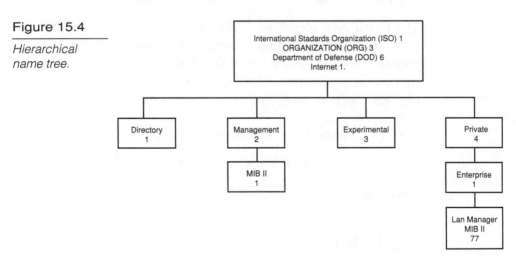

The object identifier in the hierarchy is written as a sequence of labels beginning at the root and ending at the object. It flows down the chart, starting with the International Standards Organization (ISO) and ending with the object MIB II. Labels are separated by periods. The following is an example of this labeling technique:

The object identifier for a MIB II:

Object Name	Object Number
Iso.org.dod.internet. management.mibii	1.3.6.2.1

The object identifier for LAN Manager MIB II:

Object Name	Object Number
iso.org.dod.internet. private. enterprise. lanmanger	1.3.6.1.4.77

 Note | The name space used here for the object identifiers is completely separate from that used with Unix domain names.

Microsoft SNMP Service

The SNMP Service is an additional component of Windows NT TCP/IP software. It includes the four supported MIBs; each is a dynamic-link library and can be loaded and unloaded as needed. It provides SNMP agent services to any TCP/IP host running SNMP management software. It also performs the following:

▶ Reports special happenings, such as traps, to multiple hosts

▶ Responds to requests for information from multiple hosts

▶ Can be set up on any system running Windows NT and TCP/IP

▶ Sets up special counters in Performance monitor that can be used to monitor the TCP/IP performance related to SNMP

▶ Uses host names and IP addresses to recognize which hosts it receives, and requests information

SNMP Architecture

The MIB architecture can be extended to enable developers to create their own MIB libraries, called *extension agents*. Extension agents expand the list of objects that an MIB can report on, making it not only more expansive but also directed to be specifically related to network setup and devices. Figure 15.5 illustrates the SNMP architecture.

Figure 15.5

SNMP architecture.

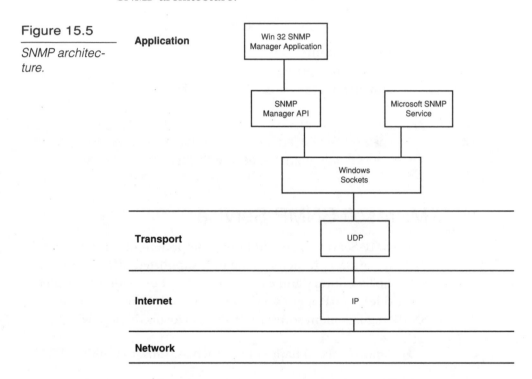

Although the Microsoft SNMP Service doesn't have management software included, it does have a Microsoft Win32 SNMP Manager API that works with the Windows Sockets. The API can then be used by developers to create third-party SNMP management utilities.

The Microsoft SNMP uses User Datagram Protocol (UDP port 161) to send and receive messages, and IP to route messages.

SNMP Communities

A *community* is a group of hosts running the SNMP Service to which they all belong. These usually consist of at least one management system and multiple agents. The idea is to logically organize systems into organizational units for better network management. Figure 15.6 illustrates SNMP communites.

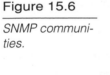

Figure 15.6

*SNMP communi-
ties.*

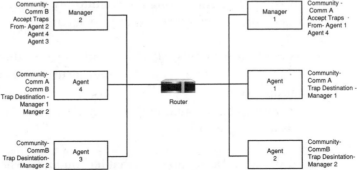

Communities are called by a *community name.* This name is case sensitive. The default community name is public and generally all hosts belong to it. Also by default, all SNMP agents respond to any request using the community public name. By using unique community names, however, you can provide limited security and segregation of hosts.

Agents do not accept requests nor respond to hosts that are not from their configured community. Agents can be members of multiple communities at the same time, but they must be explicitly configured as such. This enables them to respond to different SNMP managers from various communities.

In this example, two separate communities are defined: CommA and CommB. Only the managers and agents that are members of the same community can communicate.

▶ Agent1 can send and receive messages to Manager1 because they are both members of the CommA community.

▶ Agent2 and Agent3 can send and receive messages to Manager2 because they are all members of the CommB community.

▶ Agent4 can send and receive messages to Manager1 and Manager2 because Agent4 is a member of the CommA and CommB communities.

Security

There really is no established security with SNMP. The data is not encrypted, and there is no setup to stop someone from accessing the network, discovering the community names and addresses used, and sending fake requests to agents.

A major reason most MIBs are read-only is so that unauthorized changes cannot be made. The best security you can have is to use unique community names. Choose Send Authentication Trap and specify a Trap Destination, and stipulate Only Accept SNMP Packets from these Hosts.

You might also set up traps that let you know whether the agents receive requests from communities or addresses not specified. This way, you can track down unauthorized SNMP activity.

Installing and Configuring SNMP

The SNMP Service can be installed for the following reasons:

▶ You want to monitor TCP/IP with Performance Monitor.

▶ You want to monitor a Windows NT-based system with a third-party application.

▶ You want to set up your computer as an SNMP agent.

The following are steps on installing the SNMP Service, assuming you already have TCP/IP installed and set up. These steps also assume you have administrative privileges to install and utilize SNMP.

1. Click on Start, Settings, Control Panel.

2. Double-click Network to bring up the Network properties dialog box.

3. On the Network Settings dialog box, click Add.

4. Click the Services tab (see fig. 15.7) and click Add.

Figure 15.7

The add services screen.

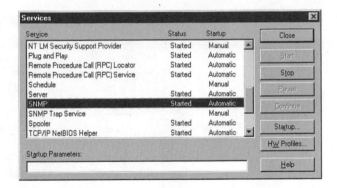

5. The Select Network Service dialog box appears (see fig. 15.8).

Figure 15.8

SNMP Service.

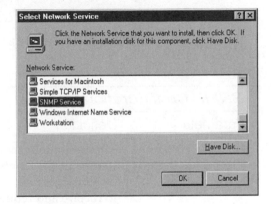

6. Click SNMP Service and then click on OK.

7. Specify the location of the Microsoft Windows NT distribution files.

8. After the files are copied, the Microsoft SNMP Properties dialog box appears (see fig. 15.9). The parameters shown in table 15.1 need to be configured:

Figure 15.9

The Microsoft SNMP Properties dialog box.

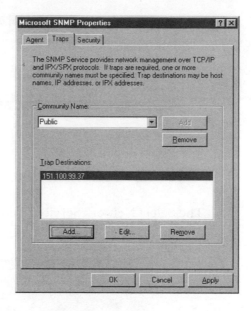

Table 15.1

SNMP Configuration Options

Parameter	Definition
Community Name	The community name to which traps are sent. Remember, it is public by default. There must be a management system in that community to receive and request information.
Trap Destination	The IP addresses of hosts to which you want the SNMP Service to send traps. Note that you can use IP addresses, host names (as long as they are resolved properly), and IPX addresses.

9. Now choose OK to close the SNMP Properties dialog box. Then choose Close to exit the Network properties dialog box. When prompted, Restart your computer.

SNMP Security Parameters

There are several options that you can set that affect the security of the SNMP agent (see fig. 15.10). By default the agent will respond to any manager using community name public. Because this can be inside or outside your organization you should at the very least change the community name.

Figure 15.10

SNMP security settings.

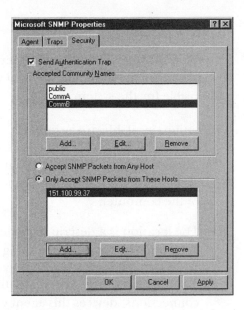

Table 15.2 describes the available options.

Table 15.2

Security Options for the SNMP Agent	
Parameter	Description
Send Authentication Trap	Sends information back to the trap initiator responding that the trap failed. This could be because of an incorrect community name or because the host is not specified for service.
Accepted Community Names	When a manager sends a query, a community name is included, this is a list of community names that the agent will respond to.
Accept SNMP Packets from Any Host	Responds to any query from any management system in any community.
Only Accept SNMP Packets from These Hosts	Responds to only the hosts listed.

SNMP Agent

In some cases you will configure other aspects of the SNMP agent. These set the type of devices that you will monitor and who is responsible for the system.

The options available are as follows:

- ▶ The contact name of the person you want to be alerted about conditions on this station—generally, this is the user of the computer.

- ▶ The location is a descriptive field for the computer to help keep track of the system sending the alert.

- ▶ The last part of the screen identifies the types of connections/devices this agent will monitor. These include:

    - ▶ Physical—You are managing physical devices like repeaters or hubs.

    - ▶ Applications—Set if the Windows NT computer uses an application that uses TCP/IP. You should check this box every time, because just by using SNMP you should have TCP/IP set up.

    - ▶ Datalink/Subnetwork—For managing a bridge.

    - ▶ Internet—Causes the Windows NT computer to act as an IP gateway, or router.

    - ▶ End-to-End—Causes the Windows NT computer to act as an IP host. You should check this box every time because you are most likely an IP host.

Any errors with SNMP will be recorded in the system log. The log records any SNMP activity. Use Event Viewer to look at the errors and to find the problem and possible solutions.

Using the SNMP Utility

The SNMP utility does not come with Windows NT. It is included in the Windows NT Resource Kit and called SNMPUTIL.EXE. Basically, it is a command line management system utility. It checks that the SNMP Service has been set up and is working correctly. You can also utilize it to make command calls. You cannot do full SNMP management from this utility but, as you will see, you would not want to due to, the complex syntax.

The following is the general syntax structure:

```
snmputil command gent community object_identifier_(OID)
```

The following are the commands you can use:

▶ **walk.** Moves through the MIB branch identified by what you have placed in the object_identifer

▶ **get.** Returns the value of the item specified by the object_identifier

▶ **getnext.** Returns the value of the next object after the one specified by the get command

To find out the time the WINS server service began, for example, providing WINS is installed and the SNMP agent is running, you query the WINS MIB with the following command:

```
c:\>snmputil getnext localhost public .1.3.6.1.4.1.311.1.1.1.1
```

In this example, the first part refers to the Microsoft branch: .1.3.6.1.4.1.311 (or iso.org.dod.internet.private.enterprise. microsoft). The last part of the example refers to the specific MIB and object you are querying: .1.1.1.1 (or .software.Wins.Par.Par WinsStartTime). A returned value might look like the following:

```
Value = OCTET STRING - 01:17:22 on 11:23:1997.<0xa>
```

What SNMP Is Really Doing

The following example tracks a sample of SNMP traffic between a manager and an agent. Remember in real life you will use management software (such as HP's Openview, which allows you to see the MIBs and query without knowing all the numbers).

1. The SNMP management system makes a request of an agent using the agent's IP address or host name.

   a. Request sent by the application to UDP port 161.

   b. Host name resolved to an IP address, if host name was used, using host name resolution methods: localhost, HOSTS file, DNS, WINS, broadcast, LMHOSTS file.

2. SNMP packet gets set up with the listed information inside, and routes the packet on the agent's UDP port 161:

   a. The command for the objects: get, get-next, set.

   b. The community name and any other specified data.

3. An SNMP agent gets the packet and puts it into its buffer.

   a. The community name is checked for validity. If it is not correct or is corrupted, the packet is rejected.

   b. If the community name checks out, the agent checks to see whether the originating host name or IP address is correct as well. If not, it is thrown out.

   c. The inquiry is then passed to the correct DLL as described in the preceding section on MIBs.

   d. The object identifier gets mapped to the specific API and that call gets made.

   e. The DLL sends the data to the agent.

4. The SNMP packet is given to the SNMP manager with the requested information.

Exercises

First, you need to install TCP/IP, then SNMP agent and monitor tools. Refer to "Installing and Configuring SNMP" earlier in this chapter for information on installing SNMP.

Exercise 15.1: Exploring Performance Monitor Counters

After you have installed SNMP, you may want to look at the Performance Monitor utility and notice the TCP/IP objects available for monitoring. To do this, use the following steps:

1. Choose Start, Programs, Administrative Tools and select Performance Monitor.

2. Click on the Edit menu and click Add to Chart.

3. Look at the list of available TCP/IP objects.

An example exercise monitoring SNMP using one of the TCP/IP related objects is as follows:

1. Follow the previous exercise.

2. Select the ICMP object from the list.

3. Click on Messages/sec in the counter box.

4. For the Scale, set to 1 and click Add.

5. Select another object IP.

6. From the Counter list, click Datagrams sent/sec.

7. Set the scale to 1 and then click Add.

8. Select Done.

9. Make certain you are using the chart view.

10. Change Vertical Maximum to 10 and click OK.

11. Go to a command prompt and ping another computer.

12. Go back to Performance Monitor and notice what happened.

continues

13. There should be two messages for ICMP and one IP datagram (two ICMP messages—one request, one reply).

14. Shut down Performance Monitor and go to the next exercise.

Exercise 15.2: Using SNMPUTIL to Access MIB Objects

This exercise is dependent on DHCP, WINS, TCP/IP, and SNMP being set up and you performing these exercises from that host machine. You may want to use the F3 key to bring up similar commands and check your number sequence carefully.

1. Copy the SNMPUtil.exe to winnt_root.

2. Go to a command prompt.

3. Type the following to find out the number of IP addresses leased by your DHCP server by querying the DHCP MIB:

```
snmputil getnext your_ip_address community_name
.1.3.6.1.4.1.311.1.3.2.1.1.1
```

4. Type the following to find out how many failed queries have been done by your WINS server by querying the WINS MIB:

```
snmputil getnext your_ip_address community_name
.1.3.6.1.4.1.311.1.2.1.18
```

5. Type the following to find out how many successful queries have be done by your WINS server by querying the WINS MIB:

```
snmputil getnext your_ip_address community_name
.1.3.6.1.4.1.311.1.2.1.17
```

6. Type the following to find out the version of Windows NT server that you are using. Notice this requires queries; you combine the results to get your full response. Notice here you are querying the LAN Manager MIB, as noted by the change in the hierarchical format.

```
snmputil getnext your_ip_address community_name
.1.3.6.1.4.1.77.1.1.1
snmputil getnext your_ip_address community_name
.1.3.6.1.4.1.77.1.1.2
```

Review Questions

The following questions test your knowledge of the information in this chapter:

1. When using an SNMP management system to query an agent, you can find out which of the following when querying the WINS MIB?

   A. The number of WINS servers available on your network

   B. The number of successful queries made on the WINS proxy server

   C. The number of unsuccessful queries processed by the WINS server

2. Through the use of SNMP, you can find out remote management information on which of the following items?

   A. Hub

   B. Router

   C. Bridge

   D. Windows NT Server

   E. Windows NT Workstation

3. When using SNMP in a TCP/IP network across a router with Unix hosts, Windows NT Servers, and LAN Manager stations, how would SNMP be able to resolve a host name?

   A. HOSTS file

   B. LMHOSTS file

   C. DNS

   D. DHCP

   E. WINS

4. The commands that you are able to implement on the management system side when making requests to the agents consist of which of the following?

A. get, set, go

B. walk, get, get-next

C. get, get-next, walk

D. set, get-next, get

5. The active component of the SNMP system that performs the trap is which of the following?

A. Management system

B. Agent

6. The part of SNMP that has specific objects related to the type of item that the management system is able to make queries against and is stored on the agent is called what?

A. MIIB

B. Management Information Base

C. MHB

D. Management Internet Information Base

7. Which of the following statements regarding the activity of SNMP and its actions are false?

A. Reports traps to multiple hosts

B. Responds to requests from multiple hosts

C. Sets up counters in Performance Monitor for SNMP

D. Uses host names and IP addresses to identify source and destination

8. A community is a group of hosts running SNMP, to which they all belong and respond to requests from a management system to agents. The default community name for all communities is _____.

A. punic

B. comm

C. community

D. public

9. When setting up security in SNMP, what is the most secure option you can select without limiting the potential for additional communities?

    A. Have a community name other than public, select Only Accept SNMP Packets from These Hosts, and set a trap to alert invalid inquiries.

    B. Have a community name of public, select Only Accept SNMP Packets from These Hosts, and set a trap to alert invalid inquiries.

    C. Have a community name of public, select Accept SNMP Packets from These Hosts.

10. When setting up an SNMP management system on a Windows NT host machine, what MIBs are supported by default under Windows NT 4.0?

    A. Internet MIB I, LAN Manager MIB II, WINS MIB, DHCP MIB

    B. Internet MIB II, LAN Manager MIB I, WINS MIB, DHCP MIB

    C. Internet MIB II, LAN Manager MIB II, WINS MIB, DHCP MIB

    D. Internet MIB II, LAN Manager MIB II, WINS MIB I, DHCP MIB

11. In order for SNMP agents and management systems to communicate with each other, they need to be set up with the same _____ name.

    A. public

    B. unity

    C. group

    D. community

12. If you are having problems with SNMP, where in Windows NT should you look?

    A. Event Viewer in Windows NT Administrative Tools

    B. Performance Monitor

    C. The SNMP log

13. Which agent services are enabled by default when setting up the Windows NT SNMP agent?

    A. Internet

    B. Physical

    C. End to End

    D. Application

14. Which SNMP operation is instituted by the agent instead of the management system?

    A. walk

    B. set

    C. trap

    D. get

15. The message sent by an SNMP agent to warn an SNMP management system of an error or specific event is known as a _____.

    A. net

    B. trap

    C. get

    D. warning event

16. What is the name of the utility found in the Windows NT Resource Kit that can be used to check if the SNMP Service

is configured correctly and working with the SNMP management system?

    A. SNMPCHECK

    B. SNMPSTAT

    C. SNMPUTIL

    D. SNMPMANG

17. What is the object identifier for a MIB II?

    A. iso.org.dod.internet.management.mib2

    B. iso.org.dod.internet.management.mibii

    C. 1.3.6.2.2

18. The MIB architecture can be extended to enable developers to create their own MIB libraries by using _____.

    A. Extension agents

    B. Extendor agents

    C. Additional dynamic link libraries

19. Why would you install the SNMP Service?

    A. You want to monitor TCP/IP with Performance Monitor.

    B. You want to remotely manage a proxy agent.

    C. You want to monitor a Windows NT-based system with a third-party application.

    D. You want to set up your computer as an SNMP agent.

20. Is it possible to have an SNMP Management utility manage multiple community names, and if so, why would you want to?

    A. Yes, for security reasons.

    B. No, it is not possible.

    C. Yes, but only for organizational purposes.

Review Answers

1. C

2. A, B, C, D

3. A, B, C, E

4. D

5. B

6. B

7. C

8. D

9. A

10. C

11. D

12. A

13. A, C, D

14. C

15. B

16. C

17. B

18. A

19. A, C, D

20. A

Answers to the Test Yourself Questions at the Beginning of the Chapter

1. SNMP provides remote management of routers, hubs, and Windows NT hosts. See "The Usefulness of SNMP."

2. SNMP uses the same host name resolution as TCP/IP: HOSTS file, DNS, WINS, broadcast, and LMHOSTS file. See "Microsoft SNMP Service."

3. SNMP fits at the application level and integrates using a socket similar to Windows sockets. See "SNMP Architecture."

4. There are none. The only type of security is to limit specific agents to the particular management systems to which they will respond and the read-write permissions on community strings.

Chapter 16

Troubleshooting Microsoft TCP/IP

This chapter helps you prepare for the exam by covering the following objectives:

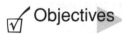 Objectives

- ▶ Diagnose and resolve IP addressing problems

- ▶ Use Microsoft TCP/IP utilities to diagnose IP configuration problems

- ▶ Identify which Microsoft TCP/IP utility to use to diagnose IP configuration problems

- ▶ Diagnose and resolve name resolution problems

Test Yourself! Before reading this chapter, test yourself to determine how much study time you will need to devote to this section.

1. What addresses can you Ping to test a TCP/IP configuration?

2. What is one address you can Ping to prove complete TCP/IP connectivity?

3. How can you determine whether a DHCP client got an IP address? If the client didn't get an address, how can you force the client to again try to get an address?

4. You can Ping an NT server's IP address but you cannot connect to a share on the server. Where are possible sources of this problem?

5. What problems can occur if a client does not have the proper address configured for the default gateway?

6. What is the effect on TCP/IP if the wrong IRQ is specified for the network card? Where do you see an indication of this problem?

7. How can you test the resolution of host names?

Answers are located at the end of the chapter.

Introduction

Your ability to successfully troubleshoot connectivity problems with TCP/IP depends upon your mastery of all the concepts of TCP/IP. For example, you must know how TCP/IP addresses work, how host names are resolved, and how routers are used to direct TCP/IP traffic. Without understanding how TCP/IP traffic makes its way from one host to another, you cannot know which tools to use to diagnose the problem and how to solve the problem itself. All the skills you mastered in prior chapters come into play as you troubleshoot TCP/IP problems.

As a client makes a TCP/IP connection, the packet prepared by TCP/IP must work its way through the TCP/IP architecture. Figure 16.1 shows the TCP/IP architecture. An incoming packet must first connect to the adapter card, as specified by the MAC address of the network card. This is the Network Interface layer. Then the packet works its way to the Internet layer, as specified by the TCP/IP address. The Transport layer is next, using the UDP or TCP protocols. The last layer is the Application layer, where the user actually sees a connection via a drive connection, printer connection, FTP session (File Transfer Protocol, a TCP/IP utility to copy files from an FTP server), Web session, or a Telnet session.

Figure 16.1

The TCP/IP architecture.

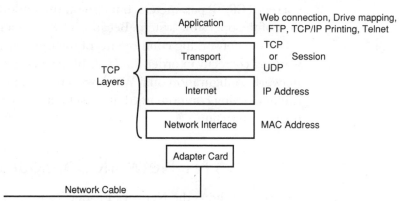

Although TCP/IP works through four layers, troubleshooting TCP/IP can be divided into just two main areas: TCP/IP address configuration and host name resolution. When configuring TCP/IP, you specify the addresses of the various components of TCP/IP that are used to route IP traffic from one host to another. With the correct configuration, TCP/IP can move a packet from one location to another through a clearly defined path. If there are configuration errors, the road for TCP/IP communications is a jumbled path, with no clear way for packets to reach other hosts. In fact, with an improper configuration, you could be telling TCP/IP to make a U-turn to route a packet while a traffic sign clearly states, "No U-turns Allowed."

If TCP/IP is configured correctly, you can contact another host by using the remote host's IP address. However, to make a connection you typically refer to another computer by its host name. If you cannot resolve host names to IP addresses, you can't establish a session with the other host, such as connecting a network drive, connecting to a Web server, or logging on to a domain. Even though TCP/IP may be configured correctly, allowing a smooth path from one host to another, if you can't resolve host names you can't accomplish the day-to-day networking tasks that almost always depend on using host names.

TCP/IP Configuration

The correct configuration of TCP/IP depends not only on entering correct TCP/IP parameters, but also on the underlying configuration of the operating system. Because TCP/IP is a networking protocol, the networking components of the operating system must be working correctly in order for TCP/IP to work. Let's examine the network configuration on a Windows NT machine to determine the underlying components that must be in place for TCP/IP to properly function.

Windows NT Network Configuration

Figure 16.2 shows the Network Properties for a Windows NT computer installed as a Windows NT Workstation or a Windows NT Server. You can access this box through Control Panel, Network. A number of things can be configured in the Network Properties dialog box that affect the capability of Windows NT to communicate over the network, and thus use TCP/IP. As Figure 16.2 shows, one of properties you can configure through this dialog box is the NetBIOS name of the computer. This name is used for any NetBIOS-related communication. When you connect to other Microsoft computers, you use NetBIOS names, which must be resolved to a TCP/IP address if you are using TCP/IP.

Figure 16.2

The Identification tab of Network Properties.

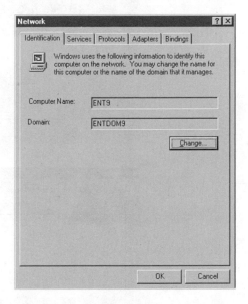

The Services tab of the dialog box shows the networking services are installed on the computer. For TCP/IP connections, you need at the very least the Workstation Service (client software). Additional services are installed by default, however, such as the Server service and the Computer Browser service. Figure 16.3 shows the Services tab of the Network Properties dialog box, with the default services that are part of a typical Windows NT installation.

The Protocols tab of the dialog box (see fig. 16.4) shows the networking protocols that are installed and enables you to configure them. TCP/IP configuration is discussed in the section "TCP/IP Configuration Parameters." If you need to add TCP/IP or simply want to see whether it is installed, however, this is the place to look.

Figure 16.3

The Services tab of Network Properties.

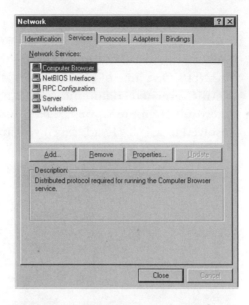

Figure 16.4

The Protocols tab of Network Properties.

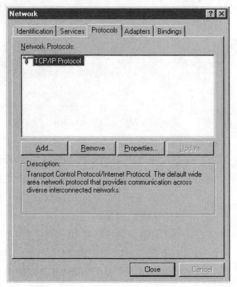

Adapter card drivers are installed and configured in the Adapters tab (see fig. 16.5). Without a properly configured adapter card driver, you cannot communicate on the network, regardless of the protocol you are using. Figure 16.5 shows the configuration for an

NE2000 adapter card. Both the IRQ and I/O Address must be correct. For other adapter cards, you may have other types of parameters, such as a slot number or port type (twisted pair or coax connection).

Figure 16.5

The Adapters tab of Network | Properties.

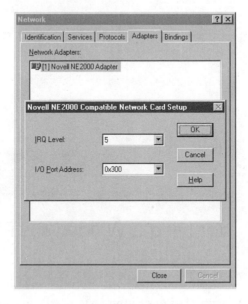

The Bindings tab (see fig. 16.6) specifies how the installed network protocols are used for the various networking services. The bindings affect performance by the order they are listed. The top binding is the one NT tries to use, and NT waits for a timeout period before using another protocol if it can't establish a session with the highest-priority protocol. In addition to changing the priority of the bindings, you can also disable the bindings of a protocol. You can turn off the TCP/IP protocol for the Workstation Service (or any other service, for that matter). With TCP/IP disabled for the Workstation Service (as shown in fig. 16.6), this computer cannot function as a Microsoft client using TCP/IP. The computer cannot, for example, map a drive to a server using TCP/IP. (Other client software, such as FTP or a Web browser, can still use TCP/IP, however.) If the binding is active for the Server service, the computer can respond to incoming requests for drive mappings from other TCP/IP clients.

Figure 16.6

The Bindings tab of Network Properties.

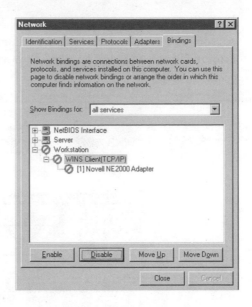

Verifying a Windows NT Network Configuration

For an exercise covering this information, see end of chapter.

You should check the Network Properties on the NT computer to verify that operating system settings are not hindering TCP/IP from connecting. You can also check the System Log in NT Event Viewer for possible error messages coming from network configuration errors. Problems with the network card configuration are usually announced in two types of messages. First, when NT boots, you should see a message saying A Dependency Service Failed to Start. This means the adapter card, on which other services depend, failed. Because the adapter card failed, these other services couldn't start. Second, you should see an error in the System Log from the adapter card. There should be other errors following it as other services that depend on the adapter card fail to start. In some cases, however, you won't see any error messages; TCP/IP simply won't connect, even with a Ping command. You should not depend on an error message to remind you to verify that the adapter card settings are correct.

In checking the Network properties, a number of things must be in place for TCP/IP to work properly. The computer must have a unique NetBIOS name. If a computer uses a duplicate name, the networking services do not start. The error generated from the duplicate name is the first chronological error in the list, at the bottom of the screen. The subsequent errors, moving from bottom to top, are a result of the duplicate name. Without a unique name, the other networking services don't start. And without networking services, TCP/IP does not work because this computer has no way to communicate on the network.

You must have client software (the Workstation service) installed on the computer to initiate TCP/IP communications. To respond to incoming requests you must have the Server service installed. You can verify their installation on the Services tab of the Network Properties dialog box. You should also check to make sure the services are started. In Control Panel, Services you can see whether services are started and how they are configured to start. The Startup parameters shown in figure 16.7 are configured to have the Workstation service start automatically when NT boots.

Figure 16.7

The Service dialog box with the Workstation service configured for automatic startup.

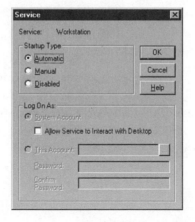

You can also check the Network properties to make sure TCP/IP is installed. Because you configure TCP/IP through the Protocols tab, you can quickly see whether TCP/IP is installed because it is listed on the Protocols tab.

You should check the configuration of the network adapter driver. If the driver is not configured properly, without the correct driver for the adapter card or without the proper settings that match the configuration of the card, you cannot communicate on the network. Figure 16.8 shows the System Log with an error resulting from the wrong adapter card parameters. The first chronological error comes from the adapter card problems. Any subsequent errors are generated from the network card not starting. Remember that by default new entries in the log are added at the top of the display.

Figure 16.8

Error messages from incorrect adapter card settings.

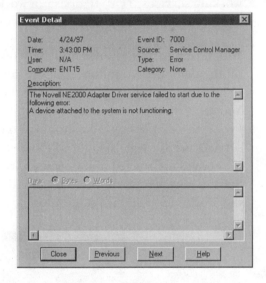

Finally, the bindings must be configured properly. All the protocols installed on the computer should be bound to the various networking services. You can check the bindings on the Bindings tab of Network Properties. Make sure TCP/IP is not disabled on any of the services.

 Tip

You can also move TCP/IP up in the binding order if you have multiple protocols installed. The binding order does not affect the computer's capability to connect using TCP/IP, but it does make TCP/IP connections faster than if TCP/IP is lower in the binding order.

TCP/IP Configuration Parameters

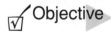 **Objective**

Three main parameters specify how TCP/IP is configured: the IP address, the subnet mask, and the default gateway, which is the address of the router. These parameters are configured through the Protocols tab of the Network Properties dialog box. Figure 16.9 shows TCP/IP manually configured on a Windows NT client. Although it is possible to receive an IP address from a DHCP server, for the moment this discussion focuses on parameters that are manually configured. (DHCP is discussed in the section **"DHCP Configuration Problems."**)

Figure 16.9

TCP/IP Properties with a manual TCP/IP address.

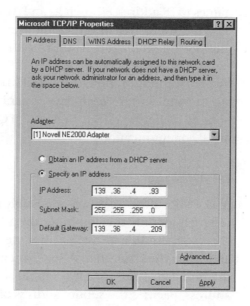

These TCP/IP parameters must be configured correctly or you cannot connect with TCP/IP. An incorrect configuration can result from typos; if you type the wrong IP address, subnet mask, or default gateway you may not connect properly or even be able to connect at all. To illustrate, if you dial the wrong number when making a telephone call, you can't reach the party you're calling. If you read the wrong phone number out of the phone book, you won't ever make a correct call even if you dial the number you think is correct time and time again.

Whether the TCP/IP configuration parameters are wrong due to a typo or due to a mistaken number, the incorrect parameters affect communications. Different types of problems occur when each of these parameters has a configuration error.

IP Address Configuration Problems

An incorrect TCP/IP address might not even cause any problems. If you configure an IP address that is on the correct subnet, but uses the wrong host ID, and is not a duplicate, the client may be able to communicate just fine. If, however, the correct IP address has been entered in a static file or database that resolves host names to IP addresses, such as an LMHOSTS file or a DNS database file, there are some communication problems. Typically, therefore, an incorrect IP address does cause some problems.

Incorrect configuration of the TCP/IP parameters can cause different symptoms for each type of parameter. The following sections examine the effects that each TCP/IP parameter can have on IP communications.

IP Address

A TCP/IP address has two or possibly three components that uniquely identify the computer the address is assigned to. At the very least, the IP address specifies the network address and host address of the computer. Also, if you are subnetting (using part of the host address to specify a subnet address), the third part of the address specifies the subnet address of the host.

Figure 16.10 shows the effect of an incorrect network address. In this example, the TCP/IP address assigned to a client is typed incorrectly. The address assigned to the client is 143.168.3.9, whereas the correct address was supposed to be 133.168.3.9. The network ID for the incorrect address is 143.168.x.x, whereas the network ID for the correct address is 133.168.x.x. With this incorrect address (143.168.3.9), the client is not able to communicate with any other TCP/IP hosts. Because the network address is incorrect, any packets this client sends will be routed to the wrong location.

If the incorrect host (143.168.3.9) sends a message to a local client (133.168.3.20), the TCP/IP configuration of the sending host indicates this is a remote address because it doesn't match the network address of the host initiating the communication. The packet won't ever reach the local client, because the address 133.168.3.20 is interpreted as a remote address.

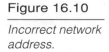

Figure 16.10

*Incorrect network
address.*

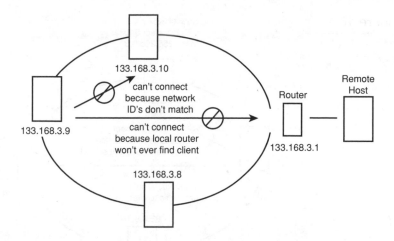

If a local client (133.168.3.6) sends a message to the incorrect
host (143.168.3.9), the message never reaches its intended destination. The message is either routed (if the local client sends the
message to the IP address as written) or it stays on the local subnet
(if the local client sends it to what should have been the address,
133.168.3.9). If the message is routed, the incorrect client does
not receive the message because it is on the same segment of the
network as the local client. If the message is not routed, the message still does not reach the incorrect client because the IP address for the destination host (133.168.3.9) does not match the
address as configured on the incorrect client (143.168.3.9).

Figure 16.11 gives another example of an incorrect IP address. In
this case, a class A address is used, 33.x.x.x. The subnet mask
(255.255.0.0) indicates the second octet is also being used to create subnets. In this case, even though the client has the same network address as the other clients on the same subnet, the client
has a different subnet number because the address was typed incorrectly. This time the incorrect address specifies the wrong subnet ID. The client 33.5.8.4 is on subnet 5 while the other clients
on the subnet have the address 33.4.x.x. In this case, if the client
33.5.8.4. tries to contact other clients on the same subnet, the
message is routed because the subnet id doesn't match the subnet
number of the source host. If the client 33.5.8.4 tries to send a
message to a remote host, the message is routed, but the message
isn't returned to the client because the router doesn't handle
subnet 5, only subnet 4.

Figure 16.11

Incorrect subnet address.

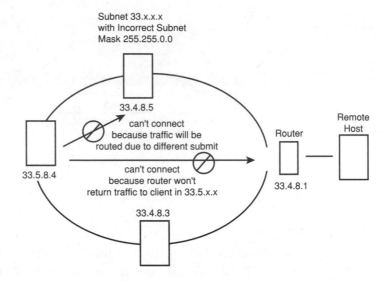

If a local client tries to send a message to 33.5.8.4, the message doesn't reach the client. If the local client uses the address as configured, the message is routed, which isn't the correct solution because the destination host is local. If the local client sends the message to what should have been the IP address, 33.5.8.4 doesn't receive the message because the IP address isn't configured correctly.

The last component of an IP address that can cause communication problems is the host address. An incorrect host address may not always cause a problem, however. In figure 16.12, a local client has the wrong IP address, but only the host address portion of the address is wrong. The network address and subnet match the rest of the clients on the subnet. In this case, if a client sends a message to the client with the incorrect address, the message still reaches the client. However, if someone tries to contact the client with what should have been the address, he doesn't contact the client. In fact, he could contact another host that ended up with the address that was supposed to be given to the original host. If the original host ends up with the same IP address as another host through the configuration error, the first client to boot works, but the second client to boot may note the address conflict and not load the TCP/IP stack at all. In this case, the second client to boot isn't able to make any TCP/IP communications.

Figure 16.12

Incorrect host address.

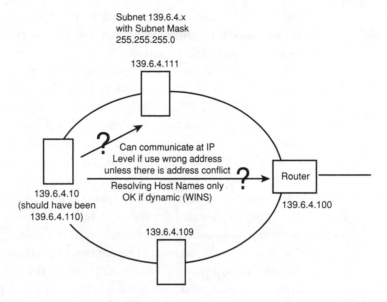

Subnet 139.6.4.x
with Subnet Mask
255.255.255.0

139.6.4.111

Can communicate at IP
Level if use wrong address
unless there is address conflict

Resolving Host Names only
OK if dynamic (WINS)

Router

139.6.4.10
(should have been
139.6.4.110)

139.6.4.100

139.6.4.109

Another problem comes in when the correct address was registered in static files, such as an LMHOSTS file or a DNS database. In this case, no one can communicate with this client by name because the name resolution for this host always returns the correct address, which can't be used to contact the host because the address has been typed incorrectly. Basically, the problems you encounter with an incorrect host address are intermittent. However, if the host was configured to be a WINS client, the host name is registered along with the incorrect address. Another WINS client trying to connect with this computer receives an accurate mapping for the host name.

Subnet Mask

The subnet mask indicates which portion of the IP address specifies the network address and which portion of the address specifies the host address. Also, the subnet mask can be used to take part of what would have been the host address and use it to further divide the network into subnets. If the subnet mask is not configured correctly, your clients may not be able to communicate at all, or you may see partial communication problems.

Figure 16.13 shows a subnet on a TCP/IP network. The network uses a Class B network address of 138.13.x.x. However, the third octet is used in this case for subnetting, so all the clients in the figure should be on subnet 4, as indicated by the common addresses 138.13.4.x. Unfortunately, the subnet mask entered for one client is 255.255.0.0. When this client tries to communicate with other hosts on the same subnet, it should be able to contact them because the subnet mask indicates they are on the same subnet, which is correct. However, if the client tries to contact a host on another subnet, such as 138.13.3.x, the client fails. In this case, the subnet mask still interprets the destination host to be on the same subnet and the message is never routed. Because the destination host is on another subnet, the message never reaches the intended destination. The subnet mask is used to determine routing for outgoing communications, so the client with the incorrect subnet mask can receive incoming messages. However, when the client tries to return communications, the message isn't routed if the source host is on the same network but on a different subnet. So in actuality, the client really can establish communications with only one side of the conversation. Contact with hosts outside the local network still works because those contacts are routed.

Figure 16.13

Incorrect subnet mask—missing third octet.

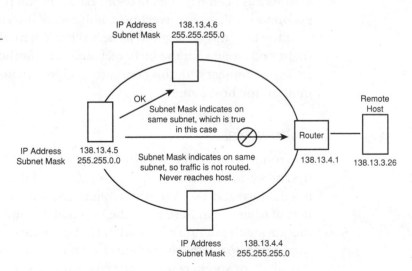

Figure 16.14 shows a subnet mask that masks too many bits. In this case, the subnet mask is 255.255.255.0. However, the network designers had intended the subnet mask to be 255.255.240.0, with four bits of the third octet used for the subnet and four bits as part of the host address. If the incorrect client tries to send a message to a local host and the third octet is the same, the message is not routed and thus reaches the local client. However, if the local client has an address that differs in the last four bits of the third octet, the message is routed and never reaches its destination. If the incorrect client tries to send a message to another client on another subnet, the message is routed because the third octet is different.

Figure 16.14

Incorrect subnet mask—incorrect third octet.

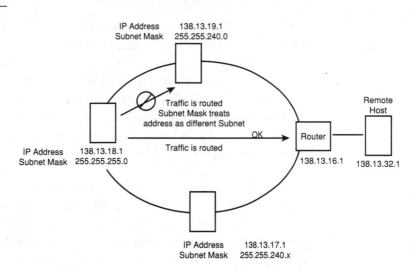

Subnet 138.13.16-31.x

IP Address   138.13.19.1
Subnet Mask   255.255.240.0

Traffic is routed
Subnet Mask treats
address as different Subnet

OK

Traffic is routed

Remote Host

Router

IP Address   138.13.18.1
Subnet Mask   255.255.255.0

138.13.16.1   138.13.32.1

IP Address   138.13.17.1
Subnet Mask   255.255.240.x

Note Problems with the subnet mask also lead to intermittent connections. Sometimes the connection works, sometimes it doesn't. The problems show up when the IP address of the destination host causes a packet to be routed when it shouldn't or to remain local when the packet should be routed.

Default Gateway

The default gateway address is the address of the router, the gateway to the world beyond the local subnet. If the default gateway address is wrong, the client with the wrong default gateway address can contact local hosts but is not able to communicate at all beyond the local subnet. It is possible for the incorrect client to receive a message, because the default gateway is used only to send packets to other hosts. However, as soon as the incorrect client attempts to respond to the incoming message, the default gateway address doesn't work and the message doesn't reach the host that sent the original message.

DHCP Client Configuration Problems

All the TCP/IP parameters mentioned previously can cause communication problems if they are not configured correctly. Using a DHCP server can greatly reduce these configuration problems. If the DHCP scope is set up properly, without any typos or other configuration errors, DHCP clients shouldn't have any configuration problems. It is impossible to completely eliminate human error, but using DHCP should reduce the points of potential errors to just the DHCP servers rather than every client on the network.

Even when there are no configuration problems with DHCP addresses, DHCP clients can get a duplicate IP address from a DHCP server. If you have multiple DHCP servers in your environment, you should have scopes on each DHCP server for different subnets. Usually you have scopes with a larger number of addresses for the local subnet where the DHCP server is located and smaller scopes for other subnets. Creating multiple scopes on one server provides backup for giving clients IP addresses. If the server on the local scope is busy or down, the client can still receive an address from a remote DHCP server. When the router forwards this DCHP request to another subnet, it includes the address of the subnet it came from so that the remote DHCP server knows from which scope of addresses to lease an address to the remote client. Using this type of redundancy, however, can cause problems if you don't configure the scopes on all the DHCP servers correctly.

The most important part of the configuration is to make sure you don't have duplicate addresses in the different scopes. On one server, for example, you could have a scope in the range 131.107.2.100 to 131.107.2.170. On the remote DHCP server, you could have a scope of 131.107.2.171 to 131.107.2.200. By setting up the scopes without overlap, you should not have any problems with clients receiving duplicate IP addresses. DHCP servers do not communicate with each other, so one server does not know anything about the addresses the other server has leased. Therefore, you must ensure the servers never give out duplicate information by making sure the scopes for one subnet on all the different DHCP servers have unique IP addresses.

Another common problem with having multiple scopes on one server is entering the configuration parameters correctly. For example, if you enter the default gateway as 131.107.3.1 (instead of 131.107.2.1) for the scope 131.107.2.100 to 131.107.2.170, the clients receiving these addresses will not be able to communicate beyond the local subnet, because they have the wrong router address. With one scope on a DCHP server, you are usually quite sure of what all the configuration parameters should be. With multiple scopes on one server, however, it is easy to get confused about which scope you are editing and what the parameters should be for that scope. To avoid this type of problem, check each scope's parameters very carefully to make sure the parameters match the address of the scope, not the subnet where the DHCP server is located.

Also, if the client doesn't receive an address because the server is down or doesn't respond in a timely manner, the client is not able to contact anyone. Without an IP address, the IP stack does not initialize and the client can't communicate at all with TCP/IP.

Tools Used to Troubleshoot TCP/IP Configuration Problems

☑ Objective ▶ A number of tools come with TCP/IP when the protocol is installed on a Windows NT computer. After you have resolved any problems caused by the Windows NT network configuration, you can then focus on using the TCP/IP tools to solve IP problems.

Some tools can be used to verify the configuration parameters. Other tools can be used to test the connectivity capabilities of TCP/IP as configured.

Using IPCONFIG to Verify a TCP/IP Configuration

If you configure the TCP/IP address and other TCP/IP parameters manually, you can always verify the configuration through the Network Properties dialog box. However, if the client receives an address from a DHCP server, the only information available in the Network Properties dialog box is that the client is receiving its address from DHCP. Because the configuration information for a DHCP client is received dynamically, you must use a utility that can read the current configuration to verify the settings.

The command-line utility IPCONFIG can be used to see how the local host is configured—whether the parameters come from manual configuration or from a DHCP server. Figure 16.15 shows the results of using IPCONFIG in a command prompt. The basic configuration parameters are displayed: the IP address, the subnet mask, and the default gateway. You can see additional information by using IPCONFIG with the /all switch. Figure 16.16 shows the results of IPCONFIG /all executed in a command prompt. In this case, not only are the standard parameters shown, but additional information, such as the WINS server address and the DNS server address, is also displayed. In the example shown in the figure the client received its IP address from a DHCP server, so additional information like the address of the DHCP server and the lease life of the IP address is also shown.

Note

A Windows version of IPCONFIG, called WNTIPCFG.EXE, is included with the Windows NT Resource Kit. WNTIPCFG reports the same information as the IPCONFIG command-utility. WNTIPCFG can also be used to release and renew DCHP addresses, as described in the following section.

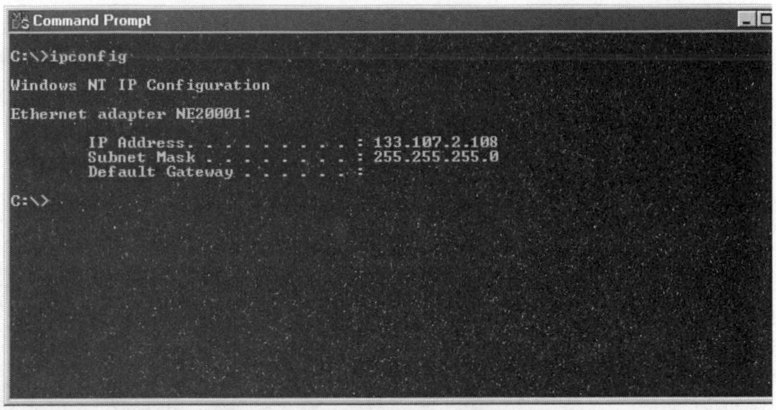

Figure 16.15

*The results of the
IPCONFIG com-
mand.*

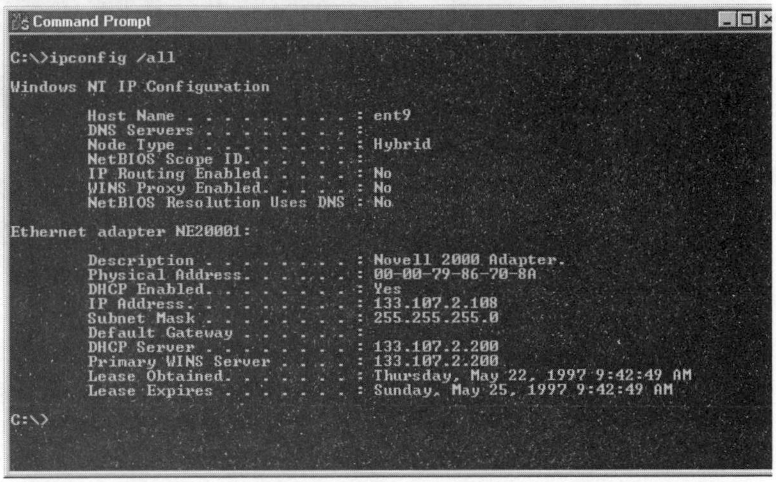

```
Command Prompt                                                    _ □
C:\>ipconfig
Windows NT IP Configuration
Ethernet adapter NE20001:

        IP Address. . . . . . . . . : 133.107.2.108
        Subnet Mask . . . . . . . . : 255.255.255.0
        Default Gateway . . . . . . :

C:\>
```

Figure 16.16

*The results of the
IPCONFIG /all
command.*

```
Command Prompt                                                _ □ X
C:\>ipconfig /all
Windows NT IP Configuration
        Host Name . . . . . . . . . : ent9
        DNS Servers . . . . . . . . :
        Node Type . . . . . . . . . : Hybrid
        NetBIOS Scope ID. . . . . . :
        IP Routing Enabled. . . . . : No
        WINS Proxy Enabled. . . . . : No
        NetBIOS Resolution Uses DNS : No
Ethernet adapter NE20001:

        Description . . . . . . . . : Novell 2000 Adapter.
        Physical Address. . . . . . : 00-00-79-86-70-8A
        DHCP Enabled. . . . . . . . : Yes
        IP Address. . . . . . . . . : 133.107.2.108
        Subnet Mask . . . . . . . . : 255.255.255.0
        Default Gateway . . . . . . :
        DHCP Server . . . . . . . . : 133.107.2.200
        Primary WINS Server . . . . : 133.107.2.200
        Lease Obtained. . . . . . . : Thursday, May 22, 1997 9:42:49 AM
        Lease Expires . . . . . . . : Sunday, May 25, 1997 9:42:49 AM

C:\>
```

Using IPCONFIG to Resolve DHCP Address Problems

When a DHCP client gets an IP that is not configured correctly or
if the client doesn't get an IP address at all, IPCONFIG can be
used to resolve these problems. If the client gets incorrect IP parameters, that should be apparent from the results of IPCONFIG
/all. You should be able to see that some of the parameters don't
match the IP address or that some parameters are completely
blank. For example, you could have the wrong default gateway, or
the client might not be configured to be a WINS client.

When a DHCP client fails to receive an address, the results of IPCONFIG /all are different. In this case, the client has an IP address of 0.0.0.0—an invalid address—and the DHCP server is 255.255.255.255—a broadcast address. Figure 16.17 shows the results of IPCONFIG /all when the client fails to obtain an address from a DHCP server.

Figure 16.17

DHCP client never received an IP address as indicated by results of IPCONFIG /all.

```
Command Prompt                                            _ □ ×

C:\>ipconfig /all

Windows NT IP Configuration

        Host Name . . . . . . . . . : ent9
        DNS Servers . . . . . . . . :
        Node Type . . . . . . . . . : Hybrid
        NetBIOS Scope ID. . . . . . :
        IP Routing Enabled. . . . . : No
        WINS Proxy Enabled. . . . . : No
        NetBIOS Resolution Uses DNS : No

Ethernet adapter NE20001:

        Description . . . . . . . . : Novell 2000 Adapter.
        Physical Address. . . . . . : 00-00-79-86-70-8A
        DHCP Enabled. . . . . . . . : Yes
        IP Address. . . . . . . . . : 0.0.0.0
        Subnet Mask . . . . . . . . : 0.0.0.0
        Default Gateway . . . . . . :
        DHCP Server . . . . . . . . : 255.255.255.255
        Primary WINS Server . . . . : 133.107.2.200

C:\>
```

To fix this problem, you can release the incorrect address with IPCONFIG /release and then try to obtain a new IP address with IPCONFIG /renew. The IPCONFIG /renew command sends out a new request for a DHCP address. If a DHCP server is available, the server responds with the lease of an IP address. Figure 16.18 shows the results of using IPCONFIG /release to release an address and using IPCONFIG /renew to acquire a new address.

 Note

In many cases, the DHCP client will acquire the same address after releasing and renewing. That the client receives the same address indicates the same DHCP server responded to the renewal request and gave out the address that had just been released back into the pool of available addresses. If you need to renew an address because the parameters of the scope are incorrect, you must fix the parameters before releasing and renewing the address. Otherwise, the client could receive the same address again with the same incorrect parameters.

Tip

Occasionally, a DHCP client will not acquire an address regardless of how many times you release and renew the address. One way to try to fix the problem is to manually assign the client a static IP address. Once the client is configured with this address, which you can verify by using IPCONFIG, switch back to DHCP.

Figure 16.18

Using IPCONFIG /release to release an address and IPCONFIG / renew to get a new address.

```
Command Prompt                                                        _ □ X

C:\>ipconfig /release

Windows NT IP Configuration

IP address 133.107.2.108 successfully released for adapter "NE20001"

C:\>ipconfig /renew

Windows NT IP Configuration

Ethernet adapter NE20001:

        IP Address. . . . . . . . . : 133.107.2.108
        Subnet Mask . . . . . . . . : 255.255.255.0
        Default Gateway . . . . . . :

C:\>
```

Using Ping to Test an IP Configuration

For an exercise covering this information, see end of chapter.

Ping is a command-line tool included with every Microsoft TCP/IP client (any DOS or Windows client with the TCP/IP protocol installed). You can use Ping to send a test packet to the specified address and then, if things are working properly, the packet is returned. Figure 16.19 shows the results of a successful Ping command. Note that four successful responses are returned. Unsuccessful Pings can result in different messages, depending on the type of problem Ping encounters while trying to send and receive the test packet.

Although Ping is a simple tool to use (from the command prompt simply type Ping with the IP address or host name you want to Ping), choosing what to Ping is the key to using it for successful troubleshooting. The remainder of this section covers which IP addresses or hosts you should Ping to troubleshoot TCP/IP connectivity problems.

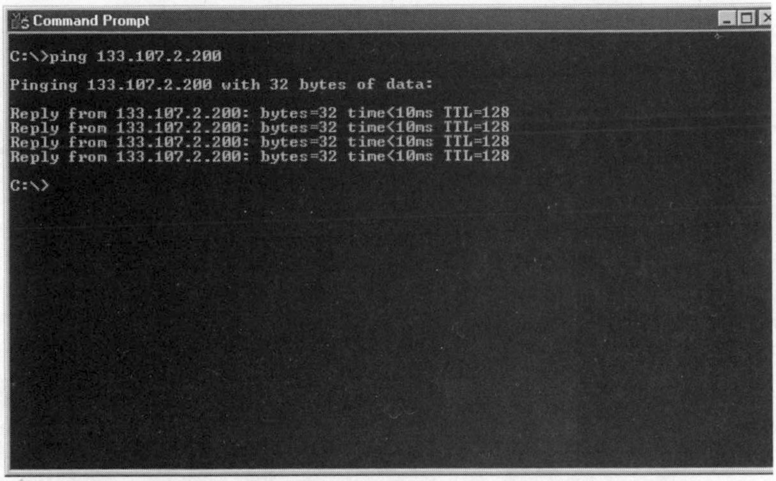

Figure 16.19

The results of a successful Ping command.

Troubleshooting IP Protocol Installation by Pinging the Loopback Address

The first step in troubleshooting many problems is to verify that TCP/IP installed correctly on the client. You can look at the configuration through the Network Properties dialog box or with IPCONFIG, but to actually test the working status of the protocol stack you should try to Ping the loopback address. The loopback address is 127.0.0.1. When you Ping this address, a packet is not sent on the network. Ping simply sends a packet down through the layers of the IP architecture and then up the layers again. If TCP/IP is installed correctly, you should receive an immediate successful response as shown in figure 16.20. If IP is not installed correctly, the response fails (see fig. 16.21).

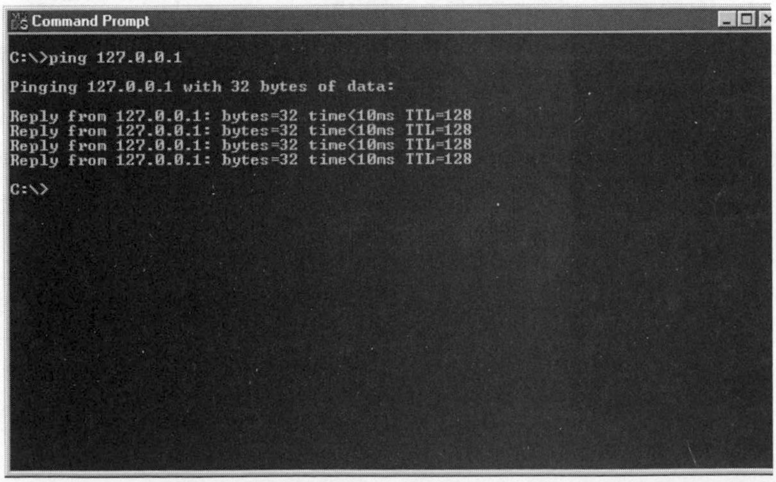

Figure 16.20

A successful loopback Ping.

Figure 16.21

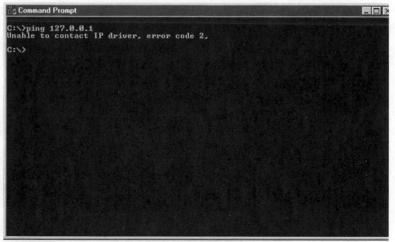

*A failed loopback
Ping.*

To correct problems of this type, you should verify the NT network configuration and the protocol installation. You can check the following items:

▶ Make sure TCP/IP is listed on the installed protocols.

▶ Make sure the network adapter card is configured correctly.

▶ Make sure TCP/IP shows up in the bindings for the adapter card and that the bindings are not disabled for TCP/IP.

▶ Check the system log for any errors indicating that the network services didn't start.

If you try the preceding steps, including rebooting the system, and have no success, you may have to remove TCP/IP and install it again. Sometimes NT gets hung up somewhere and it thinks things are really installed when they are not. Removing the protocol and then installing it again can often resolve this half-way state.

Troubleshooting Client Address Configuration by Pinging Local Address

Another step in verifying the TCP/IP configuration, after you have verified that TCP/IP is installed correctly, is to Ping the address of the local host. Simply Ping the IP address that you think is configured for the client. You should receive an immediate successful reply if the client address is configured as specified in the Ping command. You can also Ping the name of the local host, but problems with name resolution are discussed later in the section "Name Resolution Problems." For the moment, you are concerned with raw TCP/IP connectivity—the capability to communicate with another IP host by using its IP address. Figure 16.22 shows a successful local Ping; figure 16.23 shows a failed Ping.

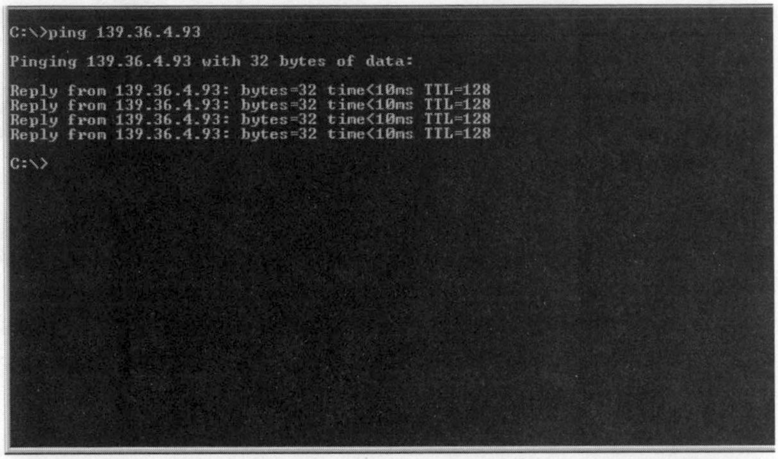

Figure 16.22

Successful Ping of the local address.

```
C:\>ping 139.36.4.93

Pinging 139.36.4.93 with 32 bytes of data:

Reply from 139.36.4.93: bytes=32 time<10ms TTL=128
Reply from 139.36.4.93: bytes=32 time<10ms TTL=128
Reply from 139.36.4.93: bytes=32 time<10ms TTL=128
Reply from 139.36.4.93: bytes=32 time<10ms TTL=128

C:\>
```

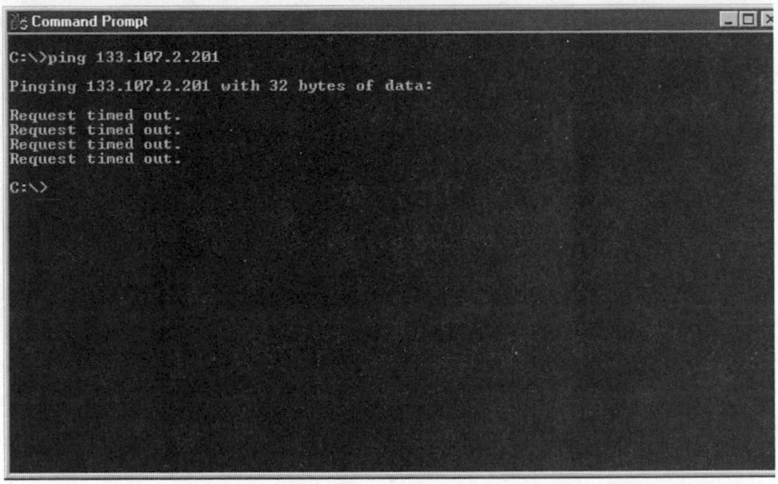

Figure 16.23

Failed Ping of the local address.

```
Command Prompt                                                 _ □ X
C:\>ping 133.107.2.201

Pinging 133.107.2.201 with 32 bytes of data:

Request timed out.
Request timed out.
Request timed out.
Request timed out.

C:\>
```

Correcting a failure at this level concerns checking the way the client address was configured. Was the address typed in correctly? Did the client receive the IP address from the DHCP server that you expected? Also, does the client have a connection on the network? Pinging the local host address does not cause a packet to be sent on the network, so if you have lost network connectivity, this Ping won't indicate a network failure.

Troubleshooting Router Problems by Pinging the Default Gateway

If you can communicate with hosts on the same subnet but cannot establish communications with hosts beyond the subnet, the problem may be with the router or the way its address is configured. To communicate beyond the subnet, a router must be enabled with an address that matches the subnet address for the clients on the local subnet. The router also has other ports configured with different addresses so it can send packets out to the network at large. Pinging the default gateway address tests the address you have configured for the router and also tests the router itself. Figure 16.24 shows a successful Ping to the default gateway. Figure 16.25 shows a failed Ping.

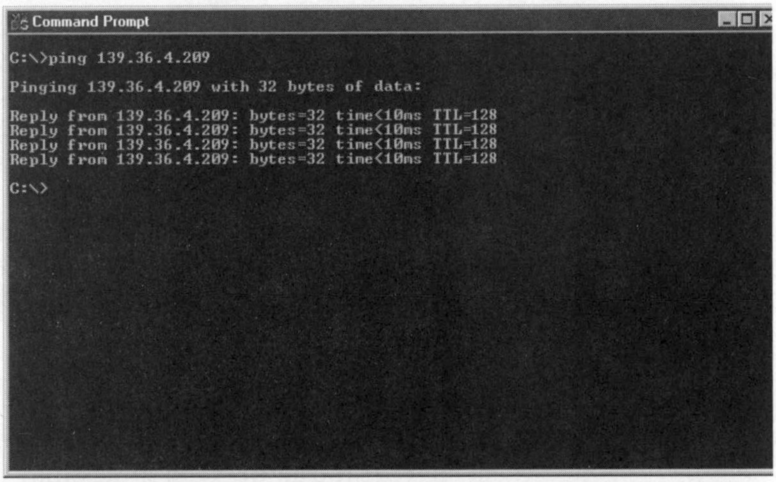

Figure 16.24

Successful Ping of the default gateway.

```
Command Prompt                                                      _□×

C:\>ping 139.36.4.209

Pinging 139.36.4.209 with 32 bytes of data:

Reply from 139.36.4.209: bytes=32 time<10ms TTL=128
Reply from 139.36.4.209: bytes=32 time<10ms TTL=128
Reply from 139.36.4.209: bytes=32 time<10ms TTL=128
Reply from 139.36.4.209: bytes=32 time<10ms TTL=128

C:\>
```

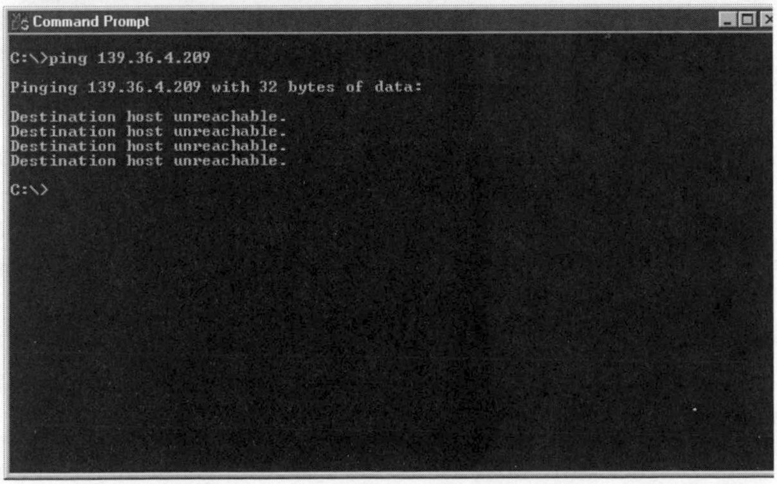

Figure 16.25

Failed Ping of the default gateway.

```
Command Prompt                                                      _□×

C:\>ping 139.36.4.209

Pinging 139.36.4.209 with 32 bytes of data:

Destination host unreachable.
Destination host unreachable.
Destination host unreachable.
Destination host unreachable.

C:\>
```

If the default gateway Ping fails, there are several possible sources for the error:

▶ **The router has failed or is down.** In this case, you cannot make connections outside the subnet until the router is brought up again. However, you should be able to communicate with hosts on the same subnet.

▶ **The client has lost a physical connection with the router or with the network.** You can test a network connection at a hardware level and also through the software by trying to establish a session with a server with another protocol, such as NetBEUI, for example. If you only have TCP/IP on your network, you can temporarily install NetBEUI on the client and on another computer on the same subnet. Test connectivity by connecting to a file share on the other computer. Remember, the computer should be on the same subnet because NetBEUI packets don't usually route.

▶ **The IP address on the router may be configured incorrectly.** The router address must match the client's default gateway address so that packets can move outside the subnet.

▶ **The client has the wrong router address.** Of course, if you Ping the correct router address and it works, you also want to make sure the default gateway address configured on the client matches the address you successfully Pinged.

▶ **The wrong subnet mask is configured.** If the subnet mask is wrong, packets destined for a remote subnet may not be routed.

You should also Ping each of the IP addresses used by the different ports on your router. It's possible that the local interface for your subnet is working but other interfaces on the router, which actually connect the router to the other subnets on the network, have some type of problem.

Pinging a Remote Host

As a final test in using Ping, you can Ping the IP address of a remote host, a computer on another subnet, or even the IP address of a Web server or FTP server on the Internet. If you can successfully Ping a remote host, your problem doesn't lie with the IP configuration; you are probably having trouble resolving host names. Figure 16.26 shows the results of a successful remote host Ping, in this case a Web server at Microsoft. Figure 16.27 shows a failed remote host Ping.

Figure 16.26

Successful Ping of a remote host.

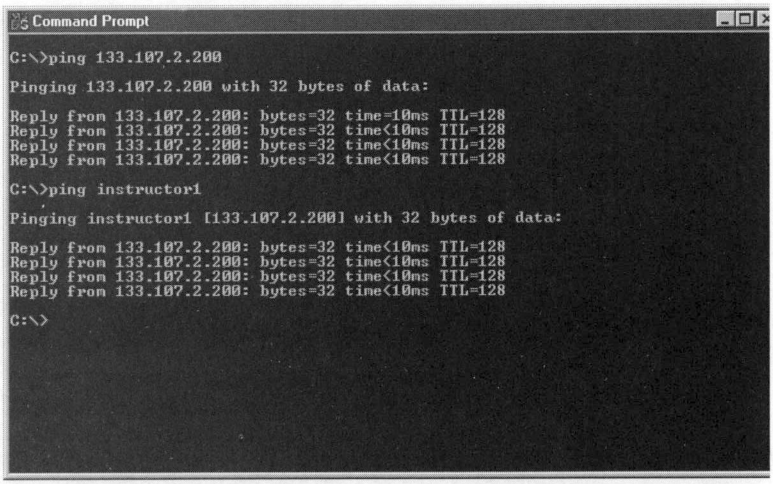

```
Command Prompt                                                    _ □ ×

C:\>ping 133.107.2.200

Pinging 133.107.2.200 with 32 bytes of data:

Reply from 133.107.2.200: bytes=32 time=10ms TTL=128
Reply from 133.107.2.200: bytes=32 time<10ms TTL=128
Reply from 133.107.2.200: bytes=32 time<10ms TTL=128
Reply from 133.107.2.200: bytes=32 time<10ms TTL=128

C:\>ping instructor1

Pinging instructor1 [133.107.2.200] with 32 bytes of data:

Reply from 133.107.2.200: bytes=32 time<10ms TTL=128
Reply from 133.107.2.200: bytes=32 time<10ms TTL=128
Reply from 133.107.2.200: bytes=32 time<10ms TTL=128
Reply from 133.107.2.200: bytes=32 time<10ms TTL=128

C:\>
```

Figure 16.27

Failed Ping of a remote host.

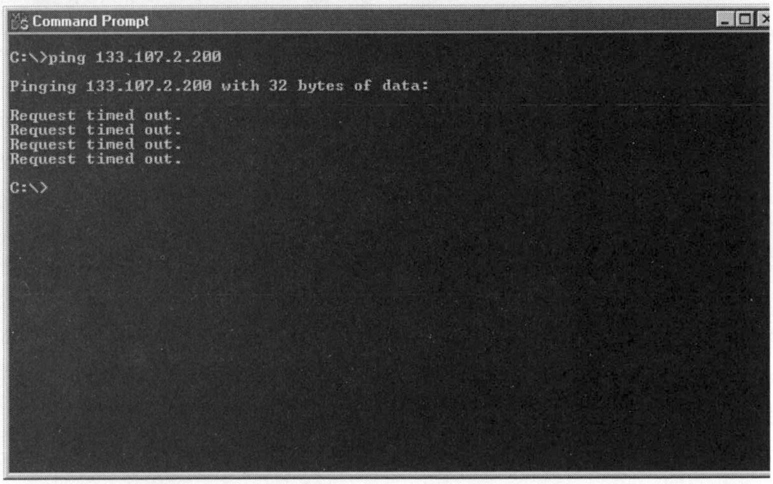

```
Command Prompt                                                    _ □ ×

C:\>ping 133.107.2.200

Pinging 133.107.2.200 with 32 bytes of data:

Request timed out.
Request timed out.
Request timed out.
Request timed out.

C:\>
```

If Pinging the remote host fails, your problems may be with the router, the subnet mask, or the local IP configuration. However, if you have followed the earlier steps of Pinging the loopback, local host address, and the default gateway address, you have already eliminated many of the problems that could cause this Ping to fail.

When a remote host Ping fails after you have tried the other Ping options, the failure may be due to other routers beyond the default gateway used for your subnet. If you know the physical layout of your network, you can Ping other router addresses along the path to the remote host to see where the trouble lies. Remember to Ping the addresses on both sides of the router: the address that receives the packet and the address that forwards the packet on. You can also use the Route command, as described in the following section, to find the path used to contact the remote host.

It is also possible that there is not a physical path to the remote host due to a router crash, a disruption in the physical network, or a crash on the remote host.

Note

Many troubleshooters prefer to simply try this last step when using Ping to troubleshoot IP configuration and connectivity. If you can successfully Ping a remote host, then the other layers of TCP/IP must be working correctly. In order for a packet to reach a remote host, IP must be installed correctly, the local client address must be configured properly, and the packet must be routed. If a Ping to the remote host works, then you can look to other sources (usually name resolution) for your connection problems. If the Ping fails, you can try each preceding step until you find the layer where the problem is located. Then you can resolve the problem at this layer. Figure 16.28 shows the methodology used to test IP with Ping. You can either start by Pinging the loopback address and working up through the architecture, or you can Ping the remote host. Of course, if Pinging the remote host works you can stop. If not, you can work back through the architecture until you find a layer where Ping succeeds. The problem must therefore be at the next layer.

Other Tools

You can use a number of tools to help troubleshoot and isolate the source of TCP/IP problems. Each tool gives you a different view of the process used to resolve an IP address to a hardware address, and then routes the IP packet to the appropriate destination.

Figure 16.28

Using Ping to test the TCP/IP configuration.

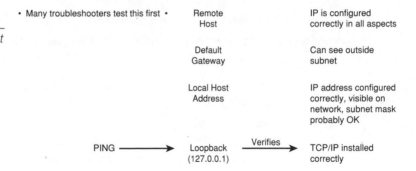

> **ARP.** ARP (Address Resolution Protocol) can be used to see the entries in the Address Resolution table, which maps network card addresses (MAC addresses) to IP addresses. You can check to see whether the IP addresses you believe should be in the table are there and whether they are mapped to the computers they should be. Usually, you do not know the MAC addresses of the hosts on your network. However, if you cannot contact a host, or if a connection is made to an unexpected host, you can check this table with the ARP command to begin isolating which host is actually assigned an IP address.

For an exercise covering this information, see end of chapter.

> **ROUTE.** ROUTE is a command-line utility that enables you to see the local routing table and add entries to it. Execute the ROUTE PRINT command to see the contents of the route table. Execute the ROUTE ADD command to add entries to the route table, and make these entries permanent with the -p switch. Execute the ROUTE DELETE command to remove entries from the route table. Execute the ROUTE command without any switches to see a help file describing all the switches for the command.

For an exercise covering this information, see end of chapter.

> **NBTSTAT.** NBTSTAT is a command-line utility that enables you to check the resolution of NetBIOS names to TCP/IP addresses. With NBTSTAT, you can check the status of current NetBIOS sessions. You can also add entries to the NetBIOS name cache from the LMHOSTS file or check your registered NetBIOS name and the NetBIOS scope assigned to your computer, if any. Execute NBTSTAT -c to display the contents of the NetBIOS name cache. Execute NBTSTAT -R to empty the NetBIOS name cache and reload it from the

For an exercise covering this information, see end of chapter.

LMHOSTS file. Execute NBTSTAT -S to display the current NetBIOS sessions with their status. Execute NBTSTAT /? for a complete description of the NBTSTAT command options.

For an exercise covering this information, see end of chapter.

▶ **NETSTAT.** NETSTAT is a command-line utility that enables you to check the status of current IP connections. Executing NETSTAT without switches displays protocol statistics and current TCP/IP connections. Executing NETSTAT with the -a switch (NETSTAT -a) displays all connections and listening ports, even those ports not currently involved with a connection. NETSTAT -r displays the route table along with active connections. Execute NETSTAT /? for a full description of the NETSTAT command options.

For an exercise covering this information, see end of chapter.

▶ **TRACERT.** TRACERT is a command-line utility that enables you to verify the route to a remote host. Execute TRACERT *hostname*, where *hostname* is the computer name or IP address of the computer whose route you want to trace. TRACERT will return the different IP addresses the packet was routed through to reach the final destination. The results also include the number of hops needed to reach the destination. Execute TRACERT without any options to see a help file that describes all the TRACERT switches.

▶ **NSLOOKUP.** NSLOOKUP is a command-line utility that enables you to verify entries on a DNS server. You can use NSLOOKUP in two modes: interactive and non-interactive. In interactive mode, you start a session with the DNS server in which you can make several requests. In non-interactive mode, you specify a command that makes a single query of the DNS server. If you want to make another query, you must type another non-interactive command. NSLOOKUP is described more completely in Chapter 12, "Domain Name System."

▶ **SNMP.** The SNMP protocol enables TCP/IP to export information to troubleshooting tools like Performance Monitor or other third-party tools. By itself, SNMP does not report any troubleshooting information. If you are using tools that depend on SNMP, however, you cannot see all the information available from these tools until you install SNMP. To install SNMP, open Control Panel, Network, and then add SNMP from the Services tab.

▶ **Performance Monitor.** Performance Monitor is a Windows tool you can use to monitor TCP/IP performance on the local computer and also on the local network segment. Performance Monitor is included in the Administrative Tools menu on any Windows NT computer. You must also install SNMP to see more complete troubleshooting information for the TCP/IP protocol.

▶ **Network Monitor.** Network Monitor is a Windows tool that enables you to see network traffic that is sent or received by a Windows NT computer. Network Monitor is included with Windows NT 4.0. To install Network Monitor, open Control Panel, Network, and then add the Network Monitor Tools and Agent from the Services tab. The version of Network Monitor that comes with Windows NT 4.0 is a simple version; it only captures traffic for the local machines (incoming and outgoing traffic). Microsoft's System Management Server, a network management product, comes with a more complete version of Network Monitor that enables you to capture packets on the local machine for the entire local network segment. You can also filter out traffic that isn't important to the troubleshooting process.

Name Resolution Problems

✓ Objective ▶

If you have configured TCP/IP correctly and the protocol is installed and working, then the problem with connectivity is probably due to errors in resolving host names. When you test connectivity with TCP/IP addresses, you are testing a lower-level of connectivity than users generally use. When users want to connect to a network resource, such as mapping a drive to a server or connecting to a Web site, they usually refer to that server or Web site by its name rather than its TCP/IP address. In fact, users do not usually know the IP address of particular server. The name used to establish a connection must be resolved down to an IP address so that the networking software can make a connection. After you've tested the IP connectivity, the next logical step is to check the resolution of a name down to its IP address. If a name cannot be resolved to its IP address or if it is resolved to the wrong address, users will not be able to connect to the network resource with that name, even if you can connect to it using an IP address.

Two types of computer names are used when communicating on the network. A NetBIOS name is assigned to a Microsoft computer, such as a Windows NT server or a Windows 95 client. A host name is assigned to non-Microsoft computer, such as a Unix server. (Host names can also be assigned to a Windows NT server running Internet Information Server. For example, the name www.microsoft.com refers to a Web server on the Microsoft Web site. This server is running on Windows NT.) In general, when using Microsoft networking, such as connecting to a server for file sharing, print sharing, or applications, you refer to that computer by its NetBIOS name. When executing a TCP/IP-specific command, such as FTP or using a Web browser, you refer to that computer by its host name.

A NetBIOS name is resolved to a TCP/IP address in several ways. Figure 16.29 shows how NetBIOS names are resolved. The TCP/IP client initiating a session first looks in its local name cache. If the client cannot find the name in a local cache, it queries a WINS server, if configured to be a WINS client. If the WINS server cannot resolve the name, the client tries a broadcast that only reaches the local subnet, because routers, by default, are not configured to forward broadcasts. If the client cannot find the name through a broadcast, it looks for any LMHOSTS or HOSTS files, if it has been configured to do so. Finally, if the client cannot resolve a name in any other way, it queries a DNS server if it has been configured to be a DNS client. However, if the client specifies a name longer than 15 characters (the maximum length of a NetBIOS name), the client first queries DNS before trying a HOSTS file or WINS.

Host names are resolved in a similar manner. The client, however, checks sources that are used solely to resolve host names before trying sources that are using to resolve NetBIOS names. In resolving host names, the client first checks the HOSTS file, then the DNS server, if configured to be a DNS client. These two sources only resolve host names. If the client cannot resolve the name, it checks the WINS server, if configured as a WINS client, tries a broadcast, and then looks in the LMHOSTS file. The last three methods to resolve a name are used to resolve NetBIOS names, but it is possible for a host name to be listed in these sources.

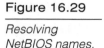

Figure 16.29

*Resolving
NetBIOS names.*

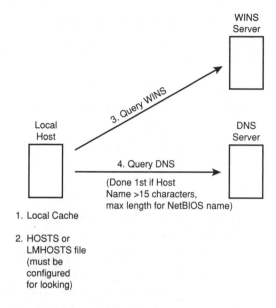

Several tools are available to test name resolution. They are discussed in the following sections.

Testing Name Resolution with Ping

Just as you can use Ping to verify the TCP/IP configuration, you can also use Ping to verify host name resolution. If you can successfully Ping a host name, then you have verified TCP/IP communication from the Network Interface layer of the TCP/IP architecture to the Transport layer. The layers of TCP/IP were reviewed in figure 16.1, earlier in this chapter. When you Ping a host name, a successful reply shows the IP address of the host. This shows that the name has been successfully resolved to an IP address and that you can communicate with that host.

Testing NetBIOS Name Resolution by Establishing a Session

The ultimate test of connectivity is to establish a session with another host. If you can establish a session through mapping a drive or by executing a Net Use command (which is the command-line equivalent of mapping a drive), you have made a NetBIOS connection. If you can FTP, Telnet, or establish a Web session with another host, you have made a Sockets connection. A NetBIOS connection or a Sockets connection are the two main types of connections made by a TCP/IP client.

After the drive has been mapped with Net Use, you can switch to the new drive letter, view files and directories, and do any other things that are specified in the permissions of the share mapped to the drive letter. To get more information about the syntax of the Net Use command, type **net help use** in a command prompt.

A common problem in making NetBIOS connections is that the wrong NetBIOS name is used. Verify that the destination host has the same name that you are using to make the connection. Another potential problem with the name configuration occurs when Net-BIOS scope IDs are used. Only NetBIOS hosts with the same scope ID can communicate with each other. The scope ID is configured through the advanced TCP/IP parameters. Incorrect share permissions can prevent you from establishing a NetBIOS session. When you try to connect a drive to a share where you have No Access, you receive an Access Denied message. This message indicates that you can connect to the server, but your rights did not allow you to make a connection to this specific share. This type of failure has nothing to do with TCP/IP connectivity. Remember that if the administrator changes your permissions to give you access, and you want to try again, you must log out and log in again to receive a new access token with the updated permissions.

To resolve NetBIOS connectivity problems, you must know what sources are used to resolve NetBIOS names. The first place a client looks to resolve a NetBIOS name is the local cache. You can view the contents of the NetBIOS cache with the NBTSTAT command. You should verify that no incorrect entry is in the cache that maps the NetBIOS name to an incorrect IP address. If there is, however, you can remove the entry and then try to make another connection.

The next place to attempt NetBIOS name resolution is in a query to a WINS server. The client must be configured to be a WINS client. You can verify the address of the WINS server through the Advanced properties of TCP/IP or by using IPCONFIG /all. You can view the contents of the WINS database by using WINS Manager on the WINS server. Verify that the host name is in the database and, if so, make sure it is mapped to the correct IP address.

If the WINS server is configured to do a DNS lookup, you have another way to get NetBIOS resolution. The WINS server queries DNS if the WINS server cannot resolve the name from its own database. You can view the contents of the DNS database files by using DNS Manager on the DNS server or by using the NSLOOKUP utility from any client.

The client next tries a broadcast to resolve NetBIOS names, although you cannot configure what the client finds through the broadcast. The next place the client looks for NetBIOS name resolution is the LMHOSTS file. You can configure the contents of this file. The client must be configured for LMHOSTS lookup in the advanced TCP/IP configuration. Also, the LMHOSTS file must be located in the correct directory path. On an NT computer, the LMHOSTS file must be in the path <winnt root>\ system32\etc.

Next, verify the entries in the LMHOSTS file. The correct host name and IP address must be entered in this file. If you have multiple entries in the file for a host name, only the first entry is used. If you added another entry for a host in the file, you must delete the other entry listed earlier in the file so that it will not be used.

Domain names are another source of potential problems with LMHOSTS files. The domain name must be registered with the IP address of the Primary Domain Controller (PDC) and #DOM (a switch that registers the server as a domain controller) on the same line. This entry is necessary to log on to the domain as well as to see the domain in a browse list.

Another problem with LMHOSTS files doesn't prevent connectivity, but it can greatly delay it. If you have #INCLUDE statements at the top of the LMHOSTS file, the files specified by #INCLUDE are included first before any other entries lower in the LMHOSTS file are searched. You can speed connections to hosts entered in the LMHOSTS file by moving the #INCLUDE entries to the bottom of the LMHOSTS file.

Testing TCP Name Resolution by Establishing a Session

Typical TCP/IP connections from a Microsoft client, such as FTP or Telnet, use Windows Sockets. To test connectivity at this level, try establishing an FTP or Telnet session or try to connect to a Web server. When you successfully connect to a Web server, you see the site's Web page, and you can navigate through the page. When the connection fails, you receive a message on your Internet browser that the connection failed.

To resolve problems with a Windows Sockets connection, you must understand how a client resolves TCP host names. The first place a client looks to resolve a host name is the local host name. You can see what TCP/IP thinks is the local host name by executing the Hostname command. Verify that if the local host is what you expect it to be. You can modify the host name in the DNS tab of the TCP/IP properties.

The next place the client looks is in a HOSTS file. This file must be located in the path <winnt root>\system32\etc. Verify that any entry in the file for the host is correct, with the correct host name and IP address. If multiple entries for the same host name are in the file, only the first name is used. The HOSTS file can also have links to HOSTS files on other servers. If links are specified in the local HOSTS file, you should make sure entries in the other HOSTS files are also correct.

The final place a client can use for host name resolution is a DNS server. The client must be configured to use DNS in the advanced properties of TCP/IP. The DNS server must have a zone file corresponding to the domain name specified in the host name, or it must be able to query another DNS server that can resolve the name. DNS is discussed in detail in Chapter 12.

Other Symptoms of TCP/IP Configuration Problems

Other symptoms can indicate problems with TCP/IP connectivity or its configuration.

Default Gateway Does Not Belong to Configured Interfaces

When you configure TCP/IP manually, you can receive the message `The Default Gateway does not belong to configured interfaces`. This message occurs when the address of the default gateway cannot logically belong to the same subnet as the host IP address. This can happen because the subnet mask is wrong, the default gateway address is wrong, or the local host address is wrong.

The TCP/IP Host Doesn't Respond

If a connection to a remote TCP/IP host is hung, you can check the status of the connection with the NETSTAT -a command. This command shows all the connections established with TCP. Successful connections should have 0 bytes in the send and receive queues. If there are bytes in the queues, then there are problems with the connection. If the connection appears to be hung but there aren't any bytes in the queues, there is probably a delay in the connection.

The Connection Is Made to the Wrong Host

You've checked everything in the IP configuration on the host and the client, yet the client connects to the wrong host. (This can happen when you establish a session using an IP address rather than a host name, such as when using Telnet.) This symptom can occur when duplicate IP addresses are on the network. You have to find the computer with the duplicate address and modify the address so it is unique. With duplicate addresses, connections are inconsistent—clients sometimes connect to one host, sometimes to another.

Error 53 Is Returned When Trying to Make a NetBIOS Session

You are trying to establish a NetBIOS session, such as mapping a drive by using the Net Use command, but Error 53 is returned. This happens because the computer name cannot be found on the network. In other words, TCP/IP can't find a computer name to resolve to an IP address. You can use the normal NetBIOS host resolution troubleshooting to resolve this problem. If the host names are correct, it's possible you are using NetBIOS scopes. If NetBIOS scopes are configured (non-blank), only hosts with the same scope ID can communicate with each other.

An FTP Server Does Not Seem to Work

FTP must be installed correctly before any clients can make connections to the server. Just as you can ping the loopback address to test a TCP/IP installation, you can also FTP the loopback address on the FTP server to test the FTP installation.

Exercises

Exercise 16.1: Correcting a Network Configuration Error

Use this exercise to see the effects that an improperly configured network card has on other networking services and protocols. Before starting, make sure you have installed Windows NT Server with a computer that has a network adapter card and that TCP/IP has been installed.

1. Clear the System Log in Event Viewer.

2. From the desktop, right-click Network Neighborhood and choose Properties from the resulting menu.

3. From the Network Properties dialog box, select the Adapters tab.

4. Select your adapter card from the list and choose Properties.

5. Change the IRQ of your adapter card to an incorrect setting.

6. Close this dialog box and choose to reboot your computer when prompted.

7. When your computer reboots, note the message received after the Logon prompt appears. The message should indicate `A Dependency Service Failed to Start`.

8. Log on and open Event Viewer.

9. Note the error message generated from the adapter card. Note the other error messages generated after the adapter card error.

10. Clear the System Log in Event Viewer.

11. From the command prompt, type **ping 127.0.0.1**. This Ping fails because TCP/IP doesn't start if the adapter doesn't start.

12. From the Network Properties dialog box, change the IRQ of your adapter card back to its proper setting and reboot.

continues

Exercise 16.1: Continued

13. Log on and check the System Log. There should be no adapter card errors or errors from networking services.

14. From the command prompt, type **ping 127.0.0.1**. This Ping succeeds because TCP/IP is started now.

Exercise 16.2: Using Ping to Test an IP Configuration

This exercise uses Ping to verify a TCP/IP installation and configuration. You should have installed Windows NT Server and TCP/IP.

1. From the desktop, right-click on Network Neighborhood and choose Properties from the resulting menu.

2. From the Bindings tab, expand all the networking services.

3. Select TCP/IP and choose Disable.

4. Repeat step 3 until you have disabled TCP/IP for all the listed networking services.

5. Close the dialog box and when prompted choose to reboot your computer.

6. When the computer reboots, log in.

7. From a command prompt, type **ping 127.0.0.1**. This Ping works because TCP/IP is installed.

8. From a command prompt, type **ping x.x.x.x**, where x.x.x.x is your default gateway address. This Ping fails because you have disabled TCP/IP from all the networking services. There isn't a way for TCP/IP packets to be sent on the network.

9. From the Bindings tab in Network Properties, enable TCP/IP for all the networking services.

10. Close the dialog box and when prompted, choose to reboot your computer.

11. When the computer reboots, log in.

12. From a command prompt, Ping your default gateway. The Ping works this time because a path now exists by which TCP/IP communications can reach the network.

Exercise 16.3:   Using ARP to Examine the ARP Cache and Add Entries

This exercise uses the ARP command to examine and modify the ARP cache.

1. From a command prompt, type **arp -g**. The contents of the ARP cache appear.

2. From a command prompt, type **arp -s 143.42.16.9 0800026c139f**. This adds a static entry to the ARP cache.

3. From a command prompt, type **arp -g** to view the revised contents of the ARP cache.

4. From a command prompt, type **arp -d 143.42.16.9**. This removes the static entry you added in step 2.

5. From a command prompt, type **arp /?** to see all the switches for the ARP command.

Exercise 16.4:   Using the Route Command to View the Routing Table and Add Entries

This exercise is used to display the contents of the local route table and to see how this table lists the default gateway address. You should have installed TCP/IP and have a default gateway address configured.

1. From a command prompt, type **route -p print**. This displays the local route table. Note the address of your client as well as the address of the default gateway in the route table.

2. Open Control Panel, Network, and then select the Protocols tab.

3. Open the TCP/IP Properties dialog box.

4. Delete the Default Gateway address.

5. Choose Apply and close the dialog box.

6. From a command prompt, type **route -p print**. Note the default gateway address is missing from the table.

continues

7. Follow steps 2–5 to restore the default gateway address.

8. From a command prompt, type **route /?** to see all the switches available with the Route command.

Exercise 16.5: Using NBTSTAT to View the Local NetBIOS Name Cache and Add Entries to the Cache from an LMHOSTS File

Exercise 16.5 examines the contents of the local NetBIOS name cache and loads entries into the cache from an LMHOSTS file. You should have installed TCP/IP and have another Windows client with TCP/IP installed and fire sharing enabled.

1. Use Notepad to open the file \WINNT\SYSTEM32\DRIVERS\ETC\LMHOSTS.SAM.

2. Add an entry to the bottom of the file for the other Windows client, specifying the NetBIOS name and the IP address of the Windows client. Make sure there is not a comment (#) in front of this line.

3. Save the file in the same directory as LMHOSTS (without an extension).

4. From a command prompt on your NT computer, type **nbtstat -c**. This displays the local cache.

5. From a command prompt, type **nbtstat -R**. This purges the cache and loads the contents of the LMHOSTS file into the local cache.

6. From a command prompt, type **nbtstat -c** to display the new contents of the local cache.

7. Using Windows NT Explorer, map a network drive to the other Windows client. The local cache was used to resolve the NetBIOS name for this connection.

8. From a command prompt, type **nbtstat /?** to see all the switches available with the NBTSTAT command.

Exercise 16.6: Using NETSTAT to Examine TCP/IP Connections

You can perform this exercise to see the information returned by the Netstat command. You should have installed TCP/IP and have access to other TCP/IP servers, such as Internet access.

1. Connect to another TCP/IP server through a Web browser or by mapping a network drive.

2. From a command prompt, type **netstat**. This displays the statistics about your current connections.

3. From a command prompt, type **netstat -a**. Note that this command also displays any listening ports.

4. From a command prompt, type **netstat -r**. Note that this command also displays the route table in addition to the connection information.

5. From a command prompt, type **netstat /?** to display all the switches available for the NETSTAT command.

Exercise 16.7: Using TRACERT to Display the Path Used to Establish a TCP/IP Connection

Exercise 16.7 displays the route used to establish a TCP/IP connection. You should have installed TCP/IP and have access to the Internet.

1. Open your Web browser and connect to www.microsoft.com.

2. From a command prompt, type **tracert www.microsoft.com**. Note the route used to connect to the Microsoft Web site and the number of hops used for the connection.

3. Connect to www.microsoft.com/train_cert.

4. From a command prompt, type **tracert www.microsoft.com/train_cert**. See if the path is the same as that used for the prior connection.

continues

Exercise 16.7: Continued

5. Connect to home.microsoft.com.

6. From a command prompt, type **tracert**. See if the path is different than connecting to www.microsoft.com.

7. Try connecting to other Web sites and viewing the path to these sites.

8. Reconnect to some of the same sites and view the path with TRACERT. Is the path the same each time you connect?

Review Questions

1. How can you see the address of the DHCP server from which a client received its IP address?

    A. Advanced properties of TCP/IP

    B. Using IPCONFIG /all

    C. Using DHCPINFO

    D. Pinging DHCP

2. Which should you do to verify that your router is configured correctly?

    A. Ping a remote host

    B. Ping 127.0.0.1

    C. Execute the ROUTE command

    D. Execute IPCONFIG /all

3. Your IP address is 136.193.5.1, your subnet mask is 255.255.240.0, and you are trying to Ping a host with the command "ping 136.193.2.23". The Ping doesn't work. What could cause the Ping to fail?

    A. The default gateway is not configured correctly.

    B. The subnet mask interprets the IP address as being on another subnet and the packet is routed.

    C. The subnet mask interprets the address as being on the local subnet and the packet is not routed.

    D. You must Ping the local host first.

4. You are using Performance Monitor but very few TCP/IP statistics are available. How can you increase the number of TCP/IP objects and counters to monitor?

    A. Install a promiscuous mode adapter card.

    B. Configure the correct default gateway in Performance Monitor.

C. Bind TCP/IP to the Monitor service.

D. Install the SNMP service.

5. TCP/IP is not working. You recall that when Windows NT first booted the message A Dependency Service Failed to Start appeared. What is a possible cause of the problem?

A. The SNMP service is not installed.

B. The network card is not configured correctly.

C. The secondary WINS server is down.

D. The PDC of your domain is down.

6. You can Ping a remote host's IP address, but you cannot connect to a share on that host. What is a possible cause of this problem?

A. The share must be configured to enable anonymous connections.

B. The Host Name Resolution Protocol must be installed.

C. The LMHOSTS file does not have any entry for this server.

D. The client has not been configured to use DHCP.

7. You made a mistake in configuring an IP address and typed the client's address as 96.82.49.208 rather than 196.82.49.208. What is the most likely result of this configuration error?

A. The client can communicate only with hosts having the network address 96.x.x.x.

B. The client cannot communicate with hosts beyond the local subnet.

C. The client cannot communicate with hosts on the local subnet.

D. The client cannot communicate with any hosts.

8. You are using NWLink and TCP/IP. How can you reduce the time that is needed to establish a TCP/IP session with another host?

   A. Move TCP/IP to the top of the bindings for the Workstation service.

   B. Configure the default gateway address to point to a faster router.

   C. Decrease the TTL for WINS registrations.

   D. Use SNMP to tune the TCP/IP cache size.

9. A DHCP client has failed to lease an IP address. What is the best way to have the client try again to get a lease?

   A. Issue a REQUEST command to the DHCP server.

   B. Reserve an address for the client on the DHCP server.

   C. Use IPCONFIG /release, then IPCONFIG /renew.

   D. Reboot the client.

10. What is the effect if you do not configure a router address on a TCP/IP client?

   A. You cannot communicate with any other TCP/IP hosts.

   B. You can only communicate with hosts connected to the default gateway.

   C. You can only communicate with hosts on the local subnet.

   D. TCP/IP doesn't initialize.

11. You have several entries for a host name in an LMHOSTS file. Which entry is used to resolve the host name to an IP address?

   A. The entry with the most current time stamp

   B. The first entry in the file

C. The last entry in the file

D. The entry with the largest IP address

12. A DHCP client has been configured to use the wrong DNS server. How can you correct the problem?

    A. Change the scope options on DHCP, then renew the lease on the client.

    B. Use IPCONFIG /update:DNS to make the change.

    C. Enter the address of the DNS server in the advanced properties of TCP/IP.

    D. Add an entry for the DHCP client on the other DNS server.

13. A TCP/IP client had a drive mapped to an NT server. You have just changed the IP address of the server and rebooted. Now the client can't connect to the new server, even though the server is configured to be a WINS client. What is the most likely cause of this problem?

    A. The WINS server hasn't copied the new registration to all its clients.

    B. The client has the old IP address cached.

    C. The LMHOSTS file on the NT Server needs to be updated.

    D. The DNS server needs to be updated.

14. On an NT computer, where does TCP/IP display its error messages?

    A. In the TCP/IP log file

    B. In the SNMP log file

    C. In the System Log

    D. In the TCP.ERR file

15. How can you test the installation of an FTP server?

    A. Ping the FTP loopback address.

    B. Ping another FTP server.

    C. FTP another server.

    D. FTP the loopback address.

Review Answers

  1. B

  2. A

  3. C

  4. D

  5. B

  6. C

  7. D

  8. A

  9. C

10. C

11. B

12. A

13. B

14. C

15. D

Answers to the Test Yourself Questions at Beginning of Chapter

1. Pinging the loopback address 127.0.0.1 verifies that TCP/IP is installed correctly. Pinging the local host address verifies that the host has a network connection and the TCP/IP stack works all the way down to the Network Interface layer. Pinging the default gateway confirms that packets can be routed to the router. Pinging a remote host verifies that the client can communicate with any client on the network.

2. Ping a remote host. If the client can communicate with a remote host, it proves that the stack is installed and configured correctly and that the router is working properly.

3. Use the IPCONFIG /all command in a command prompt. If the client received an address, the address along with the lease life and the address of the DHCP server that leased the address is listed. If the client did not acquire an address, the IP address of 0.0.0.0 is specified for the client. You can use the IPCONFIG /release command to free up any IP leases and then use the IPCONFIG /renew command to force the client to try to get an IP address.

4. Pinging the server proves you have connectivity at the IP level. When you connect to a share on the server, you are establishing a NetBIOS session with the server. NetBIOS names can be resolved by the client requesting the connections by looking in the local NetBIOS cache, looking in an LMHOSTS file if the client is configured for LMHOSTS lookup, and querying a WINS server. You can check each of these sources of name resolution for possible conflicts or incorrect entries.

5. The client can communicate with any local hosts, because those packets don't need to be routed. However, whenever the client tries to communicate with a remote host, the packet isn't routed because the address specified on the client for the default gateway isn't correct.

6. TCP/IP doesn't work, because it depends on other networking services that don't start if the adapter card isn't properly configured. You might see the `Dependency Service Failed to Start` message when NT first boots. This indicates networking services that depend on the adapter card are failing because the adapter card driver can't start based on its current configuration. After logging on, you might also see messages when you check the System Log of Event Viewer. If the messages are written to the event log, you will see an error message indicating the adapter card failed followed by error messages from other networking services that also failed to start. You might, however, see a failure of network connections as the only visible symptom of this problem.

7. One solution is to Ping the host name rather than the IP address of the host. However, the ultimate test of name resolution is to connect to the host with FTP, Telnet, or through a Web browser. If you can connect, then the name is being resolved properly and you have total connectivity with the host.

Chapter 17

TCP/IP and Remote Access Service

This chapter helps you to prepare for the exam by covering the following objective:

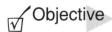 Objective

▶ Configure a RAS server and dial-up networking for use on a TCP/IP network

Test Yourself! Before reading this chapter, test yourself to determine how much study time you will need to devote to this section.

1. What service does RAS provide?

2. How many inbound RAS connections can Windows NT Workstation handle? Windows NT Server?

3. What dial-in protocols does Windows NT support?

4. When a user dials in, can she talk just to the system that she dials into?

5. What is multilink?

6. What is callback security, and what configurations can you have?

7. What are the three options that can be set for Port Usage?

8. What network protocols will the RAS server support?

9. Can a user who dials in with NetBEUI use the services of a remote server that communicates with TCP/IP?

10. What is the purpose of the Telephony API?

Answers are located at the end of the chapter.

Overview of RAS

RAS essentially enables users to connect to your network and act as if they are directly connected to it. RAS has two main components: the server (Remote Access Service) and the client (Dial Up Networking.) The RAS server can be Windows NT Server, Workstation, or Windows 95 (either with Service Pack 1 or OEM Service Release 2) and will enable users to connect to the network from a remote location. The Microsoft RAS server always uses the PPP (Point to Point Protocol) when users are dialing in to the network as the line protocol.

In addition to connecting to a Microsoft RAS server, Windows Dial-Up Networking can connect with other forms of RAS (other dial-in servers such as Unix terminal servers) by using either SLIP (Serial Line Internet Protocol) or PPP. All that is required is a communications device.

PPP versus SLIP

When clients connect to a server by using a modem, they must do so through something other than the frames that normally traverse a network (such as IEEE802.3 discussed in Chapter 3). Some other transport method is needed. In the case of dial-up servers (or terminal servers), two line protocols are popular. Serial Line Internet Protocol, or SLIP, is used frequently in Unix implementations. SLIP is the older of the two line protocols and is geared directly for TCP/IP communications. Windows NT can use the services of a SLIP server. However, it does not provide a SLIP server. Microsoft's RAS server uses Point to Point Protocol (PPP) because SLIP requires a static IP address and does not provide facility for secured logon (passwords are sent as clear text).

PPP was developed as a replacement for SLIP and provides several different advantages over the earlier protocol. PPP can automatically provide the client computer with an IP address and other configurations. It provides a secure logon and has the capability to transport protocols other than TCP/IP (such as AppleTalk, IPX, and NetBEUI.)

PPP has two important extensions: Multilink Protocol (MP) and Point to Point Tunneling Protocol (PPTP). Windows NT supports both of these extensions to the original PPP.

Multilink Protocol enables a client station to use more than one physical connection to connect to a remote server. This capability provides better throughput over standard modems. You will, however, need multiple phone lines and modems to enable this protocol. This setup can be an easy interim solution if you need to temporarily connect to offices and don't have the time or budget to set up a leased line or other similar connection.

Point to Point Tunneling Protocol facilitates secure connections across the Internet. By using PPTP, users can connect to any Internet Service Provider (ISP) and can use the ISP's network as a gateway to connect to the office network. During the session initialization, the client and server negotiate a 40-bit session key. This key can be used to encrypt all packets that will be sent back and forth over the Internet. The packets are encapsulated into PPP packets as the data.

Modems

Modems have been around for years and provide a cheap and relatively reliable method of communications over the Public Switched Telephone Network (PSTN). Installing a modem in a computer is a straightforward process. This section covers the configuring, testing, and troubleshooting of modems.

There are two main types of modems: internal and external. Internal modems are slightly cheaper, but you must open the computer to install it, and they require a free interrupt (IRQ). If you elect to go with an external modem, you should check that you have an available communications (COM) port that will be able to handle the speed of the modem.

Ports

Whether you have an internal or external modem, you will need to install the modem as a communications port. Normally, this is no problem; however, there are cases (most notably with internal modems) in which you will need to change the settings for the port. This also can cause problems with an external modem. If you cannot talk to the modem, you should check the port settings.

To check the port settings, open the Control Panel (Start, Settings, Control Panel) and double-click on the Ports Icon. The Ports dialog box appears (see fig. 17.1).

Figure 17.1

The Ports dialog box.

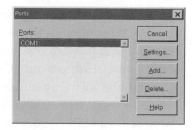

Select the port whose settings you want to check and click Settings. Another dialog box appears, showing you the settings for the port (see fig. 17.2).

Figure 17.2

The Settings for COM1 are shown in this dialog box.

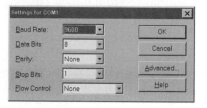

Five settings are available, but these are general settings that only deal with applications that don't set these parameters. The following list provides a description of the parameters.

▶ **Baud Rate.** The rate at which the data will flow. Serial communications move your data one bit at a time. In addition, for every byte that is sent there are (normally) 4 bits of overhead. To find the transfer rate in bytes, therefore, divide the baud rate number by 12.

▶ **Data Bits**. Not all systems use 8 bits to store one character. Some only use seven. The data bits setting allows the computer to adjust the number of bits used in the transfer.

▶ **Parity.** Parity is used to verify that information that is being transferred is getting across the line successfully. The parity can be Even, Odd, Mark, or Space, or you can set No Parity, which is what is normally used.

▶ **Stop Bits.** In some systems stop bits are used to mark the end of the transmission.

▶ **Flow Control.** This option can be set to Xon/Xoff, Hardware or None. Flow Control, as the name implies, is used to control the movement of the data between the modem and your computer. Hardware flow control uses Request to Send (RTS) and Clear to Send (CTS). The system sends a signal through the RTS wire in the cable telling the modem it wants to send. When the modem has finished transmitting what is in its buffer and signals that it has space, it will signal the computer that it can send the data using the CTS wire. Xon/Xoff is a software form of flow control where the modem sends Xon (ASCII character 17) when it is ready for data from the computer and Xoff (ASCII character 19) when it has too much data (this type of flow control does not work well with binary transfers because the Xon and Xoff characters can be part of a file).

In most cases, you can ignore these settings. They will be set and reset by the application that you will use. However, if you click the Advanced button (see fig. 17.3), you will find some settings that you do need to be aware of.

Figure 17.3

The Advanced Settings for COM1.

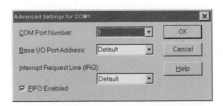

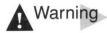 Warning

> If you make changes in this dialog box, the system will no longer be a standard system. Many applications can be affected if you make changes here.

The options that you can set here affect all applications that use the communications port. The following list provides an overview of the options that you can set.

▶ **COM Port Number.** Here you will select the port that you want to configure.

▶ **Base I/O Port Address.** When information is received from a hardware (physical) device, the information is placed in RAM by the BIOS. This setting changes where in RAM you will place the information. Unless your hardware requires a different address, do not change this.

▶ **Interrupt Request Line (IRQ).** After the BIOS places the information in RAM, it alerts the CPU to the presence of the data by using a hardware interrupt. Interrupts are a prime source for conflicts and one of the main causes of system failures. As was stated before, unless your hardware requires it, do not change this option.

▶ **FIFO Enabled.** This enables the on-chip buffering available in 16550 UARTs. Note that on some of the older revisions of the 16550, there were problems with random data loss when using FIFO. If you are experiencing unexplained problems, try disabling FIFO. With FIFO enabled, there can be a slight increase in throughput.

When you are attempting to troubleshoot a serial problem, always check that these settings are correct. Making sure that the port options are correct allows you to communicate with the modem smoothly.

Configuring Modems

Users can connect to the office network or the Internet in many ways. The most common method is to use a modem. This section deals with installing and troubleshooting modems.

Installing a Modem

Installing a modem is simple in Windows NT. After the hardware is connected, go to the Control Panel and double-click the Modems icon. If there is no modem installed, the modem installer will start automatically (see fig. 17.4). This wizard steps you through the installation of the modem. If you already have a modem, you will need to click Add.

Figure 17.4

The Install New Modem wizard.

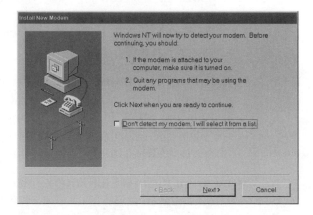

If you have already used the installer once and it was unable to detect the modem, you probably have one of two problems. Either the modem cannot be detected and you will have to install it manually, or the system can't see the modem, in which case you should check the port. If you need to install the modem manually, check the box, "Don't detect my modem; I will select it from a list." This displays a screen that enables you to select the modem (see fig. 17.5.)

Figure 17.5

The Install New Modem dialog box that lists available modems.

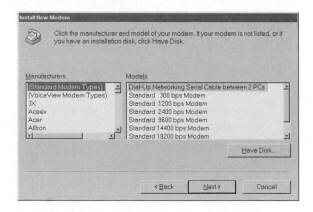

After you have the modem installed, you can check your modem properties by using the Modems icon in the Control Panel. When you open the icon, you will see a dialog box that lists all of the available modems (see fig. 17.6).

Figure 17.6

The Modems Properties dialog box, which, in this case, lists only one modem.

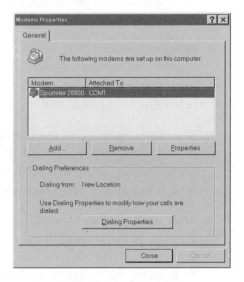

From here you will be able to check and set the properties for the modems that are installed in the computer. Several different options are of interest. Select Modem, Properties to bring up the General properties for the modem (see fig. 17.7).

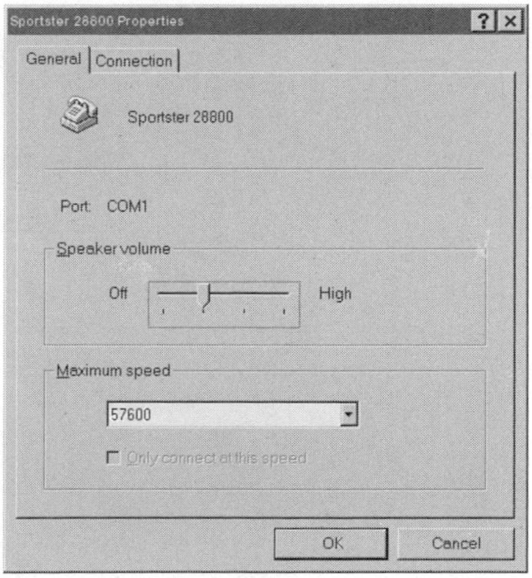

Figure 17.7

The General Properties tab for a modem.

You need to set only a couple of settings on the General tab. The following list provides the properties and what you should check for.

▶ **Port.** Displays the port that the modem was installed on. You should check the port if the hardware has been changed and the port settings if the modem is not working.

▶ **Speaker Volume.** Determines the volume of the speaker during the connection phase. Turned up the volume enough to allow you to verify that you are getting dial tone and that the other end is in fact a modem.

▶ **Maximum Speed.** Sets the fastest rate that the system will attempt to communicate with the modem. If this is set to high, some modems will not be able to respond to the system. If this is the case, lower the rate.

▶ **Only connect at this speed.** Instruct the modem that it must connect to the remote site at the same speed you set for communications with the modem. If the other site is unable to support this speed, you will not be able to communicate.

The other tab in the modem properties dialog box is the Connection tab (see fig. 17.8), which deals with the way that the modem connects. There are a couple of settings you can check when attempting to troubleshoot modems.

Figure 17.8

The Connection tab in the Modem Properties dialog box.

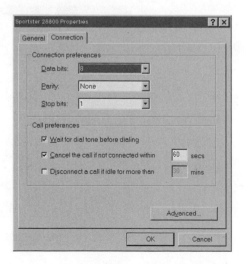

The Connection tab lets you control two properties: the Connection preferences and the Call preferences. The Connection preferences are the communications settings (which were discussed previously in the "Ports" section). These settings override the port settings. The three items from the Call preferences are listed below.

▶ **Wait for tone before dialing.** Normally, this should be selected; however, some phone systems in the world still do not have a dial tone. Make sure that this is set correctly for your area.

▶ **Cancel the call if not connected within.** This option sets the maximum amount of time that it will take for the call to be established. If line conditions are very bad, you may have to bump up this number to allow the modem more time to establish a connection and negotiate the line speed that will be used.

▶ **Disconnect a call if idle for more than.** This option enables you to set the maximum amount of time that a call can sit idle. Windows NT 4 provides an autodial service that automatically calls back a server when you get disconnected and then attempts to use a network service. This feature reduces the amount of time a user can tie up a line and can prevent massive long-distance charges. However, users need to be made aware of the time limit. If they are required to enter information for a terminal login, they should be told because the terminal screen will appear unexpectedly when the system tries to autoconnect.

Also, if a user is not aware and is using an ISP for e-mail, she needs to be told that setting the e-mail program to check for new mail at period intervals will cause the system to automatically dial the server and check—possibly using up the allowed number of hours with their ISP.

The final thing to check when doing modem configurations and troubleshooting is the Advanced Connection information (see fig. 17.9). These settings can adversely affect communications.

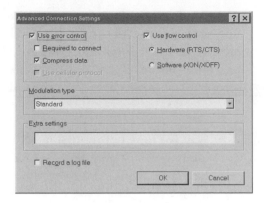

Figure 17.9

The Advanced Connection Settings dialog box.

You will want to verify a few options in the advanced modem options. The following list describes the different options and things that you should look for.

▶ **Use Error control.** This turns on or off some common settings that affect the way the system will deal with the modem. The specific options are listed here:

  ▶ **Required to connect.** This forces the modem to establish that an error correcting protocol (such as MNP class 5) be used before the connection is established. Do not use it as the default. If the modem on the other end of the connection does not support the same class of error detection, the connection will fail.

  ▶ **Compress data.** This tells the modem to use data compression. Microsoft RAS automatically implements software compression between the client and workstation if both are Microsoft. Turn on this option only if you are talking to a non-Microsoft server; otherwise, the modem will try to compress data that is already compressed.

  ▶ **Use cellular protocol.** Lets the system know that the modem you are using is a cellular modem.

▶ **User flow control.** This overrides the flow control setting for the port. Both types of flow control are available. In most cases, you should use hardware flow control. The use of flow control enables you to set the speed of the transmission between the computer and the modem. The choices are Xon/Xoff and hardware.

▶ **Modulation Type.** This enables users to set the type of frequency modulation for the modem to that of the phone system they are using. The modulation is either standard or Bell and deals with the sound frequency that is used for the send and receive channels for the communicating hosts.

▶ **Extra settings.** This enables you to enter extra modem initialization strings that you want to have sent to the modem whenever a call is placed.

▶ **Record a log file.** This probably is the most important setting from the perspective of troubleshooting. It enables you to record a file that lets you see the communications that took place between the modem and the computer during the connection phase of the communications. An example of the log is shown in figure 17.10.

Figure 17.10

The modem log as shown in Notepad.

```
ModemLog_Sportster 28800 - Notepad                                    _□×
File  Edit  Search  Help
07-25-1997 09:59:53.203 - Recv: <cr><1f>OK<cr><1f>
07-25-1997 09:59:53.203 - Interpreted response: OK
07-25-1997 09:59:53.203 - Send: ATS7=60S19=0L0M1&M4&K1&H1&R2&I0B0X4<cr>
07-25-1997 09:59:53.437 - Recv: <cr><1f>OK<cr><1f>
07-25-1997 09:59:53.437 - Interpreted response: OK
07-25-1997 09:59:53.437 - Waiting for a call.
07-25-1997 09:59:53.437 - Send: ATS0=0<cr>
07-25-1997 09:59:53.718 - 57600,N,8,1
07-25-1997 09:59:53.953 - Initializing modem.
07-25-1997 09:59:53.953 - Send: ATE0Q0U1<cr>
07-25-1997 09:59:54.234 - Recv: <cr><1f>OK<cr><1f>
07-25-1997 09:59:54.234 - Interpreted response: OK
07-25-1997 09:59:54.234 - Send: AT &F1 E0 U1 &C1 &D2 Q0 S0=0 &B1 &A3<cr>
07-25-1997 09:59:54.453 - Recv: <cr><1f>OK<cr><1f>
07-25-1997 09:59:54.453 - Interpreted response: OK
07-25-1997 09:59:54.453 - Send: ATS7=55S19=0L0M1&M4&K1&H1&R2&I0B0X4<cr>
07-25-1997 09:59:54.625 - Recv: <cr><1f>OK<cr><1f>
07-25-1997 09:59:54.625 - Interpreted response: OK
07-25-1997 09:59:54.625 - Dialing.
07-25-1997 09:59:54.625 - Send: ATDT#######<cr>
07-25-1997 10:00:11.781 - Recv: <cr><1f>CONNECT 28800/ARQ/U34/LAPM/U42BIS<cr
07-25-1997 10:00:11.781 - Interpreted response: Connect
07-25-1997 10:00:11.781 - Connection established at 28800bps.
07-25-1997 10:00:11.781 - Error-control on.
```

Note You might notice in figure 17.10 that the phone number is not shown as the modem called it. This provides added security.

Dialing Properties

From the Modem Properties dialog box (refer to fig. 17.6), you can also click the Dialing Properties button. You can the configure the system so that it knows where you are dialing from. This information is used in conjunction with Dial-Up Networking to allow the system to determine whether your call is long distance, if it should use a calling card, how to disable the call waiting feature, and so on.

When you click the Dialing Properties dialog box, the dialog box shown in figure 17.11 appears. You may create a single location or multiple locations.

Figure 17.11

The Dialing Properties dialog box.

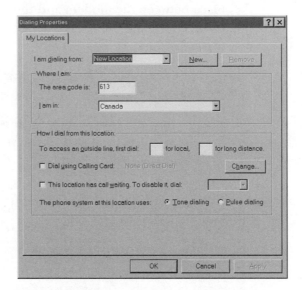

Several different items are available, and if this information is not set correctly, the client computer may attempt to connect to a local server as a long-distance call (or vice versa). The following list describes the entries that you can make:

▶ **I am dialing from.** The name of the location. To create a new entry, click the New button and enter a name in the text box. The user will need to know which entry to use when dialing.

▶ **The area code is.** The computer uses this information to determine whether it is required to dial the number as a long distance or as a local number.

- ▶ **I am in.** Sets the country code for dialing purposes so the system can connect to international numbers.

- ▶ **To access an outside line, first dial.** Set the access code for dialing out from a location. There is an entry for local calls and one for long distance.

- ▶ **Dial using Calling Card.** Enables you to have the computer enter the calling card information to make the connection with the remote host. Click the Change button to review or change calling card information.

- ▶ **This location has call waiting.** The call waiting tone often causes a connection to be dropped. You can enter the information here to disable call waiting for the location that you are dialing from.

- ▶ **The phone system at this location uses.** Enables you to select whether the system that you are calling from will use tone or pulse dialing.

If there are problems trying to connect, you should always verify the information in the Dialing Properties.

Other Communications Technologies

As stated previously, you will be able to connect to the Windows NT server in different ways. There are two principal methods by which you will be able to connect: ISDN (Integrated Services Digital Network) and X.25 (which is a wide-area networking standard.)

ISDN

One of the most common choices for connecting remote sites or even for individuals or small organizations to connect to the Internet, ISDN is becoming a very common method of communications.

Whereas a standard phone line can handle transmission speeds of up to 9,600 bits per second (compression makes up the rest of the transmission speed in most modems, such as those that transfer data at 33.6 Kbps), ISDN transmits at speeds of 64 or 128 kilobits per second, depending on whether it is one or two channels.

ISDN is a point-to-point communications technology, and special equipment must be installed at both the server and the remote site. You will need to install an ISDN card, which acts as a network card, in place of a modem in both computers. As you may have guessed by now, ISDN connections are more expensive than modems. However, if there is a requirement for higher speed, the cost will most likely be justified. Be aware, though, that in some parts of the world, this is a metered service—the more you use, the more you pay.

X.25

The X.25 protocol is not an actual device, but rather a standard for connections. It is packet-switching communication protocol that was designed for WAN connectivity.

RAS supports X.25 connections using Packet Assemblers/ Disassemblers (PADs) and X.25 smart cards. These are installed as a network card, just like with ISDN.

Dial-In Permissions

As with all other aspects of Windows NT, security is built into the RAS Server. At a minimum, a user will require an account in Windows NT, and that account will need to have dial-in permissions set.

You can grant users dial-in permission by using the User Manager (or User Manager for Domains) or through the Remote Access Admin program. If you are having problems connecting to the RAS server, this is one of the first things to check. Following are the steps to set or check dial-in permissions.

1. Open the User Manager (Start, Programs, Administrative Tools, User Manager.)

2. Select the account that you are using and choose User, Properties. You will see the User Properties dialog box, like the one shown in figure 17.12.

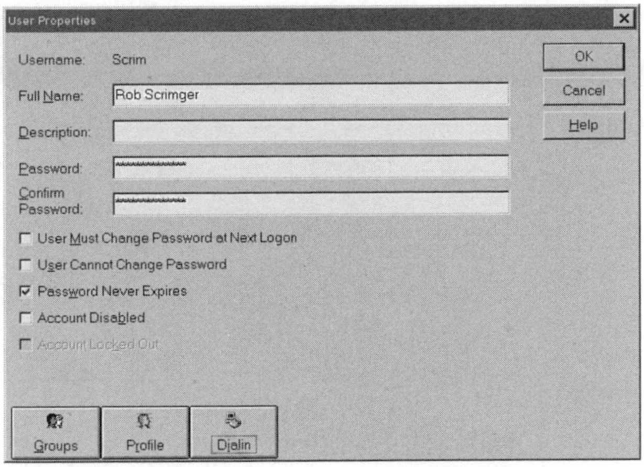

Figure 17.12

The User Proper-ties dialog box.

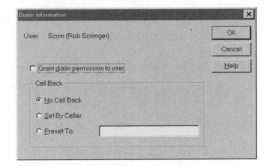

3. Click the Dial in button. The Dialin Information dialog box appears (see fig. 17.13).

Figure 17.13

The Dialin Infor-mation dialog box.

4. Check the "Grant dialin permission to user" box to allow the user to dial in.

You can also check the permissions from the Remote Access Admin utility. The following list provides the steps to do this.

1. Start the Remote Access Admin (Start, Programs, Administrative tools, RAS Admin.)

2. From the menu choose Users, Permissions.

3. In the Permissions dialog box, select the user and ensure that Dialin permission is granted (see fig. 17.14).

Figure 17.14

Dialin permission can be set in the Remote Access Admin.

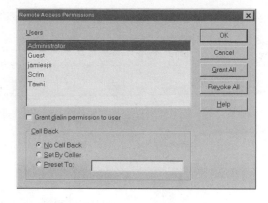

Callback Security

You probably noticed in both of the methods that there was a setting for Call Back. Call Back means that the server will do just that, call the user back. You have three options:

▶ **No Call Back.** This is the default and means that the Call Back feature is disabled.

▶ **Set By Caller.** By using this option, the user can set the number that should be used when the server calls back, which is useful if you have many users who travel and want to centralize long distance.

▶ **Preset To.** This enhances the security of the network by forcing the user to call from a specific phone number. If this is set, the user may call only from that one location.

PPP Problems

As was mentioned previously, Windows NT acts as a PPP server, which means that the client station and the server undergo a negotiation during the initial phase of the call.

During the negotiation, the client and server decide on the protocol to be used and the parameters for the protocol. If there are problems connecting, you may want to set up PPP logging to actually watch the negotiation between the server and client.

This is set up on the server by changing the Logging option under the following:

```
HKEY_LOCAL_MACHINE\SYSTEM\CurrentControlSet\Services\RASMAN\
PPP\Parameters
```

The log file will be in the system32\RAS directory and, like the modem log, can be viewed by using any text editor.

Some of the problems that you may encounter are given in the following list.

▶ You must ensure that the protocol that you are requesting from the RAS client is available on the RAS server. There must be at least one common protocol or the connection will fail.

▶ If you are using NetBEUI, ensure that the name you are using on the RAS client is not in use on the network that you are attempting to connect to.

▶ If you are attempting to connect by using TCP/IP, then the RAS server must be configured to provide you with an address.

Dial-Up Networking

✓ Objective

This section steps through the configuration of the client computer and points out the important areas. The component that is used to connect to the RAS server is Dial-Up Networking. Before you can configure Dial-Up Networking, you must install a modem or other means of communications.

By using Dial-Up Networking, you will create a phonebook entry for each of the locations you will call. The steps that are required to create an entry are given in the following list.

1. Open the My Computer icon and then open Dial-Up Networking. (If you do not have an entry, a wizard appears that will step you through creating a phonebook entry.)

2. Click the New button to create an entry. You can also select an entry in the list and click More and choose Edit the Entry.

If you choose New, the New Entry Wizard appears. You can choose to enter the information manually. Because this chapter is concerned with troubleshooting, this section covers the manual entries because they provide more options.

3. The New (or Edit) Phonebook Entry dialog box appears (see fig. 17.15). By default, it opens to the Basic tab, the options for which are discussed below. Enter or verify the information.

Figure 17.15

The Basic tab for a phonebook entry.

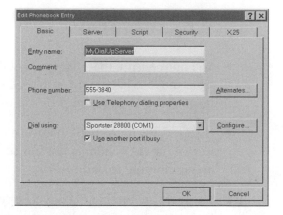

- ▶ **Entry name.** The name of the entry.

- ▶ **Comment.** Any comment you want to make about the entry.

- ▶ **Phone number.** The phone number for the entry; you should verify this. You can enter multiple entries by selecting the Alternates button. These numbers are tried in the sequence in which they are entered; you also have the option to move the most successful number to the top of the list.

- ▶ **Use telephony-dialing properties.** This tells the system to use the properties that you set for your location when dialing the number. When you are troubleshooting, turn this off.

- ▶ **Dial using.** Informs the system which modem you want to use when dialing. Verify that the modem exists and, if Multilink is selected, choose configure and verify the phone numbers that are entered for each of the modems that are listed.

▶ **Use another port if busy.** This tells the system to dial using another modem if the modem specified is busy.

4. Select the server tab and enter or verify the information (see fig. 17.16). The entries are described below.

Figure 17.16

The Server properties for a phonebook entry.

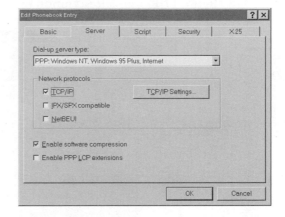

▶ **Dial-up server type.** Tells the system what type of server you are trying to connect to. You can use three different types of servers: PPP, such as Windows NT, SLIP, and Windows NT 3.1 RAS. Make sure the correct type is selected or your computer will attempt to use the wrong line protocol.

▶ **Network protocols.** Here you can select the protocols that you want to be able to use. If the client computer will be using the Internet, TCP/IP needs to be selected. If the client is going to use the services of a remote NetWare server, IPX/SPX must be selected. If you will be using only the services from a Windows NT network, then you can choose any of the protocols (remembering that the server must also use this protocol.)

▶ **Enable software compression.** If you are working with a Windows NT server, you can select this to turn on the software compression. For troubleshooting purposes, you should turn this off.

▶ **Enable PPP LCP extensions.** Tells the system that the PPP server will be able to set up the client station and will be able to verify the user name and password. This also should be turned off when you are troubleshooting.

5. If you are using TCP/IP for this connection, you should also set or verify the TCP/IP Settings. The TCP/IP setting screen will appear, the screen will be different depending on the type of server you selected. The PPP settings are shown in figure 17.17 and a description of the options is given below.

Figure 17.17

The PPP TCP/IP Settings dialog box.

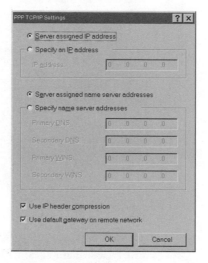

▶ **Server assigned IP address.** Tells the computer that the server assigns the IP address for this station. The server must have some means of assigning IP addresses to use this option.

▶ **Specify an IP address.** Enables you to give the station an IP address. The address need to be unique and must be correct for the servers network. The server must also allow the client to request an IP address.

▶ **Server assigned name server addresses.** Tells the system that the server assigns the IP addresses for DNS and WINS server.

▶ **Specify name server addresses.** Lets you set the addresses for DNS and WINS servers. This option enables you to see whether the server is giving you correct addresses.

▶ **Use IP header compression.** The use of IP header compression reduces the overhead that is transmitted over the modem. Disable this when troubleshooting.

▶ **Use default gateway on the remote network.** If you are connected to a network and dialed in to a service provider, this option tells Windows NT to send information that is bound for a remote network to the gateway on the dial in server.

6. Set the script options on the Script tab (see fig. 17.18).

Figure 17.18

The Script tab for a phonebook entry.

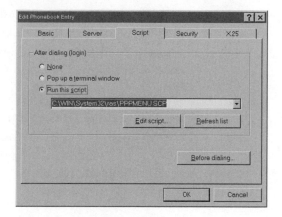

▶ **After dialing (login).** There are three different settings here. Make sure you use the correct one. For NT-to-NT communications, select None. For other connections, you may have to enter information. For troubleshooting, try the terminal window, which lets you enter the information manually, rather than using the script. If this works, then you should verify the script.

▶ **Before dialing.** If you click this button, you are presented with basically the same options. You can use this to bring up a window or run a script before you dial the remote host.

7. Check or enter the security information on the security tab (see fig. 17.19). This should be set to the same level as the security on the server or the connection will probably fail.

Figure 17.19

Setting security options for the phonebook entry.

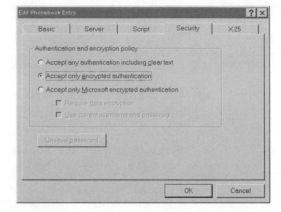

▶ **Authentication and encryption policy.** Here you can set the level of security that you want. For troubleshooting, you can try "Accept any authentication including clear text," which should be set to match the setting on the server.

▶ **Require data encryption.** If you are using Microsoft-encrypted authentication, you will have the option to encrypt all data that is being sent over the connection. Set this to match the server.

▶ **User current name and password.** Enables Windows to send the current user name and password as your login information. If you are not using the same name and password on the client as you do on the network, do not check this box. You will be prompted for the user name and password to log on just like when you attempted to connect (see fig. 17.20).

Figure 17.20

The prompt for logon information.

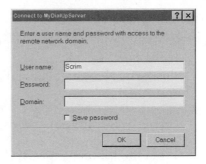

▶ **Unsave password.** If you told the system to save the logon password for a connection, you can clear it by clicking on this button. You should do this in the case of a logon problem.

8. Finally, you can enter or check the information for X.25 connections (see fig. 17.21).

Figure 17.21

X.25 settings for a phonebook entry.

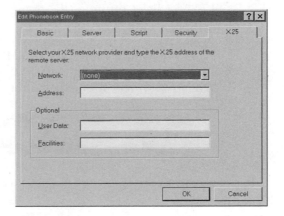

Because there are so many different options to configure, there are great potential for errors. Client errors tend either to be validation problems or errors in the network protocols. Remember that you may need to check the configuration of the server.

The RAS Server

This section covers the RAS server and the configuration of that server. Probably the best place to start would be the installation of the RAS server. After a short description of the installation, this section moves on to the configuration of the server.

Installing the RAS Server

The following steps describe the process of installing RAS.

1. Open the Network Setting dialog box (Start, Settings, Control Panel, Network).

2. From the Services tab, choose Add.

3. From the list that appears, choose Remote Access Service and click OK.

4. When prompted, enter the path to the Windows NT source files.

5. RAS asks you for the device that it should use at that point. (This includes ISDN and X.25.)

6. The Remote Access Setup dialog box appears (see fig. 17.22). Click Continue (the options for this dialog box are discussed soon).

7. From the Network settings dialog box, click Close.

8. When prompted, shut down and restart your system.

Figure 17.22

The Remote Access Setup dialog box.

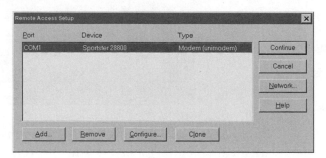

Configuring the RAS Server

If several users are all having problems connecting to your RAS server, check the modem first, and then check the configuration of the server. This section covers the basic configuration for a RAS server, which is done when you install RAS or when you verify it after installation by going to the Network settings dialog box and double-clicking Remote Access Service from the Services tab.

You will see the dialog box shown in figure 17.22. You will be able to configure each port and set the overall network preferences. Four buttons are concerned with the port settings:

▶ **Add.** Enables you to add another port to the RAS server. This could be a modem, X.25 PAD, or a PPTP Virtual Private Network.

▶ **Remove.** Removes the port from RAS.

▶ **Configure.** Brings up the Configure Port Usage dialog box, in which you can configure how this port is to be used (see fig. 17.23). Check this if no users are able to dial in.

▶ **Clone.** This setting lets you copy a port. Windows NT Server has been tested with up to 256 ports.

Figure 17.23

Configuring port usage.

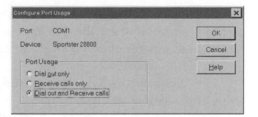

Note

Windows NT Workstation and Windows 95 (with service pack 1 or the OSR2 release) allow only one client to dial in).

After the ports are configured, you will need to configure the network settings, which affect what users will be able to see, how they will be authenticated, and what protocols they will be able to use when they dial in to the network. When you click the Network button, the Network Configuration dialog box appears (see fig. 17.24).

Figure 17.24

The Network Configuration dialog box.

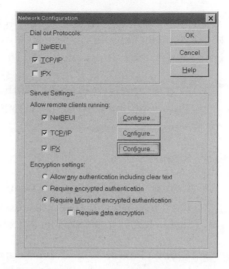

This dialog box has three main areas: the first is Dial Out Protocols, which sets which protocols you can use to dial into another server. Then there are the dial in protocols that will set the protocols that users can use to connect to you.

Finally there are the Encryption settings. The level of security that you choose must also be set on the client computer. If the client cannot use the same level of security, they will not be validated by the server.

Each of the server-side protocols has a Configuration button. The following sections deal with the configuration of each. Before you can use a protocol with RAS, it must be installed on the server.

Configuring TCP/IP on the RAS Server

If you run a mixed network that includes Unix-like hosts, then you should enable the TCP/IP protocol on the RAS server. This allows your clients to use an Internet connection on your network. The RAS Server TCP/IP Configuration dialog box includes the capability to restrict network access to the RAS server (see fig. 17.25).

Figure 17.25

*RAS Server TCP/
IP Configuration
dialog box.*

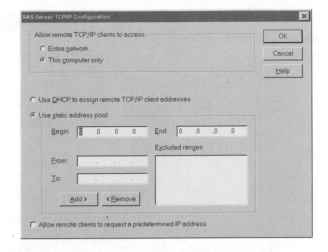

The other options all deal with the assignment of TCP/IP address
to the clients that are dialing in. By default, the RAS server uses
the services of a Dynamic Host Configuration Protocol (DHCP)
server to assign the addresses. If your DHCP server has a long
lease period, you may want to assign the numbers from a pool of
addresses that are given on the server. If you allow the client to
request an address, you must configure the client stations for all
the other parameters.

If your clients are having problems connecting, assign a range of
addresses to the RAS server; this eliminates any problems related
to the DHCP server and still allows you to prevent clients from
requesting specific IP addresses.

Monitoring the RAS Connection

After you have made the RAS connection, you will be able to monitor the connection. The client side and the server side each has a
tool of its own. This section looks at both of them because they
can be used to see what is happening with the connection.

Monitoring from the RAS Server

From the server, you can use the Remote Access Admin tool to
monitor the ports. From the Start menu, choose Programs, Administrative tools, RAS Admin. You will see the Admin tool (see
fig. 17.26).

Figure 17.26

The Remote Access Admin tool.

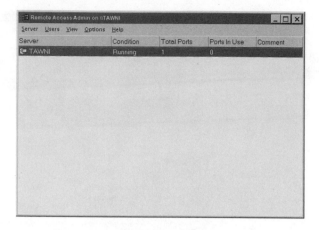

Select the server you want to look at and double-click the server. A list of the communications ports appears (see fig. 17.27). For every port that is available on the server, you will see the current user's name and the time of his initial connection.

Figure 17.27

Communications Ports on a RAS server.

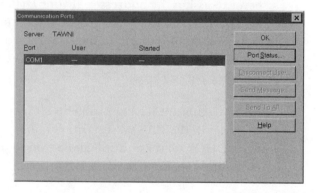

From here you can disconnect users or send a message to a single user or all users who are connected to the server. You can also check the Port Status, which shows you all the connection information for the port (see fig. 17.28).

Figure 17.28

The port status display.

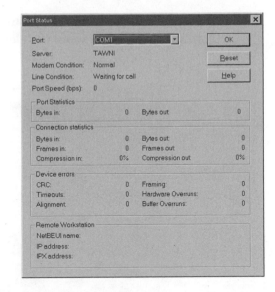

Dial-Up Networking Monitor

On the client side, there is an application called the Dial-Up Networking Monitor, which you can use to check the status of the communications. There are three tabs in the monitor.

The Status Tab

The Status tab provides you with basic information about the connection (see fig. 17.29). You have the option to hang up the connection or to view its details.

Figure 17.29

The Status tab from the Dial-Up Networking Monitor.

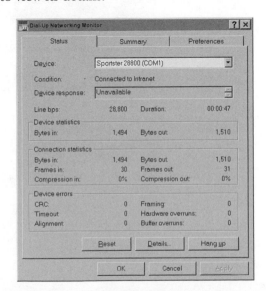

Clicking the Details tab brings up another screen (see fig. 6.30), which provides the details about the client's names on the network.

Figure 17.30

Connection Details showing the clients network identification.

The Summary Tab

The Summary tab summarizes all the connections that the client currently has open (see fig. 17.31). It is useful only cases where you have multiple connections.

Figure 17.31

The Summary tab.

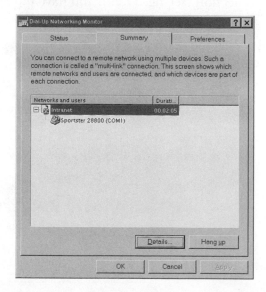

The Preferences Tab

The Preferences tab allows you to control the settings for dial-up networking (see fig. 17.32). The options break down into two main areas. You can control when a sound is played and how the Dial-Up Networking monitor will look.

Figure 17.32

Setting Dial-Up Networking preferences.

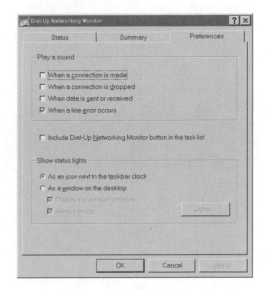

Common RAS Problems

Clients experience two common problems with RAS, which are covered here.

Authentication

Authentication can be a problem in two areas. The first is obvious. The client may attempt to connect by using the incorrect user name and password. This can easily happen if the user is dialing from a home system. The RAS client may be set to attempt the connection using the current user name and password.

The other authentication problem occurs if the security settings on the server and the client do not match. You can get around this by using the "Allow any authentication" setting or possibly by using the "After Dial terminal window."

Callback with Multilink

There is currently no way to configure Call Back security with Multilink setup. If you attempt to do this, the initial connections will be made, but then the server will hang up. The server only has one number for the client and will therefore only call back to one port.

Exercises

Exercise 17.1: Adding a Null Modem

In this exercise, you will install a Null modem that will allow those of you without a modem to proceed through some of the remaining exercises.

1. Open the Control Panel and double-click the Modems icon

2. Click the Add button to bring up the modem installer.

3. Choose "Don't detect my modem, I will select it from a list and then click next."

4. The list of manufacturers and models appears. From the Standard Modem Types, choose Dial-Up Networking Serial Cable between 2 PCs and click Next.

5. Choose any available port and click Next. NT installs your modem. When the next screen appears, choose Finish.

6. Choose OK to close the modem installer.

Exercise 17.2: Installing Remote Access Service

In this exercise, you will install the Remote Access Service. If you already have this installed, skip to exercise 3.

1. Open the Network Setting dialog box and choose Add from the Services tab.

2. Choose the Remote Access Service from the list, click OK, and enter the source files directory when prompted.

3. Choose Close on the Network Settings dialog box. When prompted, select the Null modem or the modem you already had.

4. From the RAS Setup Dialog box, choose Configure and select Dial Out. Click OK to return to the RAS Setup dialog box.

continues

Exercise 17.2: Continued

    5. Click the Continue button.

    6. When prompted, restart your system.

Exercise 17.3: Creating Phonebook Entries

You will now create a new phonebook entry. This exercise walks you through all the information that would be required to create a real phonebook entry.

1. Open the My Computer icon and double-click the Dial-Up Networking.

2. Because this is the first time you have run Dial-Up Networking, you are informed that the phone book is empty and asked to add a new entry.

Note

If you have already used Dial-Up Networking, you can click the New button, and you will be in the same position.

3. For the Name, enter **Test Entry Number 1** and click Next.

4. Select the first (I am calling the internet) and third (The non-Windows NT server) check boxes. Then click Next.

5. Enter **555-3840** as the phone number and click Next.

6. Select PPP as the protocol and click Next.

7. Choose "Use a terminal window from the next screen" and click Next.

8. Assuming the server provides you an address, click Next.

9. Enter **148.53.66.7** as the DNS server and click Next.

10. Now that you have entered all the information, click Finish.

Exercise 17.4:   Editing Phone Book Entries

In this exercise, you will edit a phone book entry and tinker with the preferences.

1. To create a shortcut to the entry, choose More, Create a shortcut to the entry.

2. Accept the default name (Test Entry Number 1.rnk).

3. Close the Dial-Up Networking dialog box.

4. On the desktop, right-click the icon and choose Edit entry and modem properties.

5. Add the alternate numbers **555-9930** and **555-6110**. To do this, click the Alternates button, type the first number in the New phone number field and click Add. Do the same for the second number.

6. Click OK to save the changes.

7. You have created a script for this entry and want to use it. Right-click the icon on the desktop and choose Edit entry and modem properties.

8. Select the Script tab and click Run this Script.

9. From the drop down list box, choose PPPMENU.SCP.

10. Click the Server tab and Enable software compression.

11. Click OK to save the changes.

Exercise 17.5:   Configuring RAS as a Server

In this exercise, you will set up the Remote Access Service to act as a RAS server; this will allow others to dial in to your machine.

1. Open the Network Setting dialog box and choose the Services tab.

2. Click on the Remote Access Service and click the Properties button.

continues

Exercise 17.5:   Continued

   3. In the dialog box that appears, select the Null Modem cable (or the modem you are using) and select Configure.

   4. Click the Dial Out and Receive Calls option and then OK to close the dialog box.

   5. Click the Network button. From here, ensure that TCP/IP is configured in the Server Settings.

   6. Click the Configure button beside TCP/IP and choose Use static address pool.

   7. Enter **148.53.90.0** as the Begin address and **148.53.90.255** as the end address. Click OK to close the dialog box and OK again to close the Server settings.

   8. Click Continue to return to the Network Settings dialog box and then choose Close.

   9. Restart your computer.

Exercise 17.6:   Assigning Permissions

You will now provide your users with dial-in Permissions and review the Remote Access Admin program.

   1. Start the User Manager for Domains (User Manager will work well in this case.)

   2. Choose User, New user and enter the following information:

Username	Bilbo
Full name	Bilbo Baggins
Description	Hobbit (small with fury feet)
Password	Blank

   3. Click the Dial-in icon and check the "Grant dial in permission."

4. Click OK to close the dial-in screen and OK to add the user.

5. Close User Manager for Domains.

6. Open the Remote Access Admin program from the Administrative Tools group.

7. Choose Users, Permissions from the menu. Click on Bilbo's name in the list. Does he have dial-in permission? (He should.)

8. Choose the account you logged on as; if you do not have dial-in permission, grant it to yourself.

Review Questions

1. Where can you enable a log that will record all of the communications between the modem and the system?

   A. In the Telephony API advanced options

   B. In the RAS Administration tool under advanced options

   C. In the Modem advanced properties

   D. In the Port Settings Advanced dialog box

2. Can the Telephony API be set to turn off the call waiting?

   A. Yes

   B. No

3. What types of security does the RAS Server accept?

   A. Clear text

   B. Kerberos

   C. Shiva

   D. Microsoft

4. Can you enter more than one phone number per phonebook entry?

   A. Yes

   B. No

5. How do you create a shortcut to a phonebook entry?

   A. From the RAS administrator

   B. From the Dial-Up Networking icon

   C. From the RAS Administrator

   D. By using Drag and Drop

6. What do you have to change in order to use a different DNS for a phone book entry?

    A. Change the Dial-Up networking properties

    B. Change the TCP/IP properties

    C. Change the settings in RAS administrator

    D. Dial-up networking will always use the default

7. What condition must be met before you can select a frame size of 1,006 or 1,500 bytes?

    A. You must use PPP.

    B. You must use PPTP.

    C. You must use SLIP.

    D. You must use CSLIP.

8. If your dial-in server requires you to log on, and this cannot be scripted, what can you do?

    A. Use NT logon

    B. Bring up a terminal window

    C. Use Client Services for Netware

    D. You will not be able to dial in

9. How can the Dial-Up Networking Monitor be displayed?

    A. As a icon on the Task Bar (beside the clock)

    B. As a regular icon on the Task Bar

    C. As a window

    D. All of the above

10. What does Auto dial do for you?

    A. Enables you to dial users from the User Manager

    B. Enables you to connect to your ISP using Windows Messaging

    C. Reconnects network resources when accessed

    D. Automatically dials at a given time

11. What events can cause the Dial-Up Networking Monitor to make a sound?

    A. On connection

    B. On errors

    C. When the program starts

    D. When the program terminates

12. Where can you grant a user dial-in permissions?

    A. From the command prompt

    B. From the User Manager

    C. From the RAS administrator

    D. From Server Manager

13. From where does the IP address for a client come?

    A. From the client

    B. From the DHCP Server

    C. From a scope of addresses on the RAS Server

    D. All of the above

14. What is the purpose of PPTP?

    A. New form of the PPP protocol

    B. Allows Tuned connections

    C. Allows secured connections across the Internet

    D. Enables the user to dial in using more than one line

15. How does PPTP show up in the Remote Access Admin?

    A. RPN

    B. VPN

    C. SPN

    D. DPN

Review Answers

1. C

2. A

3. A, D

4. A

5. B

6. A

7. C

8. B

9. D

10. C

11. A, B

12. B, C

13. D

14. C

15. B

Answers to the Test Yourself Questions at the Beginning of the Chapter

1. RAS provides dial-up networking for Windows NT Workstation and Server.

2. There is a one connection limit on inbound RAS when you are working with NT Workstation; Windows NT Server has been tested with up to 256 inbound connections.

3. Windows NT allows you to dial out using either PPP (Point to Point Protocol) or SLIP (Serial Line Internet Protocol). The dial-in for Windows NT only supports PPP.

4. Depending on the configuration of the protocol that she uses to dial in, she will be allowed to see either the one computer that she dials into or the entire network.

5. Multilink is a special protocol that allows a user to use more than one modem to connect to a RAS server. Note that the multilink protocol does not work with the callback security.

6. Callback security causes the RAS server to call back the client. There are three forms of callback security: None (no callback is done); Set by Caller (this allows the caller to enter the number they are at; though this does not necessarily increase security, it reduces the long-distance charges for the user); and Preset (this requires that the users be at a specific phone number, so they can call only from a known location.)

7. A port can be used for Dial Out, Receive Calls, or both.

8. The RAS server enables you to call in by using NetBEUI, NWLink, and TCP/IP, which are configured in the RAS Setup under the Network button.

9. If the server is using NetBIOS, then the user will be able to call in by using NetBIOS (or anything else). The RAS Server uses a system called a *NetBIOS Gateway* to forward the SMB request to the other server over the TCP/IP protocol.

10. The Telephony API allows Windows NT to be set up with different locations. You will be able to choose the location that you are calling from, and the system will know whether the call is local or long distance, what the dialing codes are, and even what calling card to use.

Appendix

Overview of the
Certification Process

To become a Microsoft Certified Professional, candidates must pass rigorous certification exams that provide a valid and reliable measure of their technical proficiency and expertise. These closed-book exams have on-the-job relevance because they are developed with the input of professionals in the computer industry and reflect how Microsoft products are actually used in the workplace. The exams are conducted by an independent organization—Sylvan Prometric—at more than 700 Sylvan Authorized Testing Centers around the world.

Currently Microsoft offers four types of certification, based on specific areas of expertise:

▶ **Microsoft Certified Product Specialist (MCPS).** Qualified to provide installation, configuration, and support for users of at least one Microsoft desktop operating system, such as Windows 95 or Windows NT Server. In addition, candidates may take additional elective exams to add areas of specialization. MCPS is the first level of expertise.

▶ **Microsoft Certified Systems Engineer (MCSE).** Qualified to effectively plan, implement, maintain, and support information systems with Microsoft Windows NT and other Microsoft advanced systems and workgroup products, such as Microsoft Office and Microsoft BackOffice. The Exchange Server 5.0 exam can be used as one of the two elective exams you must take to achieve your MCSE. MCSE is the second level of expertise.

▶ **Microsoft Certified Solution Developer (MCSD).** Qualified to design and develop custom business solutions using Microsoft development tools, technologies, and platforms, including Microsoft Office and Microsoft BackOffice. MCSD also is a second level of expertise, but in the area of software development.

▶ **Microsoft Certified Trainer (MCT).** Instructionally and technically qualified by Microsoft to deliver Microsoft Education Courses at Microsoft authorized sites. An MCT must be employed by a Microsoft Solution Provider Authorized Technical Education Center or a Microsoft Authorized Academic Training site.

You can find complete descriptions of all Microsoft Certifications in the Microsoft Education and Certification Roadmap on the CD-ROM that comes with this book. The following sections describe the requirements for each type of certification.

 Note

> For up-to-date information about each type of certification, visit the Microsoft Training and Certification World Wide Web site at `http://www.microsoft.com/train_cert`. You must have an Internet account and a WWW browser to access this information. You also can call the following sources:
>
> ▶ Microsoft Certified Professional Program: 800-636-7544
>
> ▶ Sylvan Prometric Testing Centers: 800-755-EXAM
>
> ▶ Microsoft Online Institute (MOLI): 800-449-9333

How to Become a Microsoft Certified Product Specialist (MCPS)

Becoming an MCPS requires you pass one operating system exam. Passing the "Internetworking with Microsoft TCP/IP on Microsoft Windows NT 4.0" exam (#70-59), which this book covers, does not satisfy the MCPS requirement.

The following list shows the names and exam numbers of all the operating systems from which you can choose to get your MCPS certification:

▶ Implementing and Supporting Microsoft Windows 95 #70-63

▶ Implementing and Supporting Microsoft Windows NT Workstation 4.02 #70-73

▶ Implementing and Supporting Microsoft Windows NT Workstation 3.51 #70-42

▶ Implementing and Supporting Microsoft Windows NT Server 4.0 #70-67

▶ Implementing and Supporting Microsoft Windows NT Server 3.51 #70-43

▶ Microsoft Windows for Workgroups 3.11-Desktop #70-48

▶ Microsoft Windows 3.1 #70-30

▶ Microsoft Windows Architecture I #70-160

▶ Microsoft Windows Architecture II #70-161

How to Become a Microsoft Certified Systems Engineer (MCSE)

MCSE candidates need to pass four operating system exams and two elective exams. The MCSE certification path is divided into two tracks: the Windows NT 3.51 track and the Windows NT 4.0 track. The "Internetworking with Microsoft TCP/IP on Microsoft Windows NT 4.0" exam covered in this book can be applied to either track of the MCSE certification path.

Table A.1 shows the core requirements (four operating system exams) and the elective courses (two exams) for the Windows NT 3.51 track.

Table A.1

Windows NT 3.51 MCSE Track			
Take These Two Required Exams (Core Requirements)	Plus, Pick One Exam from the Following Operating System Exams (Core Requirement)	Plus, Pick One Exam from the Following Networking Exams (Core Requirement)	Plus, Pick Two Exams from the Following Elective Exams (Elective Requirements)
Implementing and Supporting Microsoft Windows NT Server 3.51 #70-43	Implementing and Supporting Microsoft Windows 95 #70-63	Networking Essentials #70-58	Implementing and Supporting Microsoft Exchange Server 4.0 #70-75
AND Implementing and Supporting Microsoft Windows NT Workstation 3.51 #70-42	*OR* Microsoft Windows for Workgroups 3.11-Desktop #70-48		*OR* Implementing and Supporting Microsoft Exchange Server 5.0 #70-76
	OR Microsoft Windows 3.1 #70-30		*OR* Implementing and Supporting Microsoft Systems Management Server #70-14
			OR Microsoft SQL Server 4.2 Database Implementation #70-21
			OR Microsoft SQL Server 4.2 Database Administration for Microsoft Windows NT #70-22
			OR System Administration for Microsoft SQL Server 6 #70-26
			OR Implementing a Database Design on Microsoft SQL Server 6 #70-27
			OR Microsoft Mail for PC Networks 3.2-Enterprise #70-37

Take These Two Required Exams (Core Requirements)	Plus, Pick One Exam from the Following Operating System Exams (Core Requirement)	Plus, Pick One Exam from the Following Networking Exams (Core Requirement)	Plus, Pick Two Exams from the Following Elective Exams (Elective Requirements)
			OR Internetworking Microsoft TCP/IP on Microsoft Windows NT (3.5-3.51) #70-53
			OR Internetworking Microsoft TCP/IP on Microsoft Windows NT 4.0 #70-59
			OR Implementing and Supporting Microsoft Exchange Server 4.0 #70-75
			OR Implementing and Supporting Microsoft Internet Information Server #70-77
			OR Implementing and Supporting Microsoft Proxy Server 1.0 #70-78

Table A.2 shows the core requirements (four operating system exams) and elective courses (two exams) for the Windows NT 4.0 track. Tables A.1 and A.2 have many of the same exams listed, but there are distinct differences between the two. Make sure you read each track's requirements carefully.

Table A.2

Windows NT 4.0 MCSE Track			
Take These Two Required Exams (Core Requirements)	Plus, Pick One Exam from the Following Operating System Exams (Core Requirement)	Plus, Pick One Exam from the Following Networking Exams (Core Requirement)	Plus, Pick Two Exams from the Following Elective Exams (Elective Requirements)
Implementing and Supporting Microsoft Windows NT Server 4.0 #70-67	Implementing and Supporting Microsoft Windows 95 #70-63	Networking Essentials #70-58	Implementing and Supporting Microsoft Exchange Server 4.0 #70-75
AND Implementing and Supporting Microsoft Windows NT Server 4.0 in the Enterprise #70-68	*OR* Microsoft Windows for Workgroups 3.11-Desktop #70-48		*OR* Implementing and Supporting Microsoft Exchange Server 5.0 #70-76
	OR Microsoft Windows 3.1 #70-30		*OR* Implementing and Supporting Microsoft Systems Management Server #70-14
	OR Implementing and Supporting Microsoft Windows NT Workstation 4.02 #70-73		*OR* Microsoft SQL Server 4.2 Database Administration for Microsoft Windows NT #70-22
			OR System Administration for Microsoft SQL Server 6 #70-26
			OR Implementing a Database Design on Microsoft SQL Server 6 #70-27
			OR Microsoft Mail for PC Networks 3.2-Enterprise #70-37

Take These Two Required Exams (Core Requirements)	Plus, Pick One Exam from the Following Operating System Exams (Core Requirement)	Plus, Pick One Exam from the Following Networking Exams (Core Requirement)	Plus, Pick Two Exams from the Following Elective Exams (Elective Requirements)
			OR Internetworking Microsoft TCP/IP on Microsoft Windows NT (3.5-3.51) #70-53
			OR Internetworking Microsoft TCP/IP on Microsoft Windows NT 4.0 #70-59
			OR Implementing and Supporting Microsoft Exchange Server 4.0 #70-75
			OR Implementing and Supporting Microsoft Internet Information Server #70-77
			OR Implementing and Supporting Microsoft Proxy Server 1.0 #70-78

How to Become a Microsoft Certified Solution Developer (MCSD)

MCSD candidates need to pass two core technology exams and two elective exams. The "Internetworking with Microsoft TCP/IP on Microsoft Windows NT 4.0" (#70-59) exam does apply toward these requirements. Table A.3 shows the required technology exams, plus the elective exams that apply toward obtaining the MCSD.

 **Warning**

> The "Implementing a Database Design on Microsoft SQL Server 6.5" (#70-27) exam does apply toward the MCSD requirements.

Table A.3

MCSD Exams and Requirements

Take These Two Core Technology Exams	Plus, Choose from Two of the Following Elective Exams
Microsoft Windows Architecture I #70-160	Microsoft SQL Server 4.2 Database Implementation #70-21
AND Microsoft Windows Architecture II #70-161	*OR* Developing Applications with C++ Using the Microsoft Foundation Class Library #70-24
	OR Implementing a Database Design on Microsoft SQL Server 6 #70-27
	OR Microsoft Visual Basic 3.0 for Windows-Application Development #70-50
	OR Microsoft Access 2.0 for Windows-Application Development #70-51
	OR Developing Applications with Microsoft Excel 5.0 Using Visual Basic for Applications #70-52
	OR Programming in Microsoft Visual FoxPro 3.0 for Windows #70-54
	OR Programming with Microsoft Visual Basic 4.0 #70-65
	OR Microsoft Access for Windows 95 and the Microsoft Access Development Toolkit #70-69
	OR Implementing OLE in Microsoft Foundation Class Applications #70-25

Becoming a Microsoft Certified Trainer (MCT)

To understand the requirements and process for becoming a Microsoft Certified Trainer (MCT), you need to obtain the Microsoft Certified Trainer Guide document (MCTGUIDE.DOC) from the following WWW site:

```
http://www.microsoft.com/train_cert/download.htm
```

On this page, click the hyperlink MCT GUIDE (mctguide.doc) (117k). If your WWW browser can display DOC files (Word for Windows native file format), the MCT Guide displays in the browser window. Otherwise, you need to download it and open it in Word for Windows or Windows 95 WordPad. The MCT Guide explains the four-step process to becoming an MCT. The general steps for the MCT certification are as follows:

1. Complete and mail a Microsoft Certified Trainer application to Microsoft. You must include proof of your skills for presenting instructional material. The options for doing so are described in the MCT Guide.

2. Obtain and study the Microsoft Trainer Kit for the Microsoft Official Curricula (MOC) course(s) for which you want to be certified. Microsoft Trainer Kits can be ordered by calling 800-688-0496 in North America. Other regions should review the MCT Guide for information on how to order a Trainer Kit.

3. Pass the Microsoft certification exam for the product for which you want to be certified to teach.

4. Attend the Microsoft Official Curriculum (MOC) course for the course for which you want to be certified. This is done so you can understand how the course is structured, how labs are completed, and how the course flows.

 **Caution**

> You should use the preceding steps as a general overview of the MCT certification process. The actual steps you need to take are described in detail in the MCTGUIDE.DOC file on the WWW site mentioned earlier. Do not misconstrue the preceding steps as the actual process you need to take.

If you are interested in becoming an MCT, you can receive more information by visiting the Microsoft Certified Training (MCT) WWW site at `http://www.microsoft.com/train_cert/mctint.htm`; or call 800-688-0496.

Appendix

Study Tips

B

Self-study involves any method that you employ to learn a given topic, with the most popular being third-party books, such as the one you hold in your hand. Before you begin to study for a certification book, you should know exactly what Microsoft expects you to learn.

Pay close attention to the objectives posted for the exam. The most current objectives can always be found on the WWW site http://www.microsoft.com/train_cert. This book was written to the most current objectives, and the beginning of each chapter lists the relevant objectives for that chapter. As well, you should notice a handy tear-out card with an objective matrix that lists all objectives and the page you can turn to for information on that objective.

If you have taken any college courses in the past, you have probably learned what study habits work best for you. Nevertheless, consider the following:

▶ Study in bright light to reduce fatigue and depression.

▶ Establish a regular study schedule and stick as close to it as possible.

▶ Turn off all forms of distraction, including radios and televisions; or try studying in a quiet room.

▶ Study in the same place each time you study so your materials are always readily at hand.

▶ Take short breaks (approximately 15 minutes) every two to three hours or so. Studies have proven that your brain assimilates information better when this is allowed.

Another thing to think about is this: there are three ways in which humans learn information: visually, audibly, and through tactile confirmation. That's why, in a college class, the students who took notes on the lectures had better recall on exam day; they took in information both audibly and through tactile confirmation—writing it down.

Hence, use study techniques that reinforce information in all three ways. For example, by reading the books, you are visually taking in information. By writing down the information when you test yourself, you are giving your brain tactile confirmation. And lastly, have someone test you out loud, so you can hear yourself giving the correct answer. Having someone test you should always be the last step in studying.

Pretesting Yourself

Before taking the actual exam, verify that you are ready to do so by testing yourself over and over again in a variety of ways. Within this book, there are questions at the beginning and end of each chapter. On the accompanying CD-ROM, there are a number of electronic test engines that emulate the actual Microsoft test and enable you to test your knowledge of the subject areas. Use these over and over again, until you are consistently scoring in the 90 percent range (or better).

 Note

This means, of course, that you can't start studying five days before the exam begins. You will need to give yourself plenty of time to read, practice, and then test yourself several times.

The New Riders' TestPrep electronic testing engine, we believe, is the best one on the market. While described in Appendix D, "All About TestPrep," here it's just important for you to know that TestPrep will prepare you for the exam in a way unparalleled by most other engines.

Tips for Doing Your Best on the Tests

In a confusing twist of terminology, when you take one of the Microsoft exams, you are said to be "writing" the exam. When you go to take the actual exam, be prepared. Arrive early and be ready to show your two forms of identification and sit before the monitor. Expect wordy questions. Although you have 90 minutes to take the exam, there are 58 questions you must answer. This gives you just over one minute to answer each question. This may sound like ample time for each question, but remember that most of the questions are lengthy word problems, which tend to ramble on for paragraphs. Your 90 minutes of exam time can be consumed very quickly.

It has been estimated that approximately 85 percent of the candidates taking their first Microsoft exam fail it. It is not so much that they are unprepared and unknowledgeable. It is more the case that they don't know what to expect and are immediately intimidated by the wordiness of the questions and the ambiguity implied in the answers.

For every exam that Microsoft offers, there is a different required passing score. The Internetworking with Microsoft TCP/IP on Windows NT 4.0 passing score is 750 or 75 percent. Because there are 58 questions on the exam (randomly taken from a pool of about 150), this means you must correctly answer 44 or more pass.

Things to Watch For

When you take the exam, look closely at the number of correct choices you need to make. Some questions require that you select one correct answer; other questions have more than one correct answer. When you see radial buttons next to the answer choices, you need to remember that the answers are mutually exclusive and there is but one right answer. On the other hand, check boxes indicate that the answers are not mutually exclusive and there are multiple right answers. Be sure to read the questions closely to see how many correct answers you need to choose.

Also, read the questions fully. With lengthy questions, the last sentence often dramatically changes the scenario. When taking the exam, you are given pencils and two sheets of paper. If you are uncertain of what the question is saying, map out the scenario on the paper until you have it clear in your mind. You're required to turn in the scrap paper at the end of the exam.

Marking Answers for Return

You can mark questions on the actual exam and refer back to them later. If you get a wordy question that will take a long time to read and decipher, mark it and return to it when you have completed the rest of the exam. This will save you from wasting time on it and running out of time on the exam—there are only 90 minutes allotted for the exam and it ends when those 90 minutes expire, whether or not you are finished with the exam.

Attaching Notes to Test Questions

At the conclusion of the exam, before the grading takes place, you are given the opportunity to attach a message to any question. If you feel that a question was too ambiguous, or tested on knowledge you did not need to know to work with the product, take this opportunity to state your case. Unheard of is the instance where Microsoft changes a test score as a result of an attached message. However, it never hurts to try—and it helps to vent your frustration before blowing the proverbial 50-amp fuse.

Good luck!

Appendix

What's on the CD-ROM

This appendix is a brief rundown of what you'll find on the CD-ROM that comes with this book. For a more detailed description of the TestPrep test engine, exclusive to New Riders, please see Appendix D, "All About TestPrep."

New Riders' Exclusive TestPrep

A new test engine was developed exclusively for New Riders. It is, we believe, the best test engine available, because it closely emulates the actual Microsoft exam, and it enables you to check your score by category, which helps you determine what you need to study further. For a complete description of the benefits of TestPrep, please see Appendix D.

Exclusive Electronic Version of Text

Use the electronic version of this book to help you search for terms or areas that you need to study. It comes complete with all figures as they appear in the book.

Copyright Information and Disclaimer

TestPrep test engine: Copyright 1998 Macmillan Computer Publishing. All rights reserved. Made in the U.S.A.

Appendix

All About TestPrep

The electronic TestPrep utility included on the CD-ROM accompanying this book enables you to test your knowledge in a manner similar to that employed by the actual Microsoft exam.

TestPrep uses a unique randomization sequence to ensure that each time you run the program you are presented with a different sequence of questions—this enhances your learning and prevents you from merely learning the expected answers over time without reading the question each and every time.

Question Presentation

TestPrep emulates the actual Microsoft "Internetworking with Microsoft TCP/IP on Microsoft Windows NT 4.0" exam (#70-059), in that radio (circle) buttons are used to signify only one correct choice, while check boxes (squares) are used to imply multiple correct answers.

Scoring

The TestPrep Score Report follows, as closely as possible, the actual "Internetworking with Microsoft TCP/IP on Microsoft Windows NT 4.0" exam. Microsoft no longer makes available exact passing scores, but for exam #70-059, scores in the high 700s or higher have been considered passing in the past; the same parameters apply to the TestPrep. Each objective category is broken down into categories with a percentage correct given for each of the categories. Each test should include 58 questions, and each test session should last 105 minutes.

Note: Every effort has been made to maximize your test preparation by emulating the actual test experience as closely as possible. We cannot, however, guarantee that testing formats, or other details such as official passing scores, number of questions on an exam, or time given to take an exam, will not change.

Index

E

X-Z

MACMILLAN COMPUTER PUBLISHING USA

A VIACOM COMPANY

Technical ---- Support

If you need assistance with the information provided by Macmillan Computer Publishing, please access the information available on our web site at **http://www.mcp.com/feedback.** Our most Frequently Asked Questions are answered there. If you do not find the answers to your questions on our web site, you may contact Macmillan User Services at **(317) 581-3833** or email us at **support@mcp.com**.